# G. E. MOORE

# The Arguments of
# the Philosophers

## EDITED BY TED HONDERICH

*Grote Professor of the Philosophy of Mind and Logic,*
*University College, London*

The purpose of this series is to provide a contemporary assessment and history of the entire course of philosophical thought. Each book constitutes a detailed, critical introduction to the work of a philosopher of major influence and significance.

*available in paperback

# G.E. MOORE

Thomas Baldwin

London and New York

*First published 1990*
*by Routledge*
*11 New Fetter Lane, London EC4P 4EE*

*Simultaneously published in the USA and Canada*
*by Routledge*
*a division of Routledge, Chapman and Hall, Inc.*
*29 West 35th Street, New York, NY 10001*

*First published in paperback 1992*

*© 1990, 1992 Thomas Baldwin*

*Printed in Great Britain by*
*T J Press (Padstow) Ltd, Padstow, Cornwall*

*British Library Cataloguing in Publication Data*
*Baldwin, Thomas*
*G.E. Moore - (The arguments of the philosophers)*
*1. English philosophy. Moore, G.E. (George Edward), 1873-1958*
*I. Title  II Series*
*192*
*ISBN 0-415-00964-2*

*Library of Congress Cataloging in Publication Data*
*Baldwin, Thomas, 1947-*
*G.E. Moore Thomas Baldwin.*
*p. cm. - (The arguments of the philosophers)*
*Bibliography: p.*
*Includes index.*
*ISBN 0-415-00964-2*
*1. Moore, G.E. (George Edward), 1873-1958.  I. Title.*
*II. Series.*
*B1647.M74B35  1992*
*192-dc20                                    89-10324*

'The cow is over there,' said Ansell, lighting a match and holding it out over the carpet. No one spoke. He waited till the end of the match fell off. Then he spoke again, 'She is there, the cow. There, now.'

'You have not proved it,' said a voice.

'I have proved it to myself.'

'I have proved to myself that she isn't,' said the voice. 'The cow is *not* there.' Ansell frowned and lit another match.

'She's there for me,' he declared. 'I don't care whether she's there for you or not. Whether I'm in Cambridge or Iceland or dead, the cow will be there.'

It was philosophy.

(E.M. Forster The Longest Journey p. 1)

# Contents

# Preface

I was introduced to the study of philosophy by Simon Blackburn and Casimir Lewy, and both of them set me at once to read many of Moore's works (this was in Cambridge in 1965). As I recall, I was often puzzled by these assignments. Sometimes it was by Moore's writings themselves, such as the first chapter of *Principia Ethica*; at other times it seemed to me that I could understand easily enough what Moore was saying, but it was not clear why it was thought that his argument established anything of philosophical significance. Although my teachers tried to enlighten me on these matters, my attention was soon drawn away from Moore to the more obviously exciting works of Wittgenstein, Quine, and others. The result was that my attitude then was that Moore was someone whose work it was important to know about (if only to satisfy one's examiners), but not someone whose writings I studied much for their intrinsic interest.

My reaction then was, I think, not uncommon. While the writings of the other two members of the Trinity trinity, Russell and Wittgenstein, have been subjected to critical appraisal and discussion for many years, Moore's work has attracted little attention of this kind. Indeed there are those who seem to think that it should be left to fade into a series of footnotes to the history of philosophy. One result of this is that the present book is, I think, the first to attempt to deal critically with all aspects of his work, though there are distinguished studies of certain aspects of it,[1] and there has been a recent quickening of interest in Moore's early writings.[2] The reason for this latter interest has much to do with the mood of reflective appraisal which has come across recent work in the analytic tradition in philosophy. For as analytic philosophers call their own methods of argument into question, it becomes important to investigate the origins of these methods. Such an investigation must lead back to Moore's early work, since his break with idealism contributed decisively to the emergence of the analytic style. Quinton has provided a memorably bizarre analogy to represent Moore's role in that 'revolution' in philosophy which produced the analytic style: 'Moore and Russell . . . stand in a way as Lenin and Trotsky to Wittgenstein's Stalin'.[3]

I myself was partly drawn to write about Moore by the prospect of studying his early writings, which have recently become accessible thanks to the purchase of many of his papers by the Cambridge University Library. It is in these writings that his rejection of idealism is accomplished and they are crucial documents in the history of analytic philosophy. But, of course, that early break with idealism was only the start of his work and influence, and once embarked on this study I came to understand and appreciate his mature philosophy afresh. It would be foolish for me to attempt to argue here for the importance and interest of parts of this mature philosophy; my judgment about it is embodied in the latter part of this book. But no argument is required to establish the fact of Moore's influence within British philosophy throughout the first half of this century. Writing in 1920, McTaggart asserted that 'I have no hesitation in saying that I regard Dr G.E. Moore as unsurpassed in ability by any British philosopher now living'.[4]. Even when they disagreed sharply with him (as McTaggart did), other philosophers felt they had to take note of his position. By his writings and lectures on ethics and epistemology, and by the example of his analytic method, Moore set the agenda, and determined the approach, of many of the ensuing discussions within the analytic tradition. Thus to come to terms with analytic philosophy one has to come to terms with Moore.

In 1921 Moore succeeded G.F. Stout as editor of *Mind*, and in 1925 he succeeded James Ward as Professor of Philosophy at Cambridge. These appointments confirmed his pre-eminent position among British academic philosophers. He held the Professorship at Cambridge until he retired in 1939, and his tenure of it marked the golden period of Cambridge philosophy, when a succession of visitors from abroad came to study with him and Wittgenstein. Moore himself did not publish much during this period; but he exerted his powerful influence through his lectures, his presence at the Moral Sciences Club, and his hospitality to visitors. Despite the publication of his *Commonplace Book* and some of his lecture notes from this period (in his *Lectures on Philosophy*), one obviously cannot now recapture all his thoughts during that period, and for that reason a book like this which relies on his published works must fail to do him full justice. In particular, no consideration of his writings can do justice to the Socratic impact of his character upon philosophical discussions which many people have commented upon. Of the many descriptions of this, my favourite is that by Ryle, from which I will quote at length:

For some of us there still lives the Moore whose voice is never quite resuscitated by his printed words. This is the Moore whom we met at Cambridge and at the annual Joint Session of the Mind Association and the Aristotelian Society. Moore was a dynamo of courage. He gave us courage not by making concessions, but by making no concessions to our youth or to our shyness. He treated us as corrigible and therefore as responsible thinkers. He would explode at our mistakes and muddles with just that genial ferocity with which he would explode at the mistakes and muddles of philosophical high-ups, and with just the genial ferocity with which he would explode at mistakes and muddles of his own. He would listen with minute attention to what we said, and then, without a trace of discourtesy or courtesy, treat our remarks simply on their merits, usually, of course, and justly inveighing against their inadequacy, irrelevance or confusedness, but sometimes, without a trace of politeness or patronage, crediting them with whatever positive utility he thought that they possessed. If, as sometimes happened, he found in someone's interposition the exposure of a confusion or a fallacy of his own, he would announce that this was so, confess to his own unbelievable muddle-headedness or slackness of reasoning, and then with full acknowledgment, adopt and work with the new clarification.[5]

Moore's influence is most obvious within the world of academic philosophy. He was the 'philosopher's philosopher', and avoided the active public role which Russell enjoyed (and equally the public reputation which Wittgenstein unintentionally brought upon himself). But his ideas also had importance for those whose primary interests did not lie in philosophy. In his early years at Cambridge he exerted a powerful influence on some of those who were later to constitute the Bloomsbury Group – especially Clive Bell, Desmond MacCarthy, Maynard Keynes and Leonard Woolf (with all of whom he remained on close terms). Just how important Moore's influence was upon their work and that of other members of the Bloomsbury Group is disputed, and there is no general answer to this. But a comment of Virginia Woolf's is perhaps indicative; writing in 1940 to a friend, she asks 'did you ever read the book that made us all so wise and good: *Principia Ethica?*'[6] Thus paradoxically this philosopher's philosopher had at least as powerful an impact on British culture as his more obviously engaged philosophical contemporaries. In fact music was nearer to Moore's heart than the literature and the visual arts characteristic of Bloomsbury, and he also enjoyed a long friendship with Ralph Vaughan Williams. So, despite his exclusively academic career, one should not think of Moore as someone whose sole interest was philosophy. It is not for nothing that one of his sons was a poet and the other is a distinguished musician.

PREFACE

This book is, I fear, rather longer than it should be. Its structure, however, is straightforward. In the first two chapters I discuss Moore's early philosophy – his break with idealism, and his new realism. The next two chapters deal with his ethical writings, concentrating on his ethical non-naturalism and ideal utilitarianism. In chapter 5 I discuss the transition from the early to the mature philosophy, and in the last four chapters I attempt to assess critically this mature philosophy, dealing with his response to Russell's programme of logical analysis and his arguments concerning philosophical analysis, perception, and knowledge. At different times I have inflicted parts of the book on students and colleagues at York and Cambridge, and I am much indebted to them for their patience and advice. I am also indebted to Casimir Lewy, who gave me advice at an early stage of my work and permitted me to look at some of Moore's unpublished papers that are still in his care, to Peter Hylton, who helped me to understand Moore's early philosophy, to Stewart Candlish, who gave me invaluable advice about Bradley's philosophy, and to Ted Honderich, for advice and encouragment in completing the book. But most of all I am indebted to my wife, Anna, who has encouraged and supported me throughout the time I have been working on it.

# Acknowledgements

I am very grateful to Timothy Moore, for permission to quote from his father's unpublished papers. I am also grateful to Edward Arnold (Publishers) Ltd, for permission to quote the passage from *The Longest Journey* by E.M. Forster which appears on p. v; to the Hogarth Press and estate of Virginia Woolf for permission to quote the passage from her collected letters which appears on p. 65; and to Dr Jonathan Miller for permission to quote the passage he wrote for the show *Beyond the Fringe* which appears on p. 172.

# Abbreviations

This is a list of the abbreviations I have used to refer to Moore's works and books about him. It is not a complete list of his published writings (there is a nearly complete bibliography of Moore's works at the end of *The Philosophy of G.E. Moore* ed. P.A. Schilpp (*PGEM*)).

A&L    *G.E. Moore: Essays in Retrospect* ed. A. Ambrose and M. Lazerowitz (Allen & Unwin, London: 1970).

B    *Dictionary of Philosophy and Psychology* ed. J. Baldwin vols 1–2 (Macmillan, London: 1901–2).

C    'Certainty' in *PP*.

CB    *Commonplace Book* ed. C. Lewy (Allen & Unwin, London: 1962).

CCA    'The Character of Cognitive Acts' *Proceedings of the Aristotelian Society* 1920–1.

CIV    'The Conception of Intrinsic Value' in *PS*.

CR    'The Conception of Reality' *Proceedings of the Aristotelian Society* 1917–18. References are to the paper as reprinted in *PS*.

DCS    'The Defence of Common Sense' in *Contemporary British Philosophy:* 2nd series ed. J. Muirhead (Allen & Unwin, London: 1925). References are to the paper as reprinted in *PP*.

E    *Ethics* (Williams & Norgate, London: 1912). References are to the Oxford University Press (1966) edition.

EE    Moore's 1898–9 lectures on 'The Elements of Ethics with a view to an appreciation of Kant's Moral Philosophy'. These lectures have not been published, but their text survives, and it is said that an edition is in course of preparation.

EP    'Is Existence a Predicate?' *Aristotelian Society Supplementary Volume* 15 1936. References are to the paper as reprinted in *PP*.

E&E    'Experience and Empiricism' *Proceedings of the Aristotelian Society* 1902–3.

E&IR 'External and Internal Relations' *Proceedings of the Aristotelian Society* 1919–20. References are to the paper as reprinted in *PP*.

F 'Freedom' *Mind* 1898.

F&P 'Facts and Propositions' *Aristotelian Society Supplementary Volume* 7 1927. References are to the paper as reprinted in *PP*.

HP 'Hume's Philosophy' *New Quarterly* 1909. References are to the paper as reprinted in *PS*.

I 'Identity' *Proceedings of the Aristotelian Society* 1900–1.

IO 'Imaginary Objects' *Aristotelian Society Supplementary Volume* 12 1933. References are to the paper as reprinted in *PP*.

KBA 'Is There "Knowledge by Acquaintance"?' *Aristotelian Society Supplementary Volume* 2 1919.

KI 'Kant's Idealism' *Proceedings of the Aristotelian Society* 1903–4.

LP *Lectures on Philosophy* ed. C. Lewy (Allen & Unwin, London: 1966).

N 'Necessity' *Mind* 1900.

NJ 'The Nature of Judgment' *Mind* 1899.

NROP 'The Nature and Reality of the Objects of Perception' *Proceedings of the Aristotelian Society* 1905–6. References are to the paper as reprinted in *PS*.

NSA 'The Nature of Sensible Appearances' *Aristotelian Society Supplementary Volume* 6 1926.

PE *Principia Ethica* (Cambridge University Press, Cambridge: 1903).

PEW 'Proof of an External World' *Proceedings of the British Academy* 1939. References are to the paper as reprinted in *PP*.

PGEM *The Philosophy of G.E. Moore* ed. P.A. Schilpp (Northwestern, Evanston: 1st ed. 1942). References are to 3rd ed. (Open Court, La Salle: 1968).

PP *Philosophical Papers* (Allen & Unwin, London: 1959).

PS *Philosophical Studies* (Routledge, London: 1922).

RI 'The Refutation of Idealism' *Mind* 1903. References are to the paper as reprinted in *PS*.

RTD 'Russell's "Theory of Descriptions"' in *The Philosophy of Bertrand Russell* ed. P.A. Schilpp (Northwestern, Evanston: 1944). References are to the paper as reprinted in *PP*.

SJP 'Some Judgments of Perception' *Proceedings of the Aristotelian Society* 1918–19. References are to the paper as reprinted in *PS*.

SMP 'The Subject-Matter of Psychology' *Proceedings of the Aristotelian Society* 1909–10.

SMPP *Some Main Problems of Philosophy* (Allen & Unwin, London: 1953).

SSD 'The Status of Sense-Data' *Proceedings of the Aristotelian Society* 1913–14. References are to the paper as reprinted in *PS*.

ABBREVIATIONS

VR    'The Value of Religion' *International Journal of Ethics* 1901.

VSD  'Visual Sense-Data' in *British Philosophy in the Mid-Century* ed. C. Mace (Allen & Unwin, London: 1957). References are to the paper as reprinted in *Perceiving, Sensing, and Knowing* ed. R. Swartz (Anchor, New York: 1965).

WJP  'Professor James' "Pragmatism"' *Proceedings of the Aristotelian Society* 1907–8. Reprinted as 'William James' "Pragmatism"' in *PS*.

4FS   'Four Forms of Scepticism' in *PP*.

# I

# The refutation of idealism

In his autobiography Moore describes his first meeting with McTaggart:

> Russell had invited me to tea in his rooms to meet McTaggart; and McTaggart, in the course of conversation, had been led to express his well-known view that Time is unreal. This must have seemed to me then (as it still does) a perfectly monstrous proposition, and I did my best to argue against it.
>
> *(PGEM* pp. 13–14)[2]

This story suggests that from the start of his interest in philosophy Moore was antagonistic towards the idealist philosophy of McTaggart and others, and that his rejection of idealism was the response of a stubborn common-sense to the monstrous claims of that philosophy. But the truth is more complex. For, as Moore also says in his autobiography, of those who taught him philosophy at Cambridge, he was least impressed by Sidgwick, a formidable critic of idealism, and most impressed by McTaggart, who converted him to idealism, and made him an 'enthusiastic admirer' of F.H. Bradley (*PGEM* p. 22).

In this chapter I shall chart the course of Moore's critical response to idealism, from initial enthusiasm to polemical rejection. For, with the benefit of hindsight, Moore's break with idealism must strike us as a rupture of decisive significance in the development of analytic

1

philosophy, not only because of its implications for his own later work, but also because it was followed by Russell and others.[3] Of course, not all British philosophers of the latter part of the nineteenth century were idealists (Sidgwick and Cook Wilson, for example, were not), nor were all philosophers of the early twentieth century impressed by Moore's arguments against idealism. But just as the influential philosophers of the 1890s were the idealists (witness the influence of McTaggart and Bradley on the young Russell and Moore), so it was Moore and Russell who set the style for subsequent generations – including ourselves.

## 1: Moore as idealist

What excited Moore about the idealists was their denial that everything that exists is a natural object, existing in time (if not space) and to be understood through the use of the senses (including introspection). In the writings of Kant, this denial is sometimes expressed through a distinction between the world of appearances and that of things in themselves, with the natural world assigned to the former category. In his early writings Moore strongly endorsed this appearance/reality distinction; it is a distinction, he writes in 1897 (in an Apostles' paper[4]), 'than which I know none more profound'. Moore's reasons for endorsing the distinction are varied but one predominates: Kant's arguments (in his first 'antinomy' cf. *Critique of Pure Reason* A409, B436ff.) to the effect that space and time cannot be absolutely real because they are infinite. Thus in his 1898 article F, Moore argues that one must reject 'the common point of view which takes the world of experience as ultimately real' (p. 194) for

> the world as a whole is an impossible conception, if the objects of experience be taken to be its ultimate constituents, since they are necessarily conceived as in the infinite forms of space and time.
>
> (p. 195)

Hence

> the complete reason of all that appears must be placed in a supersensible reality. This supersensible reality is the world as a whole.
>
> (p. 195)

As I mentioned, the thesis that time is unreal is precisely that which astonished Moore when he first heard it from McTaggart. It is a measure of the latter's influence that Moore's first published piece contains an emphatic endorsement of this thesis[5] (even though, as I shall argue below, Moore did not always interpret this thesis in the way in which Bradley and McTaggart did). But Moore's enthusiasm for idealism is

2

most apparent in the dissertation which he submitted, unsuccessfully, in 1897 for the Trinity College Fellowship competition. Most of the text of this dissertation survives, along with that of the dissertation he submitted, successfully, in the following year. These dissertations are crucial documents for an account of Moore's response to idealism and I shall refer to them frequently in the ensuing discussion (where they will be described as the 1897 Dissertation and 1898 Dissertation).[6]

The 1897 Dissertation, on 'The Metaphysical Basis of Ethics', opens with an acknowledgement of Bradley's influence: 'It is to Mr. Bradley's *Principles of Logic* and *Appearance and Reality* that I chiefly owe my conception of the fundamental problems of metaphysics.' One is, therefore, led to expect a Bradleian study in ethical theory; and this is, to some degree, what Moore provides. He begins by using Bradley's thesis that time is unreal to criticise Kant's distinction between theoretical and practical reason. Moore takes it that any study which deals with what is real is theoretical, and argues that once it is understood that 'time seems to be a merely empirical datum, which, as such, must be discarded, when a logical test of reality is set up' the fact that what ought to be does not exist in time is irrelevant to the question of its reality. Indeed, Moore proclaims, 'what only "ought" to exist in time, certainly may *prima facie*, and (as will appear if the present discussion is successful) *must* "be" in the transcendental sense – or, to adopt the language of modern Idealism, must be real'. So the study of what ought to be is a study of a genuine aspect of reality, and therefore as theoretical a study as any.

This argument, of course, misses the point of Kant's distinction between theoretical and practical reason, which has to be understood in the context of his account of the *a priori* and its relation to the understanding and the will. As we shall see, Moore also disputes Kant's account of the *a priori*, and in that way argues against Kant's practical/theoretical distinction. But that argument need not concern us now; instead it is worth observing the connection here with the naturalistic fallacy. Where goodness is understood as the concept of what ought to be and Moore's Bradleian metaphysics is then applied, it cannot be right to identify this concept with any empirical concept that concerns only temporal appearances. Hence, as Moore writes, there arises 'the fallacy involved in all empirical definitions of the good'. This accusation of an 'empiricist' fallacy is clearly an early version of Moore's accusation of a naturalistic fallacy. However the connection between idealism and the naturalistic fallacy is complicated by the fact that in criticising the very idea of an 'empirical definition of the good' Moore does not distinguish the thesis that goodness is empirical from the thesis that it is definable. Only the accusation that the former thesis is fallacious has any direct connection with idealism: the thought that

3

there is a fallacy in defining goodness Moore took from his teacher, that implacable enemy of idealist ethics, Henry Sidgwick.

The bulk of Moore's 1897 Dissertation was devoted to a critical discussion of Kant's views about freedom. He published the parts dealing with the metaphysical aspects of Kant's views as 'Freedom' (1898), and I shall discuss these later in this chapter. But that article ends with a reference to the ethical aspect of Kant's views – to the problem of establishing 'a valid connection between the notion of Transcendental Freedom and that of End or Good' (F p. 204). This problem, to which the article offers no solution, is tackled in the 1897 Dissertation. Moore has already argued that Kant is confused about freedom, in particular that, for Kant, the freedom that is necessarily connected with ethical issues has nothing to do with the human will; instead it is the ability of the reality that is beyond sensible appearances to be the reason for all that appears (F pp. 183–5), so that the connection to be established is this: 'That, that which is ultimately real appearing to us as the reason of whatever happens, is also necessarily "good", and alone absolutely good' (this passage is not in F). And Moore does indeed assert that there is precisely such a connection between reality and the good, though I cannot say that his rather mystical prose contains any arguments for this position ('Evil . . . expresses less than good of the nature of reality and more of mere appearance').

## 2: Idealism rejected

This claim is the high water mark of Moore's youthful attachment to idealism. A year later, in the 1898 Dissertation, Moore makes no such claim; here Moore asserts that freedom has no special link with the moral law, and thus concludes that 'the whole construction of Kantian freedom seems finally to fall to the ground'. More importantly, in this dissertation Moore also begins to detach himself from his appearance/reality distinction, although since the 1898 Dissertation contains large chunks of the 1897 Dissertation, with only minor alterations, it is sometimes not clear just what his views were. But one point which is clear is that he still endorses Kant's arguments for the unreality of space and time, though now subject to an important qualification: Moore takes it that these arguments show that our ordinary conception of the world as in space and time is false; but they do not show (as he had previously assumed) that it concerns appearances conceived as in some way subjective (Moore repeats this point in *SMPP* pp. 170ff.). Thus the idealist reality/appearance distinction is, in part, replaced by a truth/falsehood distinction, with Kant's arguments interpreted as showing that all our ordinary empirical judgments are false. Moore now writes:

4

The world of phenomena, we may say, is a world consisting of existential propositions which are all of them false, because they all involve time, if not space, and therefore both of two mutually exclusive alternatives. . . . The world of noumena is the world of true propositions that are consistent both among themselves and with one or other of these two alternatives. Of this world, it may be admitted, we know little yet; but still there are some propositions, such as those of Arithmetic and Logic, which are independent of space and time, and may therefore be said to belong to it.

At the same time as he makes this move, Moore introduces an obscure distinction to which he attaches great importance for some time thereafter − between being and existence. Thus in *PE* (pp. 111–12) although idealist philosophers are praised for acknowledging (unlike the empiricists) that not everything which is exists in time, they are rebuked for thinking that whatever is timeless exists timelessly. Although Moore makes it clear that, unlike 'existence', 'being' is 'an absolutely universal term' (B vol. 2 p. 421), he never provides an account of this being/existence distinction. But we can feel our way towards his intentions by comparing what has timeless being, but not existence, with what would have timeless existence if it existed at all. To the first category belong numbers and values, and also propositions and at least some concepts (NJ p. 178, *PE* p. 111); to the second belong initially Kantian noumena, and soon afterwards God, the Absolute, and all the fictions of idealist metaphysics (*PE* pp. 112–14). Thus timeless existence would seem to be a mark of that putative reality which is introduced to account for the structure of appearances, and Moore's thought appears to be that if these appearances are thought of as grounded at all, they should be thought of as grounded in a timeless reality that actually exists. Hence what looks like a trivial verbal distinction between 'being' and 'existence' is to be understood as a sign of a distinction between pure abstract objects such as numbers and a metaphysical reality which is supposed to be the ground of our ordinary temporal experience. In the 1898 Dissertation Moore does not completely rule the latter out; but he holds that no reason for it has been given − 'Transcendental Freedom . . . is possible, as a chimaera is possible, but in no other sense. There is no ground for asserting the existence of anything timeless' (in *PE* Moore expresses the same attitude with his deliberately deflating comparison between idealist metaphysics and fiction − pp. 121–2).

Once Moore has come to regard the conception of a timeless metaphysical reality as merely chimerical, much of the content of his previous idealism has been discarded. What lies behind this change of view is his rejection of Kant's arguments concerning the need for a transcendental foundation for the possibility of synthetic *a priori* truths;

and the 1898 Dissertation opens with two new chapters sharply critical of Kant's account of the synthetic *a priori* which I discuss in the next section of this chapter. None the less, Moore still here subscribes to a vestigial appearance/reality distinction through his continued acceptance of Kant's arguments for the inherent inconsistency of judgments concerning space and time (cf. his talk of 'phenomena' and 'noumena' in the passage quoted above). Within a year, however, even this vestige has disappeared: in some of the pieces for Baldwin's *Dictionary of Philosophy* which he wrote around 1899 (cf. *PGEM* p. 23) Moore affirms the reality of space and time (cf. in particular 'Change' and 'Relative and Absolute') without any qualification.

Moore's influential paper 'The Nature of Judgment' shows his views on this matter at the moment of transition. This paper, published in 1899, is largely taken from the new chapters written for the 1898 Dissertation.[7] Since Moore advances the doctrine of the unreality of space and time in this dissertation, one would expect NJ to cohere with it. But the text of NJ itself is in fact elusive on this topic. At one point Moore writes that 'existential propositions which are false, as well as those which are true, involve the same propositions about space and time' (p. 191) which suggests that some such propositions are true; but he also writes that though 'it is not proposed to dispute the truth of particular existential propositions' the truth of any such propositions is 'merely assumed' (p. 191) and is indeed 'highly doubtful' (p. 192). Yet what is clear is that the central conception that Moore puts forward in NJ, that of the world as a system of true propositions in no way dependent upon us for their truth, does not cohere well with the belief that absolutely all empirical propositions are false. Hence it is not surprising that even if he did still accept this belief when preparing NJ Moore should have played it down and that he should have rejected it soon afterwards. Once it is rejected, Moore's abandonment of the 'Kantian' reality/appearance distinction is complete. His position in the 1898 Dissertation constitutes a temporary, and essentially incoherent, stage in the transition from idealism to realism.

I have yet to explain how Moore seeks to justify this transition. As we shall see, Moore advances a host of more or less satisfactory arguments to this end; but on the specific issue of refuting Kant's influential arguments concerning infinity, Moore is indebted to Russell. One of Russell's main purposes, and achievments, in *The Principles of Mathematics* (cf. especially chapter LII) was to provide a decisive refutation of Kant's arguments, to 'play the part of Samson' to Kant and his disciples (p. 457). Moore recognised this achievement. In 1905 he wrote a long review of *The Principles of Mathematics* (cf. *PGEM* p. 27); although this was never published, a manuscript of it survives.[8] In it Moore concentrates on Russell's refutation of Kant's arguments, and comments: 'We may conclude, then, that such arguments are one and all fallacious; and considering how many philosophical theories have been supported by the supposition that infinity is impossible, such a conclusion is not without importance.' Thus although in general Russell followed where Moore led, on this issue Moore was indebted to Russell for legitimating the final step in his passage from idealism.

### 3: The critique of Kant

In considering Moore's criticisms of Kantian idealism, it is useful to return briefly to the 1897 Dissertation. In my previous discussion of it I implied that Moore is here an uncritical Kantian idealist. That impression must now be corrected. As I have indicated, Moore's main topic in his 1897 Dissertation was Kant's account of freedom, and I have already mentioned two of Moore's main points: (i) that 'Transcendental Freedom might be taken to describe the relation between Reality and Appearance' (as Moore put it in a letter to Russell of September 1898[9]); (ii) that the Kantian thought that there is a link between freedom and the moral law is to be captured by the recognition of a necessary connection between reality and the good. There is also a third point which now concerns us: (iii) that Kant is mistaken in thinking that there is any respect in which human agents are distinctively free. Moore argues that, given Kant's determinism with respect to appearances and (cf. (i) above) the fact that noumenal freedom applies to all reality, there is simply no space left for any special relationship between the human will and freedom.

This is a frequent complaint concerning Kant's account of freedom, but what is distinctive is the way in which Moore suggests that Kant confuses himself on this matter (cf. F pp. 198–201). Kant is said, correctly, to hold that men are especially free because in the case of man alone 'reason determines the will'. Moore claims, however, that this phrase is crucially ambiguous: does Kant mean by 'reason' thoughts about the moral law or the moral law itself? If the former, then we are still on the level of phenomena, and there is no reason for supposing that there is here anything other than natural causality; if the latter were meant, however, there would seem to be something special about man. But, Moore argues, it is only through confusing this second thesis with the first that Kant makes it appear defensible. Let us not ask whether Moore is right about this; what is significant is his allegation that Kant's mistake about freedom rests on a confused assimilation of the moral law to thoughts about it. For Moore proceeds to generalise this complaint into a general complaint about Kant's idealism:

In this Kant betrays the too psychological standpoint above which he seems never to have completely risen in treating epistemological questions, in spite of the enormous services which he did to epistemology, as well as in the metaphysics of ethics elsewhere. . . . It is perhaps impossible to dispense with the term 'rational' for what is true or objective, especially after its full adoption by Hegel; but it is extremely important to avoid confusing the 'rational' in this sense which is the fundamental one for Kant's system, with the 'rational' in the sense of that which implies the psychological faculty of making judgments and inferences. The distinction between what is true and what is only believed (although only a 'rational' being can believe) is one which cannot be either done away or bridged over.

(F pp. 199–200)

With this passage from his 1897 Dissertation Moore introduces his general onslaught upon what he regards as the excessive subjectivism of Kant and his followers. We have seen that he accuses Kant of confusing thoughts about the moral law with the moral law itself; and it is only a short step from this to reject the Kantian thought that there is a necessary connection between the will and the moral law. In his 1897 Dissertation Moore takes this step, writing (this part is not in F, but Moore here refers to the passage quoted just now):

To try to obtain this objective validity out of 'Will' – this 'ought to be willed' out of 'I or you or all the world, do, or can, or must will this' – is a procedure similar to trying to prove 'this is true' from the fact that all the world believe it. The assertion of 'goodness' claims rationality in the sense explained above precisely as does the assertion of truth: the first has no more connection with volition than the latter with cognition.

The last phrase here introduces one of Moore's favourite targets, the 'vicious traditional assumption that the distinction between what is and what ought to be is identical with that between what is known and what is willed'.[10] That, in attacking this, Moore was at least attacking a central assumption of idealist philosophy is attested by Bosanquet's report as examiner on Moore's 1898 Dissertation (where the attack is developed much further). After praising Moore's dialectical skill highly, Bosanquet proceeds to say that the dissertation is intellectually worthless. He accurately discerns Moore's central aim – 'to dissociate Truth from the nature of knowledge, and Good from the nature of the Will, so as to free Metaphysic from all risk of confusion with Psychology'; and then complains that 'to get rid of mere psychology, the essential idea of consciousness and cognition as an endeavour towards unity has been abandoned, and relational truth has been hypostatised as a self-subsistent form of Reality', and that 'the divorce between "good" and the nature of the will . . . seems to me to indicate an equally

8

hopeless surrender of the most important connections'.

Hostility to subjectivism is one of the two central themes of Moore's critique of idealism, and that which predominates in his discussion of Kantian idealism. Essentially what Moore does is to simplify and then radically generalise the anti-psychologism which is a standard feature of idealist criticisms of empiricism, thereby creating an anti-subjectivist line of argument that can be turned against idealism itself. Although in relation to Kant's philosophy itself the topic is not of great interest, since it rests on an excessively subjectivist interpretation of Kant, it is none the less of central importance for Moore's philosophy since it is partly through his criticisms of Kant that Moore defines his own position. I shall therefore consider his critical discussions of Kantian theories concerning ethics, *a priori* truths, and perception.

I begin with the onslaught on Kantian ethics where, as I have observed, Moore's basic point is that Kant and his followers have erroneously sought to exhibit the moral law as internal to the structure of the will (*PE* pp. 126–7). This point is conceived by Moore as a generalisation of Kant's criticism of hedonism as heteronomous. Moore's thought is that it makes little significant difference whether or not we treat human psychology as a purely empirical, or natural, phenomenon; even if we regard people as in some respects non-empirical it is still a mistake to try to derive moral principles from psychological premises. Kant's account of the moral law, he says 'makes his Ethics ultimately and hopelessly "heteronomous" ' (*PE* p. 127).

Moore's criticism of Kant's ethical theory is best understood as the outcome of foisting a correspondence conception of moral truth upon Kant, and then arguing that in this view morality is unacceptably dependent upon the condition of a transcendental object. Given this way of putting Moore's criticism, the correct response is that it is a mistake to employ a correspondence conception of truth to interpret Kant's ethical theory; Kant's appeal to practical reason is better understood as introducing the thought that in morality, truth is rationality, that the practical reasonings of free agents embody a commitment to the moral la v. Admittedly it is not clear how this commitment arises (this is the standard criticism of Kant's theory); but the nature of the project is clear enough. Thus Moore's criticism of Kant's ethical theory largely misses the point of the theory. There is a certain irony in this: when I come to discuss Moore's ethical theory in detail in chapter 3 I shall argue that Moore's theory is best reconstructed (I do not say interpreted) as an incomplete Kantian theory. But what it crucially lacks is a foundation in a philosophy which explains how the fundamental principles of morality can be both synthetic and necessary, as Moore, like Kant, takes them to be.

This lack is no simple oversight. Moore argued that, on the contrary,

9

Kant's philosophy, both theoretical and practical, was crucially flawed by its reliance on a transcendental foundation. His attack on Kant's ethical theory rests on the claim that Kant wrongly regarded the truth of the *a priori* principles of morality as constituted by the structure of the rational will. It is easy to see how this can be generalised to apply to all *a priori* principles, and in the 1897 Dissertation this generalisation is briefly suggested. It is, however, in the 1898 Dissertation that Moore addresses himself explicitly to this task; he devotes the first chapter to arguing that Kant's account of the *a priori* embodies a radical confusion of sound logic and irrelevant psychology.

What he takes to be sound in Kant's work are the arguments of the Transcendental Aesthetic and Analytic whereby Kant is taken to show that geometry, arithmetic, and the principles of the permanence of substance and universality of causality are 'involved in' or 'logically presupposed by' ordinary empirical judgments (NJ pp. 190–2). In view of the attack on Kant that I am about to consider, it is worth stressing that at this time, and for two or three years to come, Moore did believe that Kant's arguments established important 'logical' (i.e. conceptual) truths. Thus in his one published paper on religion ('The Value of Religion'[11]) he employs an argument for determinism based on Kant's argument concerning the universality of causality. Since these claims do not occur in his writings after 1901, I assume he then changed his mind (perhaps under Russell's influence). However, the claims which Moore attributed to Kant, and believed to be correct, are of the form 'that $p$ presupposes that $q$'; these are, therefore, not the claims which more recent critics of Kant (e.g. Strawson) have commended. The claims which they have commended are of the form 'that we can know that $p$ presupposes that $q$'; and that these latter claims do indeed capture Kant's intentions better than Moore's is, I think, certainly correct.[12]

Moore's criticism of Kant's ethical theory rested on the thesis that Kant confuses two senses of the term 'rational', an objective and a psychological one. The same accusation forms the basis of Moore's criticism of Kant's account of *a priori* knowledge. In his talk of 'Reason', Moore remarks, Kant's language 'is obviously metaphorical language; but it is just this metaphorical personification of Reason, of which I think Kant never cleared his thought' (1898 Dissertation). For, Moore argues, in Kant's *Critique of Pure Reason*

> 'Reason' . . . usurps the function of a logical condition, but at the same time, since it is never identified with a proposition, it is regarded as some sort of substantial entity, and therefore as a causal condition of the *a priori*.

To this Moore has two objections. First, he accuses Kant of trying to bridge over the gulf between a thought and its truth; Kant may perhaps be able to show that we cannot but think of the world in the manner prescribed by his *a priori* principles, but from this nothing follows as to the truth of these principles. Moore asks in the 1898 Dissertation: 'how can he [Kant] prove the proposition that what is necessary to consciousness is true?' and in *PE* he is especially scornful on this point:

> That 'to be true' *means* to be thought in a certain way is, therefore, certainly false. Yet this assertion plays the most essential part in Kant's 'Copernican Revolution' of philosophy, and renders worthless the whole mass of modern literature, to which that revolution has given rise, and which is called Epistemology.
>
> (p. 133)

Moore's second objection is that Kant cannot account for the necessity of his synthetic *a priori* principles. For the assumptions about the operations of the mind, from which Kant hopes to derive his *a priori* principles, must be themselves either contingent or necessary. If they are contingent, they cannot provide a basis for the necessity of the *a priori* principles, for any such explanation of them would 'presume to deduce a necessity from a mere fact, namely that our mind is so and so constituted, and this on Kant's own principles, effectually excludes the propositions deduced from any claim to be absolutely necessary' (1898 Dissertation). Yet if they are necessary, then there must be synthetic *a priori* principles characterising these necessities, and these *a priori* principles cannot be explained by reference to the mind's operations – 'it [the mind] could not therefore be a logical basis from which their necessity could be deduced' (1898 Dissertation).

Moore was sufficiently satisfied with these objections to repeat them five times during the next ten years or so.[13] To come at Kant's arguments this way is to interpret them in the light of a correspondence theory of truth (so that 'reason' has to be 'some sort of substantial entity'); as in the ethical case, therefore, Moore's criticisms can be set aside as the outcome of a misinterpretation. In place of a correspondence conception of truth, a rationalist account of *a priori* truth is required (this is Kant's 'Copernican revolution'). Yet it does not follow that Moore's criticisms are wholly off target. In particular, when Kant's position is formulated in terms of an account of the presuppositions of knowledge there remain analogues of Moore's two objections which can be represented as objections to transcendental arguments. The first objection suggests that transcendental arguments can show only what we must take to be the case if beings like us have empirical knowledge at all; and such presuppositions might for all that be false. The second objection suggests that transcendental arguments can at best show what follows from the hypothesis that we have empirical knowledge, from

11

THE REFUTATION OF IDEALISM

which no unconditional necessity follows. Indeed these problems for transcendental arguments have been much discussed in recent literature and I shall not take the matter further.[14]

Kant's treatment of synthetic *a priori* truths is intimately related to his transcendental idealism. So it is no surprise that Moore should have extended his criticism of Kant's Copernican revolution to a criticism of transcendental idealism. In doing so Moore argues that in his treatment of empirical objects as phenomena Kant reveals himself as a phenomenalist, and this then becomes the third area within which Moore develops his anti-subjectivist critique of Kant. In imputing phenomenalism to Kant, Moore acknowledges both that Kant says that his transcendental idealism is distinct from the 'empirical idealism' of Berkeley and that it is distinct, especially in respect of Kant's account of the forms of intuition and categories of the understanding (KI pp. 128–9). But Moore argues that none the less Kant's account of what it is for us to have objective knowledge of the external world commits him to phenomenalism (KI pp. 138–40). Whether in fact a phenomenalist characterisation of Kant's position is correct is a notoriously problematic issue which it is not necessary to pursue here.[15] But what matters more than the justice of Moore's description of Kant is his objection to phenomenalism. Moore is inclined to put his objection very bluntly: to the Kantian account of objectivity as justified by the connectedness and coherence of our *vorstellungen* (which Moore translates as 'sensations'), Moore objects that these are not at all the same thing: objectivity requires real existence and 'when I say that chair exists, what I think is *not* that certain sensations of mine are connected by the categories. What I do think is that certain *objects* of sensation do really exist in a real space and really are causes and effects of other things' (KI p. 140).

Statements of this kind are not arguments; so the question arises as to whether Moore provides any argument for the position he here affirms so forcefully. In so far as he does, the argument is set out in his famous paper 'The Refutation of Idealism' (RI), whose title adverts twice to Kant; once, obviously, in respect of the phrase used, but also ironically in that Kant's idealism is among the idealisms that are supposed to be therein refuted (RI p. 30).[16]

## 4: Content, concept, and object

Moore puts his objection to phenomenalism by saying that phenomenalists mistakenly treat the object of sensation as its content (RI p. 26). So expressed, the objection makes crucial use of the terms 'object' and 'content' and I shall now digress a little from the topic of phenomenalism in order to elucidate Moore's use of these terms.

12

In his earliest writings Moore uses the expression 'content of thought' as synonymous with 'what is thought', as when he writes of the 'impassable gulf' which separates any idea from 'the content, of which it is an idea' (F p. 199). Although it is tempting to read these passages as implying that the content of a thought or idea is a thing to which a subject is just related in thought, Moore's language is not sharply delineated. But the 1898 Dissertation contains, in the two new chapters which Moore added, arguments critical of all talk of 'contents' of thought. In particular, chapter 2, the bulk of which Moore published as NJ, begins with the following thesis (not in NJ): 'Our object will be now to show that, whatever name be given to it, that which we call a proposition is something independent of consciousness' and continues with an argument that concepts, which Moore takes to be the constituent elements of propositions, are in no way 'parts of the content of ideas'. His own talk of 'contents' is quietly forgotten, and instead he criticises the account of judgment which Bradley presents in his *Principles of Logic*.[17]

Bradley's view is correctly identified by Moore as the view that the meaning of a sign is part of its 'content' – 'cut off, fixed by the mind and considered apart from the existence of the sign' (*The Principles of Logic* p. 4). This claim needs some elucidation. 'Signs', for Bradley, are things with meaning, and can be either verbal or mental; 'content' just describes the totality of a thing's properties – 'the complex of qualities and relations it contains' (p. 3) – which Bradley, assuming the identity of indiscernibles, takes to give the thing 'a character which is different or distinguishable from that of other facts' (p. 3). Bradley now observes that where a sign has a meaning, that meaning cannot be identified with the sign's total content, for another sign can have the same meaning. Furthermore, the meaning cannot be just the type of mental image associated with the sign, for the details of our images are irrelevant to the meaning of our signs. Bradley takes these misidentifications to have been characteristic of Bain, Mill, and other empiricists, who wrongly sought to reduce logic to psychology. Instead, he argues, it is our use of signs in judgment, and especially our treatment of some of them as true or false, that identifies their meaning. Furthermore, because we tend to concern ourselves solely with this role of signs we are liable to treat the meaning of a sign as an aspect of its content that can be 'cut off' and 'considered apart from the existence of a sign'. We talk of judgments as if the judgment 'that $p$' were a thing in its own right, when in fact it is just an aspect of, part of the content of, particular concrete signs.

Although this seems correct as far as it goes, it leaves much unaccounted for; in particular it does not explain how particular signs have the roles in judgment that they do have. The empiricist image theory is at least an attempt to account for this, albeit an inadequate one. But it is not necessary to pursue Bradley's account of the matter further, for when one turns to Moore's criticisms it quickly emerges that Moore misunderstood Bradley. He takes Bradley to be propounding a refined psychologism according to which the meaning of a mental sign, an idea, is an abstracted feature of its total conscious content (NJ p. 177). Moore then observes that abstraction requires judgment, and hence meanings, which cannot have been formed by abstraction on pain of infinite regress (NJ p. 178). This familiar anti-empiricist argument, though sound enough in itself, only has force against Bradley if Bradley is committed to abstraction in this sense. Bradley certainly writes of the meaning of an idea as 'a parasite cut loose, a spirit without a body seeking to rest in another, an abstraction from the concrete' (*The Principles of Logic* p. 8) but these metaphorical expressions need not imply that any mental act of abstraction is involved in the use of an idea with a particular meaning. Furthermore in this case we have Bradley's own word for it that Moore has misunderstood him; for in 1899 Bradley wrote a letter to Moore in which he responded to Moore's criticisms in NJ of his views.[18] In response to Moore's anti-abstractionist argument, Bradley denies that his talk of 'cutting off' should be taken to imply deliberate abstraction, and thus judgment, on the part of the subject:

> The first [argument] seems to be that the separation of meaning from existence required for judgement presupposes a previous judgement. Well certainly it *may* do so – a psychological judgement, that is, but then again it may not and often does not. . . . I suppose my phrase 'cut off' etc. has been taken to imply *a going about to cut off* and therefore a previous idea. I never meant this. . . . But I admit my language was loose.

Moore advances a further argument against Bradley, but its import is very obscure. He writes that 'Mr. Bradley's theory presupposes that I may have two ideas, that have a part of their content in common; but he would at the same time compel us to describe this common part of content as part of the content of some third idea' (NJ p. 178). In his response to Moore, Bradley protested that there is no such compulsion, and his protest is, I think, just: the phrase 'part of the content of an idea' just means, for Bradley, some of its properties, and his theory is explicitly designed to allow that distinct ideas may have the same meaning by treating the meaning of a sign as one among its properties. This is precisely the point of Bradley's criticism of the empiricist accounts of universals (cf. in particular *The Principles of Logic* p. 309). The only way I can make sense of Moore's argument is by supposing him to take Bradley to be advancing a conceptualist theory of universals, such that for any two things (including ideas) to have a property in common is for them to be judged to be similar in some respect. But if this right, then Moore has added insult to injury by ascribing to Bradley not only an empiricist theory of meaning he did not hold but also the empiricist theory of universals which he was arguing against in *The Principles of Logic*.

For these reasons I cannot pretend that Moore's criticisms of Bradley are satisfactory (it is arguable that Bradley himself is equally unfair to Mill). They were none the less of considerable significance both for Moore's conception of his relationship to Bradley, which I discuss further below, and for his attitude to current accounts of thought and meaning, which he took to be infected with the kind of subjectivism he had ascribed to Bradley. In conscious opposition to all such positions, Moore advanced a 'Realist' thesis (cf. *PGEM* p. 22) that meanings, or 'concepts', form a *'genus per se*, irreducible to anything else', such that 'the concept is not a mental fact, nor any part of a mental fact' (NJ pp. 178–9). Moore seems to have thought that once one rejects the abstractionism which he attributes to Bradley, there is no alternative to a simple-minded realism concerning meanings, according to which the meaning of a sign is an 'entity' (NJ p. 179) of a distinctive kind, to which subjects are related in using a sign with that meaning.

In fact, of course, this is not so. I myself favour an account of meaning in terms of convention that draws on the ideas of H.P. Grice and D. Lewis;[19] but this is not the place to pursue such matters. It may still be said that a version of Moore's early realism concerning meanings remains defensible, since alternative accounts permit the conception of meanings as entities in so far as they generate criteria of synonymy which allow one to introduce a treatment of meanings comparable to that employed by Frege in his account of directions.[20] This line of thought needs to overcome influential arguments to the effect that criteria of synonymy are never sufficiently objective to allow the treatment of meanings as entities.[21] But it is not necessary to pursue that issue here, since even if an abstract realism concerning meanings is defensible, it will not be a position that offers any support to Moore's naive realism. Moore's position is that all thought is to be regarded as fundamentally a relationship between a thinker and a proposition, conceived as composed of concepts which belong to a *'genus per se*, irreducible to anything else'; and this is not compatible with the abstract realist's dependence upon criteria of synonymy that do not themselves presuppose use of the concept of meaning.

There is more to be said about Moore's early realism concerning meanings (cf. chapter 2), but I want now to return to the context of this discussion. I have been discussing Moore's unsatisfactory argument in

NJ that the meaning of an idea is no part of the idea's 'content', but is instead a 'concept', something which exists in its own right. His argument against phenomenalism in RI is basically an attempt to establish a similar conclusion with respect to sense-perception and is anticipated in NJ in the remark that 'perception is to be regarded philosophically as the cognition of an existential proposition' (p. 183). But this extrapolation needs to be argued for; and to develop properly Moore's argument for it, we need first to attend to his use of the term 'object', which does not play an important role in NJ itself.

It is immediately after the 1898 Dissertation that Moore writes of 'objects' of consciousness as things in their own right, merely externally related to the consciousness we have of them. Such objects need not exist and are typically complex, since they are usually propositions. A good example is provided by his discussion of ends in his 1898 lectures on 'The Elements of Ethics'. He distinguishes a sense of 'end' in which it is any 'object of desire', and observes that where I desire to eat an apple the 'object' of my desire is my eating an apple, which is 'one and the same thing, whether it has existed, does exist, or will exist', so that 'the fact that I desire it, seems to make us call it an end; and yet this fact seems to make no difference whatever to what it is in itself'. It is at this time too that Moore begins to deploy an explicit 'object/content' contrast; in his article on 'Truth' he writes of 'the almost universal error, whereby the *object* of a belief or idea is regarded as the attribute or content of such belief or idea' (B vol. 2 p. 717). It is clear that Moore is here using the term 'object' to specify the intentional object of a mental act – what is desired, believed, etc. But, as these passages also show, since he thinks that the phrases which give the intentional object of a mental act denote things which *are* in their own right (whether or not they exist or are thought of), it is only to be expected that he will tend to incorporate this latter belief into his use of the term 'object', just assuming that intentional objects are real objects, if one may so speak. In discussing a version of phenomenalism which rejects this assumption for the objects of sense-experience there is then a manifest danger that questions will be begged. In fact I do not think that this is the case in RI, but it often appears to be so, and in presenting Moore's argument I shall sometimes disambiguate his uses of the term 'object' by adding the prefixes 'intentional' and 'real'.

## 5: The refutation of phenomenalism

We are now in a position to understand properly the central thesis of RI that phenomenalists mistake object for content in sensation.[22] Moore explicitly employs Bradley's account of a thing's 'content', whereby a thing's content comprises its properties, and maintains that a phenomenalist will say that the (intentional) object of sensation is just part of its content. Moore holds that this is not so: his thesis is that the (intentional) object of sensation is always a real object, something which exists in its own right.

He initially explains his use of the crucial phrase 'object of sensation' as that wherein distinct sensations, such as a sensation of blue and one of green, differ. Clearly, 'object' here need mean no more than 'intentional object', and although he proceeds immediately to characterise the object of sensation as a 'distinct element' in sensation, there is not yet anything which a phenomenalist has to reject. Moore, however, moves very rapidly to an emphatic assertion of realism with respect to objects of sensation. Taking as his example a visual sense-experience, a 'sensation of blue', he writes:

> For we can and must conceive the existence of blue as something quite
> distinct from the existence of the sensation. We can and must
> conceive that blue might exist and yet the sensation of blue not exist.
> For my own part I not only conceive this, but conceive it to be true.
>
> (RI pp. 18–19)

Assertion, however emphatic, is not argument; the question is whether Moore gives any good reasons for what he here says.

The answer to this lies in Moore's critical discussion of the phenomenalist claim that the intentional object of sensation is part of its content. Moore tacitly restricts a thing's content to its non-relational qualities, and, thus understood, it is clear why he rejects the claim. Whether a phenomenalist really has to accept it is an issue I shall discuss later. In arguing against it, Moore assumes the following interpretation of what it is to treat the intentional object of a sensation as a quality of it:

> The 'sensation of blue', on this view, differs from a blue bead or a
> blue beard, in exactly the same way in which the two latter differ
> from one another: the blue bead differs from the blue beard, in that
> while the former contains glass, the latter contains hair; and the
> 'sensation of blue' differs from both in that, instead of glass and hair,
> it contains consciousness. The relation of the blue to the consciousness
> is conceived to be exactly the same as that of the blue to the glass or
> the hair: it is in all three cases the *quality* of a *thing*.
>
> (RI p. 22)

What matters now in this strange passage is Moore's interpretation of the claim he is attacking as the claim that for a sensation to be of blue is

17

just for it to be blue. He associates this allegedly phenomenalist claim with the thought that for a phenomenalist sensations are mental images (RI pp. 23–4), related to their intentional objects as an image in a mirror is related to that of which it is a reflection; in both cases, for an image, mental or mirror, to be of blue, it must be blue.

It is a simple matter to refute the principle that for a sensation, or image, to be of $F$ is for it to be $F$: an image of a horse is not a horse. However, this makes things too easy; for Moore's allegedly phenomenalist principle seems to be restricted to colours and other sensible qualities, as in his sole, awkward, example of a sensation of blue. This restriction is not stated by Moore in RI, but I think he just took it for granted that the phrases which give the intentional objects of genuine sensations or sense-experiences describe only sensible qualities. Moore implies as much in his contemporary paper E&E when he denies that we can experience visually the woodenness of a wooden table (p. 91) and in his slightly later paper NROP (1905) this assumption is expressly enunciated: Moore here distinguishes what we normally say we see (e.g. books on a shelf) from what we 'actually see', which amounts only to 'colours, and the size and shape of colours, and spatial relations in three dimensions between these patches of colours' (p. 68).

With this restriction to sensible qualities in place, Moore's phenomenalist principle looks more plausible, and it is now Moore's objection to it that seems peculiar. Moore's objection rests on the assumption (apparent in the passage cited above from p. 22 of RI) that there is no distinction between colours as qualities of material objects (as in 'blue bead') and colours as experienced qualities (as in 'seeing blue' or 'sensation of blue'). That there is any such distinction is itself a contentious claim, though one which Moore was himself to endorse later (cf. e.g. PGEM pp. 657–8; CB p. 327) and at the time of RI the distinction was often made.[23] Discussion of its validity can be postponed until it arises in the context of a discussion of Moore's sense-datum theory in chapter 8; I shall, however, employ here the phrases 'objective quality' and 'phenomenal quality' to describe this distinction, if it is one. In RI Moore treats sensible qualities throughout as objective qualities, and it is this that makes possible his chief argument against his phenomenalist principle. His argument is just that even if visual sensations do have colours, we have no reason to suppose they have the colours that they are of (RI pp. 24–6). Clearly, if we are to think of visual experiences being coloured in the way in which material objects like beads are coloured, Moore's point is correct; but any half-awake defender of Moore's phenomenalist principle will reject its relevance by distinguishing between colours as objective qualities and as phenomenal qualities. For with this distinction, Moore's phenomenalist principle will not entail that 'a sensation of blue . . . differs from a blue bead in

18

exactly the same way in which the two latter [the blue bead and blue beard] differ from one another'; what blue is in the first case (a phenomenal quality) will itself differ from what it is in the other cases (an objective quality).

So far as I can see, therefore, Moore's influential refutation of 'idealism' (i.e. phenomenalism) in RI is a total failure. It is only fair to add that Moore himself later expressed much the same opinion (*PGEM* p. 654), and, indeed, may have held this opinion when in 1922 he commented in the preface to *PS* (p. viii) that RI was 'very confused' and embodied a 'good many down-right mistakes'. One point that Moore must have soon come to recognise is that the issue he here takes to be crucial is not really such. For the sense-datum theory he soon adopts is supposed by him to be consistent with phenomenalism, and yet it precisely does not embody the kind of treatment of the sensible qualities given in sense-experience which in RI he regards as characteristic of phenomenalism; instead of treating them as qualities of sense-experiences, it treats them as sense-data given in experience or properties of them. So even if his argument in RI were persuasive, he would have later acknowledged that it does not suffice for the falsity of phenomenalism. Nor, indeed, is it necessary: those who hold an 'adverbial' view about sensible qualities (cf. chapter 8, section 4) treat the sensible qualities we experience as qualities of our experiences; but they are not thereby committed to phenomenalism. Thus the relevance to phenomenalism of Moore's putative phenomenalist principle that for a sensation to be of sensible quality $F$ it must be $F$ is at best indirect.

From the failure, as he saw it, of the phenomenalist account of sensible qualities, Moore inferred the truth of his own strongly realist account of the intentional objects of sense-experience. According to this theory, in sense-experience we are directly aware of objects in space whose existence is as independent of our awareness of them as the existence of propositions is independent of our thoughts of them. Furthermore, by treating the sensible qualities we experience as entirely 'objective' (rather than merely 'phenomenal'), Moore is led to interpret these objects of which we are directly aware as qualities of material objects in physical space. The resulting position is the most naive of naive realisms, whose difficulties soon became apparent to him. I shall discuss the theory in more detail in the next chapter and Moore's recognition of the insuperable objections to it in chapter 5. But for now we can return to RI and conclude this examination of Moore's critical response to Kant with Moore's use of his realist position to present the conclusion of RI in explicitly anti-Kantian terms:

> When Kant supposed that the objectivity of things in space *consisted* in the fact that they were 'Vorstellungen' having to one another

19

different relations from those which the same 'Vorstellungen' have to one another in subjective experience, he supposed what was false. I am as directly aware of the existence of material things in space as of my own sensations; and *what* I am aware of with regard to each is exactly the same – namely that in one case the material thing, and in the other case my sensation, does really exist.

(p. 30)[24]

## 6: *Moore and Absolute idealism*

So far I have concentrated on Moore's critical response to Kantian idealism, in which his rejection of Kant's 'too psychological standpoint' is the predominant theme. But Moore was well aware that Hegel, while taking over much of Kant's idealism, had developed further views, some of which were endorsed by Bradley and McTaggart, with whose work he was especially familiar. One Hegelian doctrine accepted by Bradley and McTaggart was especially notorious – the doctrine that ordinary truths can only be properly understood in the context of an all-encompassing ultimate reality, the Absolute; and it is because of their acceptance of this that the kind of idealism they advanced was known as 'Absolute idealism'.

As an undergraduate Moore was introduced to Absolute idealism by Ward, Stout, and especially McTaggart (*PGEM* pp. 17–19). I have already described Moore's initial enthusiasm for some aspects of this philosophy and his special respect for Bradley; there are even favourable references to Hegel in his very early writings (e.g. F p. 200). But in 1898 Moore began to turn critically upon the doctrines of Absolute idealism. In section 1 I quoted Moore's favourable acknowledgement of Bradley from the preface to his 1897 Dissertation; the preface to the 1898 Dissertation shows a marked change – he now writes

> For my own metaphysical views I am no doubt chiefly indebted to
> Bradley. But I have come to disagree with him on so many points,
> and these points of importance, that I doubt if I can name any special
> obligations.

Over the next few years, his criticisms turn into a biting scorn, especially directed at Hegel:

> The principle of organic unities, like that of combined analysis and
> synthesis, is mainly used to defend the practice of holding both of two
> contradictory propositions, wherever this may seem convenient. In
> this, as in other matters, Hegel's main service to philosophy has
> consisted in giving a name to and erecting into a principle, a type of
> fallacy to which experience had shown philosophers, along with the

20

rest of mankind, to be addicted. No wonder that he has followers and admirers.

(RI p. 16)

Hegel, being dead, could be abused with impunity. No similar abuse is ever openly directed at Bradley, whom Moore rightly described in 1911 as 'one of the most eminent of living philosophers' (*SMPP* p. 207). But Bradley is none the less indirectly attacked through the abuse that is heaped upon claims that are all too easily recognisable as characteristically Bradleian; Bradley is, so to speak, abused by description. For example, the thrust of Moore's heavily ironical discussion of the thesis that reality is spiritual at the start of RI is unmistakable, the conclusion of *Appearance and Reality* being that 'We may fairly close this work by insisting that Reality is spiritual' (p. 552).

Moore's relationship with McTaggart was more intimate and more complex. One side of it is manifest in the two reviews of McTaggart's *Studies in Hegelian Cosmology* Moore published.[25] The high praise initially bestowed on McTaggart's book is progressively undermined as Moore remorsely exposes what he takes to be contradictions and *non-sequitur*s in McTaggart's arguments; and Moore's real opinion emerges when he writes that McTaggart's book

> has the merit of being an excellent *reductio ad absurdum* of all attempts
> to construct what Mr. McTaggart would call an 'Idealism', i.e. any
> philosophy which maintains that the universe is wholly 'spiritual' and
> perfectly good. It is equipped to perform this useful service by the
> fact that, whereas its arguments are quite as good as any that are
> commonly offered, they and their premises are stated in so
> exceptionally clear a form that their complete impotence may be easily
> exposed.[26]

It is, then, McTaggart's clarity which preserves him from Moore's abuse and this intellectual clarity is the key to the other side of Moore's relationship with McTaggart. For they remained on friendly terms and retained great respect for each other (cf. McTaggart's preface to *The Nature of Existence* and Moore's obituary note for McTaggart in *Mind* 1925). Indeed, McTaggart's work was important for Moore: it provided him with a model of a distinctively non-analytic, but respectable and recognisably philosophical, mode of reasoning (cf. Moore's references to McTaggart in *LP* pp. 179, 188, 194). In particular, McTaggart provided Moore with a paradigm case of an idealist who denied the reality of matter.[27]

Those idealist philosophers whose work lacked McTaggart's saving clarity Moore dismissed with contempt.[28] This does not entirely explain his passionate abuse of Hegel; but the explanation for this is manifest in

21

the passage quoted above: Hegel's work seemed to Moore to make self-contradiction respectable, and this, to Moore, was not merely intellectually, but also morally, reprehensible. But does Absolute idealism license self-contradiction? One might argue that Hegel's conception of the dialectic permits self-contradiction; but Moore does not pursue this charge, perhaps because both Bradley and McTaggart had denied that the Hegelian dialectic violates the law of non-contradiction.[29] In place of the dialectic, it is the concept of an 'organic whole' that Moore focuses his critical attention upon, as in the passage quoted above from RI (in fact Moore here writes of 'organic unities', but he uses these terms interchangeably; I shall keep 'organic whole' for the metaphysical concept Moore criticised, reserving the term 'organic unity' for use in formulating the ethical principle of organic unities which I shall discuss in chapter 4).

In thus focusing critically on the concept of an organic whole Moore manifests his hostility to metaphysical holism. Just as hostility to subjectivism was the dominant theme of his criticisms of Kantian idealism, hostility to holism is the dominant theme of his criticisms of Absolute idealism. His detailed criticism of the very idea of an organic whole occurs in PE (pp. 33–4). He begins by characterising an organic whole as follows: 'It is supposed that just as the whole would not be what it is but for the existence of the parts, so the parts would not be what they are but for the existence of the whole' (p. 33).[30] Moore's characterisation is couched in essentialist idioms and can be re-expressed as a pair of conditionals: $W$ is an organic whole if and only if

(i) $a$ is a part of $W \supset \text{Nec}(W \text{ exists} \supset a \text{ is a part of } W)$

and

(ii) $a$ is a part of $W \supset \text{Nec}(a \text{ exists} \supset a \text{ is a part of } W)$.

In thinking about this, an inital issue concerns the 'whole/part' terminology. Notoriously, during this period this terminology was applied very broadly, to classes and their members, to classes and sub-classes of them, to complex properties and simpler ones in terms of which the former can be defined, to propositions or facts and their constituents, and then on to the more ambitious conceptions characteristic of Absolute idealism – the Self, the State, and the Absolute. Given that different relations are involved in these cases, there is a danger of fallacies of equivocation. None the less, the conception of an organic whole is easily illustrated by taking class-membership to be a case of the 'part of' relation, so that classes are organic wholes if and only if

22

$$(iii) \ a \in W \supset \text{Nec}(W \text{ exists} \supset a \in W)$$

and

$$(iv) \ a \in W \supset \text{Nec}(a \text{ exists} \supset a \in W).$$

Condition (iii) here is uncontentious; it just asserts that it is essential to a class that it have the members that it does have, and this expresses the essential extensionality of classes. It is (iv) that is contentious: for this says that it is essential to anything that it belong to any class to which it does belong, and this implies that the existence of one member of a class entails the existence of all its other members, i.e. that their existence is internally related. This is a conclusion which flies in the face of common-sense; but it is, of course, one which Absolute idealists accepted.

Moore maintains that the concept of an organic whole is self-contradictory. His argument to this effect is, however, unsatisfactory. He starts by introducing the assumption that the parts of an organic whole 'contain analytically' the whole of which each is a part, with the result that the parts are not even 'distinct objects of thought'. The argument now runs as follows: in the case of a part $a$ of organic whole $W$, we have both '$a$ is a part of $W$' and '$W$ is a part of $a$' (since the whole is contained analytically in the parts); and Moore now concludes 'That this supposition is self-contradictory a very little reflection should be sufficient to show' (PE p. 33). But in fact it is not clear what the contradiction is supposed to be. One way of proceeding might be to argue as follows: assuming transitivity, we get '$a$ is a part of $a$', and if we now take it that parts are proper parts, this is a contradiction. This, however, is an unpersuasive argument. It is only by his assumption concerning analytical containment that Moore has obtained the premiss that '$W$ is a part of $a$', which is not implied by (ii) itself; and even if this assumption is allowed, one can hold that different part/whole relations are involved, and thus reject the use of transitivity.

A different way of interpreting Moore is to take him to be alleging, not overt self-contradiction, but pragmatic incoherence. For he goes on to argue that

> the mere assertion that *it* is a part of a whole involves that it should be distinct from that which we assert of it. Otherwise we contradict ourselves since we assert that, not *it*, but something else – namely it together with that which we assert of it – has the predicate which we assert of it.
>
> (PE p. 33)

The idea here seems to be that we want there to be some point to the assertion that '*a* is a part of *W*', but since 'that *a* is a part of *W*' is already implicit in the reference to *a*, our assertion adds nothing to our initial reference. If this is Moore's accusation, then the response to it is, first, that if the charge holds at all, then it can equally be turned against Moore himself in virtue of his own doctrine that wholes 'contain analytically' their parts (*PE* p. 34); second, that it is unclear why someone who accepts the analyticity thesis that Moore introduces should also want to treat '*a* is a part of *W*' as synthetic in the way that Moore assumes; and third, that the introduction of the analyticity thesis is gratuitous. Bradley and other Absolute idealists explicitly reject the kind of analytic/synthetic distinction employed by Moore, as is scarcely surprising in the light of their extreme holism.[31]

Moore's attempt to find self-contradiction in the concept of an organic whole is, therefore, unsuccessful. Moore in fact qualifies his position by allowing that there are natural organic wholes, such as a living human body (*PE* pp. 31–2, 34–5). For he allows that where there are relations of mutual causal dependence between parts, his argument that the concept of an organic whole is contradictory does not apply because the relations involved are not analytic. Since Absolute idealists would have repudiated Moore's ascription of analyticity to them, this admission by Moore undermines much of his case against them. But Absolute idealism requires more than just the admission that there are some organic wholes; it requires the thesis that everything is part of an ultimate organic whole, the Absolute. Since, in any organic whole, there will be necessary connections between the parts, it follows that if everything is part of the Absolute, there must be necessary connections between every aspect of things – i.e. all relations must be internal. Now we shall see that it is misleading to characterise the position of Bradley (on whom I shall concentrate in discussing the metaphysics of Absolute idealism) by reference to this thesis that all relations are internal; none the less for the moment I shall sketch a conventional account of Absolute idealism which gives prominence to it, since Moore's response to Absolute idealism is to Absolute idealism thus understood. In the next section I shall discuss the respects in which the conventional account needs to be modified in the light of Bradley's actual views, and how far these modifications affect Moore's criticisms of the position.

Returning, therefore, to the thesis that all relations are internal; this can be expressed as

$$\text{(v)} \quad xRy \supset \text{Nec}(x \text{ exists} \supset xRy)$$

and it is then clear that (v) entails the principles definitive of organic wholes (i) and (ii); so if all relations are internal, all wholes are organic.

But this does not yet justify the hypothesis of the Absolute. One way to arrive at this is to introduce the premiss that facts are organic wholes, with their constituent terms as parts; as we shall see in the next section, this is misleading if one thinks of Bradley's actual position. But if it is granted it makes possible an ascent to something like the Absolute. We need only frame the conception of the world as the totality of facts, the Master Fact: given that facts are organic wholes, this conception becomes that of the ultimate organic whole which encompasses everything. Since this whole is the only thing which is without being a part of something else, there is some point in saying that it is the only thing which *is* without qualification, a claim which approximates to the monism of Bradley's Absolute idealism — 'because everything, to complete itself and satisfy its own claims, must pass beyond itself, nothing in the end is real except the Absolute' (*Appearance and Reality* p. 555).

How is one to argue against a metaphysical juggernaut of this kind? I have already noted that Moore's attempt to show that the very idea of an organic whole is self-contradictory is unsuccessful. But it is a simpler business to argue that some relations are not internal. In his 1897 Dissertation Moore had criticised the Kantian thesis that there are necessary connections between the will and the moral law, and between the understanding and *a priori* truths; this criticism could be re-expressed as a denial of internal relations between, or an organic whole constituted by, these terms, and it is as such that Moore criticised it in RI. Indeed in NJ, Moore's rejection of the claim that cognitive relations are internal is all but explicit in such claims as that concepts

> may come into relation with a thinker; and in order that they may do anything, they must already be something. It is indifferent to their nature whether anybody thinks them or not. They are incapable of change; and the relation into which they enter with the knowing subject implies no action or reaction.

> (NJ p. 179)

Moore's rejection of metaphysical holism is clearly apparent here, and it is in his articles for Baldwin's *Dictionary*, written soon after this, that Moore begins to develop his atomist pluralism, though one should not exaggerate Moore's position at this time. It has been suggested that during this time Moore held that all relations are external;[32] but this is a mistake. Even in the article 'Relative and Absolute' (in Baldwin's *Dictionary*) in which Moore first explicitly attacked the concept of an organic whole and denied that all relations are internal, he maintained that having the parts it does have is internal to a whole's existence.

Although the atomist position thus advanced in NJ, and thereafter developed, is clearly inconsistent with Absolute idealism, it only yields good arguments against Absolute idealism if the arguments for it are any good. And here my criticisms of Moore's arguments against Kantian idealism are relevant; if, as I suggested earlier, Moore's arguments rest on misapprehensions or unjustified assumptions, one should not look to them for a refutation of Absolute idealism. This point applies especially to Moore's atomic concepts: Moore argues for his atomic concepts by way of his criticisms of Bradley's views about meaning, but since his arguments on this topic are so very unsatisfactory, there is nothing here on which any weight can be placed. What Moore should have latched on to, in order to argue against Absolute idealism, was the notion of contingency. For Absolute idealism is committed to a denial of contingency, and although this commitment was embraced enthusiastically by Bradley (*Appearance and Reality* p. 457), it is hard to regard it as welcome. But although contingency is implicit in Moore's early account of propositions, he was at this time so confused about modal concepts that he himself initially denied contingency too (NJ p. 192).

Some years later in a critical discussion in *Mind* of Joachim's Bradleian book *The Nature of Truth* Moore does, in effect, introduce contingency as an argument against Absolute idealism, though he still develops it through discussion of his thesis about the independence of subject and object in experience. Moore's debate with Joachim is illuminating, and I shall return to it in the next section. But I want now to look at Moore's famous paper E&IR in which Moore concentrates on contingency and other modal issues. This paper was written in 1919, when Moore was no longer extricating himself from Absolute idealism, and much of the paper is devoted to the development of modal predicate logic, which indeed Moore does with remarkable insight. None the less, the paper is primarily directed against the idealist thesis that all relations are internal; and Moore's argument has two elements. First, he introduces the apparent truism that there are contingent truths (Moore's example is that Edward VII might not have fathered George V[33]) in order to shift the burden of proof on to idealists; then he argues that the only argument for the doctrine that all relations are internal rests on a modal fallacy.

Moore's argument for this second thesis starts by identifying something like (v) as central to the claim that all relations are internal, though he expresses it as

$$(vi) \quad xRy \supset (u=x \text{ entails } uRy).$$

26

Moore now contrasts (vi) with an instance of Leibniz' Law, the principle of the substitutivity of identity:

$$\text{(vii) } xRy \text{ entails } (u=x \supset uRy).$$

This is an uncontroversial truth; and what Moore suggests is that (vi) has been confused with (vii). The thesis that all relations are internal requires that '$u=x \supset uRy$' be itself necessary, given $xRy$, whereas Leibniz' Law supports only the claim that it is necessarily implied by '$xRy$', a distinction which the use of 'must' in English often blurs.

Although this stage of Moore's argument is by now so familiar as to be almost trivial, Moore makes a further point about internal relations which is less familiar. He suggests that (vi) (and thus (v)) is only a weak version of the thesis that all relations are internal. Condition (vi) is equivalent to

$$\text{(viii) } xRy \supset [ \sim (uRy) \text{ entails } \sim (u=x)].$$

This asserts numerical difference; and the stronger internal relations thesis requires qualitative difference, i.e.

$$\text{(ix) } xRy \supset [ \sim (uRy) \text{ entails } (\exists G) \sim (Gx \equiv Gu)].$$

Given Leibniz' Law, (ix) entails (viii); but, more interestingly, Moore observes that (ix) also entails the identity of indiscernibles, for a case of (ix) is

$$\text{(x) } x=x \supset [ \sim (u=x) \text{ entails } (\exists G) \sim (Gx \equiv Gu)]$$

which in turn entails

$$\text{(xi) } (\forall G)(Gx \equiv Gu) \text{ entails } x=u.$$

Furthermore something like the converse holds: (ix) is entailed by the conjunction of (viii) and (xi) (to see this, contrapose (xi) and apply the result to (viii)). Hence, as Moore observes, the strong internal relations thesis (ix) is equivalent to the conjunction of the weak thesis (vi) and the identity of indiscernibles (xi).

This argument depends for its point upon the truth of the claim that upholders of Absolute idealism have maintained the strong as well as the weak internal relations thesis. If one looks to Bradley, I do not think there can be any doubt that he did maintain it (*Principles of Logic* p. 289;

*Appearance and Reality* pp. 574ff.); but, equally, since Bradley also maintained the identity of indiscernibles (*Principles of Logic* p. 288; *Appearance and Reality* pp. 587ff.) he would not have been much discomforted by this part of Moore's argument; indeed he might well say that it simply repeats his own discussions. And once one sees this, one must also ask whether there is any evidence that Bradley committed the crude modal fallacy that Moore in effect accuses him of committing. Moore adduces no evidence to support his charge, and so far as I can see there is no such evidence.[34] Bradley's reasons for his Absolute idealism simply do not, to the best of my judgment, involve the modal fallacy that Moore identifies as lying behind belief in the thesis that all relations are internal, and thus acceptance of Absolute idealism. But if this is so, then it raises the question as to whether Moore's critical response to Bradley's work makes any real contact with Bradley's actual views.

## 7: Bradley and relations

I want first to get out of the way the two places in which Moore argues explicitly against Bradley's account of time (*SMPP* ch. IX, CR; the second paper obviously incorporates much of the earlier chapter). On both occasions Moore's overall aim is to elucidate the concept of reality, and he discusses Bradley's views about time because he wants to elucidate the sense of Bradley's claims about the reality, or not, of time. He cites passages from *Appearance and Reality* in which Bradley maintains, first, that time 'has most evidently proved not to be real, but to be a contradictory appearance' (p. 43) and second, that because time is none the less an appearance, like all appearances it 'must belong to reality' (p. 132) and in that sense be real. Moore suggests that when Bradley maintains that time is not real, he is denying that there are any genuinely temporal facts (CR pp. 210–11); and that when Bradley maintains that time is none the less in some sense real, he is ascribing a minimal degree of reality to time in order to account for the fact that people genuinely do have thoughts about time. Moore compares this latter account of the minimal reality of time with the view that imaginary objects must be in some sense real simply because we can imagine them (CR pp. 214–15), although, as he acknowledges, this account of Bradley's views requires the ascription to Bradley of a 'gross fallacy' (CR p. 215). But he defends this ascription by reference to Bradley's account off error as 'truth when it is supplemented' (*Appearance and Reality* p. 195), and he could equally well have referred to Bradley's discussion of imaginary objects (*Essays on Truth and Reality* chapter III) in which Bradley maintains that whatever is imagined must be in some respect real. So it is no surprise that, in a letter to Moore about CR (now among the Moore papers in Cambridge) Bradley complains that where

28

Moore finds a 'gross fallacy' he only finds a doctrine 'certainly and even obviously true and fundamental'.

Yet although Bradley's response is no surprise, it is disappointing. His views about error and the imagination are very hard to make good sense of, and seem to involve an inference from the 'partial' (i.e. ordinary) truth that a false belief is held to the 'partial' truth of what is falsely believed. But I do not think that his views about time require that sort of nonsense. Much here depends on what it is for there to be temporal appearances which are in some sense real. Moore interprets Bradley as arguing from the existence of temporal beliefs to the minimal reality of time. But I think that when Bradley writes of temporal appearances we should understand him to be describing facts which appear to be temporal, but cannot really be so; hence, when he says that because temporal appearances exist, they must belong to reality, what he has in mind is that the facts which appear to be temporal must be such that they can somehow be accommodated within a timeless reality.

Bradley's position concerning time can be usefully compared to a line of thought concerning tense. Suppose one accepts McTaggart's argument that there cannot be any intrinsically tensed facts (since if there were, the facts would have contradictory predicates);[35] tense, one might then say, is unreal. None the less, there are facts which appear to us as tensed, and, arguably, this appearance is irreducible: so one needs a further account of the way in which facts which appear to be tensed are constituted – e.g. via an account of the token-reflexive role of tense. The structure of Bradley's argument concerning time is, I think, of this kind. Indeed, there is not just an analogy, for at one point Bradley's discussion seems to incorporate an anticipation of McTaggart's argument concerning tense (cf. *Appearance and Reality* p. 208).

Bradley's position, therefore, is that since contradictions arise if we take there to be genuinely temporal facts, we must recognise that the facts which appear to us as temporal are not intrinsically so. Since the Absolute embraces all facts, properly understood, it follows that it embraces these facts as non-temporal, but none the less with whatever aspect it was that gave rise to their temporal appearance; and this is what Bradley says: 'The Absolute is timeless, but it possesses time as an isolated aspect, an aspect which, in ceasing to be isolated, loses its special character' (*Appearance and Reality* p. 210). I do not suggest that this is a position that one can altogether make sense of, and since Bradley's arguments for the unreality of time in chapter IV of *Appearance and Reality* turn on the problems of infinity (which I mentioned before in connection with Moore's changing views about the reality of time) there is no great merit in pursuing the point further. But what I have tried to illustrate by means of the analogy with the doctrine of the unreality of tense is that Bradley's position should not be understood to require the fallacy that Moore seeks to convict him of.

With that unsatisfactory episode behind us, we can now turn to the central doctrines of Bradley's Absolute idealism. I shall start from Bradley's distinction between three modes, or levels, of experience (*Collected Essays* pp. 630ff). The basic mode is feeling (or 'immediate experience'), which is supposed to be a harmonious, non-conceptual, mode of experience. This is contrasted with judgment (or 'relational experience'), in which the subject articulates through the employment of concepts, especially concepts of relations, that which is presented in feeling as an objective spatio-temporal world of which he has experience. This distinction between non-conceptual and conceptual thought is not problematic (it is, for example, to be found in recent writing on perception[36]), though, as we shall see, Bradley's stress on the intrinsic harmony and unity of feeling is more difficult. But what is distinctive of Absolute idealism is the introduction of a third mode of experience, a supra-intellectual and supra-personal unification of feeling and judgment which is supposed to combine both the articulate detail of judgment and the harmony of feeling in such a way that the subject/object dichotomy characteristic of judgment is overcome through the realisation of their essential relatedness. This third mode of experience is what Bradley terms the 'Absolute', and it is this alone which he takes to be real in the sense that it alone is both coherent and comprehensive: 'The way of taking the world which I have found most tenable is to regard it as a single Experience, superior to relations and containing in the fullest sense everything which is' (*Essays on Truth and Reality* pp. 245–6).

I certainly do not pretend to understand Bradley's conception of the Absolute; he himself regarded it as unintelligible to us now (cf. *Appearance and Reality* p. 172), but my doubts about it extend well beyond the detailed grasp of it which Bradley denies us – I do not really understand the intellectual project whose telos the Absolute is to be. None the less I think it is possible to form some conception of this project, and essential to do so if one is to be able to form an intelligent view of Moore's critical response to Bradley. Bradley's three modes of experience are reminiscent of the Hegelian dialectical triad of particular, universal, and concrete universal; and as with all cases of Hegelian dialectic, there is a difficult question as to the intended relation between the stages of the dialectic. In Bradley's case the relation is intended to be in some sense logical, in that contradictions at one level necessitate the ascent to the next. Bradley is in fact uncertain that this applies to the transition from feeling to judgment (cf. note 8 to 'Relations' in *Collected Essays* pp. 658–63); but he is very insistent that contradictions inherent in the concept of judgment necessitate the move to the Absolute.

Since he holds that judgments essentially involve the concept of a relation between terms Bradley usually expresses this thesis that there are contradictions inherent in judgment as the thesis that all relations are unreal. Bradley's most famous, and frequently employed, argument for this thesis concerns the unity of judgments.[37] Here is a statement of it from his 1924 essay 'Relations':

> Every actual experience is a unity of the diverse and may, speaking
> loosely, be taken as a whole with parts. But the unity, so far, is
> merely that which belongs to immediate experience or feeling. . . .
> And the moment anything contained here is viewed as what is
> individual or particular, to that extent the above unity has been
> removed. But to have an experience as relational, you must have
> terms which are individuals and which therefore cannot qualify the
> former unity, but on the contrary destroy it. But when you ask for the
> unity, which in relational experience has come in and has taken the
> place of the unity so superseded – you find there is no answer. There
> is no unity left, except by a tacit and illegitimate appeal to that which
> the relational view has discarded. You can have the terms, without
> which you cannot have the relation, only so far as (in order to have the
> relation) you abstract from the former mode of unity, on which (to
> keep your relation, which requires some unity) you are forced vitally
> to depend. And this is a contradiction in its essence insoluble, except
> by a further development of experience, and by the rejection of any
> claim made on the part of relations to possess ultimate reality or
> truth.
>
> (*Collected Essays* pp. 636–7)[38]

The nub of this argument seems to be that the interpretation of experience in judgment as experience of objective facts does not satisfactorily accommodate the essential unity of judgment. But how is this claim substantiated? I think Bradley's view is that in judgment we aspire to represent things just as they are in themselves, altogether independent of us; it follows from this that there should be nothing in a true judgment which is not a feature of things themselves, but if we now ask where, amongst things themselves, we are to find that which gives rise to the unity of judgment, there is nothing to be found. From the bare assemblage of things and their properties, Bradley thinks, we cannot construct this unity (which is why it is misleading to associate him with the view that facts are organic unities, as in the argument of the previous section). Since Bradley thinks that, on the contrary, this unity is contributed by the subject (here there are echoes of Kant) he holds that it is only by transcending the subject/object dichotomy that the unity of judgment can be accommodated; but since this is precisely to abandon the essential feature of judgment, it follows that judgment itself is contradictory.

In thinking about this obscure argument much obviously depends on what the unity of judgment is supposed to be, and one easy response to it is to deny that the concept of judgment needs to be tied to the theory of truth that this argument assumes. We shall also see in the next chapter that the unity which, according to Bradley, cannot be found among things themselves is, according to Moore, unproblematically out there ahead of us. Moore's unworried presentation of this position can scarcely be regarded as providing an argument against Bradley, however; and because Moore does not directly confront Bradley on this issue, which is fundamental to the latter's metaphysics, I do not think he can be regarded as having really come to grips with Bradley's version of Absolute idealism, let alone as having refuted it.

In the present context it would not be appropriate to pursue discussion of Bradley's argument for its own sake, and I want instead to consider the bearing of the argument on the external/internal issue on which Moore and Russell focus. For although the argument is entirely general, the external/internal distinction can appear relevant to it. If one thinks of an external relation as a relation that is 'separate' from its terms it can seem that Bradley's argument shows only that no judgment can concern merely external relations; and it must be admitted that Bradley does sometimes express himself in terms which suggest this thought (cf. *Essays on Truth and Reality* pp. 237–8). But if the argument shows only this, then, it would seem to follow that all relations of which we can frame judgments are internal. Indeed, one might think that where there is an internal relation between two terms, the terms, by virtue of their essential relatedness, do form the requisite unity. Yet Bradley, though he allows that internal relations are 'truer by far than "external" relations' (*Essays on Truth and Reality* p. 312), denies the reality of internal relations and repeatedly rejects the Moore–Russell characterisation of his position (*Essays on Truth and Reality* pp. 190, 239, 290–1, 318; *Collected Essays* pp. 642ff.). The reason for this is clear enough: it is not a premiss of the argument for the unreality of relations that relations be conceived as external in the essentialist sense. Bradley states the point in a passage which shows clearly his rejection of the conventional Moore–Russell account of his position:

> Passing on now to consider relations taken as internal merely, we can reach no better result. The terms here once again are no more than abstractions. Taken each as real independently, and apart from some whole, they are things which cannot be found to exist in any actual experience.
>
> (*Collected Essays* pp. 643–4)

It is, therefore, a mistake to identify Bradley's thesis that all relations are unreal with the thesis that all relations are internal, and in so far as Moore concentrates on the latter thesis, he misses the point of much of Bradley's metaphysics. None the less, there may be a connection between these two theses. Bradley certainly did hold that 'nothing in the world is external so except for our ignorance' (*Appearance and Reality* p. 579), and the hypothesis that there is a connection between them is well illustrated by a paper by Bradley's pupil Joachim in *Mind* (1907). Joachim is here responding to Moore's challenge in a critical discussion in *Mind* of Joachim's book *The Nature of Truth* that he should justify the Bradleian claims made in the book. Joachim first presents a Bradleian argument against external relations:

> If . . . the relation is really 'external', with the *two* [terms] there is now conjoined a *third*: but the *two* are no more genuinely *one* in virtue of the added *third*, than are the contents of a waste-paper basket or of Mr. Moore's pockets.
>
> (p. 412)

In this argument, the essentialist aspect of an 'external' relation is irrelevant: the point just concerns the impossibility of grounding the unity of judgment in the terms and relation represented in the judgment. But Joachim takes it that he has established an essentialist thesis, and is therefore entitled to conclude that all relations are internal:

> The Universe is a genuine whole, and for complete knowledge there is no element utterly unrelated or merely coincident. That which, to the limited view of Mr. Moore or myself, appears at first sight merely coincident or as 'externally related', is for ideally-complete experience intelligibly coherent.
>
> (p. 414)

Is this just a confusion by Joachim – or is there a real connection here? Suppose that it is accepted that we cannot coherently suppose that the objects of experience form a world altogether independent of us; from this it follows that there is no absolute distinction to be drawn between the world and our experience. This already yields some internal relations (of a kind which Moore would have rejected); but to make the move from idealism to Absolute idealism, more is required. Even though idealism implies that truth is only a matter of coherence with experience, it does not follow that experience itself is sufficiently coherent to imply that all truths necessitate each other. Bradley's writings (cf. e.g. *Appearance and Reality* pp. 141–2) suggest that one can just add the premiss that immediate experience is sufficiently coherent or harmonious. But this does not seem satisfactory, since nothing supports this extra premiss.

I cannot at present find any better arguments for Bradley, so it may be that one should just detach his thesis that all relations are unreal from the thesis that all relations are internal. This would leave his commitment to the former unthreatened by Moore's criticisms of the latter; as I have already indicated, I am sympathetic to this conclusion. Equally, however, it leaves his commitment to the latter, which is certainly an essential feature of his Absolute idealism, vulnerable to a Moorean appeal to common-sense. The way in which this arises can be seen in the context of Moore's discussion of Joachim's book, to which I have already referred.

In his review of Joachim's book Russell had argued that the only way to refute the thesis that all relations are internal was by showing it to be self-contradictory.[39] He also acknowledged that it was hard to see how such a method of argument could succeed in this case, and I think he was right about this, as Moore's unsuccessful attempt to find self-contradiction in the very idea of an organic whole exemplifies. Moore's discussion of Joachim is also a response to Russell.[40] Moore suggests that it is not necessary to argue by *reductio ad absurdum*; it will be sufficient if one can show, by an argument *ad hominem* that the thesis that all relations are internal is inconsistent with some proposition which the protagonist of the thesis should accept. Moore takes as his proposition the proposition that different people can think the same thoughts – which he takes to show that the objects of thought, propositions, are not internally related to the occasions on which they are thought. This, although a characteristic Moorean thesis, is less than ideal, since it is open to the reply (which Joachim makes) that thought is not a relationship between a thinker and an independent object. But Moore's strategy here can be readily converted into a kind of defence of common-sense (although Moore does not here use that phrase) by taking an apparently uncontentious case of an external relation (e.g. one concerning the possibility of an alternative spatial location of an object) and asking whether we are not more certain of the truth of such a proposition than we are of an abstract metaphysical thesis inconsistent with it.

It is essential to the success of such an appeal to common-sense that there should not be reasons for accepting the disputed thesis which help to undermine acceptance of the truisms to which one appeals. In the case of Bradley's (and Joachim's) rejection of external relations, therefore, this requirement will be satisfied if it is correct to detach the thesis that all relations are internal from the thesis all relations are unreal. Without such support, Bradley can only appeal to his methodological principle that truth must 'satisfy the intellect' in a way in which brute

34

conjunctions do not (cf. *Appearance and Reality* pp. 569–70). But where a methodological principle flies in the face of common-sense, and lacks any independent support, this seems good enough reason to reject it. It may still be felt that the Moorean appeal to common-sense merely embodies a different methodology (instinct[41]); Bradley recognised that his rejection of external relations flies in the face of common-sense: 'I am not to be moved here by the charge of an insult offered to Common Sense' he writes in 1923–4 (*Collected Essays* p. 640; he might even be alluding to Moore here). Now it is certainly right that one cannot take common-sense to be an unchallengeable authority; but that is a much stronger claim than the present Moorean thesis requires, which is only that it has some intrinsic authority deriving from the fact that it is our cognitive starting-point. Bradley's methodology requires him to abandon this base, but unless he can give us good reasons for doing so, we can legitimately stay loyal to our common-sense convictions.

### 8: Evil and the Absolute

In addition to criticising the metaphysics of Absolute idealism, Moore argued that the ethical theory of Absolute idealism led to absurd conclusions. His argument is first presented in his lectures *The Elements of Ethics*, and then developed in his two reviews of McTaggart's *Studies in Hegelian Cosmology* and repeated in chapter 4 of *PE*. Having concentrated up to now on Bradley as a representative exponent of Absolute idealism, we can now follow Moore and shift our attention to McTaggart's ethical theory. Moore expresses his criticism succinctly in the following passage:

> It is, in fact, impossible for any philosophy which, like Mr.
> McTaggart's, distinguishes between a perfect timeless Reality and its
> manifestations or Appearance in time, consistently to ascribe any
> value whatever to the existence of anything in time; and this for two
> cogent reasons: (1) that it must maintain that nothing really does
> exist in time, and (2) that it cannot hold that the existence of
> anything in time can make any difference whatever to the perfection
> of the universe. Even if it allowed that things really existed in time, it
> could not allow any value to such existence; and as it is, its whole
> Ethics must consist in ascribing a value, which they cannot have, to
> things which do not exist.
> ('Mr. Moore McTaggart's "Studies in Hegelian Cosmology"' p. 195;
> cf. *PE* pp. 115–17)

Moore's criticisms here begin from the premiss that the Absolute is timeless, perfect, and the only reality; and that McTaggart endorsed such a premiss is clear from his *Studies in Hegelian Cosmology* (pp. 96–8). Moore's first objection is that it follows that human actions, being temporal, are not real, and therefore do not exist. I shall not pursue this objection, for McTaggart allows that there are temporal appearances which are, in some sense, subsumed within the Absolute (*Studies in Hegelian Cosmology* pp. 34–5). Moore's objection is therefore comparable to his criticism of Bradley's views about the reality of temporal appearances which I discussed at the start of the previous section, and similarly unsatisfactory. But Moore's second objection latches on to the crucial feature of Absolute idealism for ethical inquiry, that the Absolute is perfect. Moore infers from this that all human actions have equal value as temporal manifestations of the one perfect ultimate reality. In which case practical ethical issues evaporate, and we can do as we like in the assurance that ours is a perfect world.

Beyond the premiss that the Absolute is perfect, the crucial assumption here is that all human actions equally manifest it. McTaggart officially rejects this assumption: he writes that our limited knowledge prevents us from gaining any practical guidance from asking ourselves which course of action 'will lead us to the result least removed from the supreme good' (*Studies in Hegelian Cosmology* p. 102) and this remark implies that some courses of action are less removed from the Absolute than others. It is not clear how this spatial metaphor is to be interpreted; but there is reason for supposing that McTaggart's position here is inconsistent with the conception of the Absolute as an all-embracing organic whole. For if this is the case, then it must be equally present in all its parts; in which case the Absolute, perfect though it is, is present in the most vicious conduct as much as in the most virtuous. Alternatively, if the Absolute is not fully present in vicious conduct, then that conduct must be judged to be, in the idealist sense, unreal; in which case, why worry about it, since it is merely an appearance that will somehow be transcended?

The difficulty McTaggart faces here is analogous to the traditional theological problem of evil (without even the appearance of the 'free will defence'); and in his *Studies in the Hegelian Dialectic* McTaggart admitted that the problem of evil was an insoluble paradox for his philosophy. Indeed he more or less anticipates Moore's argument:

> To put the difficulty from a more practical point of view, either the
> imperfection in experience leaves a stain on the perfection of the
> Absolute, or it does not. If it does, there is no absolute perfection,
> and we have no right to expect that the imperfection around us is a
> delusion or transitory phase. But if it does not, then there is no reason
> why the perfection should ever feel intolerant of it, and again we have

no reason to hope for its disappearance. The whole practical interest of philosophy is thus completely overthrown.

(*Studies in the Hegelian Dialectic* p. 180)

This problem is not peculiar to McTaggart. As he observes (*Studies in the Hegelian Dialectic* pp. 175–6), the same line of argument applies to Bradley's position in *Appearance and Reality*; indeed Bradley seems to acknowledge as much in his discussion of evil (pp. 203, 412). Similarly, Green maintains in his *Prolegomena to Ethics* that the distinction between virtue and vice arises from the distinction between those courses of action which cohere with the spiritual principle in man (p. 183) and those which conflict with it; but since he also holds that this spiritual principle is the only thing 'that is real (so to speak) in its own right; the only thing of which the reality is not relative and derived' (p. 104), it seems to follow that vicious actions must derive, just as much as virtuous ones, from the realisation of this spiritual principle in man.

It will be clear by now that the problem Moore finds in the ethics of Absolute idealism arises from the hypothesis that the Absolute is perfect and equally realised in all human actions. One response might be to deny that the Absolute is perfect. It is, after all, not obvious that the metaphysical considerations that lead philosophers to introduce the conception of the Absolute have any ethical significance. To pursue this line of thought, however, would be to abandon the thesis that the truth of Absolute idealism has any ethical significance, and this is scarcely likely to appeal to Absolute idealists. The other response is to deny that the Absolute is equally realised in all human actions.

This, I think, would be Hegel's response to Moore, and although I have been unsympathetic to the possibility of McTaggart exploiting this response, the fact that Hegel, unlike McTaggart and Bradley, ascribes a temporal dimension to the dialectic perhaps makes a difference (though McTaggart gave an impressive argument that Hegel's account of the dialectic as temporal is in fact incoherent – cf. chapter 5 of *Studies in the Hegelian Dialectic*). It is because Hegel regards the dialectic as temporal that he feels that he can adopt a critical attitude in his *Philosophy of Right* to most existing political institutions. Yet since Hegel's historical dialectic is informed by the teleology of the Absolute, the matter is not entirely clear. Even when institutions are less than perfectly rational, Hegel often presents them as an essential and, in the circumstances, unavoidable stage in the development of more perfect ones, and in that way the best then available. Thus Hegel's position may after all be vulnerable to an extension of Moore's critical argument. This is, however, not the place to pursue the issue; and even if the criticism could be substantiated, it would not follow that there is not much of

37

value in Hegel's ethical theory, in particular in his conception of the state as an organic whole. For one can retain the organic analogy for the state, while rejecting the all-encompassing Absolute and the associated teleology of reason characteristic of Absolute idealism.

# II

# Pure realism

*The night of the day I left you I made an old friend see a vision. For about a minute she sat turning the pages of a missal invisible to me and describing the pictures. Hitherto I have always taken the idealist view of such visions but now, thanks to your brother's 'Refutation of Idealism', I am permitted to think they exist outside the human mind. I wish however that the missal, now that I must think it of the same stuff as the table, had lasted longer for it was a handsome book.*

*(From a letter of W.B. Yeats to G.E. Moore's brother, Sturge Moore)[1]*

In the preface to *The Principles of Mathematics* Russell wrote that 'on fundamental questions of philosophy, my position, in all its chief features is derived from Mr. G.E. Moore' (p. xviii). My aim in this chapter is to set out and discuss this early philosophy of Moore's which so influenced Russell.[2] The works I shall concentrate upon are those which Moore wrote during his Prize Fellowship at Trinity College, Cambridge, which lasted from autumn 1898 until autumn 1904. The views Moore developed during this period form a reasonably coherent position and there is a significant change in the style and content of his writing once he had left Cambridge in 1904, culminating in the lectures *SMPP* (1910–11) in which he rejects many of the central themes of this early philosophy, and begins to develop in their place the themes of his mature philosophy for which he is most famous.

I have already referred to many of the works Moore composed during this period, for Moore developed his early philosophy in the course of his rejection of idealism. The predominant themes of this were his rejection of the subjectivism which he found in Kantian idealism and the holism he found in Absolute idealism. These ensure that in his early philosophy Moore is a thoroughgoing realist and atomist; but his early philosophy also incorporates the rejection of empiricism which he took over from

39

the idealist philosophy he rejected. I have described how Moore transforms an idealist reality/appearance distinction into one between timeless being and existence in time, and it is in terms of this latter distinction that he characteristically expresses his rejection of empiricism. Empiricists are said to hold that all truths of which we can have knowledge concern what exists in time, and, as thus formulated, Moore consistently rejects empiricism (cf. NJ p. 192; E&E pp. 93–5; *PE* p. 111). Hence it would be a great mistake to regard Moore's early philosophy as a reaction of common-sense empiricism against the excesses of idealism;[3] in its commitment to timeless being Moore's early philosophy is anti-empiricist, just as in its insistent realism it is anti-idealist; it is a pure realism of which Moore wrote (to Desmond MacCarthy, August 1898): 'I am pleased to believe that this is the most Platonic system of modern times.'

### 1: Concepts as substances

Moore first presented his pure realism in NJ, and although he modified his views in important respects in the next year or two, it is worth looking with some care at NJ since he here sets out many of the central points of his position. The paper begins with Moore's unsatisfactory criticisms of Bradley's views about ideas which I discussed in chapter 1, from which Moore concludes that meanings, or 'concepts' form a *'genus per se*, irreducible to anything else' (pp. 178–9). Moore goes on to maintain that these concepts need not exist at all, are not mind-dependent, and combine to form propositions which are independent objects of thought. These claims manifest with respect to meaning his general hostility to empiricism, subjectivism, and holism; and as such they are the consequences one would expect where pure realism is applied to meaning. But none of this prepares one for the radical thesis that Moore next proclaims: that these concepts are, fundamentally, the only things that there are. 'A concept', Moore writes, 'is not in any intelligible sense an "adjective", as if there were something substantive, more ultimate than it. . . . In the end, the concept turns out to be the only substantive or subject' (pp. 192–3). It seems, therefore, as though Moore shifts without warning in NJ from what Frege would have regarded as the level of sense to the level of reference: concepts are not only the fundamental elements of meaning, they are also the fundamental elements of reality. 'The world', Moore writes, 'is formed of concepts' (p. 182). The truth of the matter is, I think, rather more complex than this initial comparison with Frege suggests, and I shall return to the comparison later. But first I want to describe Moore's development of this radical thesis.

An immediate consequence of Moore's account of reality as

constituted of concepts which are also the constituent elements of propositions is that there is nothing distinct from true propositions for a proposition to correspond to when true. Moore puts the point as follows:

> It is similarly impossible that truth should depend on a relation to existents or to an existent, since the proposition by which it is so defined must itself be true, and the truth of this can certainly not be established, without a vicious circle, by exhibiting its dependence on an existent.
>
> (NJ p. 181; cf. p. 192)

It is important to understand that the antecedent of 'it' in the phrase 'it is so defined' is 'an existent' and not 'truth'; the latter way of reading the passage would yield Frege's argument for the indefinability of truth, which is not what Moore has in mind here, although it is a view he holds. For in place of the correspondence theory, he holds that the truth or falsehood of a proposition depends on whether the concepts are 'truly' related in the proposition or not (NJ p. 181), which is not a matter that can be further analysed. This view is closely connected with his thesis that 'the world is formed of concepts'; for since concepts form propositions, it follows that the world is just the totality of true ones. Moore puts the point in the following passage from his article on 'Truth':

> a truth differs in no respect from the reality to which it was supposed merely to correspond: e.g. the truth that I exist differs in no respect from the corresponding reality – my existence. So far, indeed, from truth being defined by reference to reality, reality can only be defined by reference to truth.
>
> (B vol. 2 p. 717; cf. E&E p. 89)

Implicit in Moore's argument against the correspondence theory was the identification of existents, things which exist, with true existential propositions. This arises from the thesis that all ordinary things must be somehow composed of concepts; but since concepts combine to form propositions, ordinary things must be propositions, and Moore says (NJ p. 183) that they are true existential ones. Moore wrote excitedly about this thesis to MacCarthy (August 1898): 'I have arrived at a perfectly staggering doctrine. . . . An existent is nothing but a proposition: nothing *is* but concepts. There is my philosophy'; and in a letter to Russell at this time he tried to explain himself, but only succeeded in displaying the incoherence of his thought:

> My chief discovery, which shocked me a good deal when I made it, is expressed in the form that an existent is a proposition. . . . Of course

by an existent must be understood an existent existent − not what exists, but that + its existence. . . . True existential propositions are those in which certain concepts stand in a specific relation to the concept existence; and I see no way of distinguishing such from what are commonly called 'existents', i.e. what exists + its existence.[4]

The way to make some sense of Moore's nonsense is to interpret him as treating material objects as sums of their properties, and then treating these sums of properties as conjunctions of true propositions, which concern the existence of a property, or concept, at points of space and time (as in Moore's example of an atomic existential proposition 'Heaviness exists here and now' − NJ p. 188). On this interpretation Moore's 'staggering doctrine' is loosely comparable to the view of those who propose a fundamental ontology of events, with material objects somehow crystallised out of appropriate series of events as space–time worms. Without here entering into the issue of whether such an ontology is defensible, there are some features of Moore's version of it which are patently unsatisfactory. First, Moore's ontology of concepts requires him to treat points of space and time as concepts; but since he regards all concepts as inherently general (NJ pp. 182–3), it is unclear how this can be so. Second, Moore has no conception of the congruence relations between events which are needed if one is to make at all plausible the thesis that material objects are series of events. As we shall see, this reflects a deep failure on Moore's part to appreciate the distinction between sortal concepts and others. Third, Moore's view has some similarities with views which assign a fundamental role to 'feature-placing' propositions, such as 'it is raining here'. But what is unacceptable in Moore's position is his thought that all empirical concepts can be thus accommodated into feature-placing propositions; his own example of heaviness is a clear case of a concept not susceptible to this approach since 'heavy' is an attributive adjective.

Moore's metaphysical atomism in NJ is, therefore, deeply flawed. But it establishes the framework for the rest of his position in NJ. The outcome is an all-embracing category of being, which includes both all possible concepts and all possible combinations of concepts, i.e. propositions, both of these being 'immutably what they are' (p. 180). These propositions can be thought of as possible states of affairs, so that the true ones among them are actual states of affairs, and of these, those which concern the existence at a time and place of a concept are 'parts' of ordinary existents. Thus in so far as we see or touch ordinary things, we see or touch propositions; for perception is just 'the cognition of an existential proposition'. Nor are we exempt from this strange metaphysics: the mind itself is just a 'complex judgment' (NJ p. 193 − 'judgment' here means proposition). The resulting metaphysical system can seem almost idealist: the world is, quite literally, a world of meanings. Yet because Moore's account of meaning is thoroughly realist, his metaphysics is a case of pure realism, not idealism.

One interpretive issue must now be mentioned. I have taken Moore to hold that concepts need not exist in time; in fact he says at first that 'the concept can be consistently described neither as an existent, nor as part of an existent' (p. 181), and this suggests the stronger thesis that no concepts exist at all. Yet he is committed to there being true existential propositions such as 'Heaviness exists here and now'; and he compounds his commitment to the existence of some concepts by saying that the distinction between empirical and *a priori* concepts is that between concepts which can exist in time and those which cannot. These latter points show, I think, that one cannot ascribe the stronger thesis to Moore. His initial remark is perhaps to be understood in the context of his criticisms of Bradley concerning meaning, where it can be taken at face value; once the conclusion of that argument is transformed by the thesis that concepts are the only substances, Moore's remark has to be reinterpreted as the claim that it is not intrinsic to a concept that it exist.

Why did Moore hold that concepts are the only substances? I think it is helpful to regard Moore's position as the result of combining pure realism about meanings with the theory that an actual state of affairs just is a true proposition (I shall call this the 'identity theory of truth'), although this inverts the argument of NJ. For if reality is identical with true propositions, and these are constituted of concepts, then reality must itself be constituted from these concepts. What now needs explanation is Moore's commitment to the identity theory of truth. Much of the explanation is doubtless the (unacknowledged) influence of Bradley who had already propounded a theory of this kind.[5] But, as Frege's discussion of this theory shows,[6] it can also be regarded as an ideal case of the correspondence theory, with identity providing perfect correspondence between what is judged (a proposition) and a state of affairs.

It is difficult to overestimate the importance of this identity theory in Moore's early philosophy. It is integral to his conception of a proposition as both meaning of a sentence and possible state of affairs. Moore opens chapter 2 of his 1898 Dissertation with the remark:

Our object will be to show that, whatever name be given to it, that which we call a proposition is something independent of consciousness, and something of fundamental importance for philosophy.

and in this last remark he is not exaggerating as far as *his* philosophy is concerned. Moore's conception is best understood in the context of a comparison with those of Bradley and Frege. The disagreement with Bradley is obvious; for Bradley (and any follower of Kant), propositions could not be 'independent of consciousness', since their unity depends upon the activity of consciousness. Moore does not argue that Bradley is incorrect on this matter; it does not seem to occur to him that there is any difficulty in explaining how a proposition is composed of concepts.[7] In the case of Frege it is tempting at first to dwell on the similarities between Moore's concepts and Frege's senses, as my previous remarks suggested. But this way of comparing Moore and Frege is misleading: Moore's concepts are much better compared with Frege's referents since it is their features which determine the truth or falsity of judgments (it is relevant here that although 'reference' is the canonical translation of *Bedeutung*, it is arguable that 'meaning' would be better). So, in thinking about the relation between Moore and Frege, we need to ask, not (as I originally put it) how Moore could treat his conception of sense as also a conception of reference, but, rather, how Moore could have a conception of reference without a distinct conception of sense. It is not necessary to review here the arguments of Frege's famous paper 'On Sense and Reference' concerning this issue. But in thinking about the relation between Moore and Frege one point stands out: Frege argues that the reference of an indicative sentence is its truth-value, and in order to avoid the absurd conclusion that all true sentences have the same meaning, he must have a distinct conception of the sense of a sentence, which he calls the thought expressed by it. Now any temptation to liken Moore's conception of a proposition to that of a Fregean thought must be resisted: like all Fregean senses, thoughts are inherently intentional, in that they are modes of presentation of something else — truth-values in the case of thoughts. Moore's propositions, by contrast, are not intentional: they are possible states of affairs, and when true, actual ones. So they could only be regarded as candidates for the (Fregean) reference of a sentence, and it is because Moore, in effect, takes this view that he avoids any obvious need for a further theory of sense. For it is not obviously silly to suppose that sentences which describe the same state of affairs are synonymous (although the view is not in the end defensible).

Although the standard conception of the Fregean sense of a proper name is such that a name's having a sense does not entail that it has a reference, it has been argued recently that Frege actually took the opposite view.[8] Those who take this view sometimes describe it as the view that the content of a singular thought is a 'Russellian proposition'. Since the respect in which Russell's position is thus approached is one which he took from Moore, it might seem that this provides a way of incorporating Moorean propositions within a Fregean framework. This is, however, not the case: for even if this new interpretation of Frege is correct, it does not undermine his sense/reference distinction, even concerning proper names. And since it is precisely this distinction which Moore lacks, almost all that is characteristic of Moore's position is lacking from this new Fregean position. Thus I shall not pursue it as a possible interpretation of Moore's position, although from time to time points connected with it will arise in the course of discussion.

Although in *SMPP* Moore abandoned the identity theory of truth, and the associated conception of a proposition, he never, I think, shifted from the one-level conception of meaning which is implied by this position and which coheres with the simple act/object conception of consciousness manifest in RI. He read some of Frege's works during 1912–13, but they had no detectable influence on him. Perhaps he took it that Russell had refuted Frege's theory of sense and reference in 'On Denoting' and 'Knowledge by Acquaintance and Knowledge by Description'.[9] On one occasion he discussed a conception of meaning of roughly this kind, when reviewing a book by A. Messer (*Empfindung und Denken*) in *Mind*.[10] Following Husserl, Messer held that when we understand the phrase 'the capital of Prussia', the meaning (*Bedeutung* is his word, but his use is not Frege's) of this phrase is not the object of our act of understanding, but only the content of the act through which an object, Berlin, is presented to us. This distinction between content and object in understanding is comparable to Frege's sense/reference distinction, and Moore replies, in the way that the argument of RI would lead one to expect, that in the act of understanding, meaning is the object and not the content of the act. Moore does not explain how understanding 'the capital of Prussia' relates to the ascription of thoughts about Berlin, but a reference to Russell's views about denoting concepts (*Mind* 1910 p. 404) perhaps alludes to Russell's theory of descriptions. The important point, however, is that Moore still insists that meaning is the object of understanding, and denies that, in the sense employed by Messer, acts of the understanding have any content at all. This denial is tantamount to the denial of any role for a theory of sense in addition to a theory of reference.

## 2: *Particulars and universals*

At the end of 1898 Moore dropped the view that concepts are the ultimate substances, indeed he dropped all talk of concepts; thus although in *PE* goodness is variously described as a 'property', 'notion', 'predicate', 'idea', and 'object', it is never described as a 'concept'. In place of concepts he introduced a sharp distinction between universals and their instances: whereas universals are, but never exist, in some cases their particular instances do exist (I p. 115).[11] This new view is developed in the articles Moore wrote in 1898–9 for Baldwin's *Dictionary of Philosophy and Psychology* (cf. in particular 'Change' and 'Quality'), and then repeated in other writings; it is especially manifest in *PE*. One welcome aspect is that Moore no longer identifies existents with existential propositions: 'it must, of course, be admitted that things do exist now, which neither have always existed nor will always exist. But the *truth* is not the thing; the truth is that the thing existed at some moment of time' (N p. 296).

Moore's change of mind appears to derive from a change of mind about the identity of indiscernibles. In NJ, where concepts are the ultimate substances, Moore accepts the identity of indiscernibles: 'The material diversity of things, which is generally taken as a starting point, is only derived' (p. 182). It is precisely this derivation of diversity that Moore now rejects for the instances of universals. He expresses this new position through a contrast between 'difference in kind' and 'numerical difference'. Whereas universals are 'entities which must differ in kind from one another' ('Quality' B vol. 2 p. 406), this is not true of their instances, which 'may differ from one another not only in kind, but also merely numerically' (ibid.). Thus it is now Moore's thesis that the identity of indiscernibles applies to universals, but not to their particular instances.

Moore attempts to argue for this in his 1901 paper 'Identity', but his argument is very obscure.[12] But what matters more than his argument is a thesis concerning particular things which he now advances. He holds, not just that there are things to which the principle of the identity of indiscernibles does not apply; he holds that almost every universal, both quality and relation, has particular instances to which it does not apply ('Quality' B vol. 2 p. 406; I p. 115). Thus Moore treats almost every predicate as expressing a sortal property (i.e. as providing criteria of individuation and identity for the things which have it). Moore treats his favourite predicates, colour predicates, in this way: e.g. the universal blackness has particular 'blacks' as instances, and these are not particular shades of black, for they differ from one another merely numerically (I p. 106); and when, in RI, Moore writes about 'the sensation of blue', and about 'blue' as an object of experience, what he has in mind is a particular instance of the universal blueness which differs only numerically from other instances of the same universal.

Despite the new role for particulars, Moore's new theory resembles that of NJ in the treatment of ordinary things as sums of their properties. In this case 'the composite existents usually called "things"' ('Quality' B vol. 2 p. 407) are treated as collections of particular instances of universals. The result is a part/whole theory of predication: for most properties $P$, $a$ has $P$ if and only if an instance of $P$ is a part of $a$; thus Moore writes in *PE* that natural properties 'are, in fact, rather parts of which the object is made up than mere predicates which attach to it. If they were all taken away, no object would be left, not even a bare substance: for they are in themselves substantial and give the object all the substance it has' (p. 41; cf. pp. 33–4, 124). A further feature of Moore's construction of ordinary things is that he denies that there is any genuine persistence through time: 'Any two things which differ from one another in no respect except that they occupy immediately successive moments in time, are said to be one thing' ('Change' B vol. 1 p. 172). So the particular instances of universals which are parts of ordinary things are instantaneous, and the apparent persistence of ordinary things through time is derived from the similarity at successive moments of time of most of their parts, including their spatial parts, at those times ('Change' B vol. 1 p. 172; I p. 127).

The introduction of particulars does not mark any significant change in Moore's one-level conception of meaning. The universal/particular distinction is not a sense/reference distinction, though it does enable Moore to tidy up his anti-empiricism with respect to meaning. Instead of just holding that some concepts exist in time and some do not, he now has a categorial distinction between universals, which just 'are' and do not exist in time, and particulars, at least some of which exist in time. But particulars, just as much as universals, can be meant; they are both meanings. Moore also suggests at one point that it is essential to the conception of a particular that it should exist (I p. 115), and it would be tidier to have the universal/particular distinction coincide with the being/existence one. But he is committed to rejecting it by his views about the objects of imagination and delusive perception. This emerges most clearly in his discussion in *PE* of the strange question whether the existence of the objects of aesthetic and affectionate contemplation increases the value of such acts (Moore says that it does). For Moore takes it that that the objects of such contemplations include particulars and that it makes no difference to them as such whether or not they exist. Moore here generally writes of the objects of such contemplations as 'qualities', but he means qualities as particular instances of universals, since he writes of them differing merely numerically (*PE* p. 198); and it is of qualities thus understood that he writes that even without the existence of a material world 'a cognition of *material qualities* (though purely imaginary) would still remain' (*PE* p. 206). That Moore did not regard existence as essential to particulars is further confirmed by his position in the slightly later paper NROP (1905); he here advances a conception of existence as a simple quality of some, but not all, particulars, comparable to his conception of truth as a simple quality of some, but not all, propositions (p. 87).

One final problem arising from Moore's one-level theory of meaning and being/existence distinction concerns the status of propositions. On the one hand, Moore emphatically denies that propositions exist at all

(N p. 297; *PE* p. 111); yet if propositions include among their constituents particulars which exist in time, it might seem that propositions themselves should also exist in time; for propositions, as 'wholes', are dependent upon their 'parts', and if some parts exist in time, it seems that the whole should do so too. In thinking about this, it certainly helps that the existence of those particulars which do exist is not intrinsic: for it follows from this that the being of a proposition which includes them is not dependent on their existence. However, this does not altogether eliminate the tension here, which arises from the treatment of true propositions as actual states of affairs. For it is hard to understand why many of the latter should not be thought of as existing in time.

In reflecting critically on this early atomist metaphysics, I shall start with Moore's account of ordinary material objects. According to Moore these 'composite existents' are wholes, composed at each moment of time of those instantaneous particular instances of universals which occupy a given area of space at that time, and persisting in time by means of the occupation throughout successive moments of time of a largely similar area of space by largely similar instantaneous particulars. An initial problem here is that by treating ordinary things as wholes composed of particular instances of most of their properties, this theory implies that all such properties are essential to the things of which they are properties. However, this essentialism is relative to moments of time, and thus does not exclude change; but when the issue is considered diachronically, the problem is that too little is considered essential – there are no constraints on what changes are admissable as changes in an object.

That problem concerns persistence; there is a different problem concerning individuation. Moore's position is that almost all universals have particular instances which can differ merely numerically from other instances of the same universal. This is similar to the position later espoused by Stout, who argued that instead of thinking of qualities as universals, and thus the same in different things, we should think of them as 'abstract particulars', which are different in each of the things which have them – thus even if two pieces of paper are of exactly the same shade of white, on this view the whiteness of one piece is a different abstract particular from that of the other piece.[13] These abstract particulars are Moore's particular instances, but no longer conceived in the first instance as instances of universals; the aim instead is to regard a universal as just a set of similar abstract particulars. Moore later argued that Stout's project was mistaken, in that one could not make sense of a set of abstract particulars except by reference to universals; but, at least as presented by Moore, this objection seems question-begging.[14] But there is a different objection to both Moore and Stout, that where a

48

universal is not a sortal property, as colours are not, the fact that something is an instance of that property does not by itself individuate it; there is no way of determining how many particular instances of white, or white abstract particulars, there are in a uniformly white sheet of paper. What in fact happens is that Moore tacitly relies on space-time to individuate his bare particulars, which we might therefore identify with pairs consisting of a universal and a region of space–time (though this does not accommodate Moore's imaginary particulars which do not exist at all). It can then be questioned whether space–time suffices for individuation, and how regions of space–time are themselves individuated; but I shall not pursue these issues.

Particulars and universals, in respect of which Moore's views are conventionally Platonist (I p. 114), comprise the constituents of propositions, the objective constituents of thought. One might well think that this only applies to atomic propositions, but Moore's general theory of meaning commits him to the view that the logical constants also denote constituents of propositions. The resulting logical theory will then be a theory concerning the powers of these logical constituents, which fits with Moore's conception of logic at this time as synthetic. This is problematic in so far as it requires logical objects as constituents, though perhaps these can be thought of as primarily properties of propositions. What is none the less of interest here is the implied account of the quantifiers. In *The Principles of Mathematics* (chapter V) Russell had suggested that in propositions expressed by sentences which include a quantifier (e.g. 'Some man is talking'), although the proposition includes a constituent which is what the quantifier phrase ('Some man') means, the proposition is not 'about' this constituent, but is instead 'about' an object 'denoted' by it ('the whole procession of human beings throughout the ages is always relevant to every proposition in which *some man* occurs, and what is denoted is essentially not each separate man, but a kind of combination of all men'; p. 62). Where we may want to protest that Russell has not here characterised an object at all, Moore's protest is different. In his review of *The Principles of Mathematics*[15] he objects that it must be wrong to exclude what a proposition is 'about' from the proposition; and one can see why he takes this view, since Russell's account conflicts with the identity theory of truth in that what a proposition is about determines its truth or falsity, and must therefore, on the identity theory, be a constituent of the proposition. It is possible, indeed, that this thought had occurred to Russell and is relevant to his notoriously baffling argument against Frege in 'On Denoting', since the identity theory requires the rejection of any Fregean sense/reference distinction. In his review Moore proceeds to endorse the alternative account of quantifiers advanced by Russell in 'On Denoting'; its crucial merit, from his point of view, being that by treating quantifiers as something like second-order properties Russell avoids any need to introduce objects which are not constituents of the proposition expressed.

Having introduced the issue of Moore's relationship with Russell, it is worth briefly discussing the extent to which Russell shared Moore's early metaphysics. As I mentioned at the start of this chapter, during the period 1900–4 Russell openly expressed his great intellectual debts to Moore. One might infer from this that he completely accepted Moore's metaphysics; but this is not in fact so: Russell did not accept Moore's view that most universals determine a kind of particular. He argues the point in detail with respect to the relation of *difference* (*The Principles of Mathematics* pp. 50–2), and the example is appropriate since Moore had specifically claimed that the universal *difference* has particular differences as instances (B p. 406). Again, in his 1904 papers on Meinong[16] Russell rejects any such entity as 'the blackness of the table' as distinct from the similar blackness of any other object (p. 72) (it was Meinong's view that there are such particulars, and he shared Moore's part/whole theory of predication.)[17] This is clearly inconsistent with Moore's account of particular colours which was once expressed by means of a similar example – in which Moore maintained that even if the blackness of his waistcoat and that of his coat were exactly similar, they would not be one and the same (I pp. 105–6). Thus by 1904, despite the expression of indebtedness to Moore with which Russell commences his discussion of Meinong, he was in fact breaking away from the metaphysics of Moore's early philosophy.

### 3: Consciousness and the self

I have so far concentrated on Moore's general account of propositions and their constituents. I want now to turn to his account of the nature of consciousness, or thought. For although Moore regards propositions not simply as objects of consciousness, but as the very structure of being, it is none the less a central feature of his conception of them that they are objects of consciousness. An initial question is whether anything other than propositions can be objects of consciousness: cannot, for example, ordinary things such as trees be objects of perception? Moore thinks not; for it is not a tree, by itself, that is perceived, but the existence of a tree; and from the identity of such a state of affairs and the true proposition that such a tree exists, it follows that it is true propositions that are perceived (E&E p. 89). However, Moore does allow that there can also be sensations of simple sensible qualities, i.e. of particular instances of such qualities (E&E pp. 88–9), and it is of course the analysis of such a sensation which he discusses in RI. He says nothing explicit about universals as objects of consciousness by themselves, but implicit in his discussion in *PE* of goodness and our awareness of it is the assumption that such consciousness of universals is possible.

50

Turning now from the objects of consciousness to consciousness itself, we must ask how this is regarded. Moore of course regards it as an external relation and he initially presents it in NJ (p. 179) as a relation between subject and object. I shall discuss his views about the subject of consciousness later, and concentrate now on his account of the relation itself. He is characteristically, but unhelpfully, inclined to say that it is a kind of mental state 'of too simple a nature to admit a definition' (E&E p. 82); but in RI he makes it clear that he conceives it as, generically, a 'transparent awareness' of its object. There are two points here: first, that consciousness is always an awareness, or knowledge, of its object (B vol. 2 p. 717; RI p. 27; PE p. 134): second, that consciousness is 'transparent', i.e. an immediate presentation of its object. Both these points are problematic.

The first point is, in part, a repudiation of the associationist empiricism of Bain, Mill, and others. Moore wants to insist that our mental life is not a succession of qualitative feelings, but is essentially a stream of thoughts. This critical side of his thought is in line with the position advanced by other critics of associationism, such as Brentano, Ward, and Stout. But the details of Moore's position are idiosyncratic and problematic. In interpreting thoughts as essentially awareness of an object Moore runs into the problem that he also wants to say that what is known must be true (if it is a proposition) or exist (if it is a particular) (PE p. 134); and yet he does not want to say that in all cases of consciousness, the object exists or is true. This difficulty especially afflicts the discussion of scepticism at the end of RI. Moore here invokes his cognitive conception of consciousness to refute the sceptic: 'merely to have a sensation is already to *be* outside that circle [of our own ideas]. It is to know something which is as truly and really *not* a part of *my* experience, as anything which I can ever know' (p. 27). To render this consistent with his view that the objects of sensation need not exist, we have to suppose that the 'knowledge' which is integral to sensation does not require the existence or truth of what is known. But this 'knowledge' is not that with which the sceptic is concerned: the sceptic doubts whether we have any proper knowledge, knowledge whose objects are true or exist; and the mere occurrence of a sensation is certainly not sufficient to refute him. Moore allows himself much too easy a triumph over scepticism in RI, as he realised only too soon (cf. chapter 5).

The second feature of Moore's account of consciousness was his emphasis on its transparency. This metaphor is presented most forcefully in RI:

In general, that which makes the sensation of blue a mental fact seems to escape us: it seems, if I may use a metaphor, to be transparent – we look through it and see nothing but the blue.

(p. 20)

the moment we try to fix our attention upon consciousness and to see *what*, distinctly, it is, it seems to vanish: it seems as if we had before us a mere emptiness. When we try to interpret the sensation of blue, all we can see is the blue: the other element is as if it were diaphanous.

(p. 25)

Moore's thought seems to be that there is nothing more to an act of consciousness than the presentation of an object. As such it is intimately related to the thesis of RI, that that which has been conceived to be the 'content' of sense-experience is in fact its object. We can go on to ask whether Moore takes it that consciousness has no 'content' of any kind, in the sense of experiential qualities which contribute to the determination of the object of consciousness but are not themselves objects of consciousness.[18] One aspect of Moore's thought which confirms this hypothesis is his account of pleasure and pain: in *PE* Moore sharply separates these sensations from our consciousness of them, treating them as objects of consciousness whose *esse* is not *percipi* (pp. 87, 107, 212; but contrast *PGEM* p. 653 for a later change of mind on this point). A related point concerns his account of the difference between different kinds of act of consciousness (perception, memory, desire etc.); it would seem that if consciousness has no inner content, then these differences can arise only from differences in the objects of consciousness or other extrinsic features. And in E&E Moore does indeed seem to present this view, suggesting, for example, that the only difference between perception and imagination is that in the case of perception the object is among the causes of the act itself. Since Moore regards this difference in causality as inessential to the act of consciousness itself, it follows that there is no essential difference between perception and imagination. Yet this does not seem to have been Moore's considered view. For he also writes in E&E of 'intrinsic differences' between different kinds of consciousness, which intrinsic differences 'no one has yet succeeded in pointing out' (p. 83), although Moore is confident that by some psychological law they correspond to differences in the nature of the objects of consciousness.

The issue raised here is one that is of general relevance to Moore's philosophy. For even after he had rejected the metaphysics of pure realism, he retained the basic act/object conception of consciousness: thus in *SMPP* he treats the intentionality of consciousness, in the sense of its object-directedness, as a matter of 'Common Sense' (p. 4), and his views about sense-data presuppose the same model of sense-experience (cf. chapter 8). The occasion on which he expounded his position most clearly was in his long review in *Mind* (1910) of Messer's *Empfindung und Denken*.[19] Messer had propounded the standard act/content/object model of consciousness; to this Moore objects 'that it is impossible to verify by observation the existence of any internal qualitative difference between every pair of Acts which have different objects' (pp. 403–4). However, he does now make it clear that this repudiation of 'contents' of consciousness is not the repudiation of all qualitative distinctions between acts of consciousness. For he accepts that different kinds of consciousness do differ in 'internal quality', though he leaves it unclear how many different kinds of consciousness he wants to distinguish in this way.

I want now to turn from a discussion of Moore's conception of consciousness to his account of the self. Since in his early philosophy the only fundamental particulars are instantaneous, there is no place here for a persisting substantial subject. In his articles in B Moore seems to take the view that each act of consciousness has a single spiritual subject, which constitute a single mind or person where they are linked by self-consciousness or through connections with one single brain (vol. 1 p. 172). These brief remarks are modified and developed and at length in Moore's review of McTaggart's *Studies in Hegelian Cosmology*,[20] which is Moore's only discussion of personal identity. McTaggart had claimed that causal connectedness between the mental states of temporary selves is both necessary and sufficient for personal identity (*Studies in Hegelian Cosmology* p. 50). Moore responds that although this causal connectedness is certainly necessary for personal identity, it is not sufficient; memory is also required. His argument to this effect starts from the thought that we would not identify with a simultaneous self entirely similar to us; of such a putative double of himself Moore writes 'to confess the truth, I feel a positive repugnance to him' (p. 206). Moore now suggests that our relationship to an earlier self that was only causally connected to our present self would be no different from our relationship to this simultaneous double, and thus that we would no more identify with this earlier self than with our simultaneous double. To support this suggestion he relies on the thoughts that it is our present self-consciousness which distinguishes us from our simultaneous double, and that causal connectedness cannot substitute for this self-consciousness in the case of an earlier self, since it is not essentially a conscious relation at all. It is now obvious why Moore introduces memory; his thought is that memory is precisely self-consciousness over time:

> The only sense in which we use personal identity with 'much meaning' . . . is that in which what is meant by the past or future has the same relation to the present self, as the present self has to itself. And this relation is given by memory.
>
> (p. 208)

This is obviously a Lockean account of personal identity. As such it is vulnerable, not only to the traditional objections of Butler and Reid, but also to the duplication problem introduced by Bernard Williams and since developed by others.[21] This latter problem is especially relevant to Moore's argument for his position: there is nothing in Moore's account to rule out a situation in which two apparently distinct persons, located in different bodies, each have suitably direct perceptions by memory of the same earlier self. Moore must identify these two later selves; yet their relationship is essentially the same as his relationship to that double whom he viewed with such repugnance.

One response to this problem is to reject the conception of a subject of consciousness at all, and even in his early writings there are occasions on which Moore treats consciousness as impersonal; thus in *PE* Moore applies a part/whole analysis to the consciousness of a beautiful object and says that 'we can distinguish as parts the object on the one hand and the being conscious on the other' (p. 28), without any mention of a subject. It is this impersonal conception of consciousness which predominates in Moore's few later published comments on this topic. The paucity of these comments might suggest that Moore did not pay much attention to it, but there is reason to think otherwise: Braithwaite describes how in 1922–3 Moore lectured at length on the self (A&L p. 25), and in a lecture given in the academic year 1933–4 Moore declared that the problem of the self was one of 'the two problems of philosophy which I think interest me most, and also puzzle me most' (*LP* p. 162; the other problem was of course that of the relation between sense-data and material objects). What is surprising, in the light of this remark, is that he should have published so little on this topic (especially as compared with the topic of sense-data); even his Commonplace Book contains few entries dealing with it. The most striking feature of Moore's later comments is his tentative move towards a Humean position, according to which acts of consciousness have no subject at all (cf. SSD pp. 174–5) which leads him to cite approvingly William James's thesis that 'the present thought is the only thinker' (*LP* p. 163).[22] Sometimes what he fails to say is as revealing as what he does say: when describing the 'Common Sense' view of the world in *SMPP* (chapter 1) he includes acts of consciousness, and he accepts that, along with material objects, these are 'the only *substantial* kinds of things *known* to us' (p. 16). Even in DCS, although he initially insists on his common-sense certainty that there are selves (p. 39), at the end of the paper he undermines this by his total perplexity as to what this means (p. 59).

Moore offers little by way of argument for the Humean position he is tempted to adopt, though at one point he mentions Hume's observation that introspection does not reveal to us any such thing as the mind or self.[23] Nor does he spell out in detail what the relations are between my acts of consciousness whereby they are mine; in so far as he says anything on this topic he hints that it is some relation to a human body which is crucial and does not mention memory, despite his previous Lockean theory of personal identity.[24] This reference to the body might suggest materialist sympathies; but although in *SMPP* he maintains that all mental acts are effects of material causes in the brain (pp. 159–60) Moore's approach to the mind is too Cartesian for him to take materialism seriously. So although the general tenor of his scepticism about the subject of consciousness fits with his reaction against what he took to be the subjectivism of the idealists, one is left very much in the dark as to the nature of his view and his reasons for it.

## 4: *The* a priori

These accounts of propositions and our consciousness of them have reflected the hostility to holism and subjectivism characteristic of Moore's rejection of idealism. The third element of his pure realism is the hostility to empiricism which he took over from the idealists themselves, and I shall now pursue his development of this theme in the direction of 'analytic philosophy'.

Moore's use of the '*a priori* /empirical' terminology is idiosyncratic since it lacks some of its usual epistemological content. Thus arithmetical truths are, for him, paradigms of *a priori* truths, and yet he writes in his 1898 Dissertation that $2 + 2 = 4$ is 'a fact forced upon from outside just as much as any sensation' (cf. NJ pp. 191–2; KI p. 137). As we have seen, Moore initially founds his *a priori* /empirical distinction upon the timeless/temporal distinction (NJ p. 189), *a priori* propositions being those which include no concepts which exist in time. Once he has replaced concepts by universals and their particular instances, this account will not work, since no universals are in time; however, it is an easy matter to define an empirical universal as one whose instances can exist in time (cf. *PE* p. 41 on 'natural properties') and this yields Moore's favoured definition of empiricism as the view that 'all known truths assert something about what exists at one or more moments of time' (B p. 130; cf. *PE* pp. 111, 124; E&E p. 93). As such Moore is not an empiricist; for some ethical and arithmetical truths do not in this way concern what exists in time and are therefore *a priori* (*PE* pp. 125–6). Moore's argument for this claim concerning fundamental ethical truths is, of course, inseparable from his allegation that there is a fallacy in all naturalist systems of ethics, which I shall discuss in the next chapter.

One of the traditional marks of the *a priori* is necessity. In NJ however, Moore, argued that any proposition is such that 'if it is true, it is necessarily true, and if false, necessarily false' (p. 190). This strange claim, reminiscent of the Absolute idealism Moore was still in the process of rejecting, rests in part on the bad argument that any proposition which 'involves necessity', in the sense of entailing a necessary truth, is itself necessary (pp. 185–8). But I think it also reflects Moore's conception of truth and falsehood as relations which unify the constituent concepts of a proposition (p. 180); for if one also takes it that it is essential to any whole that it be constituted in the way that it is, then it will follow that the truth or falsity of a proposition is essential to it. This modal thesis is not repeated after NJ;[25] and it is significant that Moore also alters his view of truth and falsehood to the view that they are just simple qualities of propositions (B vol. 2 p. 717) – a thought expressed by Russell, with explicit reference to Moore, as the thought that 'some propositions are true and some false, just as some roses are red and some white'.[26] This revised view permits contingency, and Moore quickly returns to the traditional view that necessary truth is a distinctive mark of the *a priori* (B vol. 2 p. 130).

Moore develops this view in his 1900 paper N; but his position here is unusual in that he here denies that the timeless/temporal distinction has any relevance to the *a priori* /empirical distinction, on the grounds that all propositions are, if true, timelessly true (pp. 296–7). This is only a temporary abandonment of his usual position since, as he acknowledges in *PE* (p. 111), the timeless truth of all propositions does not in fact show that there are no empirical propositions, in the sense of propositions which assert the existence of things in time. None the less, this brief abandonment of his usual position leads him to develop a position of some interest. For having identified necessary truth with the *a priori*, he now interprets the *a priori* as that which has 'logical priority'. He does not define logical priority precisely, saying only that it obtains where 'one proposition is presupposed, or implied, or involved in another' (p. 300), but he gives some examples which suggest that $p$ is logically prior to $q$ just where $q$ entails $p$ because $p$ is part of any expanation of $q$. One thing he clearly has in mind is a purified version of Kant's critical philosophy (cf. chapter 1, section 3) which he thinks would show that arithmetic, geometry, and metaphysical principles of substance and causality are 'logically prior' to all empirical judgments.

The resulting conception of necessity is proof-theoretic and thus epistemological. It also implies that the concept of necessity is essentially relative: some propositions are necessary relative to others, to which they are 'logically prior'. Moore draws this consequence ('No proposition is necessary in itself' N p. 302), but suggests that where one proposition is logically prior to more propositions than another, the former is 'more necessary' than the latter. The belief that there are some absolutely necessary propositions is then to be accounted for by recognising that some propositions are logically prior to almost any propositions. This is Moore's view of the Kantian *a priori*, and he also applies it to logical truths: it is only because logic is itself logically prior to any argument that the fundamental principles of logic are necessary truths (N pp. 302–3).

As it stands, this account of necessity is incomplete, since the basic conception of logical priority is not satisfactorily elucidated. None the less, the thoughts that there is only a difference of degree between necessary and contingent truths, and that not even logic itself is absolutely necessary, are ones which have been famously developed by Quine and others in interesting and influential ways. But since these developments assume a combination of pragmatism and holism that Moore would have rejected, it cannot be said that there is an intelligible tradition which links Moore and Quine on the topic of necessity. Indeed Moore soon abandoned the position advanced in N, although at the time it had some influence on Russell.[27] Moore never explained why he abandoned this position, but I suspect that his change of mind reflects his growing scepticism about arguments for the logical priority of the Kantian *a priori*. Yet perhaps it has one lingering consequence within his thought – in his thesis that there are fundamental assumptions which we cannot prove: for in PE he explicitly advances this thesis concerning logic (p. 76 – I quote and discuss the relevant passage on p. 59). This thesis is essentially epistemological, and not presented as an account of necessity at all; but since the account of necessity presented in N is itself epistemological, it was possible for Moore to retain something of the epistemology while dropping the view that it is an account of necessity.

After N Moore reverts to his usual timeless/temporal account of the *a priori*/empirical distinction (e.g. PE pp. 110ff.) and says very little explicitly about necessity. Generally where he writes of it, it is of analytic necessity (PE pp. 29, 33, 220–1), which he treats in a very dismissive way: an analytic truth is an '*absolute* tautology', 'perfectly barren','insignificant' (RI p. 11; E&E p. 94). The important question, therefore, is whether he now thinks of all necessary truths as of this kind.

The answer is that he does not. For in RI he contrasts interpretations of '*esse*=*percipi*' which make it an analytic truth with that which makes it a '*necessary synthetic* proposition' (p. 11 – Moore's emphasis). This is the only place in his early writings (but post-1900) in which he unequivocally admits that there might be necessary but synthetic truths. In this case he holds that the proposition is false; but there are indications that he regards certain other propositions as necessary synthetic truths. He certainly regards the truths of arithmetic as synthetic (KI p. 131) and in E&E (p. 94) he describes them as 'so-called necessary truths'. Since Moore associates closely arithmetical and ethical propositions, it must also be plausible to suppose that he regards fundamental truths concerning intrinsic value as necessary and synthetic. That he regards them as synthetic is obvious; but that he regards them as necessary is not so clear since he does not state categorically in PE that this is so (though he does so later without remarking on any change in his view from that of PE: cf. E p. 27; CIV p. 259).

One reason to favour this view is simply Moore's use of the term 'intrinsic value', since the term 'intrinsic' standardly has a modal implication. But there is a further, better, reason. Moore often says that the fundamental principles of ethics and the truths of arithmetic are 'universal' (*PE* pp. 16, 23, 27, 111, 126; KI pp. 129–30), and this, I suggest, is a way of saying that they are necessary, though with a different conception of necessity from that presented in N. Thus in KI Moore says that analytic truths are unproblematically universal, but that Kant's genius lay in recognising that some universal propositions are synthetic and in raising the question of 'how we can know *universal* synthetic propositions to be true' (KI p. 130). By 'universal' Moore must here mean 'necessary', as Kant himself did when he used the term (*Critique of Pure Reason* A2). Admittedly, Moore also says (KI p. 130) that a truth is universal where it concerns all instances of a predicate, and this may seem to imply that universality is too weak for necessity, since it omits reference to the possible. This objection, however, fails to take account of the fact that the instances of Moore's universals do not have to exist in order to be; hence a Moorean universal truth concerns all actual and possible instances, and can therefore be plausibly regarded as a necessary truth (cf. *PE* pp. 118–19). The result is an essentially semantic concept of necessity, unlike that of N, and one which allows for a proposition's being necessary in itself. This becomes Moore's settled view of necessity; and as he becomes more ontologically parsimonious (cf. chapter 5), he has to introduce explicit reference to the possible as well as the actual in order to characterise necessity, with the result that his position becomes straightforwardly Leibnizian. Thus whereas in KI he contents himself with observing that '2 + 2 are always 4' (pp. 129–30), in *E* he writes:

> It seems quite clear, for instance, that it is not only true that twice two do make four, in the Universe as it actually is, but that they necessarily would make four, in any conceivable Universe, no matter how much it might differ from this one in other respects.
>
> (p. 27)[28]

As I mentioned above, in KI Moore raises the Kantian question of how we know any universal, i.e. necessary, synthetic propositions, to be true. Moore, of course, will have no dealings with Kantian transcendental deductions; and since universality embraces all possible instances, induction from observed actual instances looks a poor ground for knowledge. Equally, since the propositions are not analytic, inspection of the constitutive universals should not be sufficient by itself to yield knowledge of the proposition's truth. Yet this is in fact basically all that Moore has to offer. The position is worked out in most detail for knowledge of fundamental ethical truths, which I shall discuss in the next chapter. But Moore's general thesis is that if one prepares oneself adequately by clarifying exactly what universals one is considering, one can discern reflectively whether or not there are necessary, but synthetic, connections between them. This is a position which has a long history in philosophy; e.g. Descartes envisages something similar when he writes about 'intuition' in his *Rules on Method* (cf. rule 3); and at much the time that Moore was putting forward his view, Husserl was propounding an essentially similar account of 'eidetic intuition' (*Ideas* part 3, chapter 1). As these cases exemplify, the word 'intuition' rises irresistibly to characterise this view, and Moore himself uses it in this connection.

Before discussing further this intuitionist epistemology, however, I want to look at a passage I alluded to above, in which Moore suggests that with respect to fundamental, and hence unprovable, propositions, the best we can hope to do in any dispute concerning them is to aim to secure agreement:

> For, indeed, who can prove that proof is itself a warrant of truth? We are all agreed that the laws of logic are true and therefore we accept a result which is proved by their means; but such a proof is satisfactory to us only because we are so fully agreed that it is a warrant of truth. And yet we cannot, by the nature of the case, prove that we are right in being so agreed.
>
> (*PE* p. 76)

Moore is here writing about logic, but the context is such as to imply that he takes the same view about fundamental ethical principles. It is tempting to read into this passage the thesis that for such propositions agreement justifies a claim to knowledge. But I think that this temptation should be resisted. Moore's point here is only that in the absence of any possibility of proof, we should be content to secure agreement; he does not say that finding such agreement justifies a claim to knowledge. Indeed, a few pages later (*PE* p. 92), he unequivocally assigns authority in ethics to 'direct intuition' over common-sense. So despite the passage I have quoted Moore's position remains fundamentally intuitionist.

Any talk of intuition suggests an analogy with vision, and in Moore's case this analogy is strengthened by his frequent description of fundamental necessary synthetic truths as 'self-evident' (RI pp. 11–12). What he means by this is that these propositions themselves furnish the only evidence there is for them, and he explicitly compares them in this respect with immediate judgments of perception such as 'This is a hand' which he also holds to be incapable of proof (VR pp. 88–9, 95). This latter view is, of course, that which he was later to develop in DCS and PEW, and I shall discuss it in chapter 9. But what I want now to observe is the deep implausibility of this account of our knowledge of necessary synthetic truths. One problem is the difficulty of explaining how spatiotemporal beings such as ourselves can have reliable cognitive relations with universals, which are outside space and time. For without an understanding of how reliability might be attained in this regard, the perceptual analogy is undermined, and intuitions seem no different from deeply held convictions. Russell lucidly described the resulting conception of philosophy, in so far as it concerns itself with such supposedly self-evident principles:

> All depends, in the end, upon immediate perception; and philosophical argument, strictly speaking, consists mainly of an endeavour to cause the reader to perceive what has been perceived by the author. The argument, in short, is not of the nature of proof, but of exhortation.
>
> *(The Principles of Mathematics* p. 130)

That this is unsatisfactory Moore's practice in *PE* well shows. Where he is concerned in chapter 3 to dissuade his readers from hedonism, he advances several points which do indeed exhibit the implausibility of the hedonist position. Moore, however, insists that he cannot prove that hedonism is false; so what is to be the status of the points he advances? His theory is such that he can at best advance them with the aim of securing agreement; in fact, however, he makes a stronger claim; he presents them as 'considerations capable of determining the intellect' (*PE* p. 75). Moore is here quoting from chapter 1 of J.S. Mill's *Utilitarianism*; but Mill argues here, in the very passage from which Moore is quoting,[29] that in ethical arguments considerations of this kind are 'equivalent to proof'. Thus by this invocation of Mill Moore is tacitly acknowledging that there is a way of reasoning concerning fundamental ethical principles which his own narrow stress on intuition does not make room for. On the other hand, his practice at some other places is in line with his theory; most notably in chapter 6 where he is concerned to present his own account of what has intrinsic value, his thesis that 'personal affections and aesthetic enjoyments include *all* the greatest, and *by far* the greatest, goods we can imagine' (*PE* p. 189). For he makes no effort to present any reasons for this extraordinary thesis; and this lack of effort on his part contributes to the unconvincing nature of his discussion.

Another reason for finding Moore's intuitionist epistemology unsatisfactory is that it is dubiously compatible with the assumption that the truths in question are synthetic. For if one can discern them simply from a grasp of their constituent universals once one has cleared away misunderstandings, then, since the universals are just the meanings of the predicates in a sentence used to express the truth, it is hard to see how such a truth can fail to be analytic, not quite in the narrow Kantian sense but in that extension of it whereby a proposition is analytically true where the truth of a sentence which expresses it depends only upon the meanings of the words it contains. Were Moore to hold that there is a

60

sense/reference distinction for predicates, such that a grasp of the concept expressed by a predicate did not bring with it full knowledge of the identity of the property thus referred to, his position might be defensible. But Moore rejects any such distinction, and emphasises, on the contrary, that that once one is clear about the meanings at issue, the truth or falsity of propositions concerning them can be immediately determined, as when he presents the account of what has intrinsic value quoted above: 'Once the meaning of the question [what has intrinsic value?] is clearly understood, the answer to it, in its main outlines, appears to be so obvious, that it runs the risk of seeming a platitude.'

Moore would certainly have rejected the conclusion of this latter argument, that his supposedly synthetic necessary truths are actually analytic. It would after all have the consequence that there is no naturalistic fallacy. But then he should have provided a better account of our knowledge of them. He could with profit have tried to understand more carefully why Kant raised the question as to how there can be knowledge of synthetic *a priori* truths. As things stand, his intuitionist epistemology seems little more than a projection of the dialectical method which is manifest in the frequent use of emphasis in all his published writings and which was memorably described by Keynes:

> In practice, victory was with those who could speak with the greatest appearance of clear, undoubting conviction and could best use the accents of infallibility. Moore at this time was a master of this method – greeting one's remarks with a gasp of incredulity – *Do* you *really* think *that*, an expression of face as if to hear such a thing reduced him to a state of wonder verging on imbecility, with his mouth wide open and wagging his head so violently that his hair shook. [30]

### 5: Analysis

Since intuitions of necessary synthetic truths have such a central role in Moore's early philosophy, it cannot be right to regard this philosophy as 'analytic', where 'analytic philosophy' is philosophy informed by the belief that analysis is the central method of philosophy. None the less analysis has an important place in the method of Moore's early philosophy.

Moore's general conception of analysis is that it should reveal the structure of complex objects, or, in Moore's favoured part/whole idioms, show 'what are the parts which invariably compose a certain whole' (*PE* p. 9). In applying this method Moore reveals some of his fundamental presumptions: first, there is his commitment to simples:

> those innumerable objects of thought which are themselves incapable of definition, because they are the ultimate terms by reference to which whatever *is* capable of definition must be defined. That there must be

61

an indefinite number of such terms is obvious, on reflection; since we cannot define anything except by an analysis, which when carried as far as it will go, refers us to something, which is simply different from anything else.

(*PE* pp. 9–10)

That Moore should be thus committed to simples is only to be expected, given his rejection of holism. The Lockean argument he employs here (cf. *Essay* III.iv.5) just assumes without argument that the alternative of a circle of definitions is to be rejected. It follows from Moore's one-level theory of meaning and the associated identity theory of truth, that these semantic simples must also be ontologically simple, and he also implies that they are epistemologically basic (*PE* p. 7). A further feature of Moore's conception of analysis is that it is proper for analysis to reveal the structure not only of propositions and complex universals, but also of those 'composite existents', ordinary material objects, which are also wholes with simple particulars as parts. In NJ, where universals and particulars are not distinguished within the category of concepts, Moore writes that 'a thing becomes intelligible first when it is analysed into its constituent concepts' (NJ p. 182); and in *PE* the notorious passage about the 'definition of a horse' is to be understood in the light of his account of material objects as composed of particular instances of universals:

But (3) we may, when we define horse, mean something much more important. We may mean that a certain object, which all of us know, is composed in a certain manner: that it has four legs, a head, a liver, etc., etc., all of them arranged in definite relations to one another.

(*PE* p. 8)

Is Moore here considering a definition, or analysis, of the universal *horse*, or of a particular horse? Both: for where a complex universal is analysed into simpler ones, instances of the complex universal must themselves by likewise analysable into instances of the simpler universals.

It is easy enough to present an account in the abstract of the way in which analysis is supposed to work. But what is also required is an account of the kinds of evidence which, in particular cases, support a putative analysis. Although Moore is already emphatic that his analytic questions are not questions about the use of language (*PE* p. 6), for they are about meanings and not words, he is also forced to admit that linguistic evidence is relevant. The situation is, he says, 'peculiar' (N p. 290): though we are tempted to say 'we must know exactly what it is that we are talking about, before we can know whether what we say of it is true or false', in fact 'the order of discovery is generally just the reverse of this . . . I must examine the cases in which things are said to be necessary, before I can say what necessity is' (N pp. 290–1). Although

Moore is thus forced to admit the relevance of linguistic evidence, it plays only a small role in his early work, much smaller than that which it was to assume later as analytic philosophy developed.

The evidence to which he pays most attention concerns what we think, not what we say. Its relevance is easily explained: since analysis is the revelation of structure, it preserves the identity of what is analysed, in particular, therefore, that of propositions analysed. Hence, since propositions are objects of thought, we can subject putative analyses to the test as to whether in thinking (doubting etc.) the proposition which is the analysandum we are really thinking (doubting etc.) the proposition which is alleged to be its analysis. This is the condition of substitutivity within indirect speech. The difficulty with it lies in the question as to how it is decided whether or not two descriptions of thought are descriptions of the same thought. The obvious answer is that the thinker is the authority about the identity of his thoughts, and it is to the thinker's authority that Moore appeals in one of his arguments against ethical naturalism:

> Moreover any one can easily convince himself by inspection that the predicate of this proposition – 'good' – is positively different from the notion of 'desiring to desire' which enters into its subject: 'That we should desire to desire A is good' is *not* merely equivalent to 'That A should be good is good'.
>
> (*PE* p. 16)

The objection to this position is that it assumes that the structure of thoughts is transparently accessible to their thinker, and this is a Cartesian assumption which there is reason to reject. Thinkers are as fallible about the nature of their own thoughts as about their physical environment. Indeed, despite this argument against ethical naturalism, Moore himself denies that the thinker is the ultimate authority on his thoughts; a passage in his review of McTaggart's *Studies in Hegelian Cosmology* is especially noteworthy in this respect:

> a man may be fully convinced, in any ordinary sense of conviction –
> may even be ready to die for the truth of his opinion – that a certain
> predicate does *not* attach to a certain subject, and yet whenever he
> *imagines* that subject . . . may quite unconsciously include in it the
> very predicate of which both then and at all other times he is ready to
> asseverate the absence. . . . When the Buddhist thinks 'The soul in
> that animal will be myself, but it will not remember its present state'
> can there be any reason to suppose that when he imagines it as *himself*,
> he does not imagine it as remembering his present state? In other
> words, that the thought which is expressed by the first half of his

sentence, may firmly contradict that which is expressed by the second, without causing him the slightest uneasiness?

(p. 202)

If, as this passage implies, it is the philosopher who is the authority on the identity of a thinker's thoughts, then the substitutivity condition is no use in the search for evidence by which to test a putative analysis.

The difficulty Moore faces here is not only epistemological; it is also constitutive in that the content of his distinction between analytic truths and synthetic, but necessary, truths seems to be just that only the former warrant substitutivity within indirect speech, and if this latter condition has no content independent of a philosopher's determination, then his analytic/synthetic distinction can have none either. Philosophers with strong holistic sympathies (be they Absolute idealists or American pragmatists and their successors) will welcome this conclusion, and infer from it that there is no merit to an analytic/synthetic distinction. But I think one should be less dismissive. For there is a proper, indeed indispensable, place in philosophical arguments for inquiries into the relations (logical and epistemological) between concepts, and thus for accounts of the concepts thus related which, by elucidating their identity in relation to that of other concepts, provide analyses of them. Admittedly, since accounts of these relationships cannot be substantiated piecemeal, but require a context provided by a general theory which commands assent, acceptance of analyses cannot usually be divorced from assent to theories which range over synthetic matters of fact as well. But this fact, rightly stressed by holists, does not prove that there is nothing to an analytic/synthetic distinction. For any theory with a complex theoretical structure will legitimate a distinction between those claims about its central concepts which identify them in such a way as to clarify their logical and epistemological relationships and those claims which concern substantive matters of fact.

On this account of the matter philosophical analysis cannot be conducted in a context isolated from general theories concerning the matters which fall under the concepts under analysis. It follows that there is no reason to expect assent to analyses that are presented in an isolated fashion, and in so far as Moore's condition of substitutivity within indirect speech suggests that this should be possible it cannot be a fundamental criterion of the truth of an analysis. Yet since concepts are just ways of thinking, it looks as though the substitutivity condition should none the less be upheld as an implication of philosophical analysis; furthermore the reflective nature of philosophy implies that such analyses should be reflectively assimilable in the long run. At this point, however, there arises a difficulty concerning the possibility of non-trivial philosophical analyses. This, the 'paradox of analysis', is an issue which I shall discuss later, in chapter 7, when I return to the topic of philosophical analysis in the light of Moore's later reflections on it. So judgment on the issue of the relationship between philosophical analysis and substitutivity within indirect speech should be suspended for the time being.

In the opening sentences of the preface to PE Moore sets out his hopes concerning analysis:

> It appears to me that in Ethics, as in all other philosophical studies, the difficulties and disagreements of which its history is full, are mainly due to a very simple cause: namely to the attempt to answer questions, without discovering precisely *what* question it is which you desire to answer. I do not know how far this source of error would be done away, if philosophers would *try* to discover what question they were asking, before they set about to answer it; for the work of analysis and distinction is often very difficult. . . . But I am inclined to think that in many cases a resolute attempt would be inclined to ensure success.
>
> (p. vii)

What is implied here is an 'underlabourer' conception, not of philosophy, but of analysis; it is supposed to enable us to clear away the thickets of confusion and ambiguity which obstruct a clear intuition of philosophical truth. The grasp of such truth is not itself a product of analysis; rather analysis is supposed to bring us to the point from which alone we can grasp it. I have already argued that, on Moore's premisses, there cannot remain a truth to be discerned which analysis has not already revealed. Hence we must reject the division of labour which separates analysis of a question from the intuition of its answer; it is, rather, characteristic of philosophy that there is no way in which we can articulate a potentially satisfactory answer to a question without recognising that our answer implies much about the meaning of the question.

This conclusion conflicts with Moore's view. But his work sometimes belies it. In RI Moore says that the only alternative to interpreting '*esse = percipi*' as a 'barren' analytic truth is to interpret it as an interesting, though false, claim about a necessary but synthetic connection (pp. 11–12). Yet he proceeds to give an analysis of sensation (pp. 24–6), from which it follows that '*esse = percipi*' is false. Thus he in fact treats it as an interesting analytic falsehood. So even Moore's early philosophy reveals a more ambitious conception of the role of analysis, according to which analysis can have more than a preparatory role. In this way, despite itself, Moore's early work points towards a philosophy which takes analysis as its predominant method, towards 'analytic philosophy'; it is analytic philosophy in itself but not yet for itself.

# III

# The naturalistic fallacy

*I am climbing Moore like some industrious insect who is determined to build a nest on the top of a Cathedral spire. One sentence, a string of 'desires' makes my head spin with the infinite meaning of words unadorned; otherwise I have gone happily.*

*(Letter from Virginia Woolf)*[1]

With the publication of *Principia Ethica* Moore established his reputation as one of the foremost philosophers of his generation. Peter Geach has described the reaction of his father, Professor G.H. Geach:

> The influence of *Principia Ethica* is an extraordinary phenomenon in the history of English philosophy. Cambridge men of that generation really thought (I can remember my father continuing to think) that now for the first time in the history of philosophy ethics had been given a really rigorous foundation. This was Moore's own claim; the wonder is that men like Russell, McTaggart, and Maynard Keynes, accepted it.[2]

During the following decades the influence of Moore's ideas spread well beyond Cambridge (and Bloomsbury), partly through the establishment of an 'intuitionist' school of ethical theory at Oxford which largely agreed with him on the central metaphysical issues of ethics.[3] The result is that, for better or worse, twentieth-century British ethical theory is unintelligible without reference to *PE*; its history until 1960 or so being, in brief, that although Moore was taken to have refuted 'ethical naturalism', Moore's own brand of 'ethical non-naturalism' was thought to make unacceptable metaphysical and epistemological demands; so the only recourse was to abandon belief in an objective moral reality and accept an emotivist, prescriptivist, or otherwise anti-realist, account of ethical values.

## 1: *Background to* Principia Ethica

As will be clear from chapters 1 and 2, *Principia Ethica* is the outcome of several years of reflection. Moore's Fellowship Dissertations were much concerned with Kant's ethics and Moore starts his 1898 paper F by avowing the intention to enlarge it 'into a treatise on the whole of his [Kant's] Ethical Philosophy' (p. 179). It is clear enough what his plans were: he wanted to reject Kant's conception of practical reason and expound Kant's ethics, purified of what he took to be their illusory metaphysical foundations. It is significant therefore that Moore's first major undertaking in 1898, when he had secured his Fellowship, was to give a course of lectures in London on 'The Elements of Ethics with a view to an appreciation of Kant's Moral Philosophy'. The Kantian interest promised by this title is, in fact, little developed in these lectures, whose text survives (I refer to them as EE), and though they were followed by another course supposedly devoted to Kant's moral philosophy,[4] one rather wonders what Moore here made of Kant, since in EE he says that the Categorical Imperative 'amounts to the assertion that Good is good'! The main interest of these lectures is that they are in effect a first draft of *PE*. Moore considered publishing them, and had them typed up and circulated with this in mind. Fortunately for his reputation, he abandoned this plan; but he none the less incorporated parts of the lectures into *PE*, especially into chapters 1–3. The result is that these parts of *PE* are literally a patchwork and since understanding of the text is enhanced by knowledge of its provenance I have added an appendix in which I describe the relationship between the two works.

Apart from a few reviews and the article on 'Teleology' in B, Moore published little on ethical theory while he was developing his pure realist metaphysics. But that he continued to think about ethical theory is clear from unpublished essays which survive from this period. I shall not refer much to them, however, for most of what is said in them is better said in chapters 5 and 6 of *PE*, whose publication in 1903 was the culmination of his early philosophy. It also marks the culmination of his interest in ethical theory. For ethical theory occupies a much smaller proportion of his output than had been the case before (e.g. there are very few entries in *CB* on this topic). The explanation for this is certainly not that he felt he had said everything that needed to be said on the subject; on the contrary, he soon realised that his presentation of the main thesis of *PE* – that there is a fallacy, 'the naturalistic fallacy', in almost all previous ethical theories – was wretchedly confused, and it was probably because he was never confident that he could remove these confusions that he returned so little to the subject. But there are three significant works on ethical theory from the period after *PE*. In 1912 he published his little book *Ethics*; Moore later preferred this to *PE* ('it seems to me to be much clearer and far less full of confusions and invalid arguments' – *PGEM* p. 27), but in fact it is a much less ambitious and interesting work, and marred by the desire to elaborate unnecessary detail which disfigures parts of Moore's later writings. A few years later (*c*.1916 – though it was not published until 1922 in *PS*) Moore wrote the paper 'The Conception of Intrinsic Value' in which he returns, in effect, to the grounds for rejecting ethical naturalism. Finally, much later, in his reply to his critics in *PGEM* in 1942 he surprisingly devoted most space to ethical theory, defending himself against his critics and, in the course of doing so, developing certain of his earlier views.

I have already mentioned the influence of Kant on Moore's ethical theory. The other philosopher to whom he was especially indebted was Sidgwick, despite his lack of enthusiasm for Sidgwick as a teacher (*PGEM* pp. 16–17). Yet there is a fundamental difference between them. Sidgwick's emphasis on common-sense and the methods of ethics is that of a coherence theorist who aims to reconcile our intuitive moral convictions with the demands of reason. Moore's approach, by contrast, is that of a foundationalist. Moore does not assign a central place in ethics to common-sense; his epistemology is the intuitionism I described in the previous chapter. What is more, Moore takes it that a crucial task for the philosopher is the analysis of ethical concepts in advance of the determination of any substantive ethical theory. Only once the philosopher has settled, through his analyses, the right questions to ask and the correct way to answer them, can we place any reliance on his ethical judgments (*PE* p. 145). Thus although Moore does not hold that analysis by itself resolves ethical issues, his approach to ethical theory, unlike that of Sidgwick, is shaped by a commitment to foundationalist conceptual analysis.

This difference between Moore and Sidgwick shows up in their conceptions of the status and scope of ethical theory. Whereas Sidgwick had shied away from describing ethics as a 'science' (*The Methods of Ethics* pp. 1-2), and preferred to call it 'a department of the Theory or Study of Practice' (p. xxiii), Moore is emphatic that ethical theory should aim to be 'scientific' (*PE* pp. 3, 5, 6). He had wanted to give *PE* the Kantian title 'Prolegomena to any future Ethics that can possibly pretend to be scientific' (*PE* p. ix), but, presumably because Green had pre-empted this title, he opted instead for the Newtonian connotations of *Principia Ethica*. This stress on the 'scientific' nature of ethical theory is accompanied in Moore's thought by the thesis that ethical theory concerns more than the moral judgments concerning conduct and character on which Sidgwick concentrated. For Moore takes it that judgments of this kind only constitute knowledge where they are grounded in a general theory of value. Moore, of course, takes goodness to be the fundamental value (he standardly calls it 'intrinsic value'), and insists that it is not restricted to the evaluation of conduct (*PE* pp. 2–3). So Moore's science of ethics requires an analysis of moral concepts which makes possible (in theory, at least) the derivation of moral judgments from fundamental principles of value.

Though there was much in Moore's theory that his successors disputed, his general conception of ethical theory was not effectively challenged until Rawls rejected the application of a foundationalist analytic/synthetic distinction to ethical theory and argued that there could be no distinction between form and content in ethics in isolation from one's total ethical theory.[5] Rawls's approach to the study of ethics therefore resembles that of Sidgwick.[6] Although on this issue my sympathies lie with Sidgwick and Rawls, rather than Moore, in discussing Moore's ethical theory it is impracticable not to separate discussion of his views about the analysability, or not, of fundamental ethical concepts from discussion of his substantive moral theory – his ideal utilitarianism. The rest of the present chapter is primarily devoted to the first topic; the second is discussed in the next chapter. As will become apparent, however, it is not my view that Moore's views on these topics are as unrelated as Moore presents them as being.

## 2: *What is the naturalistic fallacy?*

The central critical contention of *PE* is that there is a fallacy, the *naturalistic fallacy*, 'to be met with in almost every book on ethics' (p. 14). Those whom Moore alleges to have committed this fallacy include Aristotle (p. 176), the Stoics (p. 113), Spinoza (p. 113), Rousseau (p. 42), Bentham (p. 18), Kant (p. 126), Mill (p. 66), Spencer (p. 50), and Green (p. 139).[7] Sidgwick is of course exempted from this company of fools (p. 17), and if one identifies commission of the naturalistic fallacy with denial that goodness is 'simple, indefinable, unanalysable' (p. 21), then, Moore also claims, it was a *discovery* of Sidgwick's that there is such a fallacy (p. 17). Whether in fact Sidgwick even maintained this is a disputable matter which I shall return to below; but the thesis that some central ethical concepts are indefinable was certainly not a discovery of Sidgwick's at all, but taken by him from such English eighteenth-century moral philosophers as Price. So far as I know, Moore never acknowledged this anticipation of his thoughts, although he was swiftly corrected on this matter by another of Sidgwick's pupils, Rashdall.[8]

But what is the *naturalistic fallacy*? Moore introduces the phrase on p. 10 of *PE* in association with an analogy between yellowness and goodness, and says that just as it is a mistake to think that yellowness can be defined in terms of those physical properties which cause us to perceive things as yellow, it is a mistake to think that goodness can be defined in terms of those properties of a thing which make it good, a mistake which he proposes to call the 'naturalistic fallacy'. This suggests that one commits this fallacy by denying that goodness is indefinable, and he proceeds (pp. 12–14) with another analogy which seems to confirm this interpretation: he compares goodness with pleasure, by which he means the property of experiences whereby they are pleasant, and having declared that this property is indefinable, he says that the mistake someone would make if he sought to define it 'would be the same fallacy as I have called naturalistic with reference to Ethics' (p. 13).

Yet at this point doubts begin to arise. For Moore also says here that 'if anybody tried to define pleasure for us as being any other natural object. . . . Well, that would be the same fallacy which I have called the naturalistic fallacy' (p. 13). What this passage suggests is that the naturalistic fallacy is committed by one who identifies goodness as something other than goodness – an interpretation suggested by Moore's use of Butler's maxim that 'Everything is what it is and not another thing'. Yet this interpretation of the naturalistic fallacy differs from the previous one: there is no denial of indefinability here, just a mistaken identification. Furthermore, the thesis that one commits the naturalistic fallacy by denying that goodness is indefinable jars with the claim that someone who identifies goodness with pleasure, as Mill is alleged by Moore to have done, thereby commits the naturalistic fallacy. For if pleasure is indefinable (as Moore maintains), and goodness is just pleasure, then goodness is indefinable. Indeed Moore's discussion of the commission of the naturalistic fallacy by those who identify goodness with pleasure suggests a further interpretation of it, as the denial that goodness is non-natural, typically because it is held to be a natural property, though 'metaphysicians' also commit the naturalistic fallacy when they treat goodness as a metaphysical property (*PE* pp. 39, 113–14).

There are here three accounts of the naturalistic fallacy: to commit the fallacy is to do one of the following:

(a) to deny that goodness is indefinable;
(b) to assert, concerning something other than goodness, that it is goodness;
(c) to deny that goodness is non-natural.

If one now asks which of these interpretations best fits the text I am afraid that one must conclude that no one of them predominates, and that Moore's discussion is hopelessly confused on this matter, the central critical thesis of a book which prided itself on establishing a new level of clarity in ethical theory (cf. the opening paragraph of the preface). Consider the following passages:

> The discussion will be designed . . . to illustrate the fact that the naturalistic fallacy is a fallacy, or, in other words, that we are all aware of a certain simple quality, which (and not anything else) is what we mean by the term 'good'.
>
> (p. 38)

Here it is (a) that predominates, although there is a hint of (b) in the parenthesis. By contrast, in the following passage, it is (b) that predominates, although there is also an element of (a):

> In this chapter I have begun the criticism of certain ethical views, which seem to owe their influence mainly to the naturalistic fallacy — the fallacy which consists in identifying the simple notion which we mean by 'good' with some other notion.
>
> (p. 58)

In the next passage, however, neither (a) nor (b) is present:

> In this argument the naturalistic fallacy is plainly involved. That fallacy, I explained, consists in the contention that good *means* nothing but some simple or complex notion, that can be defined in terms of natural qualities.
>
> (p. 73)

Here, clearly, we have (c). Nor are these isolated passages; for each of (a), (b), and (c) one can cite several passages. Wittgenstein's comment to Russell about *PE*, that 'Unclear statements don't get a bit clearer by being repeated', is certainly warranted when applied to Moore's discussions of the naturalistic fallacy.[9]

All too soon, I think, Moore himself became aware of this mess. Not only does he assert in his 1932 paper 'Is Goodness a Quality?' (reprinted in *PP*) that all his supposed proofs in *PE* that goodness is indefinable are fallacious, he had earlier (*c.*1920) more or less set out (a), (b), and (c) as alternative accounts of what he had meant in *PE* in the draft for a revised preface to *PE*.[10] But even earlier than this he must have recognised this mess; only thus can one account for the total absence of any reference to the naturalistic fallacy in *E* and *CIV*, despite the fact that in both works he criticises naturalism in ethics.

It is, I think, possible to effect two reconstructions of Moore's thoughts about the naturalistic fallacy. For the first explanation we start from (a), which undoubtedly predominates in the first chapter of *PE*. What, we must now ask, is it for goodness to be indefinable? Officially, Moore's view is that ' "good" has no definition because it is simple and has no parts' (*PE* p. 9). Unofficially, however, it is clear that Moore

71

regards identifying goodness with pleasure as defining goodness, even though he holds that this latter property is indefinable. The reason for this, as he acknowledges in the draft for the revised preface, is that he confuses use and mention by treating the identification of goodness under another description (e.g. as 'pleasure') as a definition of it. In this way the confusion of (a) with (b) becomes intelligible. The further move from (b) to (c) is made by supposing that the properties other than goodness with which goodness is identified are either natural or metaphysical properties, so that one who thus identifies goodness is committed to denying that it is non-natural.

This first account of the naturalistic fallacy is essentially a diagnosis of Moore's confusions. To get anything of philosophical interest one must concentrate, not on (a), but on (c). For if the naturalistic fallacy and the positive thesis of PE, ethical non-naturalism, are to make contact, then the naturalistic fallacy must involve the denial of ethical non-naturalism. Although this is not the most plausible interpretation of Moore's actual words, Moore sometimes puts the matter in this light, most notably on p. 125 where he writes that 'the root of the naturalistic fallacy' is that both naturalists and metaphysicians think that 'every truth must mean somehow that something exists'; since it is precisely non-natural objects which are, but do not exist, it is clearly (c) that Moore has here in mind as the naturalistic fallacy. Another passage which requires (c) is the discussion of beauty at the end of the book (p. 201). Moore here complains about the commission of the naturalistic fallacy with respect to beauty, and then proceeds to *define* beauty, as 'that of which the admiring contemplation is good in itself'. Indeed, throughout PE Moore describes goodness as the property of that which 'ought to be' or 'ought to exist for its own sake' (pp. viii, 17, 115, 118, 148, 180), and since these phrases suggest a definition of goodness an (a)-type interpretation of the naturalistic fallacy might well lead one to convict Moore of it. Finally, there is Moore's own testimony in the draft of his revised preface, in which he says that the interpretation of the naturalistic fallacy which captures what he wanted to say in PE, is that in which '$x$ is committing the naturalistic fallacy' means '$x$ is *either* confusing Good with a natural or metaphysical property *or* holding it to be identical with such a property *or* making an inference based on such a confusion'.[11]

I shall, therefore, take it that (c) is the preferred interpretation of the naturalistic fallacy. But Moore's confusions about the identity of the naturalistic fallacy infect the whole of his discussion of ethical naturalism and non-naturalism, and by opting for (c) we cannot free ourselves from a discussion of his views about the definability of ethical concepts. Before embarking on this, however, we need further clarification of Moore's conceptions of goodness and of the natural/non-natural distinction. So it is to these matters that the next two sections are devoted.

### 3: Goodness

Ethics, Moore says in *PE* (p. 2), is the general inquiry into what is good. Moore's treatment of the concept *good* is, however, radically unsatisfactory. In its typical uses the concept is attributive, as in 'good computer', where the noun ('computer') which follows 'good' specifies what the thing said to be good is good as, and thereby indicates the standards by reference to which it has been evaluated. Moore's account of goodness as a simple, non-natural, property cannot readily accommodate this feature of the concept; so it is not clear how Moore's talk of goodness is to be understood. Indeed, it has been claimed that this point by itself suffices to show that at a fundamental level Moore's ethical theory is fatally flawed.[12]

However, to draw this conclusion is to assume that one cannot incorporate within Moore's theory a recognition that 'good' is typically attributive. Central to this will be the recognition that it is the goodness of states of affairs (or 'states of things' – *PE* p. 183) that is the primary focus of Moore's ethical theory. The aim will then be to show that this focus is consistent with a recognition of the attributiveness of 'good'. Geach once argued that it is not that:

> we cannot sensibly speak of a good event or a bad event, a good or
> bad thing to happen. 'Event', like 'thing' is too empty a word to
> convey either a criterion of identity or a standard of goodness; to ask
> 'Is this a good or bad thing (to happen)?' is as useless as to ask 'Is this
> the same thing that I saw yesterday?' . . . unless the emptiness of
> 'thing' or 'event' is filled up by a special context of utterance.'[13]

The key premiss here is that the word 'event' does not convey a standard for goodness. I think there is an ambiguity here on which Geach's argument trades. If Geach meant that good events are not good *as events*, then although the premiss is true, its truth is not necessary for the meaningfulness of talk of good events; for if a phrase 'conveys a standard of goodness' as long as there is a conventional way in which such a standard is identified by the use of the phrase, then phrases such as 'event' and 'state of affairs' do convey a standard of goodness. The familiar case of 'good weather' shows the point. We readily understand this phrase without groping around for a context of utterance, even though good weather is not good *as weather*.[14] Good weather is simply weather that is good for people affected by it, and this is weather which suits their interests (so that, where interests conflict, we relativise our judgments, distinguishing between, say, weather that is good for farmers and weather that is good for holiday-makers). It is only when there are no such obvious implications for human interests that we have to return to the context of utterance for further hints in order to understand what is being said (as where someone says 'That is a good cloud'). This all suggests that where 'good' is not attached to a phrase which conveys a standard of goodness by the simple principle that a good $F$ is something which is good *as an F*, a standard for goodness is provided by reference to the implications for the interests of those affected by, or concerned with, that of which goodness is predicated. This suggestion can be readily applied to the interpretation of 'good state of affairs', and since it yields a standard of goodness which the phrase conventionally conveys, Geach's critical conclusion is avoided.[15]

So far I have argued that we can combine a recognition of the attributiveness of 'good' with the focus on the goodness of states of affairs required by Moore's ideal utilitarianism by assigning a central role to human (and perhaps non-human) interests in the evaluation of states of affairs. Moore, however, will reject any such role for the concept of human interest, on the grounds that it gives rise to an unacceptable form of ethical naturalism, and it is this rejection, rather than his simple failure to recognise the attributiveness of 'good', which makes his conception of goodness so problematic. I have not yet discussed ethical naturalism, but Moore's position on this issue can be readily discerned from his response to Sidgwick's discussion of egoism.

Sidgwick's discussion of egoism is intimately linked to an account of goodness of roughly the kind I have been presenting, except that it is couched in terms of the desires of an ideally knowledgeable and imaginative subject, instead of in terms of the subject's interests (*The Methods of Ethics* pp. 109–12; in the light of this it is not clear why Moore exempts Sidgwick from the charge of committing the 'naturalistic fallacy' with respect to goodness).[16] The important point is that in Sidgwick's account what it is for a state of affairs to be 'good in itself' is dependent upon what it is that state to be 'good for' those affected by it; hence it allows for conflict between that which is good for me, and that which, because good for the community as a whole, but not me, is good in itself. Now in his discussion of egoism (*PE* pp. 98–9) Moore reverses Sidgwick's order of explanation and insists that the expression 'good for me' can only be understood as applying to states which are good in themselves and somehow concern me. Thus, according to Moore, Sidgwick's contrast between what is good for him and what is good in itself is illusory and Sidgwick was quite wrong to regard egoism as rational. I shall return to Moore's discussion of egoism in chapter 4, but in the present context what matters is Moore's insistence that the judgment that a state of affairs is good in itself is fundamental. For this rules out any account of the goodness of states of affairs of the kind I have been examining since the evaluation of states of affairs by reference

74

to the interests, or desires, of those affected by them implies that such states are good where they are good for those affected by them.

It is this feature that makes Moore's conception of goodness so difficult to comprehend. But before proceeding further I want to revert briefly to Sidgwick's account of goodness. For even though it is not, in my view, a satisfactory account of goodness, it is a plausible account of what it is for a state of affairs to be desirable. As such it can be used to throw some light on Mill's notorious 'proof' of his principle of utility and Moore's equally notorious criticisms of Mill. Mill argued that just as 'the only proof capable of being given that an object is visible, is that people actually see it',[17] so 'the sole evidence it is possible to produce that anything is desirable, is that people do actually desire it'. Moore latches on to this analogy, and objects that although 'visible' means 'able to be seen', by 'desirable' Mill means, not 'able to be desired', but 'ought to be desired'; and, he goes on, what people actually desire is no proof of what they ought to desire (*PE* pp. 66–7). Sidgwick, however, provides an alternative account of desirability as that which would be desired under ideal conditions of knowledge and imagination. If it is this conception of desirability which is used to interpret Mill's argument, then there is good sense to it; for the best, if not the sole, evidence as to what people would desire under ideal conditions is what they actually do desire.[18] What remains problematic on this understanding of Mill's argument is just how the desirability of happiness in this sense relates to its role as 'one of the criteria of morality'.[19] It looks as though Mill takes the connection to be immediate, as it would be if whatever were desirable were *ipso facto* good for people. But if this is Mill's position, then he is open to the objection that we have experience of extremely knowledgeable people desiring things that are bad for them. So this interpretation of Mill does not yield an account of his argument which vindicates the conclusion he wants to draw from it. It does, however, save him from Moore's charge of committing 'as naive and artless a use of the naturalistic fallacy as anybody could desire' (*PE* p. 66). For, on this view, Mill's mistake is not a crude transition from 'is desired' to 'ought to be desired', but just an inadequate account of what it is for a state of affairs to be good.

Returning now to Moore's conception of goodness, I have exhausted my attempt to reconstruct a Moorean theory within the framework of the conception of goodness such as we standardly employ. The obvious conclusion would seem to be that Moore's theory cannot be interpreted without the thesis that he uses 'good' as if it denoted a simple, non-attributive, property of states of affairs. This was proposed by Ross, who maintained that there is a 'predicative' (i.e. non-attributive) use of 'good', with which alone Moore was concerned (*The Right and the Good* chapter 3). Yet there are good reasons to reject the hypothesis of any such simple property of states of affairs with the ultimate significance which Moorean goodness would have to have. Detached as it would have to be from all ordinary judgments of the value of states of affairs, and only problematically connected with their other properties, the hypothesis that the possession by states of affairs of this property is the ground of all ethical judgments could only invite indifference to ethical judgments. Why on earth should we care about the abstract 'goodness' of states of affairs if the possession of this goodness is as detached from all our recognisable concerns as Moorean goodness turns out to be? Furthermore, sceptical doubts as to whether we were denoting the same property by our use of 'good' would be unanswerable. Moore's confidence that 'we are all aware of a certain simple quality, which (and not anything else) is what we mainly mean by the term "good"' (PE p. 38) is just naive, and Mary Warnock is right to observe in this connection that there is a crucial disanalogy between 'good' and 'yellow', in that we can give an ostensive definition of the latter, but not the former.[20]

This clearly raises a substantial difficulty for any attempt to take Moore's ethical theory seriously. Fortunately, there is a way out. For Moore does not in fact leave us completely up in the air about his conception of goodness. As he later acknowledged,[21] by his distinction between 'good in itself' and 'good as means' (PE pp. 21ff), he shows clearly that his concept is to slot into his ideal utilitarian account of morality. Goodness (in itself), or, more generally, *intrinsic value*, is the concept whose application to states of affairs issues in a specification of what, in a particular situation, one ought to do. There is, therefore, the basis here for a way of understanding Moorean goodness in terms of moral obligation; but before discussing how such an analysis might run it is necessary to review Moore's own views about the relationship between goodness and obligation.

In EE Moore maintained that there is a necessary, but synthetic, relation between them: I ought to do $x$ if and only if, of the actions which it is possible for me to perform, doing $x$ will produce the best outcome. He has then added to one of the manuscripts the marginal comment: 'There is no such principle. Confusion. What is the meaning of "ought to do"? It is not good as end, hence = is a means to a good thing.' This comment is developed in PE (pp. 25, 147) as the thesis that the relationship between goodness and obligation is analytic because 'I ought to do $x$' just means 'Of the actions which it is possible for me to perform, doing $x$ will produce the best outcome'. The result is that in PE all moral concepts are analysed in terms of goodness. Russell quickly persuaded Moore, however, that this was a mistake (PGEM p. 558) because the proposed analyses fail the test of substitutivity in indirect speech. So in E (pp. 29–30) and PGEM (pp. 599–600) he returns to his initial position, that the connection between goodness and obligation is only synthetic.

Despite all this the view that goodness is analysable in terms of obligation is directly suggested by some of Moore's remarks, in particular by his treatment of phrases such as 'ought to exist for its own sake' as synonymous with 'good in itself' (*PE* p. viii). For no clear reason Moore never confronts the challenge which he here poses to his thesis that goodness is simple. Russell remarks that these synonyms 'really presuppose the notions of good and bad, and are therefore useful only as means of calling up the right ideas, not as logical definitions';[22] but how the right idea can be called up unless an analysis is involved is not explained. I do not in fact propose 'ought to exist for its own sake' as an analysis of Moorean goodness, since, as Ross observed (*The Right and the Good* p. 105), this phrase itself is so obscure. Basically, it is agents who ought, or ought not, to do things or to be something. In order therefore, to pursue the analysis of Moorean goodness in terms of obligation, the obligations should be conceived from the start as the obligations of agents to bring states of affairs of certain kinds into existence.

I want now to introduce a passage from *E*:

> To assert of any one thing, *A*, that it is *intrinsically* better than another, *B*, is to assert that if *A* existed *quite alone*, without any accompaniments or effects whatever – if, in short, *A* constituted the whole Universe, it would be better that such a Universe should exist, than that a Universe which consisted solely of *B* should exist instead.
>
> (p. 28)

This is a puzzling passage. It seems at the outset that Moore is about to give an analysis of the concept *intrinsically better*, which is not something one would expect him to undertake. But since the passage which follows concerns what 'would be better' it does not seem after all that an analysis is on offer. Yet what then is the point of the remark? And what is the intended sense here of the phrase 'it would be better that such a Universe should exist'? Moore cannot here mean that it would be intrinsically better, since this would render his remark absolutely pointless; but equally he cannot mean that it would be better as a means, since *A* and *B* are to be supposed to have no effects at all. What I think he must mean here is that it would be better, all things considered (cf. *E* p. 35 where this sense of 'good' is discussed). Yet if one follows this interpretation, there is still a problem; in Moore's official theory, the concept *better, all things considered* is surely to be understood in terms of the concept *intrinsically better*, so it is unclear what purpose the passage is supposed to achieve.

It is at this point that an analysis of goodness in terms of obligation looks attractive. Since the concept *best, all things considered* is, for Moore, necessarily equivalent to the concept *ought to be brought into existence if possible*, Moore's remark in *E* can be interpreted as profferring, implicitly, an analysis of the concept *intrinsically better* in terms of obligation. One has only to replace, in the quoted passage, the condition that the *A*-universe be better (all things considered) than the *B*-universe with the condition that, given a choice between creating the *A*-universe and the *B*-universe, one ought to create the *A*-universe. On the basis of this analysis, it is easy to provide an analysis of '*A* is intrinsically good'. Moore says that to say that *A* is intrinsically good is to say that it would be a good thing (sc. all things considered) if *A* 'existed *quite alone* without any further accompaniments or effects, whatever' (*E* p. 32). To convert this into an analysis in terms of obligation, we have to suppose ourselves to have a choice between creating an *A*-universe and doing nothing; then for *A* to be intrinsically good will be for us to be under an obligation to create the *A*-universe.

Undoubtedly, this is all highly artificial. Yet the artificiality of these analyses just re-expresses in terms of obligation the artificiality of Moore's concept of intrinsic goodness as manifested in the passage from *E* from which I started, whose analogue within *PE* is Moore's account of the 'method of reflective isolation' (pp. 91–3, 187–8). Furthermore there are simpler ways of analysing intrinsic goodness in terms of obligation; one might just say that *A*'s intrinsic goodness consists in the fact that, other things being equal, we are under an obligation to bring into existence states of affairs of kind *A*. But the apparent circle in Moore's elucidation of intrinsic goodness, and the escape from this circle which the analysis in terms of obligation offers, does not by itself establish the correctness of the analysis. Perhaps Moore's elucidations of intrinsic goodness should be set aside as errors of exposition on his part. The important question is whether or not this analysis, which is certainly contrary to Moore's intentions, serves to make his theory accessible by showing what his conception of goodness amounts to once its unsatisfactory aspects are discarded.

Since Moore always accepted that there is a necessary equivalence between goodness and obligation, the issue resolves in part around the nature of the analytic/synthetic distinction. Thus in *PGEM* (p. 600) Moore rejects this analysis, which had been proposed by Frankena in his contribution to *PGEM*, on the ground that it does not satisfy the simple test of reflective substitutivity.[23] But I have already argued that this test is useless, since thinkers are not authoritative with respect to the identity of their thoughts (cf. chapter 2, section 5), and I suggested that assessment of a putative analysis is inseparable from that of the broader context within which it occurs. Thus, my proposal should be set within the context of the project of making reasonable sense of Moore's ethical theory without either grossly misrepresenting it (as would be the

78

consequence of imposing a naturalistic conception of goodness) or leaving Moore committed to a manifestly untenable thesis (as would be the consequence of just leaving the thesis that goodness is a simple, non-attributive, property of states of affairs unquestioned). My claim is that the analysis of goodness in terms of moral obligation provides the best available alternative to these options which can claim some support from Moore's actual writings.

But I do not dispute that there is a price to be paid for adopting it. It is not that one has to abandon intuitions of the intrinsic value of states of affairs; these are just reinterpreted as intuitions of the obligatoriness of actions (I explain the structure of the resulting moral theory in the next chapter). Rather, one loses the contemplative, almost aesthetic, side of Moore's thought, in which the implications of ethical intuitions for practice can be set aside. This was undoubtedly an important aspect of the influence of Moore's thought within Bloomsbury, about which I shall say more in the next chapter, and there are several features of his theory which reflect it, most notably his thesis that goodness is not itself a moral concept. Moore really did think that judgments of intrinsic value concern a simple, immediately apprehensible, quality of states of affairs that is not to be understood in terms of our judgments about what we ought to do. This position is most emphatically presented in an essay of 1901 'Art, Morals, and Religion' where Moore's central thesis is that the 'science of morals', which deals with duties and virtues, is subservient to aesthetics, which deals with works of art, the only things with intrinsic value.[24] Moore here writes that:

> The Whole Science of Morals is doubly false, first in that it singles out as desirable for their own sake what are mere necessary evils; and secondly in that even these are not better than other necessary evils. . . . It is a science wholly abject and contemptible.

In PE the terminology is shifted around a bit, with 'ethics' introduced to describe the study of goodness and goods (which are not just works of art); but the dislike of the concepts of duty and virtue is still much in evidence.

I have argued that the presumption of this position, that Moore has a well-defined conception of goodness that we can employ without reference to our practical deliberations, is illusory, and the analysis reflects this belief. But since it conflicts with Moore's own express beliefs, the analysis is primarily intended to be a rational reconstruction of his position. There is, however, a further objection to it to be considered. It is a consequence of the analysis that moral obligation has to be treated as the fundamental ethical concept, and it may be felt that the difficulties I have been raising concerning Moorean goodness arise equally for moral obligation thus conceived. Just as we cannot readily understand what it is for a state of affairs to be good in itself, except in so far as it is good for those liable to be affected by it, likewise, it may be said, we cannot really understand how it is that a state of affairs can be such that we ought, *ceteris paribus*, to bring it into existence, except in so far as it is rational to do so in the light of our existing motivations. But no such hypothetical obligations can do justice to the intrinsic moral obligations in terms of which, on the analysis, Moore's intrinsic values should be understood. So the analysis of goodness in terms of obligation does not help.

This objection points to a serious difficulty which confronts the theory which results from the analysis of goodness in terms of obligation. I shall discuss this difficulty further at the start of chapter 4, in the context of a discussion of Moore's consequentialism. For now I shall just respond to the point as an objection to the proposed reconstruction of Moore's position. An initial response is that, except in *PE*, Moore himself regards moral obligation as a fundamental ethical concept; so the analysis does not introduce any new difficulty in this respect. Furthermore the conception of an intrinsic moral obligation is not, I think, as incomprehensible as Moore's conception of goodness. The fundamental obligations of the revised theory will be categorical imperatives, each of whose content is specified in terms of a consequentialist moral theory. The resulting position thus expresses the dominant influence on Moore of Kant and Sidgwick which I remarked earlier in this chapter. Now I certainly do not pretend that the concept of a categorical imperative is unproblematic; but we are at least relatively familiar with it, whereas once one grasps how remote Moorean goodness is from any ordinary conception of goodness, it seems unavoidable that in making sense of it we should avail ourselves of its one general connection which Moore allows – its connection with obligation.

## 4: The natural /non-natural distinction

It has often been though important to defend or refute 'naturalist' positions in ethics. But there is no consensus on the identity of this position. Thus Hume is described as an early exponent of the naturalistic fallacy; yet, equally, he is treated as an upholder of a naturalist position in ethics.[25] Since the concept of nature is one of the most contested concepts in the history of philosophy, this is not surprising. But the unclarity of twentieth-century discussions owes much to the unclarity of Moore's natural/non-natural distinction. I showed in chapter 1 how it developed out of his youthful appearance/reality distinction; but by 1903 (indeed by 1898) he had shed the grounds for that belief – his belief in the unreality of time. None the less, time seems to remain crucial to the distinction; for concerning natural objects, he writes:

If we consider whether any object is of such a nature that it may be said to exist now, to have existed, or to be about to exist, then we may know that that object is a natural object, and that nothing, of which this is not true, is a natural object.

(*PE* p. 40)

In addition to this distinction between natural and other objects, we should recall (cf. chapter 2) that the non-natural objects do not merely not exist in time: unlike metaphysical objects, which exist timelessly, they do not *exist* at all, they just *are* (*PE* pp. 110–1, 123–6).

This distinction, to which existence or not in time is central, clearly belongs within Moore's pure realism. But in the context of pure realism, nothing distinctive for goodness is proclaimed by the thought that it does not exist in time. For no general properties exist in time. One might seek to distinguish goodness by proposing that goodness, unlike other properties, cannot have particular instances which exist in time. But Moore denies this: 'I do not deny that good is a property of certain natural objects: certain of them, I think, *are* good' (*PE* p. 41). Hence to say something distinctive about goodness, Moore introduces a further distinction, between natural and non-natural *properties*:[26] natural properties, he says (p. 41), are those whose instances 'can exist *by themselves* in time' and what is distinctive about goodness is that it is not a natural property in this sense. The emphasis shows that Moore has in mind here his bare particulars; so goodness is to be distinguished by the fact that it does not have bare particulars as instances. Moore puts the point graphically as follows:

It is immediately obvious that when we see a thing to be good, its goodness is not a property which we can take up in our hands, or separate from it even by the most delicate scientific instruments, and transfer to something else. It is not, in fact, like most of the predicates which we ascribe to things, a *part* of the thing to which we ascribe it.

(*PE* p. 124)

This distinction between natural and non-natural properties is thoroughly entangled within the unacceptable metaphysics of pure realism. It is therefore not surprising that when Moore discarded pure realism, as he did in 1910, he ceased to use the terminology of 'natural' properties. It does not occur in *E*, and in the revised preface for *PE* he repudiated the account of natural properties given in *PE*, as he also did in *PGEM* (pp. 581–2). The issue that therefore arises is whether or not one can rescue from Moore's discussions sufficient material to enable one to make sense of ethical naturalism: if one cannot, then there can be no clear content to the naturalistic fallacy.

It is best to start off from the intuitive ideas of ethical naturalism, metaphysical ethics, and ethical non-naturalism as understood by Moore. Central to ethical naturalism is the view that ethical judgments concern natural objects and their properties; so on this view ethical judgments imply the existence of natural objects. This is over-simple, but it will do for now. The contrast with metaphysical ethics arises because on a theory of this kind it is held that ethical judgments concern a metaphysical object (e.g. God) as well as natural objects; so on this view ethical judgments imply the existence of a metaphysical object. What now of ethical non-naturalism? It is a mistake to try to make its definition turn on a distinctive implication concerning the being of non-natural objects; for a Moorean ethical naturalist would regard the properties of natural objects as non-natural objects. Instead, the basic idea of ethical non-naturalism must be that there are positive ethical truths which do not have any existential implications at all. Since Moore takes it that some natural objects are good, the non-naturalist position cannot be that no ethical truths have existential implications; but if attention is restricted to fundamental ethical principles, then the intended contrast with the other positions does arise.

The idea here can be illustrated by considering the judgment that the infliction of pain is intrinsically evil. On no view does this entail that the infliction of pain actually occurs, but for the ethical naturalist, it entails the existence of humans and other natural beings with feelings and interests which conflict with the experience of pain. On a metaphysical ethical theory, such as that that which is evil is so because it has been prohibited by God, the truth of the judgment entails the existence of God. Thus the ethical concepts employed by both naturalist and metaphysical ethical theories are such that the use of these concepts (in positive judgments) brings with it an existential commitment of some kind. By contrast, the core idea of Moore's ethical non-naturalism is that even though such fundamental ethical truths are synthetic, they need have no existential implications at all:

> That such a reduction of *all* propositions to the type of those which assert either that something exists or that something which exists has a certain attribute (which means, that both exist in a certain relation to one another), is erroneous, may easily be seen by reference to the particular class of ethical propositions.
>
> (*PE* pp. 125–6)

There is an aspect of Moore's conception of ethical naturalism which this initial account does not capture – his suggestion that ethical naturalism requires the reduction of ethics to a natural science:

I have thus appropriated the name Naturalism to a particular method

82

of approaching Ethics – a method which, strictly understood, is inconsistent with the possibility of any Ethics whatsoever. This method consists in substituting for 'good' some one property of a natural object or a collection of natural objects; and in thus replacing Ethics by some one of the natural sciences.

(*PE* p. 40)

The idea Moore here advances is prominent in *PE* and in the revised preface to *PE* Moore said that this was the best account of ethical naturalism he could provide.[27] Yet there is a logical gap between the thesis that ethical judgments just concern natural objects and their properties and the thesis that ethical truths can be reduced to the truths of another natural science. There must be at least one non-reducible natural science, so why not several? One should distinguish between naturalism and reductionism.

Moore does not see this in *PE*; his mistake is an extension of that which I identified in section 2 concerning the identity of the naturalistic fallacy. He seems to take it that anyone who thinks that goodness is natural is committed to analysing goodness in terms of simpler natural properties which are comprehended within another natural science. One might suppose that Moore's confusions in this regard do not matter much, because any plausible naturalist theory can be presented as reductive through the existence within it of connections between ethical and other natural properties. Certainly it seems right to suppose that any plausible theory will include such connections: otherwise it would present us with a domain of natural ethical facts whose significance within human life was unrelated to all other human activities and thoughts. But the assumption that once there are such connections, it must be possible to represent the ethical as reducible to the non-ethical is unjustified. Only if the concepts which have a fundamental role in the explanations offered by psychological and social theories are non-ethical would this be true; but the ethical naturalist is not committed to this proposition.

Similar mistakes affect Moore's discussions of metaphysical ethical theories and ethical non-naturalism. In the former case Moore takes it that the position is *ipso facto* a reductionist one, in that it involves the reduction of ethics to metaphysics (*PE* pp. 113–14). But one can hold that ethical judgments have theological implications without reducing ethical properties to theological properties. Contrariwise, Moore associates non-reductionism in ethics with ethical non-naturalism. But a Pythagorean reduction of ethical values to numbers ought to count as a case of ethical non-naturalism.

We shall have to return in the next section to the distinction between reductionist and non-reductionist ethical theories. For the rest of this section I want to take further the definition of ethical non-naturalism. One line of thought attempts to make something of the conception of goodness as a non-natural object. I argued that it is not immediately clear how this is relevant, since the ethical naturalist can also take this view of goodness. But perhaps one can use it if one asks in what the truth of an ethical judgment consists, where one assumes a correspondence theory of truth or Moore's identity theory. For where an ethical naturalist will respond by referring to certain natural states of affairs, constituted by natural objects and their properties (which he may choose to regard as instances of non-natural universals), an ethical non-naturalist will hold that the truth of fundamental ethical judgments concerning intrinsic value consists in the obtaining of a non-natural state of affairs, a relationship between two non-natural objects, the property definitive of a kind of state of affairs and intrinsic value itself. Moore's rhetoric concerning non-natural objects in *PE* suggests this picture of ethical reality, and not only is it implied by his theory of truth, it also fits with his intuitionist epistemology (as I shall argue in section 6). So this provides a plausible interpretation of his position.

An obvious reaction to this position is that the conception of a non-natural state of affairs is untenable, and this then gives rise to a different form of ethical non-naturalism, which denies that the truth of ethical judgments requires ethical states of affairs of any kind. Instead, it may be said, ethical truth is just a matter of the rationality of that which is prescribed in ethical judgment, of the fact that no contrary prescription can be coherently willed. Although this is not a plausible interpretation of Moore's position, it suggests the possibility of a Kantian reconstruction of it. But one should not assume that it is only an ethical non-naturalist who can adopt this conception of ethical truth. For once rationality is understood to consist only in the availability of internal reasons, in Williams's sense,[28] the rationality of a prescribed action will always be its rationality for an agent with a set of motivations, and the existence of such a set will be implied by any judgment of rationality. Thus the non-naturalist who pursues this strategy has to hold that our fundamental ethical judgments express external reasons for action, ones which need not engage with the motivations agents actually possess.

There are other ways of developing this non-naturalist position; but rather than pursue them, at this point a complication in Moore's own discussion of his ethical non-naturalism needs to be introduced. In his reply to his critics in *PGEM* he wrote:

> I should never have thought of suggesting that goodness was 'non-natural', unless I had supposed that it was 'derivative' in the sense that, whenever a thing is good (in the sense in question) its goodness (in Mr. Broad's words) 'depends on the presence of certain non-ethical

characteristics' possessed by the thing in question: I have always supposed that it did so 'depend', in the sense that, if a thing is good (in my sense), then that this is so *follows* from the fact that it has certain natural intrinsic properties, which are such that from the fact that it is good it does *not* follow conversely that it has those properties.

(*PGEM* p. 588)

As a gloss on *PE* this is a surprising remark, for the dependence of goodness is not a prominent feature of that work. Indeed Moore here stresses that propositions about goodness are 'utterly independent' of all other propositions (*PE* p. 60; cf. pp. 143–4) – this is the anti-reductive thesis which he treats as anti-naturalist. None the less there is one indication in *PE* of the thought that goodness is, in some sense, dependent. In his discussion of natural properties (p. 41), he says that the natural properties of an object have instances which are parts of that object, and concerning these parts, he says, 'their existence does seem to me to be independent of the existence of those objects'. Since goodness is not, according to Moore, in this sense a natural property, it follows that the goodness of a thing is not an 'independent' part, or property, of it. Hence it is a property dependent on its other properties, which is roughly the view he was later to say that he had always had in mind in supposing that goodness was non-natural.

Yet despite this basis in *PE* for his later thesis, it remains to be clarified how this kind of dependence of goodness fits with the independence of fundamental ethical propositions, and what its relationship with ethical non-naturalism is. The solution to the first issue lies in taking the dependence thesis to apply just to the goodness of particular states of affairs, whereas it is the goodness of general kinds of states that is to be independent of all other propositions. This makes possible a treatment of the second issue. That the goodness of particular states of affairs depends on their other properties requires that there be general connections between these properties and goodness; and it is these general connections that Moore regards as non-natural truths. So the derivativeness of intrinsic value is consistent with ethical non-naturalism; but it does not entail it, and the two are not as closely related as the passage from *PGEM* suggests.

In my account of Moore's ethical theory, his conception of the status of fundamental ethical truths has a central role. I have so far concentrated on his non-naturalist account of them, but a further feature of his conception of them should be introduced – his view that they are 'universal', i.e. necessary, truths, which I discussed in the previous chapter (section 4). When these two points are combined, it follows that at the heart of Moore's ethical theory lies the conception of a body of abstract synthetic *a priori* truths concerning intrinsic value; and what is problematic is why he thinks knowledge of such truths, if possible at all, should matter to us. His discussion in *PE*, which suggests the first form of ethical non-naturalism presented above, implies that we can solve these problems by simply thinking in terms of intuitions of synthetic connections between universals. I have already criticised the general presumptions of this position and will discuss it further in section 6. But the fact that this position is so unsatisfactory gives one a reason for considering the second form of ethical non-naturalism, and the Kantian model is here especially appropriate since it is precisely an understanding of synthetic *a priori* truths that is sought.

I shall discuss this further, but I want here to draw one further implication from the fact that Moore's ethical theory is based upon the hypothesis of necessary synthetic truths. Moore's theory is often taken to involve a 'fact/value' gap of the kind Hume is supposed to uphold; indeed it is common to accuse those who think that one can derive 'ought' from 'is' of committing the naturalistic fallacy.[29] But since Moore holds that obligations are derivable from intrinsic values, and that there are necessary connections between the properties definitive of kinds of states of affairs and their intrinsic value, it follows that he is committed to necessary 'is/ought' connections. In his reply to his critics he explicitly accepted this commitment: 'I have admitted, then, that at least one *natural* property is ought-implying' (*PGEM* p. 604). So it is a mistake to conflate Moore with Hume.

## 5: Is there a fallacy?

We are now in a position to begin to assess Moore's charge that there is a fallacy, the 'naturalistic fallacy', in most ethical theories. One is supposed to commit this fallacy by denying that the fundamental truths of ethics are abstract principles with no existential implications. As I have observed, however, Moore systematically confuses this thesis with an anti-reductionist thesis, and it is against this thesis that his arguments are primarily directed. Hence it appears that even if these arguments are successful, Moore will not establish his intended conclusion. I shall discuss this issue later, but we can start by looking at Moore's arguments.

Moore takes as his target the familiar conception of a reduction of ethical truths to truths of some other kind which invokes an analysis of the meaning of ethical terms (I shall discuss later how far his arguments are applicable to other types of reduction). In arguing against this, Moore does not attempt to show that there are no ethical terms whose meaning is susceptible of analysis; on the contrary, he thinks that the meanings of almost all ethical terms are susceptible of analysis – but only in terms of the meanings of the fundamental ethical terms, 'good' and /or 'ought'. It turns out, I think, that this is a crucial assumption. It certainly simplifies the reductionist's task; for, if it is assumed that this initial analysis has been accomplished, it leaves the reductionist with a target that can simply be defined by enumeration, and allows him to count any successful analysis of those concepts as a reduction of the ethical truths. But we should set aside doubts about it while looking at Moore's arguments in *PE*.

One initial distraction should be removed. Moore holds that those who propose a reductionist thesis commit a *fallacy*, by which he means that they contradict themselves. The contradiction he has in mind, other than the gratuitous accusation that reductionists deny the self-identity of goodness, arises from the charge that reductionists are bound to treat their analysis as if it were a synthetic truth, which contradicts their account of its status as an analysis of meaning (*PE* pp. 17–18). But Moore does not substantiate this charge, and I do not see why a reductionist need adopt this self-contradictory attitude, unless one wants to describe in this way all mistakes concerning the analysis of concepts. So I shall not bother with the charge that there is a fallacy in any proposal for a reduction of ethics.

Moore begins by arguing that it is a mistake to treat an account of a term's extension as an account of its meaning, and hence that it would be a mistake to take an account of the extension of 'good', a definition of 'the good', to be a definition of 'good'. There is much that might be said about Moore's presumptions here, but a point worth notice is that because he holds that fundamental ethical truths are necessary, he is committed to the view that someone who treats these as providing an analysis of the meaning of ethical terms is only moving from necessary extension to meaning, which, as he himself recognises, is a *prima facie* plausible move:

> It is very natural to make the mistake of supposing that what is universally true is of such a nature that its negation would be self-contradictory: the importance which has been assigned to analytic propositions in the history of philosophy shows how easy such a mistake is. And thus it is very easy to conclude that what seems to be a universal ethical proposition is in fact an identical proposition.
>
> (*PE* p. 16)

It is at this point (section 13 of *PE*) that Moore introduces the argument generally known as the 'open question' argument. It is notable that the section in which he advances it is the only part of the opening discussion in *PE* of the naturalistic fallacy which does not come straight from EE (cf. appendix). This suggests that Moore felt that the argument was important and needed a more careful statement than he had previously given it. However, Moore's argument is still far from lucid. He presents two alternatives to the thesis that the meaning of 'good' is unanalysable; first, that its meaning is analysable: second, that it has no meaning at all. He rejects the first on the ground that, concerning any proposed analysis, we can always raise significant doubts in a way which shows that the analysis is incorrect. The second might seem too obviously false to require refutation; but Moore reinterprets it as the thesis that 'good' has no distinctively ethical meaning, and then argues against this thesis in much the way in which he argued against the first alternative, by suggesting that because we can distinguish in thought between the meaning of 'good' and that of any putative non-ethical analysis, all such analyses must be incorrect.

Both parts of Moore's argument seem to hinge on the failure of reflective substitutivity of proposed analyses, as instanced by the possibility of doubt concerning them. Thus when considering the proposal that goodness be analysed as 'what we desire to desire', he writes:

> It may indeed be true that what we desire to desire is always also good; perhaps, even the converse may be true: but it is very doubtful whether this is the case, and the mere fact that we understand very well what is meant by doubting it, shews clearly that we have two different notions before our minds.
>
> (PE p. 16)

This argument is vulnerable to the doubts about substitutivity which I aired in the previous chapter (section 5). It is also threatened by the argument which generates Moore's own 'paradox of analysis': if analyses have to be beyond sensible doubt to be true, then they can only be trivial (I discuss this 'paradox' further in chapter 7). So if Moore's argument is interpreted in the light of this psychologistic conception of analysis, it establishes nothing of any significance; in particular, since the meaning of ethical terms need not be psychologically transparent, it does not establish the conclusion Moore hopes to establish.

To do better, it is helpful to consider what one might call his 'distinct question' argument:

> But whoever will attentively consider with himself what is actually before his mind when he asks the question 'Is pleasure (or whatever it may be) after all good?' can easily satisfy himself that he is not merely wondering whether pleasure is pleasant. And if he will try this experiment with each suggested definition in succession, he may become expert enough to recognise that in every case he has before his mind a unique object, with regard to the connection of which with any other object, a distinct question may be asked.
>
> (PE p. 16)

This may seem to be just the substitutivity point again, but I think one can take from it the different consideration that however much we may try to persuade ourselves that 'good' (as applied to human experiences) just means 'pleasant', the fact that we continue to regard the question whether all pleasures are good as significant shows that 'good' and 'pleasant' are not synonymous. What is important here is the persistence of the sense that such questions are significant, that their answer is always an 'open question' (*PE* p. 21).[30] For this persisting sense of significance, which is well attested by the popularity of Moore's argument, poses a problem for the reductionist which goes beyond the simple failure of substitutivity. I have argued that the structure of concepts need not be psychologically transparent; but it is reasonable to demand of an analysis of meaning that it should illuminate the concepts with which it deals in such a way that, because it enhances our understanding, we come to find it natural for us to guide our judgments according to it. It is in the light of this requirement that the persisting sense of the significance of Moore's questions is problematic for the ethical reductionist. It is evidence that his reductive analysis is simply not persuasive, and therefore not correct.

This point establishes a presumption against the reductionist, but no more. For the reductionist can respond that the persisting sense of significance is just evidence of the stubbornness of our attachment to an illusory conception of distinctive ethical meaning.[31] Thus like many of Moore's arguments, his 'open question' argument points to something that we feel to be true, but does not itself explain why it is. To take matters further, therefore, we have to look at explanations of the phenomenon, and thus at accounts of ethical concepts which seek to establish why reductive analyses of them are incorrect.

Moore's approach here is simply to appeal to intuitions of a 'unique object – the unique property of things – which I mean by "good"' (*PE* p. 17). For reasons which I explored in section 3, this provides no help at all. I suggested there, however, that there are other ways of thinking about Moorean goodness; so the reductionist issue needs to be considered in the light of them. One of these was to regard goodness as analysable in terms of moral obligation. When the reductionist issue is approached in this way, therefore, it hinges on the reducibility of 'ought'-judgments. Moore's comment on Mill suggests one idea why such judgments might not be reducible:

> The whole object of Mill's book is to help us discover what we ought to do; but, in fact, by attempting to define the meaning of this 'ought', he has completely debarred himself from ever fulfilling that object: he has confined himself to telling us what we do do.
>
> (*PE* p. 73)

The contrast here between 'telling us what we ought to do' and 'telling us what we do do' suggests that it is because naturalistic or metaphysical judgments are not intrinsically prescriptive in a way in which ethical judgments are that a naturalistic or metaphysical reduction of ethics must be mistaken. It is, of course, Hare who has especially developed this line of thought:

> If we admit, as I shall later maintain, that it must be part of the function of a moral judgment to prescribe or guide choices, that is to say, to entail some answer to some question of the form 'What shall I do?' – then it is clear, from the second of the rules just stated ['no imperative conclusion can be validly drawn from a set of premises which does not contain at least one imperative'], that no moral judgment can be a pure statement of fact. . . . In more recent times this rule was the point behind Professor G.E. Moore's celebrated 'refutation of naturalism'.[32]

I have already observed that it is a mistake to read Hume into Moore, and for this reason it is a mistake to interpret Moore's position in this way, despite the passage quoted above. Moore holds that some naturalistic judgments are intrinsically 'ought-implying', and is therefore committed to holding that these judgments are prescriptive. But this may be felt to be a Moorean idiosyncracy, which should be abandoned in order to establish his anti-reductionist thesis. Yet does the prescriptive/descriptive distinction really establish this?

The basic difficulty is that this distinction does not altogether match the ethical/non-ethical distinction. One problem concerns prescriptions which lack any ethical content, such as those expressive of a wholly selfish point of view, or of rules of etiquette.[33] There is nothing in this position to rule out a reduction of ethical prescriptions to non-ethical ones. A different problem comes from the other direction, from the sense that not all ethical judgments are prescriptive. Judgments about the kinds of thing that are good for people are typically premises for deliberations about what one ought to do rather than disguised versions of such prescriptions; and there does not seem anything in this respect to distinguish them from other judgments about features of the world that are relevant to one's current motivations.

I shall return at the end of this chapter to the topic of prescriptivism. But I want now to turn to a line of thought which starts from a point implied above, that it is a mistake to treat ethical judgments as consisting, fundamentally, of nothing but 'ought'-judgments. In my discussion, this treatment was reached by combining Moore's reduction of ethical judgments to judgments concerning the goodness of states of affairs with a further reduction of these to 'ought'-judgments. Once this second reduction is dropped, the non-Moorean way of thinking about the goodness of states of affairs in terms of their implications for human interests becomes relevant, and I want now to consider the reductionist issue in the light of this approach.

The first point to observe is that even though this is a naturalistic approach to the concept 'good', it is not itself a reductionist one; for the concept of a human interest is an ethical concept, linked to judgments concerning the aspects of a life which make that life worth living. It is, therefore, judgments of this latter kind that must form the target for a reductionist strategy, of which the most plausible is the Sidgwickian one which claims that they concern no more than the intrinsic desirability of aspects of human life. The details of Sidgwick's account can be modified, in particular by introducing second-order desires or preferences, and a position of this kind can appear attractive. Moore recognises this when he discusses it in *PE* (pp. 15–16; I do not know whether anything in particular had suggested it to him). His discussion is notoriously confused (cf. Virginia Woolf's reaction to it quoted on p. 65), but the substance of his objection is that it implies that the question whether a disposition which we desire to desire is valuable to us is not significant; whereas, according to Moore, the question is plainly significant.

In fact, intuitions here are not so clear. But I think that what makes the analysis in terms of second-order desires attractive is a tacit assumption of ethical knowledge. We distinguish between first-order and second-order desires by allowing the latter to be governed by ethical knowledge, such as knowledge of the value of dispositions such as kindness, loyalty, fairness, and it for this reason that we accept that the content of second-order desires provides an account of what makes life worth living. Obviously, however, a reductive analysis cannot include this ethical content; but once it is eliminated, most of the point of the distinction between first-order and second-order desires is undermined, and we are returned in effect to the simpler Sidgwickian account. To this the Moorean objection that such a position makes it impossible for us to evaluate desires themselves does appear forceful; it cannot, I think, be denied that closing off this dimension of critical thought appears to us as a loss. Yet what remains to be understood is what lies behind it, once the naive appeal to our sense of the meaning of ethical language is abandoned.

At this point a shift of focus is needed. So far I have followed Moore's approach of concentrating on the 'thin' ethical term 'good', on the assumption that his preliminary reduction of other ethical concepts to 'good' is accepted. But once we are led to such issues as that of the aspects of human life which are of value, this preliminary assumption should be called into question. For we need to consider the hypothesis that the ethical content of the thin terms is drawn from that of the 'thicker' concepts such as kindness, loyalty, and courage, i.e. that an understanding of human interests is achieved through a grasp of the virtues, rather than vice versa.[34]

This hypothesis significantly alters the issue. The reductionist can no longer just enumerate the ethical concepts to be analysed; instead, he has himself to provide a plausible characterisation of the ethical before attempting to establish that ethical truths are derivable within a theory none of whose fundamental concepts are ethical. This project is not, of itself, incoherent, and since there is clearly a descriptive aspect to the use of thick concepts, it appears that if the reductionist can isolate this through the use of non-ethical concepts he will be on the way to a reduction of some kind. The objection here, however, is that there is no satisfactory way of characterising in non-ethical terms even the extension of thick concepts such as kindness; the obvious candidates, such as a disposition to pay extra attention to the welfare of others, clearly have ethical content (what counts as 'extra'? and what is 'welfare'?). For these concepts do not just attach an evaluative label to an otherwise ethically neutral disposition; they carve up the world from a point of view that is embedded within the evaluative practices of a culture.[35] This does not imply that it is not possible to grasp these concepts without sharing the values they describe; for by exercising a sympathetic imagination we can see the point of values that we do not endorse. But the exercise of such imagination is not the identification of necessary and sufficient non-ethical conditions for the application of these concepts. It is the assumption of an ethical point of view that we do not altogether share.

The thesis I want to propose, therefore, is that Moore's 'open-question' argument draws its strength from the irreducibility of the judgments which employ these thick concepts. If, contrary to Moore, it is accepted that thin ethical concepts get their content from thick ones, then this will explain why we remain unpersuaded by proposed analyses of the thin concepts. This thesis need not conflict with a prescriptivist account of the irreducibility of many 'ought'-judgments; what it suggests, however, is that since that point concerns the irreducibility of the practical to the theoretical, if we are looking for a distinctively ethical interpretation of Moore's argument, then we should look to the irreducible role of thick ethical concepts. It should be recognised, however, that this line of thought is distinctly double-edged in its implications for Moore himself: although it substantiates his anti-reductionism, it challenges his anti-naturalism. For the use of thick ethical concepts has existential implications: there are no general truths about kindness independent of the existence of people. I shall discuss further below whether one can, none the less, substantiate Moore's anti-naturalism; but the present point shows the importance of distinguishing these two issues.

Although the argument so far supports Moore's anti-reductionist position, it has only concerned the type of reduction on which Moore concentrates. If one distinguishes (contrary to Moore's theory of meaning) between the meaning of a general term and the property it denotes, one can formulate the hypothesis that ethical properties are reducible to non-ethical ones, even though the meaning of ethical terms is not reducible to that of non-ethical ones.[36] And what is specially significant is that because this hypothesis retains a distinction of meaning between the ethical and the non-ethical, it is not immediately called into question by the persisting sense of the significance of a reductive thesis. For this reason Putnam has maintained that the possibility of such a hypothesis has a 'devastating' impact on Moore's anti-reductionist argument.[37]

It is not clear that the application of the sense/reference distinction to ethical terms is as straightforward as this hypothesis implies; but let us accept it for the sake of argument. One might now argue against this reductionist hypothesis from a further consideration of the central role of thick ethical concepts; for if their extension cannot be characterised in non-ethical terms, there is little prospect of a non-ethical characterisation of the property they supposedly denote. But this is too brief to be persuasive and I think it is helpful to pursue the issue through discussion of a possible synthetic reduction — the sociobiological hypothesis that morality is behaviour which, though often contrary to the immediate interests of the agent, has been reinforced within us because it favours the survival of the agent's genes, or his species. Before discussing this approach to sociobiology, however, I want to say a little about Moore's own attitude to evolutionary theory. Moore has been accused of misrepresenting Spencer in attributing to him a crude analytic reduction of ethical concepts.[38] In fact Moore is careful not to do this. Instead, he argues (PE pp. 46–54) that Spencer's Data of Ethics is a wretched mixture of utilitarianism and psychological egoism to which is attached, in no very clear way, some grand remarks about the fundamental importance to ethics of evolutionary theory. Though this is not a full treatment of Spencer's views, it is, I think, a fair judgment on the work it deals with. Moore's criticisms of Spencer are, in fact, very much in line with those advanced by Sidgwick in lectures which Moore had attended as an undergraduate,[39] and he does not simply employ his 'open-question' argument against evolutionary ethics. He argues directly against the thesis that conduct which is more 'highly evolved' is better, i.e. against one particularly crude evolutionary definition of the good. He is especially sarcastic about Social Darwinism:

It was very natural to suppose that evolution meant evolution from what was lower into what was higher; in fact it was observed that at least one species, commonly called higher – the species man – had so survived, and among men again it was supposed that the higher races, ourselves for example, had shewn a tendency to survive the lower, such as the North American Indians. We can kill them more easily than they can kill us.

(PE p. 47)

What is at first surprising is that Moore should have bothered to devote so much space to Spencer, whose work had been subjected to criticisms of this kind for at least two decades. But the persistence of evolutionary views is attested by the fact that Moore himself uses them in EE to support an appeal to the authority of common-sense moral beliefs. For despite the fact that these lectures also contain criticisms of Spencer similar to those propounded in PE, he here maintains that 'we shall not in general be able to think that anything is good beside what other people think so. For what we think has also been determined by the course of evolution'. Not surprisingly, this claim is not repeated in PE. For although such an appeal to evolutionary theory for epistemological purposes does not require an analytic reduction of ethics to evolutionary theory, it does not fit easily with the intuitionist epistemology and abstract ethical non-naturalism presented in PE.

None the less, the sociobiological hypothesis I mentioned before is a reductive hypothesis. In discussing it I shall be guided by the writings of E.O. Wilson, currently the most influential exponent of this position.[40] His hypothesis is, first, that there are modes of conduct which are potentially harmful to an individual, but important for the continuing flourishing of the individual's species; second, that the judgment that these modes of conduct are obligatory or ideal has evolved as a way of increasing the chances that these modes of conduct will be adhered to, thereby increasing the chances of survival for the species; and, third, that although in ethical judgments we do not normally represent to ourselves the value of actions for the survival of the species, this is in truth the property of actions with which ethical judgments are concerned. Thus we get here the combination characteristic of a synthetic reduction of ethics: there is no attempt to reduce ethical concepts to those of evolutionary theory; but it is claimed that in fact the properties of actions which ethical concepts characterise just are certain natural properties which, in the context of an evolutionary theory about the development of human thought, explain why we think of them as we do. So the natural 'real essence' of moral conduct explains its 'nominal essence', the phenomenal stereotypes we employ in thinking about certain actions as obligatory. Wilson adds that these phenomenal

94

stereotypes are typically illusory, in that we represent morality as the will of God, or some pure moral imperatives; as such 'ethics as we understand it is an illusion fobbed off on us by our genes to get us to co-operate'.[41] None the less it is only our ordinary ethical concepts that are thus illusory; for, according to sociobiology, 'ethics is seen to have a solid foundation, not in divine guidance or pure moral imperatives, but in the shared qualities of human nature and the desperate need for reciprocity'.[42] So there is a non-illusory way of thinking about ethical issues, and what sociobiology offers in a way of satisfying our 'need to turn ethical philosophy into an applied science', the science of what is requisite for the survival of the species.

The first two features of this hypothesis need not be called into question. Moore himself describes duties as actions which are beneficial to others but which agents are typically disinclined to perform (*PE* p. 168); and, at a pinch, he could accept that our moral sensibility has evolved partly in order to increase the likelihood of people doing their duty in this sense. But what Moore cannot allow is the third feature of this position, the claim that, despite what we may imagine to the contrary, ethical judgments in fact just concern the value of actions for the survival of the human species. For, he will object, this is to suppose that the survival of the human species alone has intrinsic value; and this is a significant claim whose content is not simply that it identifies clearly for the first time the property denoted by all talk of ethical value. It has an ethical significance which persists however much evolutionary theory one becomes acquainted with.

It appears at first that this objection is illegitimate, since the sociobiologist does not offer a theory about ethical concepts. But the way to press this point is by asking what ethical concepts the sociobiologist himself employs. Surely he can be assumed to have rid himself of the illusions attendant (in his opinion) upon our ordinary ethical concepts; otherwise how could he recognise them as illusions? But once he has thus 'turned ethical philosophy into applied science', what content can he give to ethical thought, other than by referring as such to the properties which in his view determine the truth or falsity of ethical judgments? But the consequence of this is that the thesis that the survival of the species is all that matters ethically comes out as a tautology. Thus although the sociobiologist does not advance a straightforward analytic reduction of ethical concepts, once we put ourselves into the position of an adherent of this position, it becomes impossible to prevent the commitment to the identity of ethical and evolutionary properties taking on the role of an account of such a thinker's ethical concepts, in so far as he has any. But this now transforms the position into one which is vulnerable to the previous anti-reductionist argument.

95

Putnam's claim that reductions which rely on analyses of properties (as opposed to meanings) elude Moore's anti-reductionist argument is, therefore, incorrect. I have concentrated on the case of sociobiology because it is the only case where anything that looks like a plausible synthetic reduction of ethics has been offered. But in arguing against Putnam I do not think anything hinges on the example chosen.

Does this conclude the case against the reduction of ethics? Perhaps not, for there are many further types of reduction which one might consider. It would be silly to try to discuss them all here, but I will briefly suggest, from consideration of an idea of Dummett's, that the prospects are not bright. Dummett's idea is that there is a kind of weak reduction which maintains that the truth of each statement of one class (e.g. the ethical – though Dummett does not suggest this application of his idea) 'can only consist in the truth of some statement of the reductive class' (i.e. some non-ethical type).[43] Dummett's meaning is not self-evident, but I think we can introduce a correspondence conception of truth to interpret this position: the weak reductionist holds that in any case in which an ethical judgment is true, it is true solely in virtue of certain non-ethical states of affairs. So far this is consistent with the kind of reduction suggested by Putnam; in order to differentiate it further, therefore, I shall take it that the weak reductionist rejects the hypothesis that there are any ethical properties at all.

Moore's thesis that the goodness of states of affairs depends on their (for him non-ethical) natural properties provides one way of approaching this idea. Moore is conscious that his commitment to this thesis might suggest a reductive construal of his position, and seeks to head this off by arguing that since there seem to be an indefinite number of natural properties thus connected with goodness, a naturalist analysis of goodness in terms of such properties would require an indefinitely long disjunction which we cannot specify (*PGEM* pp. 605–6). This argument provides just the context for the introduction of a weak reduction:[44] the weak reductionist will propose that in each case in which a judgment concerning the goodness of a state of affairs is true, it is true solely in virtue of the natural properties of the state of affairs on which the goodness of that state of affairs, according to Moore, depends. Contrary to Moore's non-naturalism, which grounds the dependence of the ethical on abstract general connections between natural and ethical properties, the weak reductionist maintains that there is no such 'ethical' fact of the matter.

An analogy with tense at first looks helpful here. In this case we do get the requisite combination of (i) the conceptual irreducibility of tense, (ii) the denial that there are any properties denoted by the concept ('the unreality of tense'), and (iii) an inclination to regard the truth of tensed judgments as correspondence to a tenseless state of affairs. Hence if one took the view that ethical concepts are irreducibly linked to 'the human point of view' in a way which makes it improper for us to regard them as characterising mind-independent properties, one might be led to the position of the weak reductionist. Yet this line of thought is vulnerable to Moore's anti-reductionist argument. For in the case of tense, even though the content of tensed statements is irreducible to that of tenseless statements, there are general claims concerning the tenseless truth-conditions of tensed statements a grasp of which is constitutive of the understanding of tense e.g. that speakers use 'now' to refer to the time at which they are speaking. Hence, if the analogy between ethics and tense is correct, there should be similar general claims about the non-ethical truth-conditions of ethical statements a grasp of which is constitutive of the understanding of ethical language − their denial should not be an 'open question'; the very meaning of the ethical language should decide their truth. This is clearly just a modified version of the position of the traditional analytic reductionist, and open to the objections to that position.

The analogy with tense does not, therefore, yield a satisfactory position for a weak reductionist to occupy. And in the absence of an intuitive grasp of what a weak reduction of ethics might be, doubts about the position receive no answer. Thus it remains unclear how it is determined in particular cases which states of affairs are decisive for ethical judgments in the absence of any general analysis of ethical concepts or properties. Furthermore, if it is held that there are no ethical properties, there seems little reason to hold that the truth of ethical judgments is a correspondence matter; on the contrary, considerations of coherence would seem to have an obvious role. But once coherence is introduced, the prospects of a reduction of ethics are much diminished. These points are not, I recognise, conclusive; but they show that the outlook for such an enterprise is not encouraging. At this point, therefore, my discussion of Moore's anti-reductionist argument is complete. I have argued that a modified version of Moore's argument does refute traditional analytic reductions of ethics and the kind of synthetic reduction whose possibility is suggested by Putnam, and although I have not provided a thorough treatment of the idea of a weaker reduction of ethics, I have offered grounds for scepticism as to whether there is really a sustainable position here.

As I have frequently stressed, however, naturalist and metaphysical ethical theories do not have to be reductionist, despite Moore's confusions on this matter; and it is obvious that the 'open-question' argument, which focuses on the persisting significance of analyses of meaning, has no purchase on non-reductive ethical theories. So the question arises as to whether Moore provides any other arguments to support his non-naturalist conclusion.

An initial issue concerns the definition of ethical naturalism. I defined it in the previous section as the view that all ethical judgments have a commitment to the existence in time of something. This is a very generic definition and there can be many forms of naturalist theory. One, which Moore's writing about naturalism suggests, adds to the general definition a correspondence theory of truth and an appropriate epistemology; on this view, then, ethical judgments are beliefs which are rendered true or false by the ethical properties of natural objects and in so far as we have ethical knowledge, we do so by virtue of being reliable indicators of the presence of these features. This is a realist version of ethical naturalism; it represents the thought that ethics might be a fundamental natural science, or, rather, that the sciences of psychology and sociology might be irreducibly ethical in content and include theories about how ethical knowledge is possible. The ethical and political theories of Aristotle come reasonably close to this conception.

Does Moore's work provide any arguments against a realist naturalism of this kind? Not explicitly; but Simon Blackburn has proposed that Moore's thesis concerning the dependence of goodness on natural properties provides the basis for an argument against this kind of realist position.[45] As we have seen, Moore himself interprets this thesis in terms of his abstract necessary connections between goodness and natural properties. These connections are definitive of his non-naturalism; but it is useful to be able to separate the dependence thesis from ethical non-naturalism by formulating it as the 'supervenience' of the ethical upon the non-ethical (this is not a term Moore actually employed though it is often attributed to him): this is the thesis that there cannot be an ethical difference between two situations unless there is some non-ethical difference between them which accounts for the ethical difference, a thesis certainly advanced by Moore (cf. E pp. 69–70; CIV pp. 260–1). Moore's ethical non-naturalism implies this thesis, as do reductionist positions. Blackburn's argument is, now, that these are the only accounts of supervenience available to a realist; and hence that non-reductive realist naturalism should be rejected.

I have already observed that once the reduction of ethical concepts to the thin concepts of goodness and/or obligation is rejected, it ceases to be straightforward to give an account of the ethical/non-ethical distinction. This has critical implications for the supervenience thesis since it is couched in terms of such a distinction. None the less, there seems to be something right about it, so it can be accepted for the sake of the argument.[46] The problem it is supposed to raise for this realist is that because he is neither a reductionist nor a Moorean non-naturalist he rejects any necessary connection between the non-ethical properties of a good situation and its goodness; but the supervenience of the ethical implies that once he has accepted the judgment that the situation is good, he is committed to accepting that any relevantly similar situation is also good. But then how does this commitment arise, in the absence of a necessary connection in the initial case? If the non-ethical properties of the first situation do not necessitate its goodness, why is it that situations which are similar in all relevant non-ethical properties cannot differ in goodness?

A central feature of this argument is the assumption that the realist cannot maintain that there are necessary connections between non-ethical and ethical properties. Certainly, the hypothesis that there are such connections is problematic, but, equally, it seems a feature of any plausible realist position to take it that they exist; according to such a realist, psychological and sociological theories should attempt to characterise these connections in a non-reductive fashion. Blackburn has recently acknowledged the possibility of a position of this kind;[47] but he argues that it still does not enable this realist to capture the supervenience of the ethical. For, he argues, supervenience is an *analytic* feature of ethical concepts, with the result that the commitments which arise from ethical judgments are themselves analytically necessary. But no non-reductive naturalist would allow that his necessary connections are analytic truths. This response is not persuasive. The realist can maintain that it is a conceptual truth that there are necessary connections between the ethical and the non-ethical, even though the particular connections themselves are not analytically necessary.

For this reason I do not think that Blackburn's use of Moore's dependence thesis to argue against a realist naturalist position is, by itself, decisive. But perhaps it should be seen as having the role of bringing out the realist's commitment to general connections between ethical and non-ethical properties. For this commitment is surely unwelcome in the light of our experience. The intellectual tradition that reaches back to Aristotle has not bequeathed to us general 'moral sciences' comparable to the natural sciences. Thus it is a truism of the philosophy of history that historical understanding is inherently particular and does not lead up to abstract generalisations comparable to those of the natural sciences. The realist may say that this only shows that our understanding of human nature is still infantile; but this is hard to take seriously.

There are other difficulties for the realist. It is not easy to combine recognition of the fact of alien cultures and apparently irresolvable differences of value with a commitment to the possibility of an ideal psychological theory which will explain how we can be reliable indicators of ethical properties. For in the absence of ethical consensus it is hard to conceive of a theory which satisfactorily explains on the basis of the real ethical properties of the world how differences of judgment

99

arise, instead of just continuing the argument.[48] Indeed the conception is so difficult to sustain in the light of experience that I think that faith in it is best combined with religious faith, so that this realist position acquires a theological (and thus, for Moore, metaphysical) dimension. Butler put well the reassurance that this religious dimension seems to offer:

> Conscience does not only offer itself to show us the way we should walk in, but it likewise carries its own authority with it, that it is our natural guide; the guide assigned to us by the Author of our nature.[49]

However, it is hard to see that the introduction of a religious element offers more than the form of a solution to scepticism about the realist ethical position; the grounds for religious faith are too indeterminate to resolve antecedent disputes about values and human nature, with the result that the unsatisfactory old disputes can continue in a theological form whose inconclusiveness is just as worrying from a realist perspective.

In the context of a discussion of ethical naturalism, however, these objections to ethical realism are not decisive. A naturalist can withdraw from the realist presumptions of Moore's characterisation of naturalism, in particular from the application of a correspondence theory of truth and the appeal to the natural sciences as a model for our understanding of ethical judgments. Indeed if the naturalist accepts the priority of the thick ethical concepts, which are to some extent culture-specific, these presumptions seem altogether out of place. But exactly what account the naturalist should then give of ethical judgment is not clear to me. It will not suffice just to invoke a rationalist conception of ethics, since much the same sceptical objections will apply to its presumptions concerning what is rational for any human being. Instead the naturalist seems to need a form of historical constructivism, which permits one to acknowledge that there are different ways in which elements of human well-being can be defined and organised. In the absence of the realist's conception of underlying general ethical properties, attention will be focused on those particular ethical institutions which shape so much of our lives, of which the modern state is the paradigm. The difficult part in the articulation of such a position is vindicating the critical pretensions inherent in ethical judgments, and thereby avoiding a lapse into vulgar relativism. It must be possible for the naturalist to represent ethical judgments as aiming at a form of objectivity without basing that description on the models of the natural sciences or mathematics. Perhaps Hegel's writings show how this project can be achieved, but I am not myself confident about the matter, and I shall not pursue it further here.

## 6: Intuitionism

Even though Moore did not refute ethical naturalism, his failure to do so does not establish it as correct. It is therefore worth looking critically at Moore's alternative, ethical non-naturalism. In section 4 I suggested that this position should be defined in generic terms as the view that there are fundamental ethical truths which have no existential implications. This position then required further specification: on one view, these ethical truths are conceived as abstract truths about the relationship between non-natural objects, the universals constitutive of these truths; on another, the truth of these judgments is not conceived of as arising from the obtaining of any state of affairs. I want to show here that Moore's intuitionist epistemology makes it fairly clear that one should attribute to him the first form of ethical non-naturalism, and that, however much one wants to, one cannot easily reconstruct his position as one of the second kind.

Before considering Moore's intuitionism in detail it is important to review the senses in which the word 'intuitionism' has been used in ethical theories. In its most generic sense, intuitionism in ethics requires no more than that there can be knowledge which is both ethical and not reducible to other kinds of knowledge. We get a more determinate sense where the manner in which fundamental ethical convictions constitute knowledge is construed by means of an analogy with sense-perception. This perceptual analogy is very general, and, as the 'moral sense' tradition shows, can be developed in a variety of ways (the issue of an analogy with secondary qualities being especially significant). But, typically, it implies that the objects of ethical judgment should be conceived of as objective states of affairs which are the objects of veridical ethical intuitions.

Intuitionism is often also taken to imply that ethical knowledge is primarily knowledge of the actions which it is our duty to perform. This implication arises from the view that it is our ordinary judgments of duty, our 'common-sense' morality, which provide the grounds for ethical knowledge; they are our common-sense perceptions of value. I shall call this view 'common-sense' intuitionism. It leads to a hostility to any general ethical theory which departs from common sense morality and sometimes to the very idea of a general theory which seeks to exhibit ethical knowledge as founded upon general principles. Typical of this is Prichard's rejection of 'general thinking' in favour of the 'direct apprehension' of obligations in particular types of situation.[50] Sidgwick, by contrast, shows his rejection of this common-sense intuitionism when he contrasts his own 'Philosophical Intuitionism', which embodies an appeal to general theory, with the 'Dogmatic' and 'Perceptional' intuitionism of those who rely exclusively on common-sense morality.[51]

A standard problem for common-sense intuitionism is that in many situations our common-sense moral intuitions conflict. Rawls distinguishes between those who think that these problems can always be resolved by an appeal to a higher-order principle which ranks the duties in conflict, and those who think that no such principle can always be found, and he calls the position of these latter theorists an 'intuitionist' one.[52] This terminology is in line with common-sense intuitionism, but it carries no commitment to the perceptual analogy. Many philosophers are intuitionists of this Rawlsian kind, but do not subscribe to perceptual intuitionism; arguably Rawls himself is a case in point.[53]

Where, now, does Moore stand? It is clear that in *PE* he is an intuitionist in my most generic sense. What is not so clear is his commitment to the perceptual analogy; thus consider the following passage from the preface to *PE*:

> In order to express the fact that ethical propositions of my *first* class
> are incapable of proof or disproof, I have sometimes followed
> Sidgwick's usage in calling them 'Intuitions' . . . I would wish it to
> be observed that, when I call such propositions 'Intuitions', I mean
> *merely* to assert that they are incapable of proof; I imply nothing
> whatever as to the manner or origin of our cognition of them.
>
> (p. x)

This passage seems to be a repudiation of an intuitionist epistemology, and, in particular, a denial of any perceptual analogy. Yet, despite what he says here about his use of the word 'intuition', Moore in fact regularly describes our consciousness of ethical propositions as 'intuition'. Sometimes he means by this not much more than immediate moral conviction, as when he acknowledges that we have 'immediate intuitions' of our duty (*PE* p. 149); and in this case he goes on to insist that what we intuit is no intuition in the sense defined in the preface. But he more commonly writes of intuition as a mode of ethical consciousness which at least presents its object as self-evident (*PE* pp. 75, 79, 143–5), and it is this which seems to invoke the perceptual analogy.

In the 1898 Dissertation there is an unequivocal commitment to the analogy; he writes here that ethical propositions are 'intuitively given' in the sense that they are 'given in the way that any sense-datum is'. There is no similar passage in *PE* or any other published writing on ethics. But Moore does here compare ethical intuition and the knowledge 'that this is a chair beside me' (*PE* p. 75); furthermore he repeatedly uses the language of descriptive contemplation to describe the method of reflective isolation by which we are supposed to attain knowledge of intuitive ethical propositions (*PE* pp. 93, 187–8, and especially p. 223 where we are encouraged to 'look and see'). So I think one can fairly confidently ascribe perceptual intuitionism to Moore, at least at the time of *PE*, with a degree of confidence enhanced by the fact that he does not offer even the beginnings of an alternative account of ethical knowledge.

Although, as the case of Hume shows, this analogy does not of itself require that the objects of ethical judgment be thought to be ethical states of affairs, Moore's thoroughly realist conception of perception is such that, for him, the analogy does have this implication. The important implication of this is that his ethical non-naturalism is of the first form specified at the start of this section. I have already criticised (in chapter 2) the resulting metaphysics and epistemology; but these criticisms can now be taken further. Although, by a strange and circuitous route Moore ends up endorsing most of common-sense morality (cf. chapter 4, section 3), he is not a common-sense intuitionist. He thinks that much ordinary moral judgment is confused, and that our common-sense judgments of duty are answerable to an ideal utilitarian analysis and therefore not genuinely intuitive (*PE* pp. 148–9). None the less, Moore is also not a 'Philosophical' intuitionist in the style of Sidgwick; he never seeks to present his fundamental ethical truths as truths of reason. Thus he is certainly an intuitionist in Rawls's sense; despite his quantitative idioms concerning intrinsic value, Moore relies on intuition, and not on any higher-order principle, to determine the relative value of intrinsic goods and evils. So what is peculiar about Moore's intuitionism is that he appeals neither to common-sense nor to reason.

In this situation Moore has to pin his hopes on the self-evidence of fundamental ethical truths. But since the appeal is to self-evidence alone, a comparison he draws in VR with religious faith is troubling:

> It is mere faith, not proof, which justifies your statement: 'God exists'. Your belief is right, because you cannot help believing: and my unbelief is right, because I have not got that intuition. . . . And so far it would seem that religious belief stands in the same position as our moral beliefs.
>
> (p. 95)

This dogmatist position interprets faith as dependent only on one's psychological disposition. Perhaps that is a defensible position with respect to religious faith, but in ethics it undermines belief in objective ethical knowledge. For in a situation of ethical disagreement concerning intrinsic value, it leaves one with nothing to appeal to to resolve the disagreement or explain why one party's intuitions are illusory. If both sides are right to stick to their positions, and have nothing to say to shift the other side, it is then just rhetoric to insist that one party's judgments are correct and the other's incorrect. That insistence can have no substantive role in ethical reflection. In fact we have just a form of subjectivism that is disguised by the dogmatic form of its pronouncements.

At the time of *PE* Moore seems to have been untroubled by this problem. He is confident that his method of reflective isolation will secure widespread agreement concerning intrinsic values (cf. preface to *PE*). This method is the opposite of an appeal to common-sense morality, and is comparable only to Husserl's contemporary phenomenological reduction; Moore asks us to bracket away the consequences and the context of a state of affairs so that we can grasp its intrinsic value. The details of Moore's method are, of course, dictated by his consequentialism and principle of organic unities; the objection to it was forcefully stated some years earlier by Bradley in a comment on Sidgwick (whose justice in that respect is not clear):

> Surely common sense must see that, to find what end we ought to
> pursue in the human life we live, by seeing what would be left us to
> pursue in an unimaginable and inhuman predicament, is not common
> sense at all, but simply bad metaphysics.
>
> *(Ethical Studies* p. 126)

Bradley is surely right here. Our ethical consciousness, to which Moore is appealing, simply does not extend to the 'unimaginable and inhuman predicaments' with which Moore faces us. Faced with a choice between a universe which consists of nothing but pleasure and one which consists of nothing but knowledge (whatever that means), the only sane response is to annihilate both universes and reject a theory which attaches significance to such a peculiar reflective exercise.

By 1912, when *E* was published, Moore's confidence in his method had receded. He opens the book with a general scepticism concerning fundamental ethical truths, and closes it with a chapter on intrinsic value in which, beyond rejecting hedonism, he refuses to commit himself significantly to what kinds of thing have intrinsic value. Thus although his intuitionism is still here worked up into the method of reflective isolation (p. 28), the results of the method are so meagre that the impression that it is a dead end is unavoidable. And once this is recognised, the collapse of Moore's intuitionism, and thus his ethical non-naturalism, is complete.

I mentioned at the start of this section that there is an alternative form of ethical non-naturalism which does not invoke non-natural objects and instead construes the truth of ethical judgments in some non-correspondence fashion. It is, therefore, worth asking whether one can find a position of this kind which enables one to reconstruct a Moorean position that is less vulnerable than his actual position. The obvious idea must be to invoke an appeal to reason; for perhaps in this way it may be possible to preserve the central conception of Moore's ethical non-naturalism, that the fundamental truths of ethics are synthetic *a priori*. In developing this, it seems appropriate to introduce the analysis of goodness in terms of obligation which I proposed in section 3. For there is no way in which the rationalist approach looks plausible if it is applied to an abstract conception of the goodness of states of affairs; whereas if one thinks of fundamental ethical principles as concerned with our obligations, there is more chance of success. The model here is, of course, Kant's ethical theory, and this reconstruction of Moore's ethical non-naturalism is, in effect, an attempt to isolate the Kantian elements in Moore's theory and present them as what he 'should have said'.

Unfortunately, however, this enterprise is doomed to failure. The difficulty arises from the need to substantiate the supposed rationality of certain kinds of action. This is, of course, a familiar problem for any Kantian theory, but the difficulty here concerns the very conception of such a substantiation, rather than problems in showing that anything in particular is thereby found to be rational for just anybody, which is what is more commonly at issue. For the Kantian route to such a substantiation lies via an understanding of human deliberations; the aim is to show that certain courses of action are ruled in, or out, for anyone who has a reflective grasp of themselves as deliberative agents, so that even if we are not ourselves sufficiently reflective to recognise these commitments, they are none the less intrinsic to our capacities. But this now introduces naturalist considerations, albeit very abstract ones; reasons for action are reasons for agents like us, so the thought that a state of affairs is of such a kind that bringing it into existence is intrinsically rational, or is, in Moore's idiom, such that it ought to exist for its own sake, includes an implicit reference to the agents for whom this is rational. Although the relevant conception of an agent is an abstract one, it suffices to render the resulting theory naturalist by Moore's standards, as Moore himself implies in his criticism of Kantian ethics (except that he construes Kant's Pure Will as metaphysical).

The only way in which a Moorean position here could be sustained would by supposing that the rationality of the kinds of action constitutive of fundamental ethical truths was not substantiated by reference to the motivations and deliberations of agents. Somehow courses of action are to be in themselves rational, i.e. such that there are reasons why they should be performed. In so far as Moore writes about rationality at all, this is how he writes of it: that which is rational is that which is 'good in itself' (*PE* p. 100). But since there is now no way in which claims concerning rationality can be substantiated, the appeal to this conception of 'external' reasons for action (in Williams's sense[54]) is no advance on the dogmatism of the first form of ethical non-naturalism which this rationalist approach was intended to improve upon. Thus although there is much to be said in favour of rationalist approaches to ethical theory, no defensible rationalist theory will accommodate the degree of abstraction characteristic of Moore's non-naturalism.

## 7: Emotivism

The judgment that Moore's ethical non-naturalism is untenable was shared by many of those who had also been persuaded by Moore that no form of ethical naturalism is tenable. Their response was to reject his assumption that ethical judgments have any ethical cognitive content, and to adopt instead the view that ethical content is just the expression of feelings or attitudes – the emotivist position. This position can be regarded as a response to Moore's criticisms of reductionist subjectivism; it deliberately avoids the kind of analysis of ethical concepts or properties that Moore would have regarded as commission of the naturalistic fallacy, and embodies a response to Moore's further charge that subjectivists mistake the nature of moral disagreement.

In $E$ Moore had argued that if '$x$ is right' just means 'I approve of $x$', and '$x$ is wrong' means 'I object to $x$', then, where two people have conflicting attitudes to the same action, each can truly report their attitudes by saying '$x$ is right' and '$x$ is wrong', with the implication that $x$ is both right and wrong. But this appears to be a contradiction. Furthermore, the nature of the disagreement is unclear, since each person can accept that the other's attitude is opposed to his own, and if their moral judgments just describe their attitudes, there is no conflict between them ($E$ pp. 45–51).[55] In his paper in $PGEM$ Stevenson responded to this argument. One aspect of his response was that Moore's argument neglects the indexical feature of this subjectivist analysis. If this is made explicit, by taking '$x$ is right' as uttered by me to be short for '$x$ is right, according to me', then, in the situation of conflicting attitudes it does not follow that anyone can truly say '$x$ is right according to me and $x$ is wrong according to me'. So the apparent inconsistency generated by the position is avoided. But the nature of the disagreement itself has still not been accounted for; each party to the apparent conflict can still regard the other's judgment as correct (a point stressed by Moore in 'The Nature of Moral Philosophy' $PS$ pp. 333–4, where the point about indexicality is already noted).

It was to deal with this problem that Stevenson introduced his distinction between a disagreement in opinion and a disagreement in attitude ($PGEM$ pp. 82–3), and proposed that in the situation envisaged by Moore the parties concerned did not disagree in opinion but in attitude. This brings with it a move from reductionist subjectivism to emotivism. Twentieth-century emotivism was first clearly propounded in Cambridge (by Ogden and Richards in *The Meaning of Meaning*),[56] and developed and discussed there by Duncan-Jones, Stevenson, Broad, and others. Moore was therefore well aware of this theory and may even have had a hand in developing it, though I know of no evidence for this hypothesis beyond the fact that at the end of CIV (p. 274) he suggests that predicates of value do not 'describe' that to which they apply.

In his reply to Stevenson in *PGEM* Moore gave a favourable response to emotivism, though he qualified his judgment in a characteristic way:

> I have some inclination to think that in *any* 'typically ethical' sense in which a man might assert that Brutus' action was right, he would be asserting nothing whatever which could conceivably be true or false, except, perhaps, that Brutus' action occurred – no more than, if he said 'Please, shut the door'. I certainly have *some* inclination to think all this. . . . But then, on the other hand, I also still have *some* inclination to think that my former view is true. And, if you ask me to which of these incompatible views I have the *stronger* inclination, I can only answer that I simply do not know whether I am any more strongly inclined to take the one rather than to take the other.
>
> (p. 545)

It is not clear how representative this passage is of Moore's views. Ewing reports that Moore had said to him some time after 1953 that he could not understand what had led him to think so well of emotivism in *PGEM* (cf. A&L p. 24 footnote 1), and in a letter of 1937 to his son Timothy he rejects an emotivist account of beauty. There are certainly central aspects of his ethical theory not consistent with emotivism, in particular his thesis that there are necessary connections between natural properties and ethical ones. For this implies that the content of ethical judgment is such that commitment to an ethical judgment arises from beliefs about non-ethical properties alone; and no emotivist account will allow this. Moore surprisingly did not note this in *PGEM*, where his indecision concerning Stevenson's emotivism occurs alongside a straightforward elucidation of this conception of the dependence of intrinsic value.

This only constitutes an argument against emotivism if there are good reasons for accepting Moore's conception of fundamental ethical truths as necessary, and we have seen that Moore at least provides none. None the less Moore's ethical theory suggests other problems for emotivism, in particular whether it is vulnerable to an extension of Moore's 'open-question' argument. For although emotivism does not purport to reduce ethical truths to truths of some other kind, there are forms of emotivism which treat ethical judgments as expressions of attitudes that need not be thought of as distinctively ethical. An important case is Hare's view that 'ought'-judgments express universalised prescriptions and evaluations express general guidance concerning choices.[57] Moore's argument certainly appears as potent as ever in relation to such a position. Choices reflect preferences and we are able to distinguish between evaluations and preferences, or recommendations made on their basis, in a way which just repeats the impact of Moore's original argument on reductionist analyses.[58]

This conclusion implies that a viable form of emotivism will have to hold that ethical judgments are expressions of distinctively ethical attitudes. An important issue concerning such a position is whether the Moorean reduction of thick ethical concepts to goodness is also to be assumed. Although I proposed before that Moore's 'open-question' argument relies on a denial of this assumption, it none the less seems natural for an emotivist to make this assumption, since judgments which employ thick concepts are clearly not just expressions of attitudes with no cognitive content; in which case, one is just left with judgments concerning goodness to be treated in an emotivist fashion, and these can be readily enough regarded as expressions of approval. Indeed, it is very natural to take just this view of Moore's actual position, given his unwillingness to permit any arguments for fundamental ethical judgments. It is no surprise, therefore, that an emotivist position of this kind has some of the unattractive features of Moore's position: where Moore relies on an unanalysable ethical concept, this position relies on an unanalysable ethical attitude.

The difficulty of the resulting position can be exhibited by considering Moore's thesis that goodness depends on natural properties. In the context of emotivist theory, this thesis will be expressed as the thesis that ethical judgments 'supervene' on judgments concerning natural properties. Simon Blackburn puts the point well:

> It seems to be a conceptual matter that moral claims supervene upon
> natural ones. Anyone failing to recognise this, or to obey the
> constraint, would indeed lack something constitutive of competence
> in the moral practice. And there is good reason for this: it would
> betray the whole purpose for which we moralise, which is to choose,
> commend, rank, approve, forbid, things on the basis of their natural
> properties.[59]

We can agree with Blackburn here, but we still need an account of what it is about approval which guarantees that it supervenes.

It seems clear, first, that it must have some cognitive content; for no commitment to supervenience can arise from the expression of a contentless feeling (if there is such a thing). Furthermore, this cognitive content must amount to something like the belief that that which is approved of has natural properties which justify favourable treatment of it (this is implied by Blackburn's remark that we commend things 'on the basis of their natural properties'). If this is right, then approval can be construed as the expression of a desire to treat something favourably

108

because one believes that its properties justify such treatment. But this now seems to be vulnerable to the extension of Moore's anti-reductionist argument: can one not feel, and express, a desire of this kind towards things which one does not judge to be valuable? The issue turns on the nature of the justification that is alluded to in the cognitive component: if this is elucidated in a way which reduces it to considerations such as the capacity to satisfy desires whose formulation involves no distinctively ethical concepts, then that objection seems as potent as ever. On the other hand, if justification is elucidated by reference to ethical concepts such as that of human interests, the objection fails.

The way in which the objection fails, however, offers no comfort to the emotivist. The non-cognitive component of approval, as expression of desire (or whatever), drops out as irrelevant, and attention is fixed on the cognitive component of approval: it is only by accepting that this has ethical content that it can be accepted that the account as a whole is satisfactory. But since the emotivist's basic thesis was the denial that there is any ethical cognitive content, to accept this is to abandon emotivism. Thus emotivism appears vulnerable to a combination of Moorean objections – the extension of the anti-reductionist argument, and the supervenience requirement.

So far, however, all of this has been premissed on the Moorean reduction of thick concepts to thin ones – leading to the conception of approval as a fundamental ethical attitude. Can the emotivist reject this – and if he does, will it help? If the thesis advanced in section 5, that the extension of these concepts cannot be characterised without use of ethical concepts, is accepted, it follows that there is an irreducible ethical content in the cognitive component of judgments which employ these concepts; hence any emotivist attempt to partition off their ethical content into a non-cognitive component seems bound to fail.

What does not follow is that these concepts have to be interpreted realistically, as denoting real properties of things which we register, more or less accurately, in our judgments. Indeed, for reasons which I briefly noted in section 5, this realist position is not a plausible one to adopt towards ethical concepts. Since the emotivist is also a critic of ethical realism, there is here the possibility of a degree of convergence in ethical theory. Those who, starting out from the traditional emotivist position, abandon their hostility to the conception of ethical cognitive content and turn their attention to the task of articulating a satisfactory form of ethical constructivism appear to be working towards much the same goal as those who, starting from the traditional naturalist position, abandon ethical realism and seek to articulate a weaker cognitivist position.[60] It is, therefore, possible to envisage a synthesis which transcends the traditional opposition between naturalism and emotivism. Such a synthesis would be a metaphysics of ethics quite different from

109

that presented by Moore; but in so far as the outcome of any dialectical process is indebted to the arguments which gave rise to it, such a theory would, like most twentieth-century ethical theory, bear the scars of Moore's arguments.

# IV

# Ideal utilitarianism

*Love and beauty are not enough.*
(Anthony Burgess *Earthly Powers* Penguin p. 102).

Sidgwick's combination of utilitarianism and intuitionism cleared the way for a moral theory which retains the structure of utilitarianism while rejecting its hedonism. Sidgwick recognised this possibility, but in the end retained a hedonist position. So it was left to Moore to complete the task by presenting his ideal utilitarian theory in *PE*.[1]

## 1: Consequentialism and deontology

Ideal utilitarianism invites one to separate discussion of the proposed ideal ends of action from discussion of its utilitarian, or consequentialist, account of moral obligation, and I shall follow this practice, starting with this latter topic. A preliminary issue here is the nature of moral obligation itself. Broadly speaking, there are two views to take: one can either regard it as a concept which just expresses the practical implications of the ethical features of situations, or one can regard it as a, or indeed, the fundamental ethical concept. Since consequentialism is usually defined by the principle that an agent ought to perform that action, of those available to him, which has the best possible consequences, it would seem that the first of these accounts of moral obligation is all that is presupposed. But if Moorean goodness is itself defined in terms of moral obligation, in the way I suggested in the previous chapter, it requires the second account of moral obligation.

Once goodness is reduced to obligation, fundamental judgments concerning the relative intrinsic value of kinds of states of affairs are represented as judgments of relative obligation, of the following form:

(a) In a situation of choice between states of affairs of kinds $X$ and $Y$, an agent ought, *ceteris paribus*, to secure the existence (by action or omission) of the state of affairs of kind $X$ rather than that of kind $Y$.

Principles of the form of (a) concern only comparative obligation. To obtain a non-comparative obligation, a further principle is required:

(b) If one can secure the existence of a state of affairs of kind $X$ and there are no other kinds of state whose existence one ought to secure rather than that of a state of kind $X$, then one ought to secure the existence of a state of affairs of kind $X$.

This principle represents the usual consequentialist principle that one ought to perform that action whose consequences are the best possible. But because goodness is here defined in terms of obligation, the principle lacks consequentialist significance; it just declares that one ought to do whatever one most ought to do. What makes the theory consequentialist is the fact that the fundamental ethical principles concern relative obligations to secure the existence or not of states of affairs of different kinds.

The type of theory that is traditionally contrasted with consequentialism is deontology (a term, ironically, coined by Bentham). The contrast is usually explained by the thought that a consequentialist treats obligation as determined by the intrinsic value of the consequences of action, whereas the deontologist holds that we have a fundamental moral obligation, or duty, to perform or refrain from actions of certain kinds. Once intrinsic value is analysed in terms of obligation, however, this contrast becomes one between a theory according to which our fundamental obligations are to secure by action or omission the existence of states of affairs of certain kinds and one according to which our fundamental obligations are to perform or refrain from certain actions (which is, in effect how Moore makes the contrast in the preface to *PE* – cf. p. viii). Yet this contrast is problematic: that an action of some kind has been performed is one of the states of affairs which the performance of that action secures, and actions can be described in terms of the kinds of state of affairs which their performance secures.

In *E* Moore tries to prevent this collapse in two ways: he restricts consequences to those states of affairs which are results (or effects) of the action, where this is understood to exclude the performance of the action itself (*E* p. 96); and he maintains that the deontologist can characterise types of actions only by reference to their intrinsic, i.e. non-consequential, properties (*E* p. 117). Both these restrictions are problematic. The familiar duties to which the deontologist appeals (keeping promises, not harming others, etc.) identify actions in terms of consequential features, and a deontology restricted to actions picked out

112

only by their intrinsic features would, as Prichard realised,[2] be limited to duties to attempt such actions. The resulting theory seems to misdescribe our responsibilities; furthermore, since consequential features are permitted within the characterisation of the types of action one ought to attempt, a thoroughly consequentialist version of the theory remains possible. Nor are matters much better with a consequentialism limited to the results of action. Classical utilitarianism, which conceived pleasure as a sensation, is a theory of this kind; but this feature of the theory is one of its objectionable features. Furthermore once one is prepared to consider a variety of intrinsic goods, there seems no reason in principle for excluding the kind of action performed from consequentialist assessment. Thus when Broad raised this point with Moore (*PGEM* pp. 48-9), Moore accepted it (pp. 559-60); indeed in *PE* Moore had explicitly supposed that it was conceivable that actions should themselves have intrinsic value (p. 147), and many of Moore's intrinsic goods in *PE* are certainly mental acts.

Yet there is a point to the contrast between consequentialism and deontology. It emerges when one considers whether a consequentialist theory which assigns positive intrinsic value only to the non-performance of harmful acts is equivalent to a deontology that restricts itself to duties not to perform such acts. This equivalence claim fails because the deontologist's principle that, e.g., one has a duty not to kill, is not equivalent to the consequentialist's principle that one ought, other things being equal, to secure the non-existence of killings. One difference here is the *ceteris paribus* clause in the consequentialist principle; but the important point is that the deontologist's principle says nothing about one's duty in respect of potential killings by others which one can intervene to prevent, whereas the consequentialist principle requires just such intervention. A similar point applies to the difference between the deontologist's positive principle that one ought to keep one's promises and a consequentialist version of it as the principle that one ought, other things being equal, to secure the existence of states of affairs in which promises are kept. In both cases, the deontologist's principles have a reflexive restriction (to 'one's own killings' or 'one's own promises') which the consequentialist principles lack; and this feature is fundamental to the distinction between consequentialism and deontology.

I have described this feature by reference to the presence or not of a reflexive pronoun in the specification of the kind of act which it is held one ought to perform. Nagel, following Parfit, calls it a distinction between 'agent-relative' and 'agent-neutral' values, and I shall follow this terminology.[3] The content of agent-relative duties varies systematically from one agent to another, which is why their specification requires the use of a reflexive pronoun. Agent-neutral duties, by contrast, are to be the same for every agent. It is easy to see that the characteristic duties of the deontologist are agent-relative (though deontologists such as Ross do not exclude agent-neutral values as well), and it is an assumption of consequentialism that the notion of an intrinsic good is agent-neutral. In the terms of my reconstruction of Moore's theory, this implies that the kinds of states of affairs whose existence one is morally obliged to secure are specified in agent-neutral terms; if one were to specify them in agent-relative terms, the resulting theory would be equivalent to a deontological theory.

This contrast does not exhaust the traditional distinction between deontology and consequentialism. Another important aspect concerns the contrast between 'side-constraint' and 'end-state' conceptions of morality.[4] Deontologists typically stress certain limited duties, such as the duty to keep one's promises and negative duties not to harm others; they regard these duties as strict, and treat open-ended positive duties of beneficence as ideals rather than strict duties (Kant distinguishes in this regard between duties of 'perfect' and 'imperfect' obligation).[5] Thus according to the deontologist as long as we act within the constraints defined by our strict duties, we do no great wrong, although our behaviour may be less than ideal. A consequentialist like Moore, by contrast, reverses the location of stringency within his theory. Obligations to secure the existence of particular intrinsic goods are always subject to *ceteris paribus* clauses, but there is a general, omnipresent, strict obligation to make the world as good as one can. Moore emphasises this in a striking passage in one of his early papers:

> It is plain, in fact, that at every moment of our lives we are either doing what we ought or what we ought not: either what will lead to the greatest possible sum of good, or else what is wicked, because it will produce less good, than it was in our power to effect.

Faced with this sort of consequentialist rigorism (whose reference to wickedness perhaps harks back to Moore's youthful commitment to evangelism – *PGEM* pp. 10–11), the deontologist's side-constraint conception of strict morality has considerable appeal.

Indeed, it is unquestionable that our ordinary moral consciousness is permeated by the conception of agent-relative duties. So there is a substantial burden of proof to be discharged by any theorist who hopes to persuade us that these values are of no fundamental importance. The possibility of a Moorean contraposition, a defence of common-sense morality, is one that Moore, at any rate, needs to take very seriously. However, in this case Moore allows himself a manoeuvre whose availability he does not always bear in mind when considering threats to common-sense – that of saving the appearances by confining his repudiation of common-sense to a level of theoretical reflection. I shall

114

discuss Moore's attempt to save most of common-sense morality in the next section; here I shall concentrate on his argument for theoretical consequentialism.

Moore's argument is simply that it is self-evident that it would be wrong to perform an action concerning which we knew that it would make the world worse than if we had performed another action available to us (*PE* pp. 147–8; *E* p. 93). In considering this, the analysis of goodness in terms of obligation is important. If this is accepted, then, given obvious connections between 'wrong' and 'ought', Moore's self-evident principle is a restatement of the principle (b) that one ought to do whatever action secures the existence of that state of affairs whose existence, in the circumstances, one most ought to secure. As such, one cannot object to it, but it provides no grounds for a consequentialism that excludes agent-relative values; for these are only excluded by the further assumption that the states of affairs whose existence one ought to secure are all specified in agent-neutral terms.

To elucidate Moore's argument, therefore, one should reject the analysis of goodness in terms of obligation, and invoke in its place an agent-neutral concept of intrinsic value which can serve as a ground for obligation. Any plausible specification of such a concept will be naturalistic, but this does not matter in the present context. Indeed, in order to support the assumption that the states of affairs whose existence one ought to secure are to be specified in agent-neutral terms, Moore himself could employ such a naturalistic concept, without accepting that it is the concept of goodness. Thus however exactly one organises the concepts here, Moore's argument rests on something like the thought that it cannot be right to act in such a way that the total situation is not as good for all those affected as it might have been. The concept of goodness employed here is relational – it is what is good for people that matters; but there is no intrinsic *agent*-relativity to it.

The strength of this argument for consequentialism is widely recognised,[6] and some familiar objections to it are ineffectual. One invokes the principle of double effect and argues that the consequentialist principle is mistaken because it fails to take proper account of the difference between intended and merely foreseen consequences.[7] The idea here is that it is wrong to do intentionally that which is in itself evil even though one foresees that the final total outcome will be the best possible in the circumstances; for, it is said, I am not responsible for the merely foreseen consequences of my actions to the same degree that I am responsible for their intended consequences. But this idea is mistaken: the central concept of responsibility is not intention, but choice, and foresight is sufficient for choice, even though not for intention.[8] Another objection concentrates on the stringency of the consequentialist demand and suggests that in some cases it is

115

permissible, though less than ideal, to act in a way which, although it does not make the world as good as possible, comes up to a respectable standard of goodness.[9] This is certainly a legitimate criticism of consequentialism; but it is rather modest, and does not vindicate the position of those who think that in some cases it is positively wrong to do that which consequentialism implies that one ought to do.

I think that one can best see what is wrong with the Moorean principle through a simple example: supposing one knew that if one kept a promise one had made then two promises (of comparable seriousness etc.) made by others would be broken which would not otherwise be broken, would one take that as a good reason (*ceteris paribus*) not to keep one's own promise? Surely not.[10] Yet in such a situation by keeping one's own promise one would be deliberately failing to make the world as good as it would otherwise have been, at least as judged by reference to the neutral goods secured by promise-keeping. What underpins this, surely uncontentious, example is the fact that the duty created by a promise is owed by the promisor to the promisee; there is no comparable duty on us to ensure that promises made by others are kept. As such the situation is characteristic of that which applies to agent-relative duties: they record the moral significance of claims which arise from our relationships with particular individuals – in this case the relationship of trust created by the voluntary act of making a promise.

Once this is understood, the denial of Moore's supposedly self-evident principle no longer appears paradoxical. The mistake made by those who find agent-relative duties irrational is that for the purpose of moral deliberation they adopt an impersonal point of view which neutralises all their actual relationships with others, so that these relationships count for them only as *someone's* relationships and they can assign value to them only as instances of generally valuable relationships. But why should the fact of my relationships with others be neutralised in moral deliberation? Indeed it is not easy to retain a recognition of the ethical significance of such relationships whilst neutralising their application to one's own case. I suggested in the previous chapter that the goodness of states of affairs depends on the kinds of life that are worth leading, and that this latter conception makes essential reference to the virtues. But virtues such as justice and loyalty give rise to agent-relative duties, and there is therefore an incoherence in the conception of a life committed to the production of good states of affairs if this implies that one should neutralise the agent-relative duties respect for which is constitutive of practice of the virtues on which the conception of a good state of affairs depends.

The reasons for belief in the neutrality of morality are varied. One important one is itself a moral judgment – that it is *unfair* to attach any moral significance to one's relationships with others except in so far as one counts them as just someone's relationships. This judgment rests on a mistake about the domain of justice: there certainly are public contexts which demand impartiality and in which it is therefore unfair to attach significance to one's relationships with particular people involved. Any context in which some public rule (e.g. a law) is being administered, or some procedure for selection to a public post is being followed, is of this kind. But what applies in this way within the public domain does not apply universally: it is not nepotism for parents to think it right that they should give more of their attention to their own children than to others, and those who literally try to show equal concern for all will end up with no significant personal relationships with anyone. One cannot sustain such relationships while at the same time neutralising the demands which arise from them as soon as one engages in reflections as to how one should lead one's life.

A related confusion which assists the neutralist position is one between the position of a moral agent and that of a political authority. Those in political authority have far-reaching responsibilities for the welfare of citizens of their state; they have to take account of the implications of their policies for all citizens, who should matter equally to them. Moral agents are not in the same position; we are not responsible for each other's welfare, and it is essential to our ability to lead a life of our own that we are not. If we did, not only would we have unlimited duties to each other, we would also have to put up with unlimited interference from each other. This may sound callous; but the denial of responsibilities at a personal level comparable to those laid upon the legitimate authorities of the state is consistent with a concern for others that does not seek to assume responsibility for them.

Once it is allowed that a place has to be made for the deontologist's agent-relative duties in a moral theory which defines our obligations, there arises the issue as to how such a theory should be organised. Ross's theories, in *The Right and the Good* and *The Foundation of Ethics*, incorporate both agent-relative duties and agent-neutral goods. But he makes little attempt to organise them, and simply relies on intuition to resolve conflicts between them. A 'theory' of this kind is not a critical tool at all. Now it may be that the pursuit of a systematic theory of this kind is misguided; this was Bradley's claim (cf. *Ethical Studies* pp. 193ff.), recently revived by Williams.[11] None the less, we still require a framework for our moral and political reflections, and it seems to me that this can only be provided by interlocking conceptions of the self and the community which show how ethical values have a place within human life. To adopt this approach, however, is to abandon an assumption shared by Moore and his deontological critics, that the all-purpose concept of moral obligation is fundamental. On the alternative approach, there is a limited concept of obligation, understood as arising

117

from voluntary undertakings; but the only generic concept is that of a reason for action, and this is not specifically moral. The mark of moral reasons is that they arise from the thicker values (including obligations in the limited sense) constitutive of a life worth living within a well-ordered community; and it is by reflecting on the nature of such a life that we are able to bring whatever order we can to our moral deliberations.

Another line of thought which points in this direction concerns the ascription of intrinsic value to the virtues. A theory that treats the concept of moral obligation as the fundamental ethical concept can regard the exercise of virtuous dispositions as obligatory, and Moore somewhat grudgingly does so (*PE* pp. 177–8; Rashdall and Ross do so more enthusiastically).[12] But this only accommodates the virtues if their significance consists in no more than an obligation to perform certain actions for certain reasons, and whether we think of the obligation as strict or ideal, this does not seem right. The obligation to be kind is not strict in the way in which the obligation to respect the rights of others is. Yet kindness is not just an 'ideal' duty; on the contrary, we expect it of our friends and there are occasions in personal relationships where the claims of kindness override the demands of justice. Hence it appears that the significance of virtues other than justice is not adequately expressed through the ascription of intrinsic value, or obligatoriness, to their exercise. Indeed in his 1921 paper 'The Nature of Moral Philosophy' (in *PS*) Moore himself suggests as much; he distinguishes between 'rules of duty', which tell us what we ought to do, if we can, and 'ideal rules', which tell us what sort of person we ought to be even if we cannot readily become such a person.

This last point is not developed by Moore, so it is unclear how he would seek to integrate his 'ideal rules' into his ideal utilitarianism. But its implication is that in order to accommodate the significance of the virtues one needs to look beyond the structure of our obligations to act to questions about the kinds of life that are worth living. The attempt to pursue such questions, however, not only carries one beyond both Moore's ideal utilitarianism and his deontological critics; it also leads one back to ethical naturalism. One cannot begin to reflect on what kind of person one 'ought to be' without some assumptions about what kind of person one might be and a view about what these assumptions imply, without, that is, a theory of the self. Yet in neither *PE* nor *E* does Moore make any attempt to elucidate the place of morality and ethical judgment within human life. Instead he directs ethical concerns towards a world of non-natural objects and just takes for granted the importance of morality in human life. But without an account of the place of ethical values in human life there is no chance of a satisfactory account of the virtues, just as there was no chance of a satisfactory account of the relative importance of different intrinsic values or obligations. In both cases the absence of such an account is not a contingent feature of the ethical writings of Moore and his deontological critics: it is a consequence of the ethical non-naturalism within which Moore imprisoned ethical theory for half a century.

## 2: Common-sense morality

One of the odd features of PE is that chapter 5 precedes chapter 6. In chapter 1 Moore maintains, as a good consequentialist, that an account of the actions we ought to perform presupposes an account of what is good in itself. But in chapter 5 he tells us, in general terms, what we ought to do, while waiting until chapter 6 to give us his account of the ideal. The explanation of this is that he thinks that the obvious route from knowledge of what is intrinsically good to knowledge of what one ought to do in any particular situation is blocked by ignorance of the consequences of the possible actions available to one: 'it follows that we never have any reason to suppose that an action is our duty' (PE p. 149). But the resulting moral scepticism is not supposed to engender total moral paralysis.[13] For our situation is alleviated by the fact that we know the probable short-term consequences of actions of various general kinds; and we can therefore be confident that the general practice of much conventional morality is beneficial without detailed knowledge of what things are good in themselves.

This last claim rests on the following thesis:

> On any view commonly taken, it seems certain that the preservation
> of civilized society, which these rules are necessary to effect, is
> necessary for the existence, in any great degree, of anything which
> may be held to be good in itself.                    (PE p. 158)

This thesis is questionable: Moore's view (PE pp. 83–5) that a beautiful world of which no one is conscious is intrinsically good is not here accommodated. More seriously, the 'heroic' ideals of valour, honour, and loyalty notoriously conflict with the demands of 'civilized society'.[14] Still, one can agree with Moore that civilised society is a precondition of the attainment of most intrinsic goods, while rejecting his line of argument at this point. For his argument embodies an individualist assumption: he takes it that intrinsic goods concern only the states of individuals and not their social and political relations with others. With this assumption Moore can take it that much of conventional morality has instrumental value, as providing the constitutive rules of society within which alone the primary intrinsic goods can be enjoyed, without committing himself to what these goods are. But once one takes the view that some social and political conditions are intrinsic goods or evils, one cannot be easily confident of the value of conventional morality in ignorance of these goods. Moore endorses the prohibition on murder, respect for private property, industry, temperance, fidelity, but rejects chastity (*PE* pp. 157–8). This odd collection does not so much point towards Moore's ideals of love and beauty as bear witness to his lack of social and political reflection.

The individualist assumption concerning intrinsic goods need not by itself lead one to endorse conventional morality. In the hands of the classical utilitarians it was part of a radical critique of existing institutions. Moore, however, commits himself to a sceptical conservatism: 'it seems doubtful whether Ethics can establish the utility of any rules other than those generally practised' (*PE* p. 161). This leads to a result which, in the context of Moore's general position, is paradoxical: in fact (though not in theory) what we ought to do is largely independent of what is intrinsically good and is largely determined by the existence of rules which express widespread desires. The practice of these rules defines and reinforces them, so that 'the general utility of an action most commonly depends on the fact that it is generally practised' (p. 164); and the lack of serious alternatives arises from the widespread persistence of desires which would be frustrated were these rules not followed. Thus the prohibition of murder does not rest on the intrinsic evil of being killed; to establish this we would have to refute 'the main contention of pessimism – namely that the existence of human life is on the whole an evil' (p. 156), and this we cannot now do (at this point Moore's faith in his intuitionist method seems to have deserted him). Instead, it rests on the fact that most people do not want to be killed – as Moore put it, in a famously absurd passage:

> So long as men desire to live as strongly as they do, and so long as it
> is certain that they will continue to do so, anything which hinders
> them from devoting their energy to the attainment of positive goods
> seems plainly bad as a means. And the general practice of murder,
> falling so far short of universality as it certainly must in all known
> conditions of society, seems certainly to be a hindrance of this kind.
>
> (p. 157)[15]

Utilitarianism does not of course have to be as silly as this. What is none the less common in utilitarian thought is some departure from act-consequentialism as a model for moral reflection. Sidgwick noted that public reliance on such reflections in a predominantly non-utilitarian society is likely to be counterproductive (*The Methods of Ethics* pp. 489ff.). Moore accepts this point (*PE* pp. 163–4), but lays most stress on the merit of general rules in the light of our limited knowledge of the future (*PE* pp. 159–61).[16] Moore certainly exaggerates here; none the less, there are good reasons within an individual's economy of practical deliberation for restricting act-consequentialist reflection to theoretical matters. Hare's position concerning the two levels of moral thinking, 'critical' and 'intuitive', well exemplifies this point of view.[17] This is not a rule-consequentialist position: the theory remains act-consequentialist, and in cases to which no general rule applies (*PE* pp. 165–7) or more than one, with conflicting prescriptions (*The Methods of Ethics* chapter 2; Moore seems to have missed this important possibility), we have no option but to have recourse to act-consequentialist reflections, even though, according to Moore, these reflections will never yield even reasonable beliefs.

Moore's formulation of this position is, however, problematic. For, as Russell spotted at once,[18] he is led into explicit contradiction by allowing that our obligations are determined both by act-consequentialist facts and by the general rules that we are familiar with. The resulting contradiction is explicit in the following passage: 'In short, though we may be sure that there are cases where the rule should be broken, we can never know which those cases are, and ought, therefore, never to break it' (*PE* pp. 162–3). The problem here arises from the conflict between 'objective' and 'subjective' accounts of obligation. On the objective view, it is the objective facts about the available actions which determine one's obligations, whether or not one is aware of them: on the subjective view, it is one's beliefs, or the reasonable beliefs one could have had, about those facts that determine one's obligations. The distinction is not one between what one ought to do and what one thinks one ought to do; rather, on the subjective view, one ought to do that which, on the objective view, one just thinks one ought to do. Clearly, if one holds both views, and allows that mistakes occur, however reasonable one's beliefs, contradiction ensues.

Moore addressed this issue in *E*. Having presented his ideal utilitarian position as an objective account of obligation, he introduces the subjective view of obligation as 'the most serious' objection to the objective position he has presented (p. 98). For, he acknowledges, where an agent has entirely reasonable beliefs about the consequences of his actions and acts, as he thinks, for the best, it seems strange to hold that he may not have acted as he ought to have done. Indeed, Moore allows, 'There does seem to be a certain paradox in maintaining that . . . it can possibly be true that he *ought* to choose a course, which he has every reason to think will *not* be the best' (pp. 99–100). Yet, Moore argues, these considerations are not conclusive. For if we distinguish the question whether an agent was blameworthy from the question whether the action he performed was that which he ought to have performed, we can hold that subjective considerations are appropriate for the former question, but not the latter.

Although Moore's distinction is relevant, it is not obviously decisive, and Moore's position was challenged by Prichard in his eccentric paper 'Duty and Ignorance of Fact'.[19] Prichard here maintains that we unhesitatingly accept that in cases of action under uncertainty an agent ought to do what he thinks the situation requires. An important feature of the examples which Prichard advances to support this claim, however, is that they are cases in which where the agent does what he reasonably thinks the situation requires, but is in fact mistaken, no significant harm ensues. The action was in the event unnecessary, but because it was not harmful we are not inclined at first to demur from the thought that it still ought to have been performed. But if one turns to cases in which the agent's mistake, however reasonable, causes serious harm (e.g. an innocent person is convicted after a fair trial) one's judgment about what ought to have been done is surely modified on coming to learn the facts (e.g. one will judge that the innocent person ought not to have been convicted); and then contradiction will ensue if one persists with one's original judgment.

It is partly the need to accommodate retrospective criticism of this kind that motivates the objective account. A related point is that we seek to convince others of the facts in discussing with them how they ought to act, even if we think their contrary beliefs are quite reasonable. Finally, it is not clear how a subjective account of obligation could be internalised, since in considering how I ought to act, I ask myself about features of the courses of action available to me, and not about my beliefs about these features. For all these reasons, therefore, Moore's objectivist position seems right. Yet to leave matters there, and rely only on the proximity of questions about culpability to defuse subjectivist intuitions, does not seem enough. I think that what needs to be added is a recognition of the virtue of integrity, of doing what one thinks one morally ought to do. This is not a virtue that can play much part in first-person moral reflection; but this does not show that it has no role in judgments about others.

The point of introducing integrity is that it enables one to assign objective significance to action in accordance with the agent's own moral deliberations, and thus to incorporate a subjectivist intuition within an objectivist position. Yet what still needs clarification is the way in which acknowledgement of this virtue, along with other good motives, should be incorporated within ethical theory. Moore himself vacillated on this issue. In *PE* (pp. 177–9), though he derides the view, which he associates with Christianity and Kant, that a sense of duty is sufficient to make an action right, he assigns some intrinsic value to love of the good and a sense of duty, which must then be taken into account in considering what course of action is obligatory. In *E*, however, Moore argues that the moral assessment of actions as right or wrong, as opposed to the assessment of agents as praiseworthy or blameworthy, is

122

independent of questions about motives (pp. 94–8). This is the position which excludes all 'subjective' considerations from questions of what ought to be done, and which recognition of the virtue of integrity will lead one to qualify.

But just how should considerations of motives be introduced? The account offered in *PE* does not seem satisfactory, since it suggests that in choosing how to act we might choose in addition from what motive to act, whereas we do not normally have any such choice; so the ethical significance of motives is not well accommodated by just assigning them intrinsic value alongside states of affairs of other kinds. Instead one is here led back to the conclusion of the previous section, that we need to turn from an ethical theory that concentrates on what states of affairs one ought to bring into existence to one that first articulates the elements of a life that is worth leading. For, as Moore's thought in *E* shows, it is clear that motives will enter directly into an account of this latter kind; and in the light of such an account it will then be possible to define the relevance, or lack of it, of motives to the different kinds of questions to be asked of actions. In particular, it should be possible to distinguish between the principles agents should take account of in deliberating how to act and those which are relevant to third-person assessments of action. Because motives are not voluntary, they can have only an indirect role in the former; but that is no reason for not including them in the latter.

### 3: Egoism

Moore's discussion of egoism is notorious. The problem it raises can be approached via his account of duty. Moore takes over from the utilitarian tradition the thought that there is no substantive distinction between duty and expedience. But he allows that there is a point to the common-sense contrast between these concepts. For, he says, the conventional classification of duties picks out those expedient actions which we are often 'strongly tempted to omit', typically because their omission has disagreeable consequences only for others (p. 168). It would seem to follow from this that there is a serious point to the egoist's question as to why we should do our duty, since we are 'strongly tempted' not to. Moore, however, denies that this question has any serious point. For, he maintains, 'the only possible reason that can justify any action is that by it the greatest possible amount of good absolutely should be realised' (*PE* p. 101), and since duties are actions which realise the greatest possible amount of good, 'no further reason can possibly be given for doing what is duty, than simply that it is duty to do so' (as he puts it in *EE*).

This position, similar to that which Prichard was to present in 'Does Moral Philosophy Rest on a Mistake?'[20] rests on the assumption that the concept of a reason for action has to be understood in terms of impersonal ethical ends. This assumption is central to Moore's disagreement with Sidgwick, to which I alluded in the previous chapter (section 3). Having defined goodness in terms of desire, Sidgwick was in a position to contrast 'my good' with 'the good', and pose what he regarded as one of the 'profoundest questions of ethics' (*The Methods of Ethics* p. 110 fn.), whether it is rational to sacrifice one's own good for the sake of the good. Since he allowed that reasons for action are not inherently linked to the impersonal conception of the good, he famously concluded that an egoist who declines such self-sacrifice cannot be shown to be irrational. By contrast, once goodness is understood in Moore's impersonal way, and reasons for action are tied to goodness thus understood, his inference that it is indefensible to hold that the only reasons for me to act concern what is good for me seems correct. For having construed that which is 'good for me' as a possible state of affairs concerning me which is good in itself (*PE* pp. 98–9) he argues that since 'The only reason I can have for aiming at "my own good", is that it is *good absolutely* that what I so call should belong to me, . . . everyone else has as much reason for aiming at *my* having it, as I have myself ' (*PE* p. 99). Equivalently, therefore, I have as much reason for aiming at things that are *good absolutely* which do not concern me as I have for aiming at good things which do concern me.

The difficulty with Moore's position, however, is to see what it has to do with egoism. For the terms in which the argument is conducted in *PE* are defined in such a way that egoism is not here discussed at all.[21] This is apparent in his argument that egoism is not merely irrational, but self-contradictory: 'What Egoism holds, therefore, is that *each* man's happiness is the sole good – that a number of different things are *each* of them the only good thing there is – an absolute contradiction' (*PE* p. 99). This 'idiocy which it seems to have been left to Moore to ascribe to him'[22] is ascribed by Moore to the egoist only by ascribing to him an impersonal conception of reason that he would immediately repudiate. Moore argues that since whatever I have reason to aim at anyone has reason to aim at, and vice versa, it follows that if the egoist maintains that I have reason to aim only at my good, he is committed to holding that my good must the only thing anyone has reason to aim at, i.e. it must be the sole good. Since the first premiss of this argument is the denial of the egoist's position, that each person has reason only to aim at his own good, it is not surprising that when combined with that position, self-contradiction results. But that is scarcely an argument against the egoist.[23]

In *E* Moore is not quite so obtuse. He here presents the egoist as challenging the consequentialist principle and maintaining that one is under no obligation to sacrifice one's own good to the general good (pp. 118–21). Though he does not suggest that this challenge is incoherent, he does not develop the issues at stake, and is content to dismiss without argument the egoist position he has presented as self-evidently mistaken. Yet to revert to my starting-point, what about the 'strong temptation' not to do one's duty? Does not Moore's acknowledgement of this give the egoist all he needs to set up his position as *prima facie* sensible? Moore will interpret this as a disinclination to promote intrinsic goods that do not concern oneself and, while recognising its psychological reality, deny it any security against rational reflective criticism. But the egoist can respond that Moore's attempts to establish this irrationality are question-begging, since they assume precisely the neutral conception of practical reason that he is challenging; and if one looks at the way in which Moore argues, this response seems just. The issue that arises, therefore, is why it is that Moore failed to comprehend what the egoist's position really is. After all, he was a pupil of Sidgwick.

I think that, at least in *PE*, Moore's incomprehension of egoism is the product of three beliefs: (i) reasons for action are propositions; (ii) propositions are objective; (iii) the self is not objective. These last two theses come from Moore's pure realism (cf. chapter 2); their implication is that propositions initially conceived as concerning oneself are, objectively, just propositions about such things as G.E. Moore. This result imposes a constraint sufficient on the first thesis sufficient to exclude the egoist from practical reason. For his reasons for action concern propositions which concern himself, and he regards this reflexive characterisation of them as essential to their being reasons for him to act. But the second and third theses rule out reasons for action of this kind: the propositions which constitute one's reasons for action are never essentially propositions concerning oneself. So in thinking how to act we should take it that we confront a world of propositions from which the self is absent.

This is only a reconstruction of a line of thought Moore never spells out. It is roughly the line of thought which Nagel develops in *The Possibility of Altruism*[24] to the effect that all reasons for action must be 'objective', and Nagel indeed says here (p. 86) that he wants to explain what Moore assumed in his discussion of egoism. As Nagel has since noted[25] the relevant conception of objectivity is that of agent-neutrality, and the objection to the egoist is therefore that his reasons for action are essentially agent-relative. Since deontology also requires agent-relative reasons for action, the argument at this point connects with my previous discussion of Moore's consequentialism. His commitment to the neutrality of reasons for action explains why he held both egoism and deontology to be irrational.

Moore's error here is not a simple mistake. There is a conception of the world from which the self is properly absent – the 'absolute' conception of the world as it is in itself.[26] Someone who abstracts from his own identity in forming such a conception of the world will indeed be unable to find any application for agent-relative reasons for action, egoistic or deontological. But, equally, it is unclear how such a person can have any reasons for action at all: for the self figures essentially in the question 'What am I to do?'; it is only if Moore acknowledges that he is GEM that the thought that GEM has reason to do something will move him to action. Thus the practical perspective requires more than the absolute, impersonal, conception of the world; it requires knowledge of where we fit into the world, and with this comes the intelligibility of egoism. It does not, of course, follow from this that egoism is defensible. But what does, I think, follow is that the question of egoism has to be taken more seriously than Moore's presumptions seem to have permitted him to do.

## 4: The principle of organic unities

Moore lays much emphasis in PE on the 'principle of organic unities'. This is the principle that 'the value of a whole must not be assumed to be the same as the sum of the values of its parts' (PE p. 28). Moore's use here of quantitative idioms implies that one should be able to set up a cardinal scale for the intrinsic value of states of affairs of different kinds. This implication is unsustainable; there is no sensible way to define a 'unit' of intrinsic value. Furthermore, the purpose of any such project is undermined by the principle of organic unities which entails that putative quantitative calculations concerning intrinsic value are always indecisive.

Once intrinsic value is analysed in terms of obligation, and quantitative idioms are eliminated, the principle of organic unities appears as the principle that our obligation to bring about a complex state of affairs does not depend only on the relative obligatoriness of those features of it whose existence, if they were to occur by themselves, we ought to bring about or eliminate. For, according to the principle, the combination of all these features in a potential state of affairs is also relevant to our obligation to bring it about. This relevance constitutes the 'value as a whole' of the state (PE pp. 214–15). Linked to this concept is that of the 'value as a part' of a feature of a complex state of affairs. Moore initially says that something is good as a part where it is any 'part' of a 'whole' which is intrinsically good (PE p. 35). But the cases he is interested in are those in which the absence of a feature from a complex state of affairs produces a state of less intrinsic value than would have been the case had the feature been present, and it is best to confine the concept good as a part to features of this kind (as Moore does later; cf. E p. 130). The principle of organic unities then assures us that a state of affairs having just that feature need not be itself intrinsically good; and the dialectical importance of the principle of organic unities is that Moore holds that some states which are often thought to be intrinsically good are in fact only, or primarily, good as parts – e.g. knowledge (*PE* p. 199) and pleasure (*PE* p. 213; *E* pp. 124–5).

One problem with the principle of organic unities, when applied in an unrestricted fashion, is that it engenders a form of moral scepticism. Since my actions belong to the total history of the universe, they may have value as parts of this history whatever their intrinsic or instrumental value. Hence, even supposing that I did have knowledge of the intrinsic and instrumental value of each course of action open to me, without knowledge of the value as a part of the history of each possible Universe of each course of action, I could not know which course of action was best overall (cf. *PE* pp. 184–5, 207). Furthermore it might be the case that a course of action which is intrinsically and instrumentally very evil is none the less an essential constituent of the best possible universe, and thus the best course of action, all things considered. In *PE* Moore disavows any such theodicy (p. 220), but in an earlier Apostles' paper he had, perhaps only flippantly, toyed with this thought; it is not, he here says, that there are no bad things, 'but that you can generally . . . by regarding them in relation to others find more good than if they were not there'.[27]

The principle of organic unities is strongly reminiscent of Absolute idealism. Indeed it is expressly stated by Bradley, who objected to Sidgwick in the following terms:

> No doubt a mere quantity is no more than the sum of its units, and
> to find the value of each unit no doubt you must isolate it by division.
> But tacitly to assume that the moral world is a mere sum of units,
> whose value can be found separately, is really nothing but an
> enormous piece of moral dogmatism.
>
> (*Ethical Studies* pp. 126–7)

The question that arises, therefore, is whether Moore can have his principle of organic unities without a commitment to the metaphysical organic wholes of Absolute idealism. For it seems irrational to hold that any 'whole' is no more than the sum of its parts (this is Moore's metaphysical doctrine) but that the intrinsic value of such a whole is not determined by the values of its parts. The intrinsic value of a whole as a whole seems to be a *deus ex machina* which is liable to interfere with the evaluation of situations in a random fashion. Indeed, the principle subverts Moore's defence of 'casuistry', i.e. the use of general principles in moral reflection (*PE* pp. 4–5). Bradley's attack on casuistry (*Ethical Studies* pp. 196–7), to which Moore is here responding, simply takes as its premiss the organic unities doctrine and then infers that reference to general principles will not determine what one ought to do in particular situations. Since Moore is committed to Bradley's premiss, he is likewise committed to the sceptical thrust of his conclusion.

The way to pursue further the role of the principle in Moore's theory is to consider why he thought he required it. At one point he uses it to defend a retributive theory of punishment, according to which 'the infliction of pain on a person whose state of mind is bad, may, if the pain be not too intense, create a state of things that is better *on the whole* than if the evil state of mind had existed unpunished' (*PE* p. 214). Moore is here using the principle because it enables him to present an alternative to the familiar utilitarian justifications of punishment. The trouble here is that the principle's role is just that of a *deus ex machina*: somehow, the infliction of pain – a condition that is, for Moore, intrinsically evil – produces an outcome that is intrinsically better than without it. This is the irrational use of the principle which will permit a theodicy. Moore's ethics and the retributive theory of punishment are better off without it.

This is, however, not a typical case. Moore generally employs the principle to justify such thoughts as that an appropriately pleasant consciousness of beauty is a state of affairs of very great intrinsic value, even though pleasure, consciousness, and beauty, are by themselves of little or no positive intrinsic value, and a similarly pleasant consciousness of what is ugly would be intrinsically evil (*PE* p. 190; cf. pp. 28–9, 93–4). In cases of this kind there seems some point to the principle: the value of a pleasure is not independent of the value of that in which pleasure is taken. However, the principle has some point here only because of connections between the features involved which make its application strained.[28] It is because taking pleasure in an activity is a way of thinking about the value of the activity that the value of pleasure is inseparable from the value of the activity in which pleasure is taken. Moore does not approach the point in this way. He treats pleasure as a simple feeling (*PE* pp. 12–13) which occurs as a discriminable aspect of complex states of consciousness, which he calls 'enjoyments' (*PE* p. 188). Where pleasure is conceived in this way, as comparable to physical pain, the application of the principle of organic unities to pleasures is both straightforward (it is a 'part' of the 'whole' enjoyment) and irrational – why does the context in which the feeling occurs make a difference to its value? By contrast, once pleasure is conceived as itself intentional, and intentionally related to that in which pleasure is taken, the application of the principle to pleasures becomes strained, but the result is none the less acceptable. Where someone takes sadistic pleasure in causing suffering to another, the thought that this pleasure mitigates even slightly the evil of the situation is undermined when the sadist's pleasure is interpreted as enjoyment of cruelty, so that we recognise him as someone who thinks that cruelty is worth practising for its own sake.

My conclusion is, therefore, that the principle of organic unities has some merit just where the grounds for its application are at best strained. It applies best to complex states of mind, whose intentional interrelationships are such that the 'part/whole' terminology fits them badly; and in so far as it can be applied elsewhere, e.g. to works of art and social situations, I think analogous points apply. The difficulty in all such cases is to characterise the nature of the connections between the elements of a whole. One wants more than causality but less than the mutual necessitation characteristic of Absolute idealism. The case I have discussed involves intentional relationships, but it is not clear how far this point should be generalised. This difficulty, however, does not controvert the general point that Moore cannot have his ethical organic unities without some more substantive organic wholes.

### 5: The ideal

The last chapter, on *The Ideal*, is the best in the book. . . . It is quite extraordinary and surprising with what certainty the author is able to appeal to our intuitive perception of values, not only in regard to fairly simple matters, but even in very complex and elaborate organic unities. There is a keen pleasure, as we read, in the sure assent with which we follow his estimates.

Thus Russell, in his review of *PE*.[29] It is hard now to tell how striking Moore's commitment to the primacy of love and beauty appeared to his contemporaries. If one looks back to *PE* with the perspective supplied by Bloomsbury, parts of its final chapter read like a manifesto. Yet McTaggart had for some years extolled the value of love, and the value of art is a central theme of romanticism. But these values had never before been so straightforwardly proclaimed as they are in the final chapter of *PE*. For since Moore's judgments concerning intrinsic value are supposed to be intuitive, he presents his values without the discursive justifications with which they occur in other works, and it is the directness of this proclamation which gave Moore's ideal its impact. Equally, because it is just a direct proclamation, it will not do. Values are not in this way discerned; which is not to say that love and beauty are not values.

Moore's early writings include many affirmations of the value of love and beauty. The most emphatic affirmation of the value of beauty occurs in the 1901 essay on 'Art, Morals, and Religion':

What is beautiful is certainly an end-in-itself. But further I cannot see but what that which is meant by beautiful is simply and solely that which is an end-in-itself. The object of art would then be that to which the objects of morals are means, and the only things to which they are means. The only reasons for having virtues would be to produce works of art.

As this passage shows, Moore's affirmations of the value of beauty sometimes merge into definitions of beauty as intrinsic value which threaten to trivialise the initial claim. This certainly happens in *PE*. Moore says here (p. 189) that the admiring contemplation of beauty is one of the greatest of intrinsic goods, but he goes on to define beauty as that of which the admiring contemplation is good (p. 201); and the same vacuousness afflicts his account of intrinsic evils (pp. 208–9). These problems are compounded by the fact that Moore's theory has a quasi-recursive structure, in which complex goods and evils are defined in terms of simpler ones, of which aesthetic enjoyment is supposed to be a prime case. Thus, his account of the value of love turns into a thesis about the great value of the appreciation of another person's appreciation of beauty:

> Though . . . we may admit that the appreciation of a person's attitude towards other persons, or, to take one instance, the love of love, is far the most valuable good we know, and far more valuable than the mere love of beauty, yet we can only admit this if the first be understood to include the latter.
>
> (*PE* p. 204)

But if the love of beauty is just love of that which it is good to love, then the love of love, Moore's greatest good, is itself defined in terms of goodness. Clearly, this is not a deep problem. Once Moore drops the definition of beauty in terms of goodness (as he does implicitly in CIV – cf. p. 253) this problem does not arise. Yet the definition at least explains why beauty is of such great intrinsic value (the only trouble is that it succeeds too well); without it, Moore needs an aesthetic theory which provides such an explanation. Despite Moore's scattered remarks about aesthetic issues in chapter 6 of *PE* and elsewhere, it is hard to envisage him doing so.

There are two goods whose identification as such in *PE* is not affected by Moore's unsatisfactory definition of beauty. Significantly, these are pleasure and the absence of pain (or, rather, consciousness of these states); of these, the latter is far more important, for 'pain appears to be a far worse evil than pleasure is a good' (p. 212). Their presence in Moore's ideal raises the question of his attitude to hedonism. Though Moore says that his practical conclusions are largely in line with those proposed by hedonists (p. 62; Moore has Sidgwick in mind here), he strongly opposed hedonism itself. His objection is basically that of Carlyle to J.S. Mill: hedonism is the pig's philosophy (*E* p. 25). Perhaps

130

relying on the experience of some of his Apostolic brethren, Moore invokes common-sense to repudiate this philosophy: 'it is commonly held that certain of what would be called the lowest forms of sexual enjoyment, for instance, are positively bad, although it is by no means clear that they are not the most pleasant states we ever experience' (p. 95). Moore cannot of course allow himself to argue against hedonism; even common-sense is only invoked *ad hominem* against Sidgwick. All we can do, officially at least, is to isolate reflectively the consciousness of pleasure and by comparing it with other isolated states (e.g. the contemplation of beauty) see that it is not the only good thing. As I have observed, this is a hopeless method for ethical reflection. None the less Moore's discussion of pleasure provides the basis for an effective argument against hedonism. I suggested in the previous section that although Moore himself seems to have conceived pleasure as a uniform type of sensation (which fits well with the hedonist position), his application of the principle of organic unities to types of pleasure suggests a more complex conception according to which pleasure includes a judgment about the positive value of that in which pleasure is taken. Once this conception of pleasure is adopted, the hedonist position is undermined.

Although Moore rejected generic hedonism, it does not follow that he is not a refined hedonist, with intrinsic goods which largely match Mill's top-quality pleasures (in chapter 2 of *Utilitarianism*). Moore rightly criticises Mill's attempt to combine his qualitative distinctions between pleasures with his generic hedonism (*PE* pp. 77–9); but once the generic hedonism is rejected, Moore is free to affirm the top-quality pleasures without Mill's problems, and in *E* he does indeed advance this position (p. 214). This position is, however, a modification of the view propounded in *PE*, that there are intrinsic goods which are not pleasures – indeed they are not even personal states or relationships.

The reason for this claim is embodied in his famous two-world argument (*PE* pp. 83–4): independent of any reference to states of consciousness, actual or possible, it is better that there should exist an exquisitely beautiful world than a disgustingly ugly one, a 'heap of filth'. Moore presents his argument as a thought-experiment for whose conclusion no further considerations need be advanced; if anything, my intuitions go the other way. Suppose I am confronted by a machine concerning which I know that it will produce an object of great beauty if I press one button, and a heap of filth if I press another, and that the machine will destroy whatever it produces a moment later, before any being of any kind can appreciate what was produced. It seems wholly immaterial which button I press. Yet there are real issues which connect with Moore's intuition that there are intrinsic goods which do not concern human life, arising from conflicts between human goods and the needs of other species. For although conservationists rightly appeal to a human interest in the preservation of non-human species in their natural habitat, they also encourage us to abandon our speciesist concern with human goods, and find intrinsic value in the preservation of the variety of evolved species.

There is much to be said on this issue. I think that any defence of the Moorean thesis that there are non-human intrinsic goods requires the articulation of an ethical perspective which places human life within a context which reveals an exclusive concern with human goods as parochial. Many religions provide such a perspective (though Christianity does so to a lesser extent than most others).[30] But in the absence of any religious or metaphysical assumptions it is not easy to achieve this, and Moore's actual thought-experiment in *PE* is unpersuasive partly because it lacks any such general ethical perspective.

Some time between *PE* and *E* Moore changed his mind on this point, and took up the characteristic Bloomsbury view that it is only states of consciousness that have intrinsic value (*E* p. 129). He never explains why he changed his mind on this point, nor does he consider the view that there are human goods which are not states of consciousness. But there is a phrase which he employs in *PE* and thereafter which is revealing: in the passage which leads up to the proclamation that personal affections and aesthetic enjoyments are by far the greatest goods, Moore says that we must 'consider strictly what things are worth having purely for their own sakes' (p. 188). The phrase 'worth having for their own sakes' is here (and, I think, only here in *PE*) being used as a synonym for 'intrinsically good'; Moore later proposed it as an informal account, though not an analysis, of intrinsic goodness.[31] What is significant about this phrase is, first, that there are things to which it cannot be sensibly applied – e.g. a beautiful world experienced by no one (unlike states of consciousness). Second, the phrase is most naturally understood to apply to those things which we have an intrinsic interest in having. That is, the use of the phrase 'worth having for their own sakes' as a synonym for 'intrinsically good' strongly suggests a naturalistic account of goodness. Moore is of course deeply committed to repudiating any such naturalist account of goodness. But it is by covertly presenting his greatest goods to us as natural goods, things which it is worth our having for their own sake, that his claims for them have whatever plausibility they do have.

Moore takes the greatest goods to be, not love and beauty themselves (the latter of which is not a state of consciousness at all), but a pleasurable appreciation of them by those who understand them properly. It is this feature of Moore's ideal which warrants the imputation of a refined hedonism to him, of the kind manifest in the lives and writings characteristic of Bloomsbury. Moore's friend Clive

Bell, who formulated the influential definition of beauty as 'significant form', linked this with a conception of 'aesthetic ecstasy', the emotional appreciation of beauty, which he regarded as one of the greatest of goods because the pleasure involved is of a specially intense variety.[32] In the following passage Bell invokes Moore's authority for this view (presumably Moore is exempted from the strictures of the last sentence, which matches Moore's views about his contemporaries):

> It is not denied that the civilized man in search of exquisite pleasure is, and must be, an amateur of exquisite states of mind. Wherefore let the professors of ethics give him their blessing.
>
> But ethical systems are dull at best, and the tendency of professors to confound ethics with conventional morality too often renders them downright disgusting.[33]

This refined hedonism has two distinctive features. First, it is elitist: for even though knowledge is ascribed no intrinsic value, knowledge of certain kinds, especially that relevant to the appreciation of art, is a crucial element within these ideal pleasures (*PE* p. 199). Hence those who lack this knowledge cannot participate in the ideal; their pleasures are of very little intrinsic value. Second, it is a private ideal, a sort of religion, as Keynes described it.[34] For the public affairs of state are largely irrelevant to the attainment of the ideal pleasures. As such it underlines Moore's lack of concern for the social and political dimensions of ethics. Describing Cambridge in 1900, Bell wrote 'Philosophically we were dominated by Moore, and politics we despised'; the juxtaposition is no accident.[35] It does not follow that there is no place in an ethical theory oriented towards Moore's ideal for a concern with institutions which protect personal relationships (e.g. the family) and nurture the practice and appreciation of the arts. There is in fact a direct line of influence from Moore through Keynes and Bell to the present day British Arts Council. But the central concerns of politics are by-passed by this refined hedonism. Leonard Woolf once sought to defend Moore from Keynes's description of his ideal as wholly unworldly.[36] But when one sees that Moore's 'divine voice of plain common sense', as Woolf put it, proclaimed only a cautious conservatism with respect to conventional morality and nothing at all with respect to politics, Keynes's description is confirmed. And it is because Moore's ideal is essentially private that those who try to live by it alone may find that their respect for the ties of friendship makes them victims of the treachery of their friends, as the fate of that erstwhile Apostle and art historian, Anthony Blunt, shows.

The elitism and the unworldliness of Moore's ideal rules it out of consideration as a satisfactory basis for a theory of justice, which has to concern itself with more mundane, and thus more universal, goods. None the less Moore's ideal does have a place in ethical reflection – as a personal ideal, in the sense that it articulates the possibility of a life distinctively committed to friendship and art, at least where the circumstances of individual freedom and the demands of public affairs permit such a commitment. *Moore's* ethical theory does not readily accommodate this way of conceiving his ideal. For him, it is the *summum bonum* within a supposedly all-embracing account of moral obligation; but this was one of the unsatisfactory aspects of his theory, and an ethical theory liberated from it can find a different place for Moore's ideal. In this sense, Bloomsbury took its ideal from Moore, and Bell, the most perspicacious exponent of the implications of Moore's ideal, spelled it out thus:

> The best man – if good mean anything – will be he who is capable of the best states of mind and enjoys them longest. It is among artists, philosophers, and mystics, with their intense and interminable ecstasies of contemplation and creation, that we must look for our Saints.[37]

The fact that this ideal was initially misrepresented as resting on 'the ultimate and fundamental truth of Moral Philosophy' (*PE* p. 189) should not blind us to the great value of the works produced by those whose lives were informed by it.

### 6: Free will

Although much of Moore's *Ethics* is only a rather pedestrian restatement of themes from *PE*, there is one famous chapter in which Moore discussed a topic he had not discussed in *PE* – free will. Moore had of course discussed this topic before, in F, and there is a very long (and very poor) discussion of it in EE. On both these occasions Moore had endorsed determinism, in the belief that Kant had established its truth, and I think that the absence of any discussion of free will in *PE* is connected with Moore's loss of faith in this argument. In *E* he does not commit himself to determinism (although in *SMPP* he rather implies that he still accepted it – cf. pp. 159–62). But it is still a compatibilist thesis that he advances in *E*, albeit rather tentatively – 'this chapter must conclude with a doubt' (p. 115).

Unfortunately, Moore commences his discussion in *E* in a thoroughly unsatisfactory manner. In chapter 1 he introduces the conception of a 'voluntary action' as an action which the agent could have avoided, and says that the theory he is going to discuss is a theory about the conditions under which voluntary actions are right or wrong. He adds here: 'whether any actions, except voluntary ones, can be properly said to be right or wrong . . . is again a question which our theory does not presume to answer' (p. 6). However, in the opening paragraphs of chapter 6, he implies that it is only voluntary actions that are right or wrong and this connects with his belief that determinism poses a threat to his theory. For if it is only voluntary actions that are right and wrong, then the view that determinism entails that no action is voluntary implies that determinism entails that 'no action of ours is ever right and none is ever wrong' (p. 104), which is supposed to conflict with the ideal utilitarian theory which 'implies, on the contrary, that we very often do act *wrongly*, if never quite rightly' (p. 104).

What reason does Moore offer for the thesis that only voluntary actions are right or wrong? So far as I can see, he takes it to be a prerequisite of his ideal utilitarian theory:

> It [the ideal utilitarian theory] does, therefore, hold that the question whether an action is right or wrong does always depend upon a comparison of its consequences with those of all the other actions which the agent *could* have done instead. It assumes, therefore, that wherever a voluntary action is right or wrong (and we have throughout been talking of *voluntary* actions), it is true that the agent *could*, in a sense, have done something else instead. This is an absolutely essential part of the theory.
>
> (*E* pp. 102–3)

This is a difficult passage. Since voluntary actions are by definition those where the agent could have done something else instead, the second sentence does not need the support of the first. Furthermore from this analytic truth, and the fact that the theory applies only to voluntary actions, nothing follows about whether non-voluntary actions can be said to be right or wrong. But the intended conclusion of this passage, which is employed throughout the following discussion, is that the theory requires that only voluntary actions are right or wrong. To find anything like this conclusion within the quoted passage one has to omit the word 'voluntary' and the parenthesis from the second sentence. Thus emended the sentence is not an analytic truth and is the thesis employed in the ensuing argument. It is also a claim which might be thought to be supported by the first sentence which mentions the need for a comparison between an agent's actual action and those which he might have performed instead. Yet there is still no good argument here for the intended conclusion. The ideal utilitarian theory does not require that there were possible alternatives to an agent's actual course of action, unless the theory is stipulatively restricted to voluntary actions. If an agent's action was the only one possible for him, then *ipso facto*, it was the best possible, even though it was not voluntary.

The result is that Moore provides no good reason for his thesis that only voluntary actions can be right or wrong, which provides the context for his discussion of free will. To do better, we need to introduce a familiar thought about moral responsibility, to the effect that it is not just to praise or blame agents for actions which are not voluntary. It will only follow that only voluntary actions are right or wrong if one assumes that what is neither justly praised nor justly blamed is neither right nor wrong. Such an assumption can be defended, but Moore explicitly rejects it in *E* (pp. 97–8). Still, this does not matter, for the issue as to whether or not praise and blame are ever just provides an adequate context for a discussion of free will. What is, none the less, worth observing is that this familiar thesis concerning moral responsibility is an ethical thesis, which determinism cannot show to be false. So determinism cannot pose a threat to all ethical judgments in the way that Moore supposes. Furthermore, it is a much-debated question whether ideal utilitarianism itself implies this ethical judgment concerning moral responsibility. If, as I believe, this implication does not hold, then on any understanding of voluntary action, determinism poses no threat at all to ideal utilitarianism – a conclusion which is the opposite of Moore's view that it poses 'an extremely serious and fundamental objection to our theory' (p. 104).

Once Moore's discussion of free will is re-oriented around the issue of moral responsibility, the threat posed by determinism is obvious. Moore's response is that the sense in which a voluntary action is one which the agent 'could have avoided' is consistent with the determinist's belief that the agent 'could not have done otherwise'. For the determinist employs an 'absolute' (p. 103) sense of 'could not have done otherwise', and this is consistent with the conditional freedom constitutive of voluntariness, which Moore initially expresses by saying that the agent 'could have acted differently, if he had chosen' (pp. 5, 12, 103) and later expresses by saying that the agent 'would have acted differently, if he had chosen' (pp. 110ff.).

Moore argues for his conditional account of voluntariness by introducing the topic of abilities. He gives three examples of contrasting abilities and inabilities: his ability to walk a mile in twenty minutes that morning, as contrasted with his inability to run a mile in two minutes then: the ability of cats to climb trees, as contrasted with the inability of dogs to do so: the ability of one ship to steam at twenty knots, as contrasted with the inability of another to do so. He then claims that these contrasts, and thus the possession of the abilities, are not called into question by determinism; for, he suggests, possession of an ability depends upon whether an agent can secure performance of an appropriate action at will. Both of these points are problematic. The first comes close to begging the question when applied to Moore's first example; and the second point is not readily applicable to the second and third examples. Moore suggests that the contrasting abilities of the two ships can be elucidated by reference to the different ways in which the ships

136

would perform if those in control of them made appropriate choices. But the capacities of inanimate objects need not be under human control (consider the speeds at which sailing boats can sail). And Moore's failure to say anything at all about the application of his second point to the abilities of cats and dogs is eloquent.[38]

Moore's treatment of abilities was famously criticised by J.L. Austin in his 1956 lecture 'Ifs and Cans'.[39] Austin certainly showed that the topic was more complicated, more of a 'can of worms' (in Dennett's nice phrase[40]), than Moore had envisaged. Austin's lecture in its turn has attracted criticism, especially from Chisholm and Pears,[41] and the outcome seems to me to be that a roughly Moorean position concerning abilities can be defended. But I do not propose to cover all that ground here. For although Moore treats voluntariness as the ability to do otherwise and then argues for his conditional analysis and compatibilist conclusion via his general treatment of abilities, this argument is not essential to his analysis; and what I want to do in the rest of this chapter is to see how Moore's position stands up to criticisms of it that derive from arguments advanced more recently by van Inwagen, Chisholm, and Frankfurt, which can be assessed without the need to explore fully the 'can of worms'.

Moore's position can be reconstructed in terms of three propositions: first, that an agent's action is free, in the sense that she is morally responsible, just where she could have done otherwise; following Frankfurt, I shall call this the 'alternate possibility' condition. The second proposition is the conditional analysis of this condition; and the third proposition is that where the alternate possibility condition is thus analysed its satisfaction is consistent with the truth of determinism. My three critics of Moore can now be regarded as raising objections to each of these propositions.

I shall start by discussing van Inwagen's argument against the third proposition.[42] Let us suppose that at the present time $t$ Jane does not raise her hand; could she have raised her hand at $t$, if determinism is true? Van Inwagen argues that, even if a conditional analysis is assumed, she could not. He starts from a characterisation of determinism: he takes it to imply that the laws of nature ($L$) are such that, in conjunction with a description of the state of the world many millions of years ago ($Po$), they entail a description of the state of the world at the present time $t$ ($Pt$), which includes the fact that Jane does not raise her hand at $t$; i.e.

(1) If determinism is true, then ($Po$ & $L$ entails $Pt$).

Van Inwagen next introduces an idiom 'renders false' whose sense is to be such that if Jane raises her hand at $t$, she 'renders false' $Pt$; thus, if Jane could have raised her hand at $t$, she could have rendered false $Pt$.

But if Jane could have rendered false $Pt$, and $Pt$ is entailed by $L$ and $Po$, then Jane could have rendered false the conjunction of $Po$ and $L$; i.e.

(2) If determinism is true and Jane could have rendered false $Pt$ then Jane could have rendered false ($Po$ & $L$).

But, van Inwagen argues, since $Po$ concerns the distant past, and one cannot alter the past, it is in general true, for all propositions $q$, that:

(3) If Jane could have rendered false ($Po$ & $q$) then Jane could have rendered false $q$.

Furthermore, since $L$ is the set of laws of nature, we must also accept that:

(4) Jane could not have rendered false $L$.

But the result of combining (2),(3), and (4) is that the antecedent of (2) must be false; i.e. that it cannot be the case both that determinism is true and that Jane could have rendered false $Pt$, contrary to the compatibilist's hypothesis.

As van Inwagen observes, although this conclusion conflicts with Moore's compatibilist thesis, the argument does not invoke any particular conception of possibility. Hence there is no reason to suppose that a Moorean conditional analysis enables one to elude van Inwagen's conclusion. I think that there is in fact a connection here, but it is best first to introduce the issue on which critical discussion of van Inwagen's argument has largely focused – the status of his proposition (3).[43] Van Inwagen presents it as something we should accept on its own merits, but in thinking about it it helps to consider the related issue as to whether Jane could have rendered false $Po$. Where 'renders false' is understood as van Inwagen originally defined it, this is not true: for he defined it in such a way that the falsity of $Po$ would have had to be entailed by Jane's doing something which she could do, and since the laws of nature are not logically necessary, no such entailment obtains. The truth of (4) is similarly uncontestable, where 'renders false' is so understood. This might seem to give van Inwagen all that he wants, without the need to employ (3) at all; but this is not so. For, thus understood, one cannot infer 'Jane could not have rendered false ($Po$ & $L$)' from 'Jane could not have rendered false $Po$' and 'Jane could not have rendered false $L$'; the fallacy would be comparable to that of supposing that because '$x$ is human' entails '$x$ is male or $x$ is female' then either '$x$ is human' entails '$x$ is male' or '$x$ is human' entails '$x$ is female'.

I am not accusing van Inwagen of committing this fallacy; he wants

(3) to be acceptable on its own merits, and (3) and (4) certainly do produce the conclusion he wants. The difficulty, however, is to see on what grounds (3) should be accepted when 'renders false' is understood in the original sense. Since the idiom 'renders false' is van Inwagen's artificial idiom, he cannot here appeal to unreflective modal intuitions; and the compatibilist can explain away any initial inclination to accept it by referring to the fallacy I have just described. In his later work van Inwagen, recognising that he needs to say more in support of (3), has modified his account of 'renders false': he now suggests that the propositions Jane renders false are those whose falsity is entailed by the conjunction of the fact that she acts as she does and the fact that the past has been as it actually was.[44] This certainly seems to help, for (3) is now indisputable: since $Po$ is definitely entailed by the conjunction of Jane's action and the past being as it actually was, if that conjunction also entails $\sim (Po \And q)$ it must entail $\sim q$. But now the problem has been shifted to (4); for where 'renders false' is understood in this revised sense, the compatibilist will want to say that Jane can 'render false' the laws of nature (for, given the deterministic assumption (1), their falsity is entailed by the conjunction of $Po$ and $\sim Pt$). And although this sounds odd, the compatibilist can maintain that the oddity is a consequence of van Inwagen's revised definition of 'renders false', not of his own position.

At this point the dispute is in danger of becoming bogged down in an artificial debate about what it is to 'render false' a proposition, and the argument is therefore best conducted in other terms. The Moorean compatibilist will certainly allow that something like (2) is correct: because determinism is true, if Jane could have raised her arm at $t$ then either the laws of nature need not have been as they are or the past could have been other than it was. Furthermore, he will allow that since, by the standards of natural necessity the laws of nature could not have been other than they are, by those standards, that Jane could have raised her arm implies that the past could have been different. But he will say, this is indeed possible where the possibility is conditional; for although van Inwagen's determinism implies that the past was itself determined of natural necessity, this determination is always relative to some earlier past. So another past was possible (if the earlier past had been different, which it would have been if . . .). In this way therefore, the Moorean compatibilist will want to say, not that Jane could have altered the past, but that, even allowing for determinism, there could have been a past which led to Jane's doing something which she did not do.

Although this point embodies the substance of the Moorean response to van Inwagen, more needs to be said to undermine the plausibility of his argument. The intuition behind (3) can be expressed in terms of an asymmetry between the past and the future: we allow that Jane could have altered the future where she could have done something which implies that the future would not be as it will be; but since we do not allow that Jane could alter the past, should we allow that she could have done something which implies that past would not have been as it was? The answer is that it is the temporal direction of causation that accounts for the asymmetry concerning what Jane can alter, and not any further difference in the possibilities. Indeed, it is this fact which explains the initial plausibility of van Inwagen's argument: because 'rendering false' is naturally understood as a verb of action, it is naturally understood with the usual implication concerning the direction of causation. Hence it is not surprising that van Inwagen should confidently appeal to our intuitions that we can only render false '$Po$ & $q$' by rendering false '$q$', however 'render false' be precisely defined. But the compatibilist does not have to allow that there is any verb of action which expresses the relation between an agent and a possible past whose existence is implied (given the laws of nature) by the possibility of her action.

I now turn to Chisholm's criticism of the second Moorean proposition, that which embodies the conditional analysis of the alternate possibility condition.[45] Chisholm argues that the condition that Jane would have done otherwise if she had so chosen does not suffice for the truth of 'Jane could have done otherwise'; the further premiss that Jane could have chosen to do otherwise is also required. After all: that Jane will get to New York tomorrow if she gets a seat on an aeroplane today does not show that she can get to New York tomorrow; the further premiss that she can get a seat on an aeroplane today is also required. Furthermore, Chisholm argues, since the extra premiss employs the concept of possibility, its addition to the conditional analysis deprives that analysis of any value for the compatibilist cause.

Chisholm's argument is best considered with reference to the following triad of propositions:[46]

(a) Jane would have done otherwise if she had so chosen.
(b) Jane would not have done otherwise, if she had not so chosen.
(c) Jane could not have chosen to do otherwise.

The problem for Moore is that (b) and (c) entail that Jane could not have done otherwise; so if (a)–(c) are consistent, as they seem to be, (a) cannot be equivalent to 'Jane could have done otherwise', contrary to Moore's conditional analysis of the latter.

An immediate response is that if the sense in which (c) is true is just that entailed by determinism, then the sense in which (b) and (c) entail that Jane could not have done otherwise is just the bare sense entailed by determinism. But this does not threaten Moore; for he holds that there is another sense, central to the alternate possibility condition for moral responsibility and captured by his conditional analysis (a), in which Jane could none the less do otherwise even if determinism is true. Yet Chisholm's argument threatens this position as well. For if one thinks of a case in which (c) is substantiated, not by a determinist hypothesis, but by the condition of Jane's will, then one may well judge that in such a case the ascription of moral responsibility to Jane would be unjust despite the truth of (a); for example, Jane might be acting under hypnosis, or suffering from an irresistible obsession. Hence the alternate possibility condition seems to require the condition that Jane could have chosen to do otherwise, which employs the problematic concept of possibility which Moore had hoped to eliminate by the conditional analysis.

At this point we should briefly return to Moore himself. For the conclusion for which Chisholm argues is one that Moore himself came to accept. In *E* he only acknowledges that 'there is some plausibility in this contention' (p. 113), but in his reply in *PGEM* he unequivocally accepts it: 'the proposition that the agent was morally responsible for it [his action], certainly *entails* that the agent *could* have made a different choice from the one he did make' (p. 624). The issue between Moore and Chisholm is not, therefore, whether the condition that Jane can choose to do otherwise is necessary; it is, rather, whether this condition can be explicated in a manner which is satisfactory from the point of view of compatibilism. Moore makes two suggestions to this effect in *E* (pp. 113–14). First, he suggests that by 'Jane could choose to do otherwise' we might mean that Jane did not know prior to her choice what choice she would make, a suggestion he had also made in F (pp. 189–90). This certainly captures a genuine concept of possibility, *epistemic* possibility – that which is possible for all one knows – and in this sense alternate choices are indeed typically possible. But there is no obvious connection between this kind of epistemic possibility and moral responsibility. The fact that the hypnotised subject does not know in advance what choice she is going to make does not show that her choice is such that she is responsible for what she does. Equally, the fact that on some occasion one did predict with certainty one's choice, and thus that no alternative was epistemically possible, does not by itself furnish one with an excuse for doing what one chose to do.

Moore's second suggestion in *E* (which he had rejected in F) is that by 'Jane could have chosen to do otherwise' we might mean that Jane would have chosen to do otherwise if she had chosen so to choose. At first sight this seems no help. It is not clear what content there is to 'choosing to choose'; furthermore, the suggestion invites the same objection as before – could the agent choose to choose otherwise? One can recycle Chisholm's argument to show that in the absence of this condition Moore's conditional analysis is unsatisfactory. This last point admits of a

141

general application: in principle, one can recycle Chisholm's objection to any conditional analysis of 'Jane could have chosen to do otherwise'.

At this point a new strategy is needed. The key to this is that too much was conceded to Chisholm when it was allowed that his argument showed the need for the further condition 'Jane could have chosen to do otherwise' in the analysis of the alternate possibility condition. For all that was shown was that in addition to the truth of the conditional analysis (a), a further condition on Jane's choice is necessary for the ascription of moral responsibility, a condition which excludes choices such as those made under hypnosis. And instead of incorporating this in the analysis of the alternate possibility condition, one can add it to the first Moorean proposition as a further condition of free action. As the ensuing argument then shows, this condition is not best formulated as the condition that Jane could have chosen to do otherwise. It is better regarded as a causal condition, that Jane's choice was the product of a free will.

It is not easy to say what it is for Jane's will to be free. Legal experience with the concept of diminished responsibility shows that there is a range of cases which do not easily come under one description. Rationality is one obvious suggestion here; but since, as Locke observed,[47] the insane are often perfectly rational, given their beliefs, it cannot be sufficient. A better suggestion arises from Feinberg's observation that the insane are often incapable of understanding their own motivation:[48] for this connects with Frankfurt's thesis that 'it is in securing the conformity of his will to his second-order volitions, then, that a person exercises freedom of the will'.[49] This thesis can be regarded as a reformulation of Moore's unsatisfactory suggestion that to have a free will is to be such that one would have chosen otherwise if one had chosen so to choose; the difference comes from replacing Moore's conditional analysis by the causal thesis that the agent's choice was one which she chose to choose, i.e. accords with her second-order volitions.

This causal condition needs further refinement, but it can be accepted here for the sake of the argument. The resulting position is that moral responsibility is held to require both freedom of action and freedom of choice, and that although freedom of action is constituted by the existence of an alternate possibility, the same idea is not applied to freedom of choice. This does not directly threaten More's compatibilist strategy, but it invites the following objection: since freedom of choice is here given a causal analysis, why cannot a causal analysis be likewise given for freedom of action, without the need for the alternate possibility condition?

This objection leads to Frankfurt's challenge to the first Moorean proposition,[50] to the necessity of the alternate possibility condition at all. The challenge arises from reflection on cases of potential causal overdetermination. Suppose Jane is considering whether or not to kill Charles, and this fact is known to the Evil Genius, who also wishes Charles to be killed but prefers that Jane, rather than he himself, should kill Charles. Suppose, further, that the Evil Genius, unknown to Jane, can somehow monitor Jane's deliberations and will cause Jane to kill Charles if Jane decides, prior to his intervention, not to kill Charles. It does not matter how the Evil Genius has this power over Jane; what matters is that the situation is such that Jane cannot but kill Charles, whatever she initially decides. We are now to suppose that Jane decides that she will kill Charles, and does so. Does the fact that she could not have done otherwise provide her with any excuse? Frankfurt argues that it does not:

> Thus it would have made no difference, so far as concerns her action or how she came to perform it, if the circumstances that made it impossible for her to avoid performing it had not prevailed. . . .
> When a fact is in this way irrelevant to the problem of accounting for a person's action, it seems quite gratuitous to assign it any weight in the assignment of her moral responsibility.[51]

Frankfurt is surely right about this. Where an agent's action is quite unaffected causally by the fact which makes that action unavoidable, the fact that the action was unavoidable is irrelevant to the issue of the agent's moral responsibility. That issue must be settled by reference to the actual causes of the action, by whether the agent acted deliberately and whether her will was free. So the alternate possibility condition is not even a necessary condition of moral responsibility. This obviously assists the compatibilist case, though it remains open for the libertarian to argue that 'agent-causation' is incompatible with deterministic 'event-causation'. I shall not pursue that issue; I want to consider instead whether dropping the alternate possibility condition induces such a radical change in questions about responsibility that Moore's conditional analysis of it is rendered irrelevant.

Certainly, the focus of intellectual interest must alter. Once a causal analysis is adopted, its details will be the central issue in debates about moral responsibility (e.g. Davidson's notorious deviant causal chains have to be excluded[52]). But one thing which it is easy to understand from this perspective is why it is that Moore's conditional analysis seemed relevant to questions about responsibility. Usually, where $x$ causes $y$, if $x$ had not occurred $y$ would not have occurred. Given a causal analysis of free action, it follows that where an action was free it is usually the case that if the agent had not made the choice she did make, she would not have done what she did. Since the agent would not have made the choice she did if she had chosen not to do what she did in fact do, it follows that where an action was free it is usually the case that if

143

the agent had chosen not to do what she did do, she would not have done what she did – which is what Moore's conditional analysis yields. Of course, the connection between 'x caused y' and 'if x had not occurred y would not have occurred' breaks down in cases of potential overdetermination, but since it is precisely these cases that Frankfurt appeals to, we have here an explanation of the applicability of the conditional analysis to the ordinary cases of free action from which potential overdetermination is absent (and perhaps that is all actual cases of free action).

This explanation shows that the conditional analysis provided much of the substance of the causal theory of responsibility within an approach dominated by the alternate possibility condition. When the tables are turned and a causal theory is itself recognised as fundamental to questions of responsibility, Moore's conditional analysis is not needed for that purpose. But I think it still has a role, more or less the reverse of its previous one, as a way of legitimating within a causal theory the concept of possibility which figures in our practical deliberations. In deliberating we think of ourselves as choosing between courses of action which it is possible for us to attempt; but these courses of action need be neither causally nor epistemically possible for us, nor need we think of them as such. What Moore's analysis implies is that there is another concept of possibility – practical possibility – which gives point to our practical deliberations since it interprets the thought that certain courses of action are possible for us as the thought that these are actions such that if we choose to attempt them, we will. Someone who believes that only one action is possible, in the sense captured by Moore's conditional analysis, has nothing to deliberate about. Since practical deliberation is an essential feature of the life of a moral agent, Moore's analysis of the alternate possibility condition has in this way a central place within our beliefs about ourselves.

My conclusion, therefore, is that although Frankfurt's argument shows that Moore's conditional analysis does not have the fundamental importance which it seemed to have, even within the perspective of a causal theory of responsibility the analysis retains an important analytical role in elucidating the concept of practical possibility which is central to practical deliberation.

# V

# Pure realism rejected

---

*A philosopher is a man who has to cure many intellectual diseases in himself before he can arrive at the notions of common sense.*

(L. Wittgenstein *Culture and Value* p. 44)

In September 1904 Moore's Fellowship at Trinity College came to an end, and he moved from Cambridge to Edinburgh, where he lived for the next three years. This change in the circumstances of his life is marked by a change in his intellectual style. The naive but engaging self-confidence of the early period (which even led him to think that he should have been appointed in 1900 to succeed Sidgwick as Professor of Philosophy at Cambridge[1]) is replaced by anxious self-criticism. One manifestation of this is a tendency to devote a great deal of space to clarifying the issues he wants to discuss. In his 1905 paper NROP, after two pages of such clarification, he writes:

> But I am sorry to say that I have not yet reached the end of my
> explanations as to what my meaning is. I am afraid that the subject
> may seem very tedious. I can assure you that I have found it
> excessively tedious to try to make my meaning clear to myself. I have
> constantly found that I was confusing one question with another, and
> that, where I had thought I had a good reason for some assertion, I
> had in reality no good reason.
>
> (p. 38)

There then follow several more pages of tedious explanation. To criticise Moore in this respect is not, of course, to say that his aim is misguided; it is just that the means employed are often disproportionate to the results achieved and, in the worst cases, make his writings barely readable.

Part of the explanation for this change is, I think, his separation from

145

many of his Cambridge friends who had admired and encouraged him. In their absence there was little to check the anxiety which is manifest in the diaries he kept of the number of hours he had worked each day. But he also recognised quickly some of the faults in his early work, and the positive side of this self-criticism is that it led him, in the course of the next few years, to abandon many of the characteristic doctrines of pure realism. The changes were not immediate, but by the winter of 1910–11, when he gave the lectures 'Some Main Problems of Philosophy', Moore had developed a reasonably coherent new position from which he was never to depart far for the rest of his life. Thus the period 1904–10 is a period of transition; it is also the period of his absence from Cambridge. For in 1911 Moore was appointed to a University Lectureship at Cambridge, and, apart from an extended visit to the United States during the Second World War, he never again lived away from Cambridge.

## 1: Naive realism and its problems

Moore was led to abandon pure realism by his recognition of problems inherent in its naively realist account of the objects of perception and in its conception of false propositions. It is problems concerning his account of the objects of perception that appear first. Moore's account of perception had been that in sense-perception we are directly aware of instances of sensible qualities which typically constitute some of the parts of material objects. This direct awareness, Moore held, was a form of knowledge, and it was for this reason he thought that there was no serious problem about scepticism. However, as I observed in chapter 2, in order to account for illusory perceptions, Moore allowed that there can be objects of perception which do not exist. Hence there is plenty of room here for sceptical doubt as to how we ever know that any of the objects of our consciousness actually exist. Moore does not voice this doubt explicitly; but its pressure is apparent in his writings immediately after leaving Cambridge.

'The Nature and Reality of the Objects of Perception' (NROP) is the first substantial piece of writing Moore completed after leaving Cambridge. I have already commented on its tedious style; and matters are not helped by the fact that although Moore takes up a great deal of space trying to explain what he means, his arguments are rather condensed. He begins with a brief discussion of the analysis of knowledge, and suggests that $a$ knows that $p$ just where $a$ truly believes that $p$ and has a good reason for his belief that $p$. What is notable here is his account of a good reason for a belief – it is, he writes, 'a true proposition, which would not be true unless the belief itself – what is believed – were also true' (p. 40). This sounds similar to the position recently advanced by Dretske and others,[2] but everything depends on what it is to have a good reason – is it merely required that the proposition in question be true (as Dretske and other 'externalists' maintain[3]) or does the subject have to know that the proposition is true (as 'internalists' maintain)? Moore takes the latter option (p. 35) although it threatens the regress familiar from traditional accounts of knowledge; and the 'internalism' of his approach is further apparent in the way in which he takes it that to know that $p$ one must not only have a good reason for one's belief that $p$, one must also know that one's reason is a good reason (p. 47) – a requirement on which he then concentrates in the bulk of the paper.

Most of the discussion concerns knowledge of other minds, a topic Moore does not elsewhere discuss at length. Not surprisingly, it is the argument by analogy that forms the basis of his discussion, and what interests Moore is the kind of general correlation whose observation provides one with a good reason for holding that one's reasons, in particular cases, for ascribing mental states to others on the basis of their behaviour are good reasons. He argues that if one takes the observed correlation to be exemplified by that between one's perceptions of one's body writhing and one's feelings of one's own pains, then observation of one's perception of another body writhing can only give one reason to postulate the existence, unobserved by one, of another feeling of pain of one's own. Whereas if the observed correlation is taken to be between one's own writhings and one's own pains then observation of the writhing of another body gives one reason to postulate the existence of a pain felt by the person whose body is writhing. Moore's argument hinges on the difference between subjective and objective correlations, and seems correct as far as it goes, though it does not address doubts about the role of induction in knowledge about others. But the interesting aspect of the argument is what it leads Moore to say about the subjective/objective distinction, about 'the nature and reality of the objects of perception'.

One point is clear: Moore still upholds the being/existence distinction. In discussing the objective items correlations between which provide reasons for belief in other minds, he separates the issue of their existence from that of their independence from our perception of them: 'It is not self-contradictory to suppose that what *is* perceived, does not exist' (p. 79). This position is further confirmed by his discussion of perceptual illusion at the end of the paper; he here advances the account characteristic of his pure realism: '*some* of the sensible qualities which we perceive do not exist at the places where they appear to exist, though others do' (p. 94).

But what are the things we perceive? In E&E Moore had distinguished between those properties of material objects which are

147

experienced by us by virtue of their role in causing our experience of them and those properties which we merely imagine as occupying the space occupied by the properties we do experience. In NROP he takes this distinction much further, leaving out all reference to causality and the imagination, and introducing a sharp distinction between those properties which we actually perceive and the rest:

> But when we say, as in ordinary talk we should, that the objects we perceive are *books*, we certainly mean to ascribe to them properties, which, in a sense which we all understand, are not actually seen by us, at the moment when we are merely looking at two books on a shelf two yards off. And all such properties I mean to exclude as not being then *observed* or *directly perceived* by us. When I speak of what we *observe*, when we see two books on a shelf, I mean to limit the expression to that which is *actually seen*. And, thus understood, the expression does include colours, and the size and shape of colours, and spatial relations in three dimensions between these patches of colour, but it includes nothing else.
>
> (p. 68)

In this way Moore, in effect, introduces sense-data into his philosophy. They are not so called here; he writes of the ' "things", "objects", or "contents", which we perceive, as we say, "by the senses" ' (NROP p. 70), and he usually calls them 'sense-contents' (within quotation marks). The issue of how these 'sense-contents' relate to material objects is not explicitly confronted. But the closing discussion of perceptual illusions implies the naive realist position that some of the 'sense-contents' we observe really exist in the places in which we perceive them to be (cf. the passage quoted above from p. 94), and I think we can add in the pure realist account of these perceived qualities as parts of material objects.

In NROP Moore says little about scepticism. He seems to think that he can defuse Berkleian arguments for the subjectivity of 'sense-contents' by means of his being/existence distinction, and he ends the paper with an affirmation of his realist faith in the objective existence of some 'sense-contents':

> The more I look at objects round me, the more I am unable to resist the conviction that what I see does exist, as truly and as really, as my perception of it. The conviction is overwhelming.
>
> (p. 96)[4]

But in his 1909 paper 'Hume's Philosophy' (HP) he shows a greater sensitivity to sceptical arguments. Although he asserts that in ordinary life we cannot dispense, not only with our belief in the existence of the external world, but also with our belief that we know of its existence, he accepts that the existence of this belief is no proof of its truth and that there is real value in reflective enquiries into philosophical scepticism, such as the position advanced by Hume. In discussing this Moore employs many of the anti-sceptical gambits that he was to re-use several times. I shall postpone discussion of most of these until chapter 9, but I want to look now at his treatment of what he takes to be Hume's argument for scepticism concerning the external world.

Moore concentrates on the argument Hume employs in his *Treatise* against the 'philosophical system' (1.4.2). Moore presents it as resting on two assumptions: '(1) that we cannot know any fact, which we have not observed, unless we know it to be causally connected with some fact which we have observed, and (2) that we have no reason for assuming any causal connection, except where we have experienced some instances of conjunction between the two facts connected' (HP p. 160). Suppose it is further assumed that we never observe any external objects; then, according to Moore, Hume argued that, given (1) and (2), scepticism about the external world must ensue. As an account of Hume's criticism of Locke, this is fair enough, although it is by no means a full treatment of Hume's views. What matters to us, however, is Moore's response to this argument. He sketches the contraposition move that he was to make much more of later, and then remarks that Hume's criticisms of the 'vulgar' theory that we do observe external objects are 'obviously inconclusive' (HP p. 162), though he has said nothing at all about them. But, finally, he waives this point and claims that even supposing we never observe any external objects, (1) and (2) do not imply Hume's sceptical conclusion. For, he suggests, if we assume that external objects are very like things which we do observe, then we can infer the existence of an external object from observations of things which, although not external objects, are very like them. This is not a persuasive line of thought, and one year later, in *SMPP*, Moore rejects it. So we shall return to 'Hume's argument'; but for the moment it suffices to note Moore's formulation of it in HP and his unsatisfactory response to it.

### 2: Sense-data introduced and scepticism confronted

This discussion of NROP and HP has revealed Moore's growing awareness of difficulties in the naive realism characteristic of his pure realism. He confronts these difficulties in his lectures on 'Some Main Problems of Philosophy', which he delivered in London in the winter of 1910–11.[5] After an introductory lecture on the question 'What is Philosophy?', which I shall discuss in the next section, Moore turns to discuss the evidence of the senses and the way in which this evidence forms the basis for our knowledge of the external world.

149

In considering the question 'what sort of thing this evidence of the senses is' (p. 29), Moore asks: 'What exactly happens, when (as we should say) we *see* a material object?' (p. 29); he then holds up an envelope and, inviting his audience to look at it, describes his visual experience:

> But now, what happened to each of us, when we saw that envelope? I
> will begin by describing *part* of what happened to me. I saw a patch
> of a particular whitish colour, having a certain size, and a certain
> shape, a shape with rather sharp angles or corners and bounded by
> fairly straight lines. These things: this patch of a whitish colour, and
> its size and shape I did actually see. And I propose to call these
> things, the colour and size and shape, *sense-data*.
>
> (p. 30)

Thus does the term 'sense-datum' enter Moore's writings, with the sense that it is to bear throughout his writings hereafter, as descriptive of what is 'actually' perceived.[6] His views about what is thus perceived change, and it is worth describing the position he holds in *SMPP*. First, sense-data are sharply distinguished from all acts of consciousness, including perceptions. Moore does not here argue for this way of thinking about perception – he just assumes the conclusion argued for in RI. Second, our perceptual consciousness of sense-data is 'direct' – it is not accomplished by means of our consciousness of anything else. Moore's usual term for this type of consciousness, to which our introspective awareness of our own mental states also belongs (p. 49), is 'direct apprehension', and he contrasts it with 'indirect apprehension', which is our consciousness of $x$ when we are thinking about $x$ but not directly apprehending $x$, as when we remember some sense-datum we directly apprehended yesterday. This contrast is similar to Russell's contrast between knowledge by acquaintance and knowledge by description with which Moore must have been familiar (Russell had already presented it in 'On Denoting'[7]).

A further feature of direct apprehension is that it is 'a way of knowing'. Moore means by this that direct apprehension of an object suffices for knowledge of its existence at the time that one is directly apprehending it, and indeed later when one remembers it; furthermore, the knowledge thus obtained is indubitable (pp. 52–3). Moore regards this epistemic feature of direct apprehension as absolutely straightforward (p. 91). When, in order to elude scepticism, he later distinguishes between direct apprehension and immediate knowledge, he still accepts that one knows immediately of the existence of that which one directly apprehends (p. 123).

So far the features of sense-data are much as one would expect. What is unexpected about the position presented in *SMPP* is Moore's method of individuating sense-data. In the passage quoted above from p. 30 he describes 'the colour and size and shape' as sense-data; thus, as he notes in his 1952 footnotes, his view was not that the patch of colour he apprehends is a sense-datum, with certain apprehended qualities (colour, size, and shape). Instead his view was that the colour is one sense-datum, the size another, and the shape a third; and this is a view which is manifest in the pages which follow (e.g. 'Of the three kinds of sense-data, then, which you all saw when I held up the envelope, namely, the whitish colour, its size, and its shape' – p. 38). What we have here, as the discussion of numerically different, but qualitatively identical, shapes shows (pp. 36–7), is an implication of his previous view that most properties are sortal concepts and particulars are bare instances of these properties. Where these particulars are directly apprehended, they are sense-data.

In his pure realism, this view of the objects of perception was combined with the view that, when they exist, the objects perceived are parts of material objects. In *SMPP* this view appears as the hypothesis that material objects are just collections of sense-data. Moore frequently adverts to this naive realist position as the 'natural' view to take (cf. esp. pp. 137, 326), and he suggests that even when, as philosophers, we have rejected this naive realist view, we typically think and act as if it were true (p. 327). None the less in *SMPP* he accepts the traditional 'argument from illusion' – essentially Berkeley's argument from the relativity of appearances – against naive realism, and for the thesis that none of the sense-data we directly apprehend are parts of material objects.

Once naive realism is rejected, Moore has to provide a new account of the nature of sense-data and of their relationship to material objects. In *SMPP* he falls back, not very confidently, on what he calls 'the accepted view' of sense-data, that they exist only when directly apprehended, that no two people ever directly apprehend the same one, and that the sense-data directly apprehended by one person have no spatial relationship to the sense-data apprehended by anyone else (pp. 40–4). As he acknowledges, on this view they are essentially subjective items. But he still insists that they are not acts of consciousness, neither are they just aspects of such acts. They are particulars (p. 304), objects in their own right, and Moore considers two ways of thinking about the relationship between such objects and material objects – phenomenalism and indirect realism.

Moore's discussion here of phenomenalism is brief and unsatisfactory. He takes it as obvious that the content of thoughts about presently existing, but unobserved, material objects is not captured by construing them as about possible sense-data which we would apprehend directly if various hypothetical conditions were realised (pp. 134–5). There is a

151

point here, but Moore's discussion is based on a misapprehension: he imputes to the phenomenalist the view that 'if you know that your carriage is running on and supported by wheels, *what* you know is that it is running on and supported by the possibility that certain sense-data should exist in the future. This possibility is what the wheels of the carriage *are*, if it has any wheels at all' (p. 134). The phenomenalist will reject any such piecemeal identification of particular material objects with possibilities for the existence of sense-data and will hold instead that it is only the content of total thoughts that is susceptible of a phenomenalist analysis. Admittedly Berkeley's language does sometimes suggest the position Moore attacks: Moore alludes (p. 235) to the passage in *The Principles of Human Knowledge* (section 38) in which Berkeley says that we eat and drink ideas. But Berkeley acknowledges that his language here is unsatisfactory, and a clear-minded phenomenalist will avoid these idioms.

This just leaves indirect realism, which is indeed the position Moore affirms in *SMPP*. Moore's discussion is unsatisfactory in that he does not develop his position in any detail. But his commitment to it is manifest in the following passage (Moore is here talking about a pencil which he is holding up):

> I, for instance, claim to *know* that there does exist now, or did a
> moment ago, not only these sense-data which I am directly
> apprehending – seeing and feeling – but *also* something else which I
> am not directly apprehending. And I claim to know not merely that
> this something else is the *cause* of the sense-data which I am seeing or
> feeling: I claim to know that this cause is situated *here*; and though by
> *here* I do not necessarily mean *in* the space which I directly apprehend,
> yet I do mean *in space* – somewhere in *some* space. And moreover I
> claim to know, not merely that the cause of my sensations is situated
> here in space, and has therefore some shape, but also roughly *what* its
> shape is. I claim to know that the cause of the sense-data I am now
> directly apprehending is part of the surface of something which is
> really roughly cylindrical; . . . It is, I think, plainly things like these
> that we all of us believe, when we believe in the existence of material
> objects.

(p. 116)

The issue that now arises is how Moore intends to avoid the sceptical conclusion traditionally associated with indirect realism, but emphatically repudiated in passages such as that quoted above. The issue is precisely that which he had discussed a year before in HP; but his views are now quite different. Not only does he now reject the naive realist position of the 'vulgar' that he was then prepared to entertain; he also rejects the unpersuasive line of thought he had employed before to argue that

Hume's sceptical conclusion does not follow from his premisses (pp. 117–19). So he now accepts that Hume's argument is valid. But he refuses to draw the sceptical conclusion that Hume wanted to attach to indirect realism. For, Moore rightly observes, one who accepts the validity of Hume's argument can legitimately contrapose and use the argument to argue from the negation of Hume's sceptical conclusion to the negation of one of the premisses of the argument. This is one of Moore's most famous anti-sceptical gambits; I shall discuss it fully in chapter 9, but one feature of it is to be noted now. Moore recognises that it is not enough for him just to contrapose; he has to make it plausible to suppose that his anti-sceptical premiss is more certain than the premisses of Hume's argument (pp. 121–2). And to this end he formulates his anti-sceptical premiss in terms of a particular case – in terms of his knowledge of the existence of the pencil that he is holding; for, he claims, our certainty concerning particular cases such as this is always greater than is our certainty concerning the general premisses of an argument for philosophical scepticism (pp. 125–6, 142–4).

I shall return to this kind of appeal to a particular cases, which is a feature of Moore's philosophical style which first emerges in *SMPP*. The issues I want to explore now, however, are just what Moore's anti-scepticism in *SMPP* amounts to and which of the premisses of Hume's argument Moore rejects. The first of these issues is raised by the following passage: 'we can never know *what* a material object *is in itself*, but can only know what properties it has, or how it is related to other things' (p. 131). The implication of this passage is that despite his robust appeal to our conviction that we do have knowledge of particular material objects (pencils etc.), his rejection of naive realism has led him to concede that there are limits to this knowledge. In this respect Moore's position in *SMPP* makes more of a concession to sceptical arguments than his anti-sceptical rhetoric at first suggests.

Hume's argument, as construed by Moore, has, in effect, four main premisses. Two are central to Moore's philosophy of perception in *SMPP* – that in sense-perception we directly apprehend sense-data, and that sense-data are in no case parts of material objects. We might well want to reject the approach to perception which these premisses embody, but Moore does not regard Hume's argument as even bringing them up for scrutiny. He concentrates on the other two premisses: those which I set out before when discussing Moore's reaction in HP to the argument. Frustratingly, despite his method of contraposition, he does not clearly identify which of these premisses he proposes to reject. None the less I think one can discern his position.

One line of thought frequently advanced by indirect realists is that we can justify the hypothesis of the existence of material objects as a way of explaining the similarities among the sense-data we apprehend and simplifying our overall conception of the world. This requires the rejection of the Humean premiss 'that nobody can ever know that the existence of one thing A is a *sign* of the *existence* of another thing B, unless he himself (or, under certain conditions, somebody else) has experienced a *general conjunction* between *things like A* and *things like B*' (as Moore puts it in *SMPP* p. 109); for this justification of belief in the existence of material objects does not invoke experience of regularities between material objects and sense-data. I do not think, however, that this is Moore's position. For the treatment of the existence of material objects as just a theoretical hypothesis conflicts with his robust insistence on his certain knowledge of the existence of the pencil he is holding, and in particular with his claim that this knowledge is *immediate* (p. 125).

Moore considers the other Humean principle, 'that nobody can ever know of the existence of anything which he has not directly apprehended, unless he knows that something which he has directly apprehended is *a sign* of its existence' (*SMPP* p. 109), in the following passage:

> It might be said: I certainly do not know immediately that the pencil exists; for I should not know it at all, unless I were directly apprehending certain sense-data, and knew that they were signs of its existence. And of course I admit, that I should not know it, unless I were directly apprehending certain sense-data. But this is again a different thing from admitting that that I do not know it immediately. For the mere fact that I should not know it, unless certain other things were happening, is quite a different thing from knowing it *only* because I know *some other proposition*.
>
> (p. 125)

The implication of this passage is that Moore rejects this Humean principle, for he here insists that he does know immediately of the existence of something which he does not directly apprehend. However he wants to retain the thought that in some sense he has 'the evidence of the senses' for it; for he allows that he would not have this knowledge unless he were directly apprehending certain sense-data. He does not, however, explain the basis of this conditional. One might take it to be causal – that one of the things which makes his belief that the pencil exists a case of knowledge is that it is caused by appropriate sense experiences, so that the occurrence of these experiences provides him with a 'good reason' for his belief, to use the idiom of NROP. But it is difficult to see how to combine this conception of a purely causal role for sense-experience with the conception of sense-experience which he advances in *SMPP*. For if sense-experience consists of the direct apprehension of sense-data, one would expect our apprehensions of them to have a causal role in the explanation of our knowledge of the existence

154

of things such as pencils, which are not directly apprehended, only in virtue of their possession of the evidential role which Moore denies them.

As it is the matter is left undeveloped, and never taken up in Moore's later writings. This unclarity is symptomatic of a general unclarity in *SMPP* about the relationship between the philosophy of perception and the theory of knowledge. It is all very well, and a striking departure from his earlier pure realist position, for Moore to distinguish sharply between 'direct apprehension' and 'immediate knowledge' (p. 123). But we still need a coherent account of how we have 'the evidence of the senses' for our knowledge of material objects. And this Moore does not provide. In this respect *SMPP* is only too typical of Moore's mature philosophy.

### 3: Common-sense

When discussing Moore's response to 'Hume's argument' I noted his stress on our certainty concerning our knowledge in particular cases. This is a feature of Moore's philosophical style that is first self-consciously applied in *SMPP*. In his discussion of 'Hume's argument' its purport is anti-sceptical; but its application is broader than this. He introduces his conception of a sense-datum through discussion of the visual experience involved in seeing him hold up an envelope, for the reason that 'it is, I think, very important for every one, in these subjects, to consider carefully single concrete instances, so that there may be no mistake as to exactly what it is that is being talked about. Such mistakes are, I think, very apt to happen, if one talks merely in generalities' (p. 29). Again, when discussing the relationship between sense-data and material objects, he writes, concerning one account of this relationship:

> Many philosophers have, I think, really believed the theory, and it also may seem very plausible so long as you merely state it in general terms, such as: All that we know of material objects is that they are the unknown cases of our sensations; and this is what we mean by 'material objects'. But it also seems to me to lose its plausibility, so soon as you consider what it implies in particular concrete instances.
>
> (pp. 136–7)

This appeal to the particular, once introduced, becomes a hallmark of Moore's style, reaching its climax in his 'Proof of an External World'. It is also a feature of his style that much influenced others; in the foreword to *SMPP* Wisdom writes (in 1952) that in Moore's work 'we find a habit of thought which, carried further by Wittgenstein, led to enormous advances – the study of the meaning of general terms by consideration of

155

concrete cases'. Its main purpose is to enable us to assess general theories by reference to their implications concerning particular cases. This strategy assumes that judgments concerning particular instances have epistemic priority over general philosophical beliefs, an assumption explicit in Moore's discussion of Hume's argument:

> In short, the attempt to prove by means of such a principle as
> Hume's, that we cannot know of the existence of any material object,
> seems to me a characteristic instance of a sort of argument which is
> very common in philosophy: namely an attempt to prove that a given
> proposition is false, by means of a principle which is, in fact, much
> less certain than the proposition which is supposed to be proved false
> by its means.

(p. 143)

This attitude contrasts with that characteristic of his early philosophy. In *PE* he is dismissive of our 'immediate judgments' concerning our duty in particular situations, and relies instead on abstract general intuitions concerning the goodness of kinds of state of affairs. This is not a sign of different attitudes to ethics versus the rest of philosophy; instead it exemplifies the change in his philosophical perspective as he abandoned the abstract intuitionism of his youth, and replaced it with the concept central to his new approach to philosophy – common-sense. He does now think that in important respects philosophy is answerable to common-sense – which is why he commences his lectures in *SMPP* with a lecture on 'What is Philosophy?' which is mainly given over to an exposition of 'the Common-Sense view of the Universe'.

It is, I think, no accident that common-sense comes to occupy this central place in Moore's philosophy just after his residence in Edinburgh. For while there he had studied not only Hume, but also Hume's great critic – Reid, the philosopher of common-sense (there are many references to Reid in NROP). Just what Moore took from Reid it is hard to say; certainly there are similarities – e.g. Reid stresses the epistemic priority of particular instances of common-sense principles over the principles themselves.[8] But there is one important difference (apart from the fact that Moore is unmoved by Reid's critique of the theory of ideas): Reid takes over Hume's naturalism, and this not only leads him to treat common-sense as a natural cognitive disposition to judge in accordance with certain principles, but also to regard this as a reason for treating these principles as first principles.[9] Moore's conception of common-sense lacks this second feature: our common-sense beliefs are just 'things which we all commonly assume to be true about the Universe, and which we are all sure that we know to be true about it' (*SMPP* p. 2). Thus although common-sense has a critical role within Moore's philosophy, it is not a source of first principles and it is not incorporated within a naturalised epistemology.

In addition to Reid, Moore was obviously influenced by Sidgwick, who defined the morality of common-sense as 'a collection of such general rules, as to the validity of which there would be apparent agreement at least among moral persons of our own age and civilization' (*The Methods of Ethics* p. 215). There is an indexical relativity here which Moore's conception shares. This is manifest in Moore's view that common-sense has changed with regard to astronomical and religious beliefs (*SMPP* pp. 3, 8, 17), and connects with the point that Moore does not treat common-sense as a source of first principles. The epistemic authority of common-sense derives instead from fact that our common-sense defines our starting-point in our reflections upon the world and our place within it. This authority is clearly defeasible; so the task of philosophy, as Moore conceives it in *SMPP* at least, is not the unyielding defence of common-sense: in his discussions of the paradoxes of the infinite and their implications for space and time Moore allows that we may have to revise some of our common-sense convictions (chapters IX, X). And there are other limitations to common-sense: although we have common-sense beliefs about what sorts of thing there are in the world and about what we know about them, we can legitimately add to these categories, through scientific inquiry and philosophical reflections. Furthermore, we do not have common-sense beliefs about the world as a whole (p. 2) nor about the limits of human knowledge (p. 14). Since Moore recognises in *SMPP* that it is an essential feature of philosophy to present, and justify, accounts of these last two matters, it is clear that the task of philosophy cannot be accomplished just by explicating and defending common-sense.

Another feature of Moore's approach in *SMPP* which goes beyond the appeal to common-sense is his use of introspective analysis. This is manifest in *SMPP* in the way in which he presents his account of visual perception; though he makes it clear that his question is not one about the physiology of visual perception, his approach is still that of intro-spective psychology:

> the occurrence which I mean here to analyse is merely the *mental* occurrence – the act of consciousness – which we call *seeing*. . . . This mental occurrence, which I call 'seeing', is known to us in a much more simple and direct way, than are the complicated physiological processes which go on in our eyes and nerves and brains. A man cannot directly observe the minute processes which go on in his own eyes and nerves and brain when he sees; but all of us who are not blind can directly observe this mental occurrence, which we mean by seeing.
>
> (*SMPP* p. 29)

For much of this century it has been usual to distinguish the philosophical analysis of concepts from scientific analysis of the facts, and in the light of this the sense-datum analysis would be regarded as a conceptual analysis. This is indeed roughly the way in which Moore presents it in later writings (e.g. DCS pp. 54–5). But, as the passage quoted shows, this is not how Moore viewed the matter in *SMPP*: here he treats the analysis of perception as an empirical matter, but one for which no special expertise is required, since the mental processes are ones which all of us can 'directly observe'.

Moore's approach here is, in part, due to his continuing attachment to the one-level theory of meaning characteristic of his pure realism. Without a sense/reference distinction, the philosophical analysis of perception cannot be an analysis of the concept of perception without also being an analysis of the facts of perception. But his introspective method also bears witness to his Cartesian assumption that the structure of mental states is 'directly observable' by their subjects, an assumption apparent elsewhere in *SMPP*, especially in his discussions of the nature of thought. Moore argues that there is more to thought than the direct apprehension of sense-data and similar mental images since no account of such direct apprehensions suffices for an account of the way in which we perceive, remember, and imagine things which are not sense-data, let alone an account of what it is for us to have thoughts about them capable of truth or falsity (pp. 65–6, chapter XIII). In order to describe this aspect of thought Moore introduces the concept of indirect apprehension, his variant of Russellian knowledge by description. But Moore is not happy about this concept, and what is striking about his anxieties about it is his repeated complaint that introspection does not enable him to form a clear conception of it:

> if we try to discover by introspection, what is before our minds when we remember or imagine, it is extraordinarily difficult to discover that anything whatever is ever before them except some image; . . . The difficulty is the same as in the case of sense-perception. When I look at this paper, *is* anything before my mind except the sense-data which I directly perceive? and if anything else is before my mind, in what way is it before it? In general, I think we may say that it is extraordinarily difficult to discover by introspection that conscious processes or mental events ever consist in anything else at all except the direct perception of sense-data, either impressions or ideas.
>
> (*SMPP* p. 244; cf. pp. 48, 72–3)

Moore's difficulty here arises largely from his empiricist assumptions about the deliverances of introspection. But that he takes it seriously indicates his commitment to an introspective criterion of truth in psychology that we no longer accept.

In his early philosophy, Moore's reliance on introspection was closely allied to his intuitionism; in *SMPP* this is apparent in his conception of self-evident truths as propositions such that 'as soon as you really understand what the proposition means, you can *see* that it is true' (p. 90). In chapter 2 I commented unfavourably on this conception and argued that, despite Moore's intentions, it applies at best to analytic necessities. In *SMPP* Moore still accepts that there are synthetic necessities (p. 152); but a striking feature of many of his arguments throughout the book is his denial of self-evidence to propositions which he would regard as synthetic necessities if true – this applies to 'the accepted view' of sense-data (p. 44), to all propositions about the limits of knowledge (pp. 141–3), and to several propositions about space and time (chapters VIII, IX). Thus in practice Moore is chipping away at this problematic category. At the same time he is developing a more sophisticated conception of analysis and thus of analytic truths. The conception to be found in his early work was founded upon a criterion of substitutivity within indirect speech that was unworkable in practice. In theory Moore retains the same criterion in *SMPP*, but when he seeks to employ it, as in his discussion of truth, it is as useless as ever:

> The only point as to which I can see any room for doubt whether these definitions do fulfil all the requirements of a definition of the words 'true' and 'false' as we should apply them to this particular belief, is that it may be doubted whether when we say that the belief is 'true' or 'false', these properties of 'corresponding to a fact' and 'not corresponding to a fact' are the properties which we actually *have before our minds* and express by those words. This is a question which can only be settled by actual inspection; and I admit that it is difficult to be quite sure what result the inspection yields.
>
> (p. 287)

Despite passages of this kind in *SMPP* Moore also presents a different line of thought. Central to this is the thesis that there are two kinds of question about meaning. One concerns our ordinary understanding of language; we can ask about the meaning of a word which we do not understand. If, as Moore puts it, 'a Polynesian, who knew no English, asked: "What is the meaning of the word 'real'?" ' (p. 218) the content of his question is just the request 'Please, call up before my mind the notion which Englishmen express by the word "real" '. Questions of this kind, Moore claims, are of no intrinsic philosophical significance. But there is another kind of question about meaning which is important for philosophy, that in which we concern ourselves with that which is meant by some word, and ask how it relates to that which is meant by some other words or words. It is questions of this latter kind about meaning which raise issues of philosophical analysis.

Moore's distinction is a scope distinction, between questions about what certain words mean and questions, concerning the meanings of certain words, about their relationship. This is obviously problematic, for it is not clear how questions of the second kind can be partitioned from the first. What I want to focus on here, however, is the fact that in the passages in which he advances this conception of philosophical analysis (pp. 205–6, 216–23) Moore is happy to say that those who understand a word perfectly well in the ordinary sense may yet be puzzled or mistaken about the analysis of its meaning: 'we may, therefore, know quite well, in one sense, what a word means, while at the same time, in another sense, we may not know what it means. We may be quite familiar with the notion it conveys, and understand sentences in which it occurs, although at the same time we are quite unable to *define* it' (p. 205). The crucial implication of this thesis is that philosophical analyses do not have to satisfy any criterion of introspective assent, and in the context of Moore's use of philosophical analysis this is a potentially liberating thought.

Moore's failure to make much use of this implication derives from the fact that he does not yet have a self-conscious grasp of the power of logical and epistemological analysis. This is reflected in his insistence that the resolution of issues concerning the philosophical analysis of the meanings of 'real' or 'exists' does not enable us to settle the more important, and still philosophically relevant, question as to what is real or exists (pp. 222–4). This view is comparable to his earlier characterisation of analytic truths as 'perfectly barren'. But just as then his practice did not conform to this characterisation, so here much of his argument hinges on issues of analysis – the sense-datum analysis of perception and the analysis of the relationship between sense-data and material objects. Indeed there is a more striking instance of this: much of the second half of *SMPP* is devoted to issues concerning the nature of belief and imagination, and Moore repeatedly expresses his conclusion as revealing an important truth of semantic analysis: that 'single words and phrases which we use will constantly seem to be names for something, when in fact they are not names for anything' (p. 290). This is a clear case in which Moore's argument hinges on an analytic thesis; furthermore Moore himself presents the issue as one concerning the semantic roles of elements of language. So not only does he here assign a more substantive role to philosophical analysis than his official theory allows, he also employs here a notion of analysis that is much closer to questions about the meaning of words than his official account of philosophical analysis allows.

Having thus introduced the central thesis of his critique of the pure realist theory of propositions, I will now discuss it in detail.

## 4: Propositions denied

In my account of pure realism in chapter 3 I picked out Moore's realist conception of a proposition and his associated identity theory of truth as central to this position. If, then, in *SMPP* he abandons pure realism, his views on these subjects should undergo radical revision. This is indeed so; but one would not think this as one starts the work. For, having introduced his audience to sense-data in chapter 2, Moore turns in chapter 3 to propositions:

> The fact is that absolutely all the contents of the Universe, absolutely everything that *is* at all, may be divided into two classes – namely into *propositions*, on the one hand, and into things which are not propositions on the other hand. There certainly are in the Universe such things as propositions: the sort of thing that I mean by a proposition is certainly one of the things that *is*.
>
> (p. 56)

So far Moore has not departed from pure realism. The change comes when he turns, halfway through the lectures, to the issue of truth and falsity, in particular to the issue of false belief.[10] His pure realist account of this had been that the proposition which is the object of one's belief has the simple property of falsehood, which implies that the proposition believed is not an actual state of affairs or a fact. Now this is not in fact a position Moore puts forward for discussion in *SMPP*. The view he does consider, and reject, is that facts consist, not of true propositions, but of the truth of true propositions, where truth is, as before, a simple property of propositions (p. 261). So before considering Moore's discussion of this revised position it is worth considering what reasons might have led him to adopt it. I think the answer to this is implicit in the following passage in *SMPP*:

> we can at once say two things about the difference between the truth and falsehood of this particular belief – the belief that we *are* now hearing the noise of a brass-band. We can say, in the first place that since the belief is false, there simply *is* not in the Universe one thing which would be in it, if the belief were true. And we can say, in the second place, that this thing . . . which would be present, if it were true, *is* that fact, whose nature is so unmistakable . . . the fact which would consist in our actually being now hearing it.
>
> (*SMPP* p. 225)

The pure realist identity theory does not meet these conditions. For since, on this theory, the fact which is, or obtains, where a belief is true, is just the proposition believed, and this proposition would still have *been* had the belief been false, the truth of the belief does not require that there *be* something which would not have *been* at all had the belief been false.

This line of thought embodies a claim about the point of the difference between truth and falsehood with which it is difficult to quarrel, and the revised theory which Moore advances in *SMPP* does, in a way, satisfy this reequirement. For if the fact that *p* is just the truth of the proposition that *p*, then, where the proposition is false, there is no such fact. Yet Moore rejects this theory in *SMPP*, albeit not very confidently (p. 262). He gives two reasons for doing so: the first is essentially an extension of the previous point. Facts should have an explanatory role, as that in virtue of which beliefs are true where they are. But on this account the direction of explanation runs the opposite way: it is the truth of a proposition which explains why there is a fact. The other point concerns the remaining commitment to false propositions. Here he does not offer much of an argument, only a conviction:

> But this is the sort of objection I feel. It is that, if you consider what happens when a man entertains a false belief, it doesn't seem as if his belief consisted merely in his having a relation to some object which certainly *is*. It seems rather as if the thing he was believing, the *object* of his belief, were just *the* fact which certainly is *not*.
>
> (p. 263)

Although intuitive, this objection is more radical than the previous one. It strikes at the heart of pure realism's proposition-centred metaphysics. In thinking about it it is again essential not to confuse Moorean propositions with Fregean thoughts. With a sense/reference distinction one can distinguish, in the case of a true belief, between the thought which constitutes the content of the belief and the fact, or state of affairs, in virtue of which the belief is true (of course Frege himself would not have accepted this talk of states of affairs, but that is not important here). Hence there is no reason to think that in the case of a false belief, the absence of any appropriate state of affairs threatens the existence of the thought which constitutes the belief's content. This line of thought is not accessible to Moore, since his propositions straddle the sense/reference distinction. His conception of a proposition was formed in the light of the identity theory, as is shown by his objection here to false propositions: the problem is that even in the case of a false belief it seems as if the proposition believed 'were *the* fact which certainly is *not*'. So conceived, false propositions are bound to be an embarrassment: they do not differ in any intrinsic respect from actual states of affairs, but since in their case there is no such state of affairs, it is not easy to grasp how there is none the less a proposition, which has all the substance of an actual state of affairs, but just lacks its actuality.[11] Switching to

Moore's new theory of facts helps a bit with this problem, since on this theory false propositions are not assigned the same metaphysical status as actual states of affairs. But they are still taken to be around, 'in the Universe', and thus an embarrassment in the light of their falsehood. Furthermore, their falsehood will be as much a fact as is the truth of a true proposition; so it looks as though, alongside facts as Moore now conceives them, there should also be a domain of 'false facts' with exactly the same metaphysical status.

Moore formulates his conclusion with reference to his previous account of belief:

> The whole expression 'I am believing in the existence of lions' is, of course, a name for a fact. But we cannot analyse this fact into a relation between me on the one hand, and a proposition called 'the existence of lions' on the other. This is the theory of the analysis of belief which I wish to recommend. It may be expressed by saying that there simply are no such things as *propositions*.
>
> (p. 265)

However, he continues in the following terms:

> It might be thought that if there *are* no such things as propositions then whenever we make statements about them (as we constantly do and must do) all these statements must be nonsense. But this result does not by any means necessarily follow. Of course we can, and must, still continue to talk *as* if there were such things as propositions.
>
> (p. 265)

What are we to make of this?

It is not difficult to see here the influence of Russell, and the ideas associated with his theory of descriptions. One might think, Moore suggests, that if there is no such thing as the proposition that lions exist, then the statement 'I believe the proposition that lions exist' must be, not false, but nonsense – just as Russell had suggested that one might think that there if there is no King of France, then the statement 'The King of France is bald' is nonsense.[12] Russell showed that this latter implication does not hold if one adopts his theory of descriptions; and in his discussions of the nature of truth, he argued that the former implication does not hold if one adopts his 'multiple-relation' theory of judgment. One can continue to characterise judgment as a 'propositional attitude', 'as if' it were a relation between a subject and a proposition, even though one takes the view that 'a judgment does not have a single object, namely the proposition, but has several interrelated objects'.[13] Moore does not endorse this theory in *SMPP*, indeed he here declines to offer any positive theory of judgment to replace the pure realist one he has rejected (p. 266). But several of his comments suggest sympathy with Russell's theory – his description of propositions as 'imaginary things' (pp. 290–1, 309), and his view that the mistake which has led people (such as himself) to a realist conception of propositions is that 'they suppose that every expression which seems to be a name of something must be so in fact' (p. 266).

I shall say more in the next chapter about Moore's response to Russell's theory of 'incomplete symbols' which is suggested by these remarks. But the fact that Moore's position is influenced by Russell's ideas in this regard is surely indicative of the way in which he was led to adopt it. As one reads *SMPP* it appears that Moore came to reject the pure realist theory of propositions while delivering his lectures; there is evidence in the lectures of a change of mind on this issue (cf. p. 300). But one should not think that Moore's arrival at this conclusion was just a matter of the internal dialectic of his own thoughts. For the objections to the pure realist theory which Moore advances had been aired by Russell since 1906 in papers which Moore will certainly have studied.[14] So on this issue Moore's discussion in *SMPP* begins to catch up with lines of argument Russell had already developed – whereas on the philosophy of perception at this time Russell still followed Moore.

## 5: Truth

Ramsey observed in his paper 'Facts and Propositions' that 'if we have analysed judgment we have solved the problem of truth'.[15] In his rather unsatisfactory reply to Ramsey, Moore dissented (F&P p. 82); but the truth of Ramsey's thesis is born out by Moore's discussion of truth in *SMPP*. His pure realist theory of judgment had been intimately linked to the identity theory of truth; having rejected these, Moore needs a new theory of truth, but in the absence of a positive theory of judgment, he finds himself unable to provide more than the familiar formula that a belief is true just where it corresponds to a fact (*SMPP* pp. 276–7). To develop this formula into a theory one needs an account of correspondence, and it is here that Ramsey's point applies – without a theory of judgment Moore cannot give such an account. Instead he indulges in some characteristic reflections on our direct apprehension of the relation of correspondence – his audience is instructed 'to hold it before your mind, in the sense in which when I name the colour "vermilion", you can hold before your mind the colour that I mean' (*SMPP* p. 279).

What Moore wants is an account which has the consequence that the belief that $p$ corresponds, when true, with the fact that $p$, and he expresses this at one point as arising from 'the partial identity of name between the belief and the fact in question' (p. 276). But he also remarks that one cannot use this as a definition of correspondence, since it would imply that no belief could be true unless it had a name (pp. 257–8). This objection can be set aside by employing propositional quantifiers, which enable one to formulate Moore's view as the thesis that for all $p$, to say that the belief that $p$ is true is just to say that it is believed that $p$ and that it is a fact that $p$. In the light of this one can ask whether Moore's use of the concept of a fact has any importance, or whether his position can be simplified into that of a redundancy theorist whose position is that for all $p$, to say that the belief that $p$ is true is just to say that $p$, and that it is believed that $p$.

In *SMPP* it sometimes looks as though this is so, for one finds Moore citing as evidence for his 'correspondence' theory instances of the redundancy theorist's position – for example:

> The main recommendation of this theory seems to me to lie in the fact that it does take account of, and does not conflict with, many millions of the most obvious facts. One such obvious fact is that my friend's belief that I have gone away for the holidays certainly will be true, in one common sense of the word, *if* and only if I actually have gone away.
>
> (*SMPP* p. 281)

But when he directly confronts the redundancy position in *SMPP* – 'to say that the belief that I have gone away is *true*, is to say the same thing as to say that I have gone away' (*SMPP* pp. 275–6) – he rejects it. The reason he gives for doing so is very poor: it is just that in saying that I have gone away I don't say that anyone believes that I have gone away; this is of course true, but no objection to the redundancy theory (and the introduction of facts makes no difference to the point Moore has raised). None the less there is, I think, a better reason for his rejection of the redundancy theory in *SMPP*, namely that it does not explicate the concept of truth by reference to that of a fact. For Moore insists here on the reality of facts: they are 'one of the largest and most important classes of things in the Universe' (*SMPP* p. 296). This diagnosis is supported by the position he takes in his reply to Ramsey in F&P, and in his earlier 1925–6 lectures in which he discussed W.E. Johnson's presentation of a redundancy theory in his *Logic* (the name comes from Johnson – cf. *Logic* part I p. 52). On both occasions he objects to the redundancy theory's failure to take account of the relation of 'direct verification' (*LP* p. 145) or 'correspondence' (F&P p. 83) that obtains between a belief and a fact just when the belief is true, and in which the truth of the belief consists. So it is his realist, non-periphrastic, conception of facts which prevents Moore from adopting the position of the redundancy theorist.

But what are these facts? It is only in *SMPP* that Moore discusses the matter in any detail. His position is best understood if one regards his facts on the model of the old true propositions of the identity theory of truth. One cannot quite identify facts with the old true propositions, since, in the old theory, propositions *are* whether or not they are true, whereas in the new theory, truth depends on the existence of facts (*SMPP* pp. 308–9). None the less, the similarities are manifold and represent part of the legacy of pure realism within Moore's later philosophy. He insists that facts must be complex in just the way that propositions had to be, and treats them as having universal properties and particulars as constituents, which were just the constituents of the old propositions. He also writes that in some inexplicable way they are not just the sum of their constituents (*SMPP* p. 309) – just as, in response to Bradley, he acknowledged that propositions have a kind of unity that he could not explain. Finally, at the end of the book he makes concerning facts almost exactly the same ontological claim as he had made at the start of the book about propositions; compare the following two passages:

> The fact is that absolutely all the contents of the Universe, absolutely everything that *is* at all, may be divided into two classes – namely into *propositions*, on the one hand, and into things which are not propositions on the other hand.
>
> (*SMPP* p. 56)

> We may divide all the constituents of the Universe – all the things which are, into two classes, putting into one class those which we can only express by a clause beginning with 'that' or the corresponding verbal noun, and in the other all the rest. Thus we have, in the first class, such things as 'the fact that lions exist'.
>
> (*SMPP* p. 296)

Facts thus conceived will be as varied and complex as the contents of true beliefs, and they constitute a central ontological category of Moore's philosophy for most of the rest of his life. But not, it appears, for all of it: there is an entry in notebook V (1942–3) of *CB* in which he advances the redundancy theorist's position:

> We can say that to call an idea 'true' means that there is a fact *corresponding* to it; but this only means that, if the idea you are talking of is somebody's idea *that* the sun is larger, then in asserting that *this* idea is true, all that you are asserting besides its existence is that the sun is larger: you are asserting 'he believes that the sun is larger & the sun is larger'.
>
> (p. 231)

Was this really Moore's view then? If so, when did he come to hold it? I do not know.

In addition to advancing his 'correspondence' theory of truth in *SMPP*, Moore here criticises coherence and pragmatist theories. I have already discussed Moore's criticisms of the coherence theory of Bradley, Joachim, and others, but his critical discussion of James's pragmatist theory of truth is worth attention. The remarks in *SMPP* (pp. 281–3) are a brief summary of the argument of his 1908 paper WJP, which, remarkably, escaped his usual retrospective self-criticism – in his autobiography in *PGEM* he singles it out as 'a good piece of work' (p. 27). I shall try to show that, despite much unfair and irrelevant rhetoric, Moore's estimate is, in one respect, sound.

James presents his theory as the conclusion to be drawn from two premisses: first, that the criterion of truth is coherence – 'what fits every part of life best and combines with the collectivity of experience's demands, nothing being omitted' (*Pragmatism* p. 80[16]): second, that for truth as for all other concepts, meaning is given by criteria for application, so that for truth 'the reasons why we call things true is the reason why they are true' (*Pragmatism* p. 64). The theory is, therefore, a coherence theory. Moore, however, regularly treats James's pragmatist theory as if it were an alternative to the coherence approach, which he associates exclusively with Bradley. Of course, as James stresses, his theory does not require Bradleian monism; his hope is that by means of evidential relations he can achieve in a respectable way what Bradley, with his internal relations, could only postulate as an article of metaphysical faith.

Symptomatic of Moore's unsatisfactory approach is his interpretation of James's thesis that a belief is true if and only if it is useful or 'works' (cf. *SMPP* pp. 281–2). Since Moore interprets utility by reference to the total utility, or value, which arises from action on the basis of a belief, it is not difficult for him to find fault with this thesis (WJP pp. 113–14). But when James declares that the true is the 'expedient in the way of thinking' (*Pragmatism* p. 222) he is usually just expressing his coherence doctrine, that for a belief to be true is for it to cohere with our other beliefs and in particular with those engendered by our future sense-experiences.[17] So in this respect Moore largely missed the point. Admittedly James also employs the pragmatist conception of belief as a guide to action, and at some points when he talks of the utility of true beliefs he implies that this consists in their enabling us to secure outcomes that are of value to us, as when he says that true beliefs have the function of a 'leading that is worth while' (*Pragmatism* p. 205). But as long as utility, or value, is here interpreted strictly with reference to satisfaction of the desires which motivate action, this pragmatist thesis is not 'intensely silly', as Moore alleged (WJP p. 115). For it is a mark of truth (though not a definition of it) that actions which are guided by true beliefs enable agents to satisfy the desires which motivated them (even if the desires themselves are for worthless ends).

None the less Moore does make one telling criticism of James's position. This arises in the context of his discussion of James's thesis that the truth of a belief consists in its verifiability in the light of sense-experience – i.e. the coherence aspect of James's theory. Moore argues against this by introducing the topic of beliefs about the past, and arguing that James's position conflicts with the application of the law of excluded middle to these beliefs (WJP pp. 101–6). If we take a hypothesis about the past for which there is not now, nor will there ever be, any evidence for or against its truth (Moore's example is the hypothesis that he had the seven of diamonds in the third hand of whist last night), we may well still want to insist that such a hypothesis is either true or false even though we accept that it is neither verifiable nor falsifiable by us.

One response open to James would be to deny that such unverifiable hypotheses have any content, and thus to deny that we can properly make sense of the situation as characterised. This fits with his verificationist conception of meaning, but it seems a desperate move since there is nothing objectionably 'metaphysical' about the case Moore adduces.[18] Another response would be to argue that Moore's problem only arises because verifiability has been too narrowly construed as verifiability in practice. There is, it may be said, no belief about the past which is in principle unverifiable. This response would not get much support from James, who is dismissive of Peirce's conception of 'absolute truth' defined by reference to the long run (cf. *Pragmatism* pp. 223–4), and is content with a weaker conception of 'relative truth' that can always be shown later to be falsehood after all. Furthermore the response is not intrinsically attractive since it seems just an article of metaphysical faith, reminiscent of Bradley's monism, to suppose that in the long run verifying or falsifying evidence will always turn up.

Moore's objection, therefore, raises a serious challenge to James's position, as to any verificationist, or otherwise anti-realist, conception of truth.[19] But Moore's discussion does not take account of the response which Dummett has advanced in recent years: that unverifiable hypotheses about the past are neither true nor false, and that bivalence, or the law of excluded middle, which Moore takes to be 'an obvious fact' (WJP p. 106) concerning such hypotheses, is to be abandoned.[20] I shall not pursue here the issues raised by this response, since a proper discussion of it would take one well away from positions explored by Moore. But it seems clear that the burden of proof lies with those who wish to limit the application of the law of excluded middle to the past for purely epistemological reasons; for it is hard to interpret the contingent unavailability of evidence concerning some hypothesis as a

168

reason for refusing to allow that the past is itself determinate on the matter of the hypothesis.

### 6: Being and existence

Few distinctions were as central to pure realism as that between pure being and existence in time. Moore's anti-empiricism was precisely the thesis that some of the things we know concern objects which certainly are, even though they do not exist in time – such objects being numbers, values, universals, propositions, and also illusory and imaginary objects. So it is not surprising that as Moore thinks through the implications of his rejection in *SMPP* of some of the central doctrines of pure realism, and in particular his rejection of propositions, he should come to call into question the distinction between pure being and existence in time. He puts this change in his thought in the following passage:

> I used to hold very strongly, what many other people are also inclined to hold, that the words 'being' and 'existence' do stand for two entirely different properties; and that though everything that exists must also 'be', yet many things which 'are' nevertheless emphatically do *not* exist. I did, in fact, actually hold this view when I began these lectures; and I have based the whole scheme of lectures upon the distinction, having said that I would deal first with the question what sort of things exist, and then separately, as a quite distinct matter, with the question what sort of things *are*, but don't exist. But nevertheless I am inclined to think that I was quite wrong, and that there is no such distinction between 'being' and 'existence' as I thought there was.
>
> (*SMPP* p. 300)

The division among the lectures to which Moore refers here is that between those concerned with sense-data and material objects, and those concerned with propositions, imaginary objects, and universals. So it is these latter kinds which he initially took to be objects which are but do not exist; but having come to the conclusion that there are in reality no propositions or imaginary objects, he is led to think that the whole being/existence distinction is spurious.

It may be felt that in this respect Moore must have progressed beyond the pure realist position long before *SMPP*; after all Russell's famous attack on Meinong commenced in 1905. But, as I mentioned, in his 1906 paper NROP Moore explicitly mentioned that in cases of illusory perception there is an object of perception which does not exist; and although that possibility is not canvassed in *SMPP*, he does here devote a good deal of space to the denial that imaginary objects 'are' in any

169

sense at all. So I think that on this issue, as on that of propositions, Moore was feeling his way towards Russell's position during the period 1905–11, and only fully accepted it in *SMPP* itself, signalling this acceptance by his abandonment of the being/existence distinction. Indeed, there may be a connection between Moore's abandonment of this distinction and his adoption of a sense-datum theory in *SMPP*. For once Moore has abandoned naive realism, there is no need for him to invoke a being/existence distinction to cope with perceptual illusions. Thus in *SMPP* he takes it that in all cases where sense-data are directly apprehended, the sense-data exist; perceptual illusion arises where the sense-data apprehended do not stand in the relationship to a material object characteristic of veridical perception.

At one point Moore even suggests that all existence is existence in time: 'For my part, I cannot think of any instance of a thing, with regard to which it seems quite certain that it *is*, and yet also that it is not *now*' (*SMPP* p. 294); but I think this is a casual remark which one should set aside. He is more concerned to insist that there is one univocal sense of 'exists' which applies to particulars, universals, and facts. He discusses briefly the objection one can imagine his earlier self raising – that facts and universals do not exist at all; in response he argues that perhaps we normally use the word 'exists' in such a way that only particulars exist, but the property thereby attributed to particulars is no different from that possessed by facts and universals which 'are' (*SMPP* pp. 295–6). And it is certainly this thesis of the univocity of 'existence', or 'being', which he carries forward into his later writings. The further thesis that all existence is existence in time is not one that, I think, is ever even implied elsewhere, and on at least one occasion he makes it clear that he does not think that facts are in time (F&P p. 64).

It may seem that without this further thesis there is here no more than a verbal shift from pure realism. For whereas Moore used to distinguish between existence and being and held that not everything that is exists, he still distinguishes between existence in time and existence *per se* and holds that not everything that exists exists in time. However, the change is more than verbal in the light of Moore's change of view about the kinds of thing which have being or exist. His pure realist view had been that some particulars have being even though they do not exist – imaginary objects, for example. This possibility is excluded by his new way of thinking. Even if facts and universals exist, but not in time, there are no similarly timeless particulars, such as imaginary objects. It is not clear whether one should go further and say that his new view requires that all particulars exist in time. Since the kinds of particular whose existence he acknowledges are mental acts, sense-data, material objects, spaces, and times, my feeling is that Moore's view was that all particulars do in fact exist in time (perhaps his remark quoted above that all existence is existence in time is to be understood as applying only to particulars). But I do not think he would want to regard this as a conceptual truth about the existence of particulars, for he did not want to rule out the conception of a God who exists outside time (p. 17), and the status of time and space themselves in his description of the universe is not clear (p. 16). But even without this further thesis, his new position embodies a significant, and welcome, change from the uncritical ontological generosity of pure realism.

# VI

# Logic and fictions

*'Moore', I said, 'have you any apples in that basket?' 'No', he replied and smiled seraphically as was his wont. I decided to try a different logical tack. 'Moore', I said, 'do you then have some apples in that basket?' 'No', he said once again. Now I was in a logical cleft-stick, so to speak, and had but one way out. 'Moore', I said, 'do you then have apples in that basket?' 'Yes', he replied, and from that day forth we remained the very closest of friends.*

(J. Miller *et al. Beyond the Fringe*)

The importance for Moore of his lectures 'Some Main Problems of Philosophy' is easily seen from the use he makes of ideas presented there in papers published during the next few years (*SMPP* itself not being published until 1953). The introductory chapter 'What is Philosophy?' obviously foreshadows his 1925 paper 'A Defence of Common Sense'. The next chapter on 'Sense-Data', and some of the ensuing discussion of perception, is reworked into his 1914 paper 'The Status of Sense-Data'. The treatment of scepticism about the external world which he presents in his 1918 paper 'Some Judgments of Perception' is similar to that presented in chapter 6 of *SMPP*. The critical discussion of Bradley on reality and appearance is repeated almost verbatim in his 1917 paper 'The Conception of Reality'. Finally, although his rejection of propositions is never set out in detail in his published writings, the position he puts forward in his 1928 paper 'Facts and Propositions' owes much to lines of thought which go back to the arguments considered in *SMPP*.

The remainder of this book is given over to a critical examination of the philosophy which develops out of the positions presented in *SMPP*. In the last two chapters I shall discuss Moore's views about perception and scepticism. Here, and in the next chapter, I shall discuss Moore's

172

work as an 'analytic philosopher'. Since analytic philosophy is as much a style as a doctrine, there is no consensus as to the commitments an analytic philosopher has to have. But the thesis that analysis, and especially logical analysis, has a central role within philosophy seems central. Moore was not himself a logical theorist; but he was one of the first people to appreciate the importance of Russell's achievements in this area, and a critical appreciation of Moore's work as an analytic philosopher must begin with a discussion of Moore's own critical evaluation of Russell's logical theories.

## 1: Logical fictions

One theme of this critical evaluation is a recognition of some degree of misfit between ordinary language and Russell's logic. Moore recognised at an early date that there are uses of definite descriptions to which Russell's theory does not apply, as in 'The right hand is often slightly longer than the left' (*LP* p. 162; cf. RTD pp. 185–6). He was likewise critical of Russell's treatment of the material conditional as an account of implication (E&IR pp. 303–4; Moore's critical thoughts here can be traced back to his unpublished review of *The Principles of Mathematics*). Furthermore, in a series of late entries in *CB* he rejected the treatment of the English conditional as a material conditional (cf. esp. pp. 295–8). But he never sought to develop these thoughts into a general critique of logical analysis as such; he never tried to make a case for the logical ineffability of ordinary language of the kind that Strawson suggested in his *Introduction to Logical Theory*.[1] In particular, in his mature work (though not in his early philosophy) Moore was sensitive to the distinction between meaning and conversational implicature; he makes this distinction very clearly in a letter to Malcolm of 1949:

> It is perfectly possible that a person who uses them [certain words] senselessly, in the sense that he uses them where no sensible person would use them because, under those circumstances, they serve no useful purpose, should be using them *in their normal sense*, & that what he asserts by so using them should be *true*.[2]

Although Moore is here discussing his claim to know such things as that 'This is a tree', he would surely have said much the same about 'The present King of France is not bald'. Moore did not doubt that logical analysis was essential to determine the propositions expressed in ordinary language; his criticisms of Russell's accounts of descriptions and conditionals were essentially that Russell's logical analyses were in some respects too simple; and subsequent work has of course confirmed Moore's position on these issues.

But Moore's critical reflections on Russell's work do not just concern the details of Russell's logical analyses. More fundamentally, they concern the significance of logical analysis, of Russell's 'logical-analytic method in philosophy'.[3] The place to begin an inquiry into Moore's account of this is by considering his response to Russell's theory of logical fictions. Moore discussed this in lectures whose influence can be seen in the references to them in two classic works of this period which deal with issues raised by Russell's analytic programme: Susan Stebbing's *A Modern Introduction to Logic* (especially the second edition) and John Wisdom's *Logical Constructions* (especially the first article).[4] Although Moore himself published little directly on this topic, we can now study Moore's views on this matter from his lecture notes, published in *LP*, on the topic 'Classes and Incomplete Symbols'.

Moore's starting-point here is Russell's ambivalence concerning the truth-value of the sentence 'There are classes'. It is because Russell regards classes as 'logical fictions' that he thinks there is a sense in which there are classes and a sense in which there are not. But what does it mean to say that classes are 'logical fictions'? Moore observes that this is to be understood in the light of Russell's theory of incomplete symbols. Russell defines what it is for a symbol to be incomplete in a variety of ways, but Moore cites one typical formulation from *Principia Mathematica*: an incomplete symbol is one 'which is not supposed to have any meaning in isolation, but is only defined in certain contexts',[5] and although this is not the most lucid of definitions, the two clauses here capture important aspects of his thought.

The thesis that incomplete symbols have no meaning in isolation is to be understood in terms of the Russell–Moore one-level theory of meaning; it asserts that the meaning of an incomplete symbol does not consist in there being some one thing which the symbol means, or stands for. Russell sometimes put this point by saying that incomplete symbols do not stand for things which are constituents of the propositions, or facts, expressed by sentences in which the incomplete symbol occurs and Moore once suggested that one might use this feature of incomplete symbols to define them.[6] The other part of Russell's definition – that incomplete symbols are 'defined in certain contexts' – suggests his positive account of the meaning of incomplete symbols. For although they have no meaning 'in isolation', they are not meaningless adjuncts of sentences in which they occur. Instead, according to Russell, their meaning can be identified by means of analytic definitions of what is meant by sentences which include them.

It is largely in terms of this latter aspect of Russell's theory that Moore discusses it in *LP*. Since Moore accepts much of what is unsatisfactory in Russell's theory, and does not take into account the semantic role of logical constants, his discussion does not go very deep. But he does make the important observation (*LP* pp. 118–19) that in

174

practice Russell limits the application of the term 'incomplete symbol' to expressions such as definite descriptions and class abstracts which, as far as surface grammar goes, appear to be names. For example, Russell's account of incomplete symbols implies that he should regard the predicate 'exists' as one; but in fact he never does so. Moore therefore suggests that most of what matters to Russell concerning incomplete symbols is captured by defining them as expressions which look like names but which logical analysis reveals not to be such.

Russell makes the transition from incomplete symbols to logical fictions in a very straightforward manner: $a$ is a logical fiction iff '$a$' is an incomplete symbol. The underlying thought here is obvious, given the amended definition of an incomplete symbol: logical fictions are the fictitious entities which we suppose incomplete symbols to stand for when we fail to realise that they are not the names they appear to be. Those who grasp logical form correctly are freed from any such ontological commitment, even if they still frame their thoughts as if there are such things, as Russell does in the case of those 'quasi-things', classes.[7] Yet, despite the naturalness of this thought, Moore saw that Russell was here blurring an important distinction (*LP* pp. 121–2).

The distinction is that although Russell does not regard 'the author of Waverley' as a name, his theory of descriptions is such that propositions expressed by sentences in which the description has primary occurrence assert the existence of at least one author of Waverley; but the analogous point does not hold of his analysis of class abstracts. In this case the propositions assert only the existence of propositional functions. The point can be expressed in a Quinean way: in the case of descriptions, the analysis quantifies over just the things which it looks as though the description names: in the case of class abstracts, this is not so. Now it is only where this latter condition obtains that it is appropriate to talk of 'logical fictions'; for here the conception of things of a certain kind is liable to be fictitiously projected on to the world through a failure to grasp the logical form of what is said. This does not apply to definite descriptions; a failure to grasp that 'the author of Waverley' is not a name will not lead one to think that there is something it names to which the Russellian analysis does not commit one anyway. Admittedly, in the case of empty descriptions ('the present King of France') one might make a fictitious (Meinongian) projection; but one who takes definite descriptions to be names certainly does not have to take this view (as Russell knew) and the possibility of it does not suffice for it to be true that the present Queen of England is a logical fiction.

A different way of approaching the relationship between incomplete symbols and logical fictions is by observing that the occurrence of '$a$' in ' "$a$" is an incomplete symbol' is non-extensional, whereas that in '$a$ is a logical fiction' appears to be extensional. Since it is the conception of an incomplete symbol that is basic, this implies that one should not speak of a thing as a logical fiction *tout court*, but only, e.g., of the class of men as a logical fiction *qua* class of men (i.e. in so far as 'the class of men' is an incomplete symbol). In fact, as applied to classes and propositions, this point has little significance, for it is a consequence of Russell's treatment of classes, and his multiple-relation theory of judgment, that all apparent names of classes and propositions are incomplete symbols. But the point would certainly have application if one were to accept Russell's view that the present Queen of England is a logical fiction: it could only be *qua* Queen of England that she is a logical fiction. However, this shows, in a different way, why Moore was right to object to Russell's treatment of her as a logical fiction at all. For the possibility of referring to her by means of a genuine name is internally related to the fact that Russell's theory of descriptions involves quantification over precisely the sort of thing which the definite description appears to name.

Moore puts the point I have been discussing by saying that 'A is a logical fiction' is true iff 'A' is an incomplete symbol and is not a description. This is rather *ad hoc*, though it produces the right results. Nonetheless the general direction of Moore's critical reaction to Russell's use of the expression 'logical fiction' is right. In particular, it enables one to identify the source of Russell's ambivalence concerning the truth of 'There are classes' and to assess its significance. The sense in which it is true is that in which its truth is to follow from the truth of sentences such as 'My fingers form a class'; and the sense in which it is false is that which the thesis that classes are logical fictions implies. As long as it is also accepted that an analysis of what is meant by a sentence presents its content more clearly than the unanalysed sentence (a crucial assumption to which I shall return in the next chapter), then it must follow that more significance is to be attached to Russell's denial of existence to classes than to his acceptance of them. There is a sense in which the latter is only verbal: it just tells us that sentences of certain kinds express true propositions; whereas the denial of existence purports to tell us how things 'really' are – how things are if they are just as our language, properly analysed, shows them to be.

This way of putting things conflicts with what Moore says; for he says (*LP* p. 122) that it is only when Russell is denying existence to classes, on the grounds that they are logical fictions, that his claim is one about symbols. But he is doubly mistaken on this point. His reason for maintaining that the denial of existence is about symbols is that the conception of a logical fiction is defined in terms of that of an incomplete symbol. However, as we have seen, one who maintains that classes are logical fictions does not just maintain that symbols for classes are incomplete; he must also establish that the analysis of the incomplete symbols involved does not embody any ontological commitment to classes, and the content of this latter commitment is not 'about' symbols at all. Equally, where Moore claims that in the sense in which 'There are classes' is true it is not about symbols, he is mistaken. Moore thinks that it is not about symbols because its truth follows directly from the truth of 'My fingers form a class' which is not about symbols. But it does not thus follow; for once it is accepted that class abstracts are incomplete symbols, one cannot apply to sentences including them the principle of existential instantiation ('$Fa \supset (\exists x)(Fx)$'). Thus the only way to derive 'There are classes' from the fact that 'My fingers form a class' expresses a true proposition is to interpret it as something like: 'Some sentences apparently about classes express true propositions.'

Moore's mistake on this issue is an instance of his general thesis, which I shall discuss further in the next chapter, that analysis is neutral concerning questions about what exists (DCS p. 53). In *LP* it connects with his attitude to Russell's logical constructions. Moore interprets the term 'logical construction' as just a stylistic variant of 'logical fiction', but does not want to draw the conclusion that logical constructions are fictions. For he holds that one should not infer from the hypothesis 'Pennies are logical constructions of appearances' that they do not exist. So he objects to Russell's talk of logical fictions as fictions (*LP* p. 122).

Several issues are combined here. An initial point to make is that although Russell often uses the terms 'logical fiction' and 'logical construction' in close proximity, they do not have the same sense. He never says that classes themselves are logical constructions, though they are paradigm logical fictions. Nor does he attempt to argue directly that numbers or material objects are logical fictions; rather, in advancing the thesis that they are logical constructions, he takes this to follow from the thesis that they are classes (of equinumerous classes in one case, of appearances in the other). Admittedly it will follow that for him numbers and physical objects are logical fictions, since he thinks that classes are logical fictions. But, as he usually observes, this conclusion requires this extra premiss.[8] I think Russell's conception of a logical construction is to be understood as follows: 'As are logical constructions' means that although As do not appear to be classes, all our thoughts about As can be analysed as thoughts about classes of things which are not As. The basic idea is that once we have things of one kind, appearances, for example, and we allow ourselves to form classes of these things, then we do not need a separate category of material objects *as well*; we can 'substitute' the conception of a class of appearances for that of a material object beyond appearances.[9]

It follows from this that if one rejects Russell's conception of classes as logical fictions, one can in principle hold both that pennies are logical constructions and that they really exist, as Moore wants. But much here depends on the way in which the logical construction is carried out. In the case of Russell's theory of natural number, there is a straightforward identification of particular numbers with particular classes, such that all properties of numbers are interpreted as properties of the corresponding class. In this case, therefore, the thesis that numbers are logical constructions does nothing to undermine the thesis that numbers exist. In other cases, however, there is no such straightforward identification. Instead, the claim is that propositions expressed by sentences concerning things of one kind are to be analysed as propositions concerning classes of things of some other kind. Thus the proposition expressed by 'This penny looks brown' is not analysed by Russell as a proposition, concerning a class of appearances which 'is' this penny, that it looks brown; instead it is analysed as a proposition, concerning that class of appearances which are of this penny (whatever that means), that it includes a brown appearance now. This logical construction clearly does not preserve our common-sense ontology of persisting substances; although the theory talks of classes of appearances in addition to appearances, these classes are not our familiar pennies under a new description. In this case, therefore, the theory of material objects as logical constructions is a theory of logical fictions. I shall discuss further in chapter 7 (section 4) how Moore reacted to this kind of challenge to common-sense; but a remark of Wisdom's shows that he certainly grasped the underlying point:

> We must not say that a table *is* the string of events which make up its life-history. For then to say of a table that it collapsed is to say of a string of events that they collapsed. On the other hand, the fact that the table collapsed is perhaps nothing but the fact that a set of suitably interrelated events includes a collapse. We may claim that this is so and avoid the mistake of saying that a table *is* a string of events by saying that the table is a logical construction out of events (I owe this point to Prof. Moore).[10]

### 2: Existence

I noted in chapter 5 that one of the clear indications of Moore's abandonment of pure realism in *SMPP* is his rejection of the contrast between being and existence, and his insistence instead that there is just one property, existence, which belongs to all things, be they particulars, universals, or facts. We have just seen that in his reflections on Russell's doctrine of logical fictions, Moore qualifies this thesis; there is a sense in which the sentences 'There are classes' and 'There are propositions' are true, and a sense in which they are not. I suggested, however, that despite Moore's views to the contrary, the sense in which they are true is such that they are somewhat misleading – for it is a sense in which they just assert the truth of certain kinds of thought or utterance. So the doctrine of logical fictions presents no deep challenge to the univocity of existence. In his later writings about existence, however, Moore is led to postulate a deeper ambiguity in 'exists', between a sense in which it does not 'stand for an attribute', and a sense in which it does 'stand for an attribute' (EP pp. 124, 126).

In thinking about this it is useful to start from his response to Russell's treatment of existence – that 'when you take any propositional function and assert that of it that . . . it is sometimes true, that gives you the fundamental meaning of "existence" '.[11] In *SMPP* Moore shows no awareness of this thesis (which, I think, Russell first explicitly advanced in *Principia Mathematica* pp. 174–5, so I doubt if Moore would have encountered it at the time of *SMPP*). But a notable feature of his 1917 paper CR is that although most of it comes straight out of *SMPP* he adds a couple of pages (pp. 212–13) in which he puts forward the view that 'the terms "real" and "unreal" cannot . . . be properly said to stand for any conception whatever'. Moore's argument for this Russellian view is that in saying 'Lions are real' we are not saying that all lions have a property – the property of being real – in the way in which in saying 'Lions are mammals' we are attributing the property of being a mammal to all lions. Instead, Moore maintains, in saying 'Lions are real' we mean that the property of being a lion belongs to something; but, he insists, it does not follow that the word 'real' here stands for the property of belonging to something. On the contrary, if it did, in saying 'Lions are real' we would be saying that lions belong to something. Since this is plainly not the case, Moore concludes, 'real' does not here stand for a property at all.

In EP an account of this kind of use of 'exist' (which in CR Moore does not distinguish from 'real') is set alongside the thesis that there is another use of 'exist' in which it does stand for a property (or attribute, as he says here). For, Moore observes, we can surely say truly of something at which we are pointing 'This *might* not have existed', and this can only be so if 'This exists' is itself significant. But where 'exists' is the sort of incomplete symbol which, he has argued, it is in such sentences as 'Lions exist', the sentence 'This exists' is literally meaningless. So we have to recognise that the sense of 'exists' in which it occurs in 'This exists' is distinct from that with which it occurs in 'Lions exist'; and in the former sense it does 'stand for an attribute', since the property expressed by 'exists' is here predicated of that to which 'this' refers, i.e. some particular. Moore complicates his argument for this last conclusion by introducing the assumption that sense-data are the objects

179

of demonstrative reference and suggesting that one might construe 'This exists' as 'The thing which this sense-datum is "of" exists', and thereby conclude, with the help of Russell's theory of descriptions, that 'exists' here does not stand for an attribute after all. But he goes on to observe that we can take 'This might not have existed' to be saying of a sense-datum itself that it is possible that it should not have existed. So the possibility, if there is one, of interpreting 'This exists' in such a way that 'exists' does not here stand for an attribute does not affect Moore's conclusion that there is a way of interpreting it – which is indeed the obvious way of interpreting it – in which it does stand for an attribute.[12]

Moore's argument here was, I think, one of the first substantive criticisms of the thesis that 'existence is not a predicate', and is, I think, decisive; obviously it does not require his assumption that sense-data are the objects of demonstrative reference. It is worth noting that it does not only straightforwardly establish a need for existence as a first-order property; it also challenges the familiar view that this point can be encompassed within a theory which holds that the basic concept expressed by 'exists' is that which is captured by the use of the existential quantifier, the idea here being that the first-order predicate '$(\exists x)(x = \ldots)$' captures all that one needs by way of a first-order property of existence.[13] The Moorean challenge to this view is to explain what it is for '$a$ might not exist' to be true without employing existence as a first-order property in addition to the existential quantifier and identity. The natural suggestion that '$(\exists x)(x = a)$' is false in a possible world just where in that world there does not exist something identical to $a$ obviously fails. One might relativise identity to possible worlds, and then propose '$(\exists w) \sim (\exists x)(x = $in $w\ a)$'; but it is not easy to think of any non-question-begging reason for insisting where $a$ does not exist in $w$, $\sim (a =$in $w\ a)$. It may appear that Lewis's counterpart theory offers a way out; for there is no difficulty with '$(\exists w) \sim (\exists x)(x = C(a,w))$'. But the difficulty now recurs in the need to express the thought that nothing exists in more than one possible world; within Lewis's theory, this requires an existence predicate.[14]

Moore's argument concerning 'This might not exist' occurs right at the end of EP, in a way which rather suggests that it was an afterthought on his part. In fact Moore had been thinking about the matter for many years, perhaps stimulated by Russell's claim that 'the word "existence" cannot be significantly applied to subjects immediately given'.[15] He presents much the same argument as occurs in EP in his lecture notes for 1928–9 (LP pp. 40–1). Moore also makes several related claims in his 1927 paper F&P, when responding to Ramsey's argument for the thesis that 'what things there are in the world . . .[is] something presupposed by logic or at best a proposition of logic'.[16]

Ramsey sought to show that if $a$, $b$, and $c$ are the only things in the world, then it is a necessary truth that this is so. For, he argued, if it is not, then there might be something else, which does not in fact exist – say $d$. But since the numerical difference between different things is necessary, $d$'s difference from $a$ will be a necessary truth, and this implies that $d$'s existence itself is necessary, which conflicts with the assumption that $d$ does not in fact exist. Moore correctly replies that numerical difference is only a necessary relation in the sense that, '*if a and b* both exist, then $a$ must be other than $b$' (F&P p. 88); hence, even where $a$ is different from $b$ it is not a necessary truth that $a$ is different from $b$ since this 'would entail besides that "*a* exists" is necessary, and that "*b* exists" is necessary, which I should deny'.[17]

This reply explicitly commits Moore to the contingency of some propositions of the form '*a* exists'. He also shows here an awareness of the implications of this view for logical theory. He rejects Ramsey's claim that '$(\forall x)(Fx)$' entails '$Fa$' on the ground that the further premiss '*a* exists' is required, and he goes on to observe that Ramsey was mistaken in supposing that '$\sim Fa$', where this expresses the contradictory of '$Fa$', is inconsistent with '$(\forall x)(Fx)$'; what is inconsistent with '$(\forall x)(Fx)$' is the conjunction of '$\sim Fa$' and '*a* exists'. Moore is thus making a move towards free logic, and introducing the distinction between the internal and external negation of sentences of the form '$Fa$' which is essential once one allows that there can be empty names and that existence is a predicate (Moore discusses internal and external negation further in *CB*, pp. 262, 264).

It is clear from all this that Moore's commitment to existence as a first-order property was deep and well thought out. But he was also aware that there is something strange about the claim that sentences such as 'This exists' express contingent truths. For, he observes, the sentence 'There is no such thing as this sense-datum' '*couldn't* have been true, because it is self-contradictory' (*LP* p. 129). What seems to lie behind this is the thesis that it is a condition of the significance of demonstrative reference that the demonstrative should actually refer to something. This is in one way similar to the position advocated recently by Evans,[18] though Evans lacks Moore's reliance upon sense-data as objects of demonstrative reference, which ensures that for Moore a hallucinating subject refers to something (a sense-datum) by his demonstrative even if there is no appropriate object in physical space. Setting aside this complication, however, we can ask how Moore proposes to hold both that 'This exists' does not express a necessary truth and that its negation is self-contradictory.

There are verbal distinctions to be drawn here, between necessary truths and truths whose denial is self-contradictory (Moore sometimes calls these latter 'tautologies' – e.g. *CB* pp. 239–40). But what matters is the underlying semantic theory within which the modal distinctions are to be incorporated. In *LP* Moore says that the contingency of 'This exists' arises from the fact that 'there *might have been* no such prop. as "There is such a thing as this sense-datum"' (p. 129). It is not obvious how this helps; but one can perhaps read into Moore's notes at this point an intimation of the need to distinguish two types of meaning in order to handle demonstratives and other indexicals satisfactorily. Just how one best proceeds on this matter is controversial; but the distinction which Moore's remarks suggest is one between, on the one hand, the proposition expressed by the utterance of a sentence, and, on the other, the conditions constitutive of the fact that that proposition is expressed by that utterance, which I shall call the 'character' of the utterance. Employing this distinction one can now hold that the character of any utterance of 'This exists' is such that such utterances express no proposition unless they are true (which is why their denial is self-contradictory) even though the proposition expressed by an utterance of 'This exists' said of *a* is simply that *a* exists, and there is no inherent problem about the contingent truth of this. Thus as long as one is prepared to distinguish the character of an utterance from the proposition thereby expressed, the problem Moore identified can be resolved.[19]

The fact that, despite this last point, Moore well understood the role of existence as a first-order property raises the question as to why he held on to the view that there is another sense of 'exists' which 'does not stand for an attribute', and I now turn to his arguments for this view in EP. He begins the paper by expressing some doubts as to what this thesis means, but as the paper proceeds he advances two main interpretations of it which essentially rest on a comparison between the use of 'exist' in 'Tame tigers exist' and related sentences, and the use of 'growl' in 'Tame tigers growl' and related sentences. The first interpretation he offers is that to say that 'exists' does not stand for an attribute, whereas 'growls' does, is to say that whereas the meaning of the sentence 'Some tame tigers don't growl' is unproblematic, the sentence 'Some tame tigers don't exist' is meaningless if 'exist' has here the meaning that it has in 'Tame tigers exist'. The second interpretation he offers that whereas 'This growls', uttered by someone pointing at a tiger, makes perfectly good sense, 'This exists', uttered in the same circumstances, is meaningless where 'exists' has the sense that it has in 'Tame tigers exist'. Moore does not connect these two interpretations; but the implicit connection must be that if 'Some tame tigers don't exist' is meaningless, it is so because the form of words 'Some *F*s don't *G*' only makes sense where '*G*' stands for a first-level property, and it is just this which is denied by one who says that 'This exists' is meaningless. Hence whichever interpretation is fixed on, the thesis is essentially that, as it occurs in 'Tame tigers exist' 'exist' does not stand for a first-level property, but is instead to be construed as having the semantic role of the existential quantifier.

Yet so far from the two intermediate interpretations of the thesis offering it any support, they suggest reasons against it. As Moore himself recognises, we can make sense of both 'This exists' and 'Some tame tigers don't exist'. I have already discussed the former of these, and in this sense 'Some tame tigers don't exist' will also be meaningful, though perhaps obviously false. Moore in fact implies that in order to give 'Some tame tigers don't exist' a sense we have to interpret it as 'Some imaginary tame tigers don't exist' which, although it gives us a sense in which it is true, raises the question of the status of imaginary and fictional things. Now this question is certainly worth discussing, and the next section is devoted precisely to Moore's interesting views on this matter. But it is not essential for someone who thinks that existence is a first-order property to hold that there are things (e.g. imaginary objects) which do not exist; thus the thesis that 'Some tame tigers don't exist' is meaningless can be criticised without introducing the issue of imaginary objects (and to do Moore justice, he recognises this in his lecture notes on this topic – cf. *LP* p. 41).

It is because he recognises that his interpretations of the thesis that 'exists' does not stand for an attribute are vulnerable to this kind of criticism that Moore formulates his interpretations of the thesis with constant reference to the sense of 'exists' that it bears in 'Tame tigers exist' and compares our use of this sentence with our use of 'Tame tigers growl'. So the question is whether Moore is able to point to aspects of our use of these two sentences (and related ones) which show that his thesis, essentially as he first interprets it, is correct. Although his discussion here is famous, it is not easy to take from it a clear line of argument, but I think the following reconstruction does him justice. He begins by setting up three related contrasts: (i) whereas 'Tame tigers growl' means, according to context, 'All tame tigers growl', or 'Most tame tigers growl', or 'Some tame tigers growl', 'Tame tigers exist' means only 'Some tame tigers exist'; (ii) whereas the meanings of 'All tame tigers growl' and 'Most tame tigers growl' are unproblematic, it is not obvious that 'All tame tigers exist' and 'Most tame tigers exist' have any meaning; (iii) whereas the meaning of 'Some tame tigers don't growl' is unproblematic, it is not obvious that 'Some tame tigers don't exist' has any meaning. Moore then takes this last point to be crucial; he claims that where 'exists' means what it does in 'Some tame tigers exist' 'Some tame tigers don't exist' is meaningless, and that from this it follows that 'All tame tigers exist' and 'Most tame tigers exist' are meaningless, which accounts for points (i) and (ii) above.

In thinking about this, I think we need to separate an assessment of the linguistic data which Moore offers (points (i)–(iii) above) from an assessment of the use which Moore himself makes of them. For, as the widespread fame of Moore's paper shows, there is something in Moore's linguistic observations; but it is far from clear that he deals with them satisfactorily. The crucial claim in Moore's argument is that, in the requisite sense, 'Some tame tigers don't exist' is meaningless. His argument for this is very brief: since 'Some tame tigers exist' means just 'There are some tame tigers', 'Some tame tigers don't exist' must mean, if anything, 'There are some tame tigers which don't exist' – which is, however, meaningless (p. 118). This argument has two unsatisfactory aspects: first, the starting-point is question-begging since one who holds that 'exist' stands for an attribute will want to say that 'Some tame tigers exist' means 'There are some tame tigers which exist'. If he were to allow Moore's rendering of it, he would certainly be ill-placed to explain the role of the negation in 'Some tame tigers don't exist' since the only negations of 'There are some tame tigers' are 'There are no tame tigers' and 'There are some non-tame tigers', neither of which are candidates for the meaning of 'Some tame tigers don't exist'. Moore, however, does not exploit the potential of the premiss he has given himself; so we can forget about its question-begging nature. But his argument that 'There are some tame tigers which don't exist' is meaningless consists just of a rhetorical question – 'Is it possible that there should be any tame tigers which don't exist?' (p. 118). The answer Moore clearly expects is 'No'; but, and this is the second unsatisfactory aspect of Moore's argument, the conclusion he wants does not follow from this answer to his question. Someone who thinks that existence is an attribute can also hold that it is necessary truth that everything exists, and thus that it is not possible that there should be things – e.g. tame tigers – which do not exist. So Moore's direct argument for his thesis that 'Some tame tigers don't exist' is meaningless is thoroughly unsatisfactory.

None the less there is perhaps an indirect argument from the linguistic data which Moore adduces. For if the best explanation of the data were the hypothesis that 'Some tame tigers don't exist' is meaningless then this fact would be a good argument for it. But what are the data? Moore's thesis implies, as he rightly says, that 'All tame tigers exist' and 'Most tame tigers exist' are meaningless (for we have no way to construe these without using 'exist' as a first-level predicate); but the data were not that these sentences are meaningless – only that there was something strange about them. And this observation is consistent with the thesis that 'exists' stands for an attribute; for if it is also held to be obvious that everything exists, then it is not clear what point there is in 'All (or most) tame tigers exist'. Moore's opponent will say that the oddity here is pragmatic, rather than semantic, and if anything, I think, naive reflection supports Moore's opponent on this point. Of course, one

184

can deny that everything exists (perhaps imaginary objects do not); but if one takes this line then one will certainly want 'All tame tigers exist' to be meaningful. However, this does not quite deal with Moore's linguistic data. For there remains his starting-point, the observation that 'Tame tigers growl' can mean, according to context, 'All tame tigers growl', 'Most etc.', or 'Some etc.', whereas 'Tame tigers exist' typically means only 'Some tame tigers exist'.

Moore's observation needs to be assessed in the light of other similar linguistic data. Three further observations are *prima facie* relevant: (i) if one considers, not 'Tame tigers exist' but 'The tame tigers exist', then the situation is exactly like that which Moore describes for 'Tame tigers growl' – i.e. what is said means, according to context, 'All of the tame tigers exist', 'Most of the etc.', or 'Some of the etc.' with the first of these the dominant interpretation, as is the case with 'Tame tigers growl' (the point is perhaps clearer if one considers 'The Old Testament prophets exist'); (ii) there are similar cases which do not require the definite article – e.g. 'Historical characters exist', or 'People depicted in portraits exist'; (iii) there are sentences of the form of 'Tame tigers growl' which seem to admit only, or at least predominantly, the 'Some' interpretation – e.g. 'Women do take drugs', 'Students do fail examinations'. These facts suffice by themselves, I think, to show that there is not the simple contrast between 'exists' and 'growls' which Moore suggests. What is less clear is just what is going on in all these cases.

The third group is perhaps to be explained by treating the auxiliary verb 'do' here as an existential operator, comparable to 'sometimes', and if that is right these cases are not directly relevant to 'Tame tigers exist'. The first group relies on the use of the definite article to introduce reference, in some sense, to some perhaps contextually specified group in such a way as to allow that questions of existence can be sensibly raised concerning its members. This, I think, shows that what is essential to the most important group, the second, is that the subject term involved be one such that either there might be a sensible question as to whether things to which it applies actually exist or else it is a restriction of a predicate for which this is true (e.g. it is because not all pictures depict actual persons that we naturally interpret 'People depicted in portraits exist' as 'All people depicted in portraits exist'). If this is right, it implies that the reason why we normally take 'Tame tigers exist' to mean just 'Some tame tigers exist' is essentially pragmatic: it is so obvious that anything which is a tame tiger actually exists that we cannot take that obvious truth to be the significance of an utterance of 'Tame tigers exist' – and instead we take it to have the non-trivial significance of 'Some tame tigers exist'. Furthermore, this point can be incorporated in the view that the primary semantic interpretation of

'Tame tigers exist' is, like that of 'Tame tigers growl', the universal one as 'All tame tigers exist'. For if one takes it that such universal propositions have existential import (as Moore does in EP – p. 119), then 'Tame tigers exist' means 'Some tame tigers exist and there is no tame tiger which does not exist'; but since the second conjunct of this is a trivial truth, we typically pay it no attention and, focusing only on the first conjunct, interpret 'Tame tigers exist' as just 'Some tame tigers exist'. When the second conjunct is non-trivial, as in the case of the existence of people depicted in paintings, we cannot just take the first conjunct to exhaust the point of what is said and we recognise the existential claim for the universal claim that it usually is.

The conclusion to be drawn from all this is that Moore's linguistic data, though clever and interesting, do not provide evidence for the claim that existence is not a first-order property. And with this conclusion, the case against Moore's arguments for this thesis is complete. Obviously, it does not follow from the fact that Moore's arguments are unsatisfactory that there are no other, better, arguments for this thesis; in particular, the issue of negative existentials needs to be resolved satisfactorily before one can be happy about any general thesis in this area. Moore does not address this issue directly, but I think that some of his remarks about imaginary objects, which I discuss in the next section, point towards a treatment of this issue which does not require more than a first-order property of existence.

### 3: Imaginary objects

Moore devotes one of the central chapters of *SMPP* to 'The Meaning of "Real"'. He is drawn into this by his attempt to provide a 'general description of the whole Universe', and, in particular, by Bradley's views about the unreality of time. Once embarked he characteristically finds it difficult to call a halt and launches into a long discussion of imaginary objects via the thesis that 'the commonest usage of "real" in ordinary life is that in which it is opposed to "imaginary"' (*SMPP* p. 211). Moore's practice here anticipates Austin's famous claim that 'with "real" . . . it is the *negative* use that wears the trousers';[20] for he takes it that since to be unreal is to be imaginary, an account of the the meaning of 'real' requires an elucidation of the concept of an imaginary object.

Having begun to think critically about this topic, Moore returned to it several times. In *SMPP* the discussion is largely negative; Moore is just concerned to reject the naive view of his pure realist self – 'we mustn't suppose that there *is* such a thing as a chimaera, merely because we can do something which we call thinking of it and making propositions about it' (p. 291). But in CR Moore suggests that thinking of a unicorn is something like thinking that there is a unicorn (CR

p. 217; cf. *LP* p. 26); and if this were right it would help. For, by treating 'thinking of' as an incompletely specified propositional attitude, Moore assimilates the question 'How can I think of a unicorn when there aren't any?' to 'How can I think that there is a unicorn when there aren't any?', and the latter question does not raise quite the difficulty that the former seems to raise, since there is not here the appearance of a relation ('thinking of') which obtains between me and a unicorn. Admittedly, there remains the issue of the possibility of false beliefs, but that was there anyway.

Although this idea, or some variant of it, is widespread,[21] I do not myself regard it as satisfactory. It is, for example, clearly possible to think of a unicorn without thinking that there are any; and in my view, pictorial modes of representation, which are central to the imagination (cf. *SMPP* p. 248), are not propositional at all. But we can leave this issue to one side, for it is largely independent of the issue of the reality of imaginary objects, on which I want to concentrate. It is in his 1928–9 lecture notes that we find Moore's most extended treatment of this issue, although it recurs in his published papers EP and IO.

Moore begins his discussion in *LP* with the following puzzle: since from 'There are material objects' we can infer 'Material objects are real', why is it that we cannot infer 'Imaginary material objects are real' from 'There are imaginary material objects' (p. 21)? He suggests, as a solution, that 'There are imaginary material objects' just means 'There are properties such that, if anything had them, it would be a material object, but nothing has them' (p. 22). Since this is satisfied by properties such as having a mass of exactly 2.56789 grams if, in fact, nothing has that mass, it will not do. In EP Moore says that 'Some tame tigers are imaginary objects' just means 'People have imagined, or told fictional stories about, some tame tigers' (p. 120), and this implies that 'There are imaginary objects' means something like 'People have imagined, or told fictional stories about, things of some kind'. This is clearly an improvement, but it will not quite do by itself, since 'Some tame tigers are imaginary objects' implies that those tame tigers do not exist, and that implication is not present in the analysis. Furthermore, it is not easy to see how to add it; it is not implied that no tame tigers exist, so some way must be found of predicating non-existence of the ones which people have imagined without the existential commitment that is normally implied by the use of quantifiers and variables.

In *LP* Moore confronts what is in effect this issue by asking how it is possible for different people to think of one and the same imaginary object – e.g. Aladdin's lamp (p. 26). He begins by considering Russell's account of what it is for two people to think of the same real object. In this case, according to Russell (and Moore agrees with Russell here), there will be properties which apply only to the object (e.g. Julius

Caesar) such that both people know, with respect to one of the properties, that there is just one thing with that property and think that something is true of the thing with that property. This account is of course based on Russell's conception of knowledge by description, and is a consequence of Russell's thesis that no two people are acquainted with the same particulars. There are many criticisms that could be made of it; but my aim at present is just to explore Moore's reasons for thinking that no account of this kind will work where two people are thinking of the same imaginary object.

His main reason is very simple: in the case of an imaginary object there simply are no properties which uniquely apply to the object, since it does not really exist. This point might be disputed: for surely Cinderella is the girl with the two ugly step-sisters etc. The brief answer to this is that although this is indeed true *in the story*, it is not true in the real world, and Russell's account requires properties which really apply to the same object. This in turn might be disputed, but since I think that to make good its denial one will have to introduce the conception of imaginary objects as non-existent objects which Moore is aiming to show to be unnecessary, the point is not worth pursuing. It is at least clear that if the requirement of Russell's theory is stated in terms of properties which *really* apply, then the theory will not yield an account of two people thinking of the same imaginary object.

Moore adds two further objections to a Russellian account of the matter. First, he rightly observes that in thinking of an imaginary object we do not typically think of it as *the* unique bearer of certain properties. Instead, we just think that something had the properties without thinking that many things had those properties; to take Moore's example of the parable of the Good Samaritan, we think: 'A certain man was going down from Jerusalem to Jericho; and he fell among robbers, which both stripped him and beat him and departed, leaving him half dead.' Moore connects this point with a criticism of Russell's view of fictional names as disguised definite descriptions (the definite descriptions under which, according to Russell, we think of the imaginary objects): on Russell's view of the matter 'Apollo does not exist' need not involve a denial of existence. For since 'Apollo' is a disguised definite description, 'Apollo does not exist' is construed as just a denial of the conjunction of existence and uniqueness. But this, as Moore observes, has the absurd result that when we deny that Apollo exists, 'we're only saying with regard to the properties mentioned in the Classical Dict. under Apollo, that it's not true that only *one* person possessed them all, & are leaving it perfectly open that there may have been several who did' (*LP* p. 32).

The central idea of Moore's alternative account is that the inapplicable condition that the properties the people are thinking of should apply to the same thing is to be replaced by a causal condition on the thoughts –

either that one person's having his thought is caused by the other's having his, or that they both derive ultimately from a common source. Moore adds to this causal condition the further condition that the properties the people are thinking of should be similar – i.e. the people should be prepared to tell much the same story. It seems to me, however, that this condition is not really necessary, although it is a useful evidence concerning the identity of the objects of thought; for behind the causal condition is the ideal of one person deliberately repeating a story told by another. This ideal guarantees the same story in the two cases; but human hearing, memory, and inventiveness being what they are, this ideal is not often realised and we usually only get approximate similarity of stories. But as long as the similarity is such that we can plausibly take it that the second story is an attempt at a repetition of the first, then the constitutive causal condition is satisfied. Thus Moore's similarity condition is to be regarded not as a separate necessary condition on thinking of the same imaginary object but as important evidence that the constitutive causal condition of repetition is satisfied.

Moore's assignment of a central role to the concept of causality seems clearly right, though I shall suggest below that there is a further detail to be added. As Moore notes (*LP* p. 34) one virtue of this account is that it explains the fact that where exactly similar stories in fact have different sources, we do not regard them as stories about the same things, and we therefore judge them to be, in a sense, different stories. David Lewis has recently used one of Borges' stories to make this point: 'When Pierre Menard re-tells *Don Quixote*, that is not the same fiction as Cervantes' *Don Quixote* – not even if they are in the same language and match word for word. (It would have been different if Menard had copied Cervantes' fiction from memory . . .).'[22] But there is a further, and more significant, point on which Moore anticipates Lewis (and others); returning to the parable of the Good Samaritan, Moore writes:

> I pointed out that it may quite well have been the case that there really were many men who went from Jerusalem to Jericho & fell among thieves: not only so, there might quite well have been several of whom the whole story was true. In saying then that the man is an imaginary one, we are not necessarily saying of the character, *F*, with regard to wh. we conceive that there was something which had it, that *nothing* had it. What we are saying in such a case is, I think, something about the original author of the story: . . . *what* we are saying is that the original author was not telling the story about a real person.
>
> (*LP* p. 35)

Moore then gives an account of what it is to tell a story about a real person in terms of Russellian knowledge by description of the person, and thus, ultimately, acquaintance with some particulars (typically sense-data) whose relational properties uniquely determine the real person. But it is not necessary to follow him in this respect to see the merit of his thought. For it is an essential feature of fiction that even though, in a sense, the story may fit some one real thing, still the story is not about that real thing.

One implication of this point is that the way to capture 'Some tame tigers are imaginary objects', which previously seemed problematic, is by taking it to mean roughly 'There are stories about tame tigers, and those who tell them do not thereby refer to any real things' (Moore in effect propounds this account in *CB* p. 244). But Moore adds a further twist to his discussion of this matter in IO (especially pp. 113–14). Moore is here considering the possibility that there might have been a real person, called 'Mr Pickwick', to whom all the events related in Dickens's novel actually occurred, and he rightly insists that even in this hypothetical situation we should not say that Dickens was referring to this Mr Pickwick. So far the position does not differ from that propounded earlier, but Moore now adds the thesis that Dickens's novel would not even be true of the real Mr Pickwick. For, Moore says, Dickens introduces us in his novel to his Mr Pickwick as *the person about whom he is going to tell us* who also has certain properties – e.g being called 'Mr Pickwick'; and since the real Mr Pickwick, even if all the rest of Dickens's story fits him, is not someone about whom Dickens is in fact telling the story, it follows that he does not in fact fit the whole of Dickens's story.

This thesis that the storyteller, by including in the story the pretence that he is telling a story about real persons, ensures that his story is fiction, and not fact, seems right and is an important feature of Lewis's recent account of fiction.[23] Furthermore it enables one to clarify an aspect of his position in *LP* that seems to me otherwise puzzling. Moore, it will be recalled, argued against Russell that, in thinking of an imaginary object, it is not necessary to think of it as the unique bearer of certain properties. But it is then puzzling how one can properly draw the conclusion that I am thinking of the same man as you when I repeat your story about a man travelling from Jerusalem to Jericho; how, one wants to know, can the first story define a single object of thought which the second telling of the story picks up. Part of the solution to this puzzle is surely provided by Moore's thesis of IO that the storyteller alludes to his own storytelling; for, in telling a story about a man travelling from Jerusalem to Jericho, the storyteller implies that there is only one such man about whom he is telling his story. It is this reference to his own storytelling that, as Moore says in IO (p. 113), gives 'unique reference' to all his later references to him and ensures that the story defines a unique object of thought. In the case of repetition, then, the second storyteller alludes not to his own storytelling, but to the first storyteller's telling of the story, and thereby picks up the same object of thought: in telling the story of a man travelling from Jerusalem to Jericho we tell it as the story of *the man about whom Jesus tells* who was travelling from Jerusalem to Jericho.

This move does not undercut the causal condition; it complements it. For one could not take an apparent reference to an earlier telling of a story by someone else as such unless the causal condition of attempted repetition were met. On the other hand, there are cases of people thinking of the same imaginary object where there is no reference in the later thought, or story, to the earlier telling of it. The situation, as I conceive it, is essentially similar to that proposed by Lockeans in their account of personal identity. In both cases it is the ancestral of the basic relation which secures identity, and not the relation itself, since this is not transitive (Moore makes this point for his account too – cf. *LP* p. 35). This analogy with personal identity suggests that the possibilities of fission and fusion should raise interesting issues concerning the identity of imaginary objects. This is indeed the case: fairy-tale characters provide a good range of examples to think about in this context.

Although the account I have presented is not systematically presented by Moore, it is largely a development of his ideas and it seems a great pity that he did not take the opportunity provided by his reply (IO) to papers by Ryle and Braithwaite on this topic to do so himself. The extent to which Moore anticipates recent discussions of fiction and imaginary objects is striking. Indeed a stronger claim may be made: does not his account of thought about imaginary objects show up defects in Russell's theory of names and suggest the route for an alternative theory? Moore's remark that in thinking of Apollo we do not typically have in mind properties which he uniquely instantiates certainly reminds one of Kripke's remarks about Cicero and Feynman;[24] and the role of causality in Moore's account is strongly reminiscent of Evans's theory of reference.[25]

Moore, so far as I can tell, never made this extrapolation (though he was aware that the topic of proper names was a complex and difficult one: there is an amusing little note in *CB* (p. 248) in which he sets out seven different names by which he is called and discusses briefly the different ways in which they are used to name him). On this issue of thought about particular objects, he remained largely loyal to Russell's theories of names and descriptions. This is, I think, to be explained by his continuing acceptance of a one-level theory of meaning; for Russell's theories enable one to accommodate many of the obvious cases of referential opacity in the attribution of thoughts without introducing a

Fregean sense/reference distinction. This is in many ways over-simple, and in truth Russell's theories merely postpone the need to recognise the role of sense, rather than eliminating it altogether. But the extent to which Russell's theories enable one to save the appearances in this regard explains, I think, Moore's continuing commitment to them. None the less it remains a striking fact that in his discussion of thought about imaginary objects he sketched out the lines of thought which later critics of Russell were to follow.

# VII

# Philosophical analysis

*In 1922–23, when I attended both courses of Moore's lectures, we hunted the correct analysis of propositions about the self on Monday, Wednesday, and Friday mornings and the correct analysis of propositions of the form 'This is a pencil' on Tuesday, Thursday, and Saturday mornings throughout the year. By the end of May, when lectures had to stop because the triposes started, Moore would have got through about two-and-a-half of the possible kinds of analysis. The lectures were quite inconclusive.*

(R. Braithwaite's obituary talk)[1]

Moore struck his contemporaries and pupils as a paradigm analytic philosopher: Wisdom wrote 'Philosophy is concerned with the analysis of facts – a doctrine which Wittgenstein has lately preached and Moore long practised',[2] and the message of Braithwaite's description, quoted above, is the same. Yet Moore was always hostile to the view that philosophy is just philosophical analysis. He rejects it in his 1933–4 lectures on the nature of philosophy (cf. *LP* pp. 172–90) and most emphatically in his reply to Wisdom in *PGEM* (pp. 675–6):

> But it is not true that I have ever either said or thought or implied that analysis is the only proper business of philosophy! By practising analysis I may have implied that it is *one* of the proper businesses of philosophy. But I certainly cannot have implied more than that. And, in fact, analysis is by no means the only thing I have tried to do.

It is not clear what Moore had in mind in this last remark, but one candidate would be the discussions of proof, knowledge, and scepticism with which he had just then been much occupied in his papers PEW, 4FS, and C. For in his lecture notes on the nature of philosophy in *LP* he explicitly distinguishes questions of knowledge and scepticism from

193

issues of philosophical analysis, offering a four-fold division of philosophy:

> (1) Questions about the meaning of words, phrases & forms of expression: Analysis, (2) Questions about Reality as a whole, (3) A number of questions about human knowledge, (4) Still more questions about what it's *reasonable for us to believe & in what degree.*
>
> (*LP* p. 190)

Yet despite this characterisation of philosophy, with its limited role for analysis, Moore could not hold back from pursuing analytic issues when discussing other matters. In the papers I have just mentioned Moore devotes at least as much space to the analysis of concepts such as 'external thing', 'possibility', and 'certainty', as to arguments which directly address the issues he is discussing. And there is a revealing parenthetical remark in his lecture notes, at a point where he is supposed to be discussing questions about knowledge: '(how difficult it is to distinguish clearly between questions of analysis & others)' (*LP* p. 184).

The fact is that the situation concerning the role of analysis in Moore's mature works does not differ greatly from that which I discussed in chapter 2 concerning his early philosophy, although his conception of the possibilities of analysis is greatly enhanced: in both cases, Moore's practice does not cohere with his official prescriptions. In theory, the role of analysis is to distinguish the distinct senses of ambiguous expressions that occur in the formulation of philosophical issues and analyse them so that it is clear what questions are being asked. One should not, however, hope to obtain an answer to these questions from the practice of analysis. Just how one should obtain answers is not clear, and though it is a mark of his mature philosophy that the appeal to common-sense has some authority in philosophical debates, Moore offers no general account of the matter (cf. *LP* p. 191: 'It seems to me there is nothing wh. can be described as *the* method of philos.').

That is Moore's official account of the role of analysis in philosophical argument; in practice, he concentrates on issues of analysis, and acknowledges that some familiar questions of philosophy turn on then. This is his view, for example, about phenomenalism, solipsism, and philosophical materialism (*LP* pp. 172–9); and it is in this context that he remarked in DCS concerning the proposition '*This* is a human hand':

> It is the analysis of propositions of the latter kind which seems to me to present such great difficulties, while nevertheless the whole question as to the *nature* of material things obviously depends upon their analysis.
>
> (p. 53)

The result is that the residue of philosophical issues which Moore supposes not to be resolvable by reference to either philosophical analysis or the appeal to common-sense is a rather unappealing collection whose typical instances are '(1) Does God exist? (2) Are there, as Spinoza said there were, an infinite number of "attributes" besides extension and thought' (*LP* p. 180). So although one should not doubt the sincerity of the response in *PGEM* to Wisdom, his practice reveals a rather different conception of philosophy whereby it is supposed that the important questions of philosophy can be resolved by a combination of philosophical analysis and a reflective use of common-sense.

This is certainly a conception of philosophy which many of Moore's pupils acknowledged as their own (Duncan-Jones wrote in 1937 of it as 'the intellectual background of many of us in recent years'[3]). But one striking feature of Moore's discussions of analysis and its philosophical significance is that he does not attempt to back it up with the considerations characteristic of logical atomism or logical empiricism which motivate much of Russell's 'logical-analytic' programme. For this raises the question of just what considerations are operative in the cases of analysis which he recognised as philosophically significant. Before one can answer this, however, it is necessary to become clearer about Moore's conception of philosophical analysis itself.

### 1: Propositions and sentences

A prominent feature of Moore's later discussions of philosophical analysis is his insistence that this is the analysis of propositions. Indeed this is so prominent that one might well think that he had retracted the denial of propositions propounded in *SMPP*. There is certainly one change in his views during the years after *SMPP*. In chapter 5 (section 4) I mentioned that although Moore does not advance a theory of judgment in *SMPP*, much of what he says suggests sympathy with Russell's multiple relation theory; this is further confirmed by a remark about Russell's theory in his 1919 paper 'Is there Knowledge by Acquaintance?' that 'though it does not seem to me certain that Mr. Russell was right in this contention, I am strongly inclined to think that he was, and should be prepared, on a proper occasion, to defend that view'.[4] But no such occasion arose, and within a few years he had changed his mind, as his 1925–6 lectures notes show:

> There is *a* sense of prop. such that whenever anybody believes *that* so-&-so or conceives the hypothesis that so-&-so, he can be truly said to be believing the *proposition* that so-&-so or conceiving the *proposition* that so-&-so. . . . This gives a vague descr. of one (or several) uses of prop.; but it does not profess to give any analytic def. of p is a

proposition; & it leaves open the question whether propositions are single entities, or, as R. at one time believed, are logical constructions. . . . The question *what* a prop. is, in this sense, can only be answered by an analysis of this kind of expression & I don't think anyone knows what the analysis is.

(*LP* pp. 133–4: cf. F&P p. 76)

The reasons for this change of mind can be found in his notebooks (from *c*.1919 and *c*.1926), for he here raises two objections to the multiple relation theory: first, that the content of a judgment has a unity which the Russellian analysis threatens: 'a judgment is a single act – *not* a mere collection of ideas simultaneously present' (*CB* p. 27). Second, that, since no one relation can have a variable number of terms, Russell's theory requires not just one belief-relation, but an indefinite number of them to relate the constituents of ever more complex beliefs (*CB* pp. 28, 93–4). The first of these objections is, in effect, the old Bradleian point about the unity of judgment, and Russell was indeed embarrassed by it.[5] He was also aware of the second, but in this case he seems to have been happy to accept the implication of his own theory: 'Belief will really have to have different logical forms according to the nature of what is believed. So that the apparent sameness of believing in different cases is illusory.'[6] In truth, however, if Russell's theory did have this implication, it would constitute a serious objection to it; but it can be reformulated to avoid it.[7]

As Moore recognised in *SMPP*, the multiple relation theory enabled Russell to talk *as if* there were propositions while repudiating any commitment to their existence (or being). Having rejected this theory, it might seem as though Moore's continuing talk of propositions should carry an ontological commitment, and he sometimes expresses himself in terms which imply such a commitment: in lectures on 'Necessity' delivered during 1925–6 he says that where a proposition includes among its constituents a particular whose existence is contingent, the proposition 'subsists contingently', by which he means that 'there *might have been* no such proposition' (*LP* pp. 129–30). Later in the same course of lectures, however, he shows, in the passage quoted above, that he does not want any such commitment, though he replaces the rejection of propositions characteristic of *SMPP* with a suspension of judgment on the issue.

This passage suggests that Moore's continuing talk of propositions was just a convenient way of talking of the content of propositional attitudes, without any commitment to any one way of explicating what there really is in the world when someone has a propositional attitude with a particular content. His characterisation of the conditions for the 'subsistence' of propositions has then to be interpreted as an account of conditions for the possibility of attitudes with that content. But Moore is not entirely neutral between different accounts of propositional attitudes. He regularly rejects the view that attitudes such as belief are to be understood as relations between a subject and a sentence, such that to believe that Caesar is dead is to believe-true 'Caesar is dead', and expresses his rejection by an insistence upon the need to distinguish between sentences and propositions. In the light of this, therefore, although Moore's talk of propositions does not carry a commitment to any positive theory, it signals his rejection of the quotational analysis of belief and other attitudes.

The quotational analysis was made famous by Carnap's presentation of it in *The Logical Syntax of Language*,[8] though Moore's discussion of it in his 1925–6 lectures (*LP* pp. 132–49) pre-dates Carnap's book and relates to the position advanced by J.M. Keynes.[9] There are, I think, two main reasons for this analysis. One is ontological: the aim is to give an account of truth without introducing reference to abstract entities by taking sentences, or utterances of them, to be fundamental bearers of truth. This then requires that the truth of beliefs and other propositional attitudes be elucidated by construing them as, somehow, relationships involving sentences. The other reason, which connects with the position advanced in Wittgenstein's *Tractatus*, is the wish to present all logical structures as extensional (cf. *Tractatus* 5.54–5.542, where Moore's early theory of judgment is explicitly rejected). Wittgenstein's own theory of judgment is enigmatic, but his programme requires that the apparent intensionality of propositional attitudes be dissipated, and the quotational analysis provides a way of doing this without introducing reference to intensional entities.

Moore had two chief arguments against the quotational approach. One is embodied in the famous 'translation' argument, which, I believe, can be attributed to him, although he never employed it in his published writings.[10] This is the argument that one can see that someone who says that Brutus believes that Caesar is dead does not say that Brutus believes-true 'Cacsar is dead' by observing that a correct translation of the first statement into French would be 'Brutus croit que Caesar est mort', whereas a correct translation of the second would be 'Brutus croit-vrai "Caesar is dead"', which obviously differs from the first. Moore's other objection, which comes from the earlier lectures, is expressed in the following passage:

> A prop. is true if & only if there is some fact wh. directly verifies it, & false if & only if there is some fact wh. directly negates it. And the relation of the prop. in each case to the fact is *necessary*, not accidental: that *prop. couldn't* have been verified or negated by any *other* fact than this one. Of all token-expressions, even in the wide sense, this is not

197

true: the connection of any expression with the fact wh. verifies or negates it is accidental.

(LP p. 142)

Moore's point here is that there is a necessary connection between the content of an attitude and that attitude's truth-conditions which is not preserved when the content is specified simply by reference to a sentence; for the relation between a sentence and its truth-conditions is not essential – sentences might not mean what they do mean.

Both of these arguments raise important issues in the philosophy of language. The standard objection to the translation argument is that the principles of correct translation are not as simple as is assumed in this argument; in particular that it is often correct to translate occurrences of phrases within quotation marks, contrary to the presumption of this argument.[11] I think that this is an effective rejoinder, for it has to be acknowledged that the conception of a 'correct translation' is typically guided by pragmatic criteria which may lead one to translate phrases within quotation marks. None the less, a revised version of the argument is, I think, defensible. This is best formulated by dropping the issue of translation altogether and considering instead what someone who understands the ascription of a propositional attitude needs to understand.[12]

It is clear that anyone who understands the sentence 'Brutus believes that Caesar is dead' must understand the sentence 'Caesar is dead'. But must anyone who understands the sentence 'Brutus believes-true "Caesar is dead"' understand the sentence 'Caesar is dead'? It is not so clear. What is clear is that if this requirement does not obtain, then the quotational analysis will be incorrect. For an analysis is supposed to explicate our understanding of the analysandum; hence a putative analysis which implies that we do not need to understand phrases which it is quite clear that we do need to understand in order to understand the analysandum must be incorrect.

The problem with the translation argument was that there was no non-question-begging way of ensuring that the quoted sentence did not get translated. The analogue of that problem is that the quotational analysis is such that understanding it does require an understanding of the quoted sentence. Yet the upholder of the Moorean position can challenge his opponent to explain how this requirement arises. For the substance of the quotational analysis is that attitudes such as belief consist of a relation between a subject and sentence, and this does not readily yield any requirement that, in understanding that this relationship holds, one should have to understand the sentence to which a subject is said to be related. Understanding that someone assents to a sentence, for example, does not require any understanding of the sentence assented to. The only way in which this requirement would

198

arise is if the analysis were such that the sentence were explicitly specified in it as having a specific meaning, as in Field's account of belief, according to which Brutus' belief is analysed as his believing-true a sentence which means that Caesar is dead.[13] But since this approach employs the intensional connective 'means that' within the analysis itself, it does not further the quotational analysis itself (this is no objection to Field).

Davidson's 'paratactic' analysis of propositional attitudes, however, can be regarded as an attempt to reformulate the quotational analysis in such a way as to avoid this objection.[14] Davidson argues that the overt grammatical structure of indirect discourse is misleading, in that it represents as one sentence, with a subordinate clause, what are in fact two sentences. The sentence which is usually regarded as a subordinate clause should be regarded as a separate sentence, whose utterance by the speaker is referred to by the occurrence of the word 'that' which standardly follows propositional attitude verbs such as 'believe'. Thus, on Davidson's analysis, what we normally regard as the single sentence 'Brutus believes that Caesar is dead' is better represented as the pair of sentences 'Brutus believes that. Caesar is dead', understood as uttered in such a way that the speaker refers by his use of 'that' in the first sentence to his forthcoming utterance of the second sentence. This account does now seem to meet the challenge posed by the reformulated translation argument. For there seems no reason to deny that, in order to understand the pair of sentences Davidson offers as his account of 'Brutus believes that Caesar is dead', one needs to understand both of them.

Yet the challenge posed by the reformulated argument can, I think, be refined to apply to Davidson's analysis. The essential step is that the requirement on understanding be taken to be a requirement on what one needs to understand if one is to know what assertion is made by one who makes an assertion by uttering a sentence such as 'Brutus believes that Caesar is dead'. It is clear, first, that the requirement that one understand the sentence 'Caesar is dead' still holds. The challenge for Davidson, therefore, is to show that his analysis also generates this requirement. On his analysis, one who makes an assertion by the utterance of 'Brutus believes that Caesar is dead' makes his assertion by his utterance of the sentence 'Brutus believes that'; for he certainly does not himself need to assert that Caesar is dead. But what assertion does he make by his utterance of the first sentence? According to Davidson he asserts that Brutus believes the content of his next utterance. But someone can grasp this assertion without understanding the sentence which follows. Certainly his knowledge is enhanced if he also understands the second sentence; but this enhancement carries his state of knowledge beyond that required for an understanding of all that, on Davidson's account, is strictly asserted by one who employs indirect discourse. Hence Davidson's analysis fails to generate the requirement that content sentences in indirect discourse be understood by those who know what is asserted by those who make an assertion by means of an utterance employing indirect discourse.

The fact that Davidson's analysis falls foul of this reformulated version of the translation argument should occasion no surprise. For his paratactic analysis is essentially the product of applying to the quotational analysis Moore's demonstrative theory of quotation which he himself advances elsewhere.[15] What is surprising is that Davidson should have thought that his paratactic analysis is not vulnerable to the translation argument since he himself employs it against standard versions of the quotational analysis.[16] But that is an issue internal to Davidson's philosophy which need not concern us, and I want now to turn to Moore's other argument against the quotational analysis of propositional attitudes.

This turned on a supposed modal distinction which one can present as follows: on the one hand:

(1) (Caesar is dead & Brutus believes that Caesar is dead) entails (Brutus has a true belief);

but, on the other hand:

(2) (Caesar is dead & Brutus believes-true 'Caesar is dead') does not entail (Brutus has a true belief).

To get an entailment analogous to (1), Moore maintains, one needs the further premiss:

(3) 'Caesar is dead' means that Caesar is dead,

which, being contingent, is not dispensable in modal contexts.

Since the truth of (1) is indisputable, an upholder of the quotational analysis has to dispute (2), and will typically want to maintain that, as it stands, it is not properly formulated, since it omits the essential relativity to a language of the predicate 'believes-true'. Once this is restored, it will be said, we do get a correct analogue of (1), namely:

(4) (Caesar is dead & Brutus believes-true in English 'Caesar is dead') entails (Brutus has a true belief)

since the extra premiss analogous to (3)

(5) 'Caesar is dead' means in English that Caesar is dead

is a necessary truth.

But how is this last claim to be substantiated? One can think of languages as individuated in such a way that the meanings of the sentences of a language are essential features of the language. The resulting conception of a language is not altogether natural, since it implies that as words change their meanings, the language to which they belong changes its identity; but this position can be defended as an abstract model of the individuation of languages to which our ordinary practice approximates. The trouble, however, for an upholder of the quotational analysis is that introduction of reference to a language of this kind in (4) defeats the purposes of the quotational analysis. Not only are languages thus conceived abstract, they are themselves thoroughly intensional since they are individuated by reference to meaning.[17]

There is, however, an alternative tactic for an upholder of the quotational analysis. This is to make the reference to a language a reference to the language of the same sentence, so that (4) is replaced by:

(6) (Caesar is dead & Brutus believes-true in the language of this sentence 'Caesar is dead') entails (Brutus has a true belief).

The further premiss (3) is now specified as:

(7) 'Caesar is dead' means in the language of this sentence that Caesar is dead,

and this, it will be argued, we can see to be a necessary truth without reference to the conception of a language employed above.[18]

In response to this the Moorean must challenge the claim that the self-reference characteristic of (7) suffices for it to be a necessary truth, and this is in effect what Moore himself does when discussing the claim that (3) cannot be denied without absurdity (RTD pp. 175–6). He argues that this absurdity does not show (3) to be a necessary truth; instead, he suggests, the absurdity arises from a conflict between that which is asserted by one who utters ' "Caesar is dead" does not mean that Caesar is dead' and that which is implied by the use of that sentence to make that assertion. This seems right as far as it goes, but it does not complete the argument concerning the denial of (7), where the self-referential demonstrative threatens to bring what is implied by the use of the sentence into the assertion made by its use.

At this point it is useful to recall a point made in the previous chapter in the context of Moore's discussion of the modal status of 'This exists'. I suggested that where one is dealing with sentences which include indexicals, one needs to distinguish between the proposition expressed by the utterance of a sentence and the conditions which determine that that proposition is then expressed, which I called the 'character' of the sentence. The same distinction can be applied to (7): thanks to the self-referential indexical it contains, its character is such that it cannot be uttered falsely; any proposition thereby expressed will be true. But it' does not follow that these propositions are necessary truths. To substantiate this thesis one has to provide an account of the relationship between the meaning of the sentences of a language and the identity of the language. Arguably, languages are such that a change of meaning implies a change of language; but that just returns us to the line of thought explored earlier in considering the modal status of (5), to which the present line of argument was supposed to be an alternative.

I conclude, therefore, that Moore's modal argument, like the revised version of his translation argument, is an effective objection to the quotational analysis of propositional attitudes. Since this analysis is closely related to Tarski's influential semantic conception of truth, important issues are at stake here. But I do not want to exaggerate the implications of Moore's arguments. They do, I think, show that there is no chance of dissipating the apparent intensionality of indirect discourse, in the way that those proponents of the quotational analysis who wanted to substantiate the thesis of extensionality hoped to achieve. But, as I think Moore's own agnosticism concerning the analysis of propositional attitudes implies, they do not show that the ontological aim of elucidating truth and falsehood without reference to abstract entities cannot be attained. For Moore's arguments do not imply that the contents of propositional attitudes have to be understood by reference to Fregean thoughts, propositions conceived as in Moore's early philosophy, or sets of possible worlds. The conclusion of the arguments is for example consistent with the Prior–Quine 'attitudinative' construal of indirect discourse.[19]

Similarly, Moore's arguments do not threaten the central thesis of Field's account of belief, according to which beliefs are constituted by a relationship between a believer and a sentence (perhaps of 'mentalese') whose meaning gives the content of the belief.[20] For, as I stressed above, as long as the meaning of the sentence in question is explicitly given in the analysis (as is the case in Field's account), Moore's objections do not apply. Indeed in this case Moore himself acknowledged something like this possibility. Field's account is similar to the account of belief proposed by Russell in *The Analysis of Mind* (lecture XII); Russell invokes 'image-propositions' where Field has sentences of mentalese. In his 1925–6 lectures Moore raises no objection to Russell's account, which he reformulates along the lines of Field's account (*LP* pp. 139–42): he suggests that belief might be constituted by a relation between a subject and a particular 'token-proposition', such as a Russellian image-proposition, which has a predicate in terms of which the content of the belief can be explicated. Of course, the nature of this predicate, whose role is analogous to that played by the concept of meaning in Field's account, remains to be elucidated and Moore himself offers no suggestions. But one can envisage lines of thought concerning it which do not incur objections based upon Moore's arguments against the quotational analysis of propositional attitudes.

### 2: Conceptual analysis and the paradox of analysis

The arguments of the preceding section support Moore's insistence that philosophical analysis is primarily the analysis of propositions, of the content of mental and linguistic acts. But, as Moore himself recognised (cf. *LP* pp. 162–3), this is not altogether satisfactory, in that philosophers are not typically concerned with the analysis of single propositions, but rather with the analysis of certain kinds of proposition, e.g. propositions concerning numbers; and for this reason it is often better to regard philosophical analysis as the analysis of the *concepts* characteristic of the kinds of proposition at issue, e.g. of the concept of number. This way of putting the point, which Moore regularly employs in his later writings, implies that philosophical analysis is typically conceptual analysis. Though this is a familiar enough thesis, in thinking about Moore's assertion of it, one needs to consider what significance it has for him.

In his early philosophy, concepts, as constituents of propositions, are not distinguished from properties, whose possession by something constitutes an actual state of affairs. The question, therefore, arises whether Moore's later talk of concepts is to be similarly understood, so that for him conceptual analysis is the analysis of properties. I think that this is the case. The concept/property distinction is an application of the general Fregean sense/reference distinction for which Moore nowhere indicates any sympathy. Furthermore, Moore seems not to regard second-order concepts as concepts; thus he does not regard Russell's theory of definite descriptions as an analysis of a concept (*LP* p. 161). This is intelligible if one thinks of concepts as properties of particular things; but less so otherwise. Finally, one of Moore's favourite idioms for expressing conceptual analyses is 'To be an *F* is to be a *G*' (e.g. 'To be a brother is to be a male sibling' – *PGEM* p. 665). This idiom strongly suggests the interpretation of concepts as properties, since it is primarily appropriate for the expression of property identities.

This is obviously not a major issue. It is easy enough to reinterpret Moorean conceptual analysis as the analysis of sense; and, as far as Moore's favourite examples of analysis are concerned (e.g. Russell's theory of descriptions and his own sense-datum theory), this seems entirely beneficial. But there is a further unfamiliar aspect of Moore's conception of conceptual analysis which one cannot so easily set aside. This concerns the role of references to language in statements of philosophical analyses. Moore maintained that the analysis of a concept such as the concept of a brother should not be expressed by a sentence such as:

(a) 'Brother' means the same as 'male sibling'.

In place of this he sometimes allows (*LP* pp. 156–8) that an analysis can be expressed by a sentence such as:

(b) 'brother' means male sibling;

but he later seems to prefer the elimination of all explicit reference to language, as in:

(c) to be a brother is to be a male sibling

(*PGEM* p. 664; but in RTD, which is contemporary with this, Moore allows that either form is acceptable – cf. pp. 163–7). Moore's position here is to be understood in the light of the arguments presented in the previous section: if an understanding of the assertion made by one who utters (a) does not even require an understanding of 'male sibling', then it cannot present a philosophical analysis of the concept of a brother. For grasp of an analysis requires a grasp of the concepts employed in the analysis itself. One can also appreciate his inclination to favour (c) over (b): for, by the same argument, it does not seem that an understanding of (b) requires an understanding of the word 'brother' – but then how can it be such that it is understood as presenting an analysis of the concept of a brother? Surely a proper grasp of an analysis requires an understanding of the analysandum, as well as the analysis.

Yet the conclusion, that all philosophical analysis should have the form of (c), seems wrong. In his own writings Moore refers repeatedly to our uses of language in presenting his analyses, and the references to language are not eliminable from his arguments and conclusions. In his discussion of whether existence is a predicate, the issue is precisely that of the logical form of sentences like 'Tame tigers exist' and 'Tame tigers growl'; none the less the conclusion concerns the *concept* of existence. Similarly, Moore's critical discussion of Russell's conception of a logical fiction revolves around the issue of what is, and what is not, an 'incomplete symbol'; but, as Moore acknowledged, the implications of Russell's position are central to the analysis of such concepts as number, class, and belief. Finally, Moore himself regularly presents his sense-datum analysis as an analysis of the proposition expressed by one who utters a sentence such as 'This is a hand', and the use of the demonstrative ensures that the reference to language is not eliminable.

There is therefore a conflict between the theoretical conception of philosophical analysis presented in Moore's later writings and his philosophical practice. This is not just another case of the conflict between theory and practice which I have noted when discussing Moore's views about the role of analysis within philosophy. For in this case the theoretical position concerning analysis is substantiated by a serious argument. So the conflict arises from a genuine unclarity about the role of references to language in philosophical analysis.

The issues that now arise are complex, but central to a critical understanding of Moore's conception of philosophical analysis. In thinking about them, it helps to generalise Moore's alternatives (a), (b), and (c) by treating them as putative cases of, respectively, analysis conducted wholly within an object-language, metalinguistic analysis of an object-language expression, and analysis conducted wholly within the metalanguage employed by a philosopher. Schematically, therefore, the alternatives might be represented as follows:

(A) OL ⇒ OL – Syntactic analysis
(B) OL ⇒ ML – Semantic analysis
(C) ML ⇒ ML – Explicatory analysis

The symbol '⇒' is intended to represent, ambiguously, the relation that holds between analysandum and analysis in each case (clearly it belongs to the metalanguage). Analyses of type (A) are syntactic because they typically involve the identification of features of the 'logical' syntax of object-language sentences. Analyses of type (B) are semantic because they involve assigning meanings to object-language sentences. And those of type (C) are explicatory since the analysis aims to explicate the concepts employed in the analysandum.

There certainly appear to be clear cases of each type of analysis. Accounts of the 'logical form' of indirect discourse and sentences concerning existence are cases of syntactic analysis: operationalist accounts of the use of theoretical terms in scientific theories are cases of semantic analysis: and explicatory analysis is exemplified by many traditional cases of philosophical analysis, such as occur in debates about knowledge or causation. In presenting this typology, however, I do not want to imply that it is always clear what kind of analysis one is dealing with – Russell's theory of descriptions and possible world analyses of modal concepts are cases in point here. The type of an analysis typically depends upon the dialectical context within which it occurs: syntactic and semantic analyses occur where arguments concerning language and our understanding of it are prominent, whereas explicatory analyses occur where considerations from the philosophy of language are not adduced as reasons for a putative analysis.

In the terms I have introduced, the strong Moorean thesis is that it is only explicatory analyses of type (C) that constitute philosophical analyses. Even though those who present syntactic and semantic analyses may intend thereby to present philosophical analyses, and may be understood as so doing, this can only be because their mode of expression is being systematically reinterpreted. As I have indicated, this seems wrong. Although one can often transform a syntactic or a semantic analysis into an explicatory analysis, such a transformation will typically separate the analysis from the considerations which give it its point. So there is reason to resist any such reinterpretation of syntactic and semantic analyses.

How then is one to combine respect for syntactic and semantic analyses as such with acceptance of Moore's point that conceptual analysis demands an understanding of the concepts employed? It is best here to start with the case of semantic analyses of type (B). A reason in favour of permitting analyses of this kind is that since the analysis provides an account of the meaning of the object-language expression named, Moore cannot object that it is possible to have a grasp of the analysis without an understanding of the analysandum; for the analysis precisely provides an account of that in which this understanding consists. Yet Moore can still object that on this account semantic analysis does not differ from the interpretation of a foreign language; an interpretation of this kind tells us what (in our own terms) the foreign words mean, and thereby what those who understand them thereby understand. But philosophical analysis is a reflexive project, whereby we seek to elucidate concepts expressed by expressions of which we already have an uncritical understanding; it should not itself be represented as if it were itself radical interpretation. Moore makes essentially this point in the course of his defence of common-sense, through his distinction between understanding a sentence and being able to give a correct analysis of its meaning (DCS p. 37). His claim is that, by and large, we can rely on our ordinary understanding of sentences when asking ourselves whether or not they are true, while leaving open the question of the correct analysis of the proposition expressed. This is surely correct; debates about the analysis of a concept such as knowledge start from a stock of judgments about whose truth-value a large measure of agreement is assumed.

The way to eliminate the unwanted conception of semantic analysis as radical interpretation is, I think, to make explicit the reflexive nature of the analytic project; to take Moore's example, one should not just present the analysis as

(b) 'Brother' means male sibling

but as

(b)' 'Brother', as used in this language, means male sibling.

Not only does this eliminate the possibility of conceiving of analysis as interpretation of words of a foreign language; it also makes possible the derivation of an explicatory analysis of type (C), and thereby shows how one can legitimately regard a semantic analysis as a conceptual analysis. The extra premiss required here is just

(d) 'Brother', as used in this language, means brother.

This is the sort of proposition which, I argued in the previous section, one should not regard as a necessary truth. Without going back on that claim, I now want to use (d) as an uncontentious way of describing our own understanding of our own language; the character of the self-reference in (d) is such as to ensure the proposition it expresses is obviously true. Putting together (d) and (b)', therefore, one can infer (c), or some similar form of words to the effect that the concept of a brother is the concept of a male sibling.

The hypothesis I want to propose, therefore, is that once one incorporates linguistic self-reference into a semantic analysis, and adds the uncontentious assumption about our understanding of the analysandum, Moore's objections to treating semantic analyses as conceptual (philosophical) analyses can be met. This position implies that that the philosopher's metalanguage will include the vulgar idioms which occur in the analysandum; but the philosopher can still partition off a restricted set of idioms in which he thinks it best to talk and think when in his study, and regard this as his strict philosophical metalanguage. Furthermore, having effected this division within his own metalanguage, the philosopher can easily distinguish between the significance of a semantic analysis of some vulgar idiom in the terms of his restricted metalanguage, and that of a homophonic interpretation which merely reflects his own ability to employ the vulgar idioms. All that this accommodation of Moore's requirement requires one to give up, therefore, is the conception of analysis as the total abolition of the vulgar idioms that are analysed. But this was never plausible anyway; for philosophical analysis is not a self-deceptive attempt to repress one's understanding of the idioms whose content one seeks to analyse.

In the case of a syntactic analysis of type (A), a similar strategy concerning our understanding of the analysandum is available. But there is the further problem in this case that, on the face of it, there is no need to understand the expression which gives the analysis in order to understand the whole sentence which is supposed to constitute the analysis, whereas Moore's thesis is that the analysis must be understood if one is to regard knowledge of it as possession of a conceptual analysis. I might come to know that some complex expression employed by an adherent of Montague grammar[21] gives the logical form of a sentence of English without understanding the expression itself, through believing on the basis of reliable authorities that Montague grammar provides the best treatment of the logical form of English sentences. Yet surely, I do not thereby possess a conceptual analysis of the analysandum, even though I can point to what, *ex hypothesi*, I do in fact know to be a syntactic analysis of it.

207

In this case it seems question-begging to repeat the strategy used before. Although propositions similar to (d) will be true, and such that anyone who understands the expression giving the analysis can recognise their truth, the point at issue is precisely whether the expression which gives the analysis needs to be understood and one cannot pass this off as an uncontentious assumption about the philosopher's understanding of his own language. Instead one needs to show how this understanding of the expression which gives the analysis is, in fact, required for a full grasp of a syntactic analysis. The way to establish this is by considering the connections between syntactic analysis and semantic theory. Since the purpose of syntactic analysis is to identify the semantic roles of expressions (and especially to unmask those whose surface appearance is misleading), syntactic analysis can only take place in the context of a theory which identifies the implications of assigning particular roles to particular expressions. Thus syntactic analysis is always guided by its semantic implications, and an understanding of these implications must include a grasp of a semantic interpretation of the expression which gives the syntactic analysis, since this determines the semantic implications. One cannot attain an understanding of the reasons for a particular syntactic analysis without understanding the analysis itself. The case envisaged earlier concerning Montague grammar is essentially parasitic.

The considerations I have advanced do, I think, suffice to vindicate the status of both syntactic and semantic analyses as conceptual analyses, despite Moore's argument to the contrary. Semantic analysis tells one what concepts are employed in the analysandum, and syntactic analysis elucidates the way in which they are there combined. The fact that one can derive an explicatory analysis from a semantic analysis confirms this claim, and if one makes explicit the tacit semantic interpretation which guides syntactic analysis a similar derivation is possible in this case too. These derivations raise the question whether the conception of explicatory analysis itself is really a self-sufficient conception of philosophical analysis, or whether explicatory analyses are in fact always just implications of semantic or syntactic analyses and best understood as such. Such a thesis is almost as counterintuitive as Moore's critical thesis concerning syntactic and semantic analysis. But there is an argument for this thesis: ironically, it is, I believe, an argument first constructed by Moore – the paradox of analysis.

So far as I have been able to ascertain, the paradox first appeared in print in Langford's contribution to *PGEM* (p. 323); but it is clear from the way in which Langford here refers to it as 'the so-called paradox of analysis' that he did not take himself to be stating anything altogether novel, and it seems to me likely that Moore had himself formulated and discussed the argument of the paradox, perhaps with Langford himself, who had studied with him in Cambridge. Moore presents and discusses the paradox in RTD (pp. 177–84), and his discussion here appears (on internal grounds) to have been written earlier than the reply to Langford in *PGEM* (though it was published two years later in 1944). Furthermore, he does not here acknowledge the argument as anyone else's puzzle, and since in his later writings he was usually scrupulous about acknowledging others, this suggests that the argument was his own idea.

I shall first state the argument of the paradox in Moorean terms, with a Moorean example – the analysis of free action which I discussed in chapter 4. This looks a straightforward case of an explicatory analysis, which may be formulated as follows:

(1) the proposition that Jane acts freely =
the proposition that Jane can act otherwise if she so chooses.

Given Moore's conception of propositions, this should imply that:

(2) Tom's belief that Jane acts freely =
Tom's belief that Jane can act otherwise if she so chooses,

and this certainly implies that:

(3) Tom believes that Jane acts freely iff
Tom believes that Jane can act otherwise if she so chooses.

The presumption underlying the move from (1) to (3) here is that analyses license substitutions within indirect discourse. For Moore this presumption is implicit in his official conception of analysis as propositional, or conceptual, analysis (though we shall see in a moment that he himself had doubts about this matter). The paradox arises when we apply the same considerations to second-order thoughts, such as:

(4) Susan doubts whether (Tom's belief that Jane acts freely =
Tom's belief that Jane can act otherwise if she so chooses);

(5) Susan doubts whether (Tom believes that Jane acts freely iff
Tom believes that Jane can act otherwise if she so chooses).

For if (2) is true, then, surely, so are the following:

(6) Susan's doubt whether (Tom's belief that Jane acts freely =
Tom's belief that Jane can act otherwise if she so chooses)
= Susan's doubt whether (Tom's belief that Jane acts freely =
Tom's belief that Jane acts freely);

(7) Susan doubts whether (Tom believes that Jane acts freely iff
Tom believes that Jane can act otherwise if she so chooses)
iff Susan doubts whether (Tom believes that Jane acts freely iff
Tom believes that Jane acts freely).

But it seems obvious that (6) and (7) are false, and any analysis with non-trivial content will give rise to an analogous result. So the difficulty is how one is to conceive analyses in such a way that an analysis legitimates claims such as (2) and (3), but not claims such as (6) and (7).

It is clear that the paradox revolves around the issue of substitutivity within indirect speech. When I discussed the conception of analysis in Moore's early philosophy (chapter 2 section 5) I observed that although Moore presents this kind of substitutivity as a criterion of analyticity, in practice he nullifies its significance as such by allowing himself to be the authority about the content of people's thoughts. It does not follow from the uselessness of substitutivity as a criterion of analyticity, however, that it is not an implication of it, and Moore pretty clearly takes it to be such in his early philosophy. The question which must now be faced, however, is whether this implication should be accepted, for one way of dealing with the paradox is just to deny that analyses need to license substitutivity at all (and thus that (1) does not even imply (2) or (3)).

Despite his talk of propositions and his conception of analysis, Moore himself vacillated on this issue. In his 1933–4 lectures on philosophy he writes:

> I said I thought that for the purpose of philos. it doesn't matter what the answer is to the question: What was I thinking when I thought p? If you've discovered a more analysed expression, expressing a prop. which entails & is entailed by p, you've done all a philosopher need want to do. I still think this is so, but I don't know.
>
> (LP pp. 192–3)

In RTD Moore is similarly indecisive; for although he accepts that where we use a sentence to give an analysis of the proposition expressed by another we are committed to holding that the two sentences express the same proposition, he also allows that there may yet be a sense in which the two sentences 'do *not* "mean the same"', because, when we understand the one, "what we are thinking" is not the same as what we are thinking when we understand the other' (RTD p. 181). On the other hand, Moore's acceptance in his reply in *PGEM* of Langford's epistemological conception of analysis suggests acceptance of the substitutivity implication, and this is supported by his remark that one can express an analysis by using the form of words 'to say that *p* is to say that *q*' (*PGEM* p. 664). But since he also says here that he does not know how to distinguish an analytic necessary connection from a synthetic one (*PGEM* p. 667) I do not think one can be confident about his views on this issue at the time.

The explanation of Moore's vacillations lies partly in his recognition of the threat posed by the paradox. But I think he was also moved by the difficulty of combining substitutivity with his Cartesian conception of the content of thought as transparently available to the subject. Yet I do not think that this is really a tenable position for Moore to take up. For, as I explained in the previous section, the account of propositions which he offers in his later writings is in terms of the contents of thought and other attitudes, and where an analysis takes the form of a propositional identity (as in (1)), this must imply the kind of first-order substitutivity manifested in (2) and (3). So Moore could only abandon first-order substitutivity by giving up the conception of a proposition in terms of which not only the argument for the paradox of analysis but much of his mature philosophy is presented.

In one respect this perhaps overstates the point. For there are attitudes which, arguably, do require a Cartesian conception of their content, e.g. awareness of something as such. Again we sometimes distinguish, in accounts of people's statements, between what they said and what they meant, where an account of the former has to stick much closer to the words used than the latter. In these cases substitutivity will be less permissive than in the case of normal ascriptions of thought. But the explanation for this is that these attitudes are not simply propositional; an account of their content includes an indication of the 'matter' (verbal or mental) by means of which a proposition is grasped or presented. So they are not counter-examples to the thesis that, in the case of thoughts and other standard propositional attitudes, a conceptual analysis does imply first-order substitutivity.

It is in fact easy enough (now) to reject the Cartesian conception of content. But this still leaves the argument which generates the paradox: if (1) implies (2) and (3), why does it not likewise imply (6) and (7)? One influential response was proposed by Church, who argued that the situation here is similar to that discussed by Frege concerning judgments about identity.[22] Frege argued that in order to account for the cognitive significance of judgments of identity one should recognise that it is the ordinary sense, and not the ordinary reference, of the proper names used to specify such judgments which determines whether reports of such judgments are true. Church's idea was that since the paradox of analysis concerns a second-order judgment of identity (such as (6)) one should reapply Frege's strategy and take it that it is not the ordinary senses of the expressions used to specify the initial judgment which determine whether reports of judgments about it are true, but the modes of presentation of these senses. One can call these the first-order senses of the expressions, since they will be the senses of the expressions when they occur in first-order indirect discourse. Church then generalised the idea, so that the truth of reports of $n$th-order judgments is determined by the $(n-1)$th-order senses of the expressions which occur in them, each of which is a mode of presentation of the $(n-2)$th-order sense of the expression, if there is one.[23]

211

Church's basic idea (to some extent anticipated by Morton White) seems to me correct. But the way in which he generalises it gives rise to problems. For since reference does not determine sense, and likewise sense does not determine its own mode of presentation, there is no constructive route up Church's hierarchy of senses. Hence there is a difficulty, as Davidson observed,[24] in understanding how one can ever have a complete grasp of the sense of an expression, that is to say, a capacity to understand occurrences of it in contexts of arbitrary complexity.

The way around this problem is to stop the hierarchy of senses at level 1; having distinguished between the ordinary sense of an expression and its first-order sense, one should take it that the latter determines the truth of reports of indirect discourse of order two and greater. For although the paradox of analysis argument shows the need to distinguish between conditions for substitution in first-order and second-order indirect discourse, there is no similar argument to show that one needs to distinguish between conditions for substitution in third-order and second-order indirect discourse. Any such argument would have to show that conditions for substitution in second-order indirect discourse were satisfied (and thus that analogues of (6) and (7) were correct) but that substitution in third-order discourse was not acceptable. Since the only cases in which substitution in second-order indirect discourse is guaranteed to be truth-preserving are cases in which the substitution is licensed by a judgment of identity which is as trivial as an explicit self-identity, there is no reason to think that such judgments would not license substitution in third-order indirect discourse.

This modification of Church's proposal provides the abstract framework for a solution to the paradox of analysis. But it is incomplete without an account of what a mode of presentation of a sense might be. To provide this it is best to drop Church's abstract realism concerning senses, and concentrate instead on mental states and their modes of presentation. If we go back to (4) and (5), the reason we want to allow that Susan's doubt is not silly despite the assumed truth of (1) is that Tom's *belief* is presented to her in two different ways: as the belief that Jane acts freely and the belief that Jane can act otherwise if she so chooses. So what needs elucidation is the way in which one and the same belief has these different modes of presentation. If one considers how another's belief is presented to a subject, the answer is clearly via some medium of representation, of which language is far and away the obvious candidate (though in first-person cases there are also sensory and imagistic modes of presentation). Tom's belief can have two different modes of presentation for Susan because it can be expressed in two different ways in her language, and these two ways are of course indicated by the two different names of the belief.

212

A natural way of taking this thesis is to take it as the suggestion that Susan's doubt (4) is really something like the following:

(4)' Susan doubts whether the belief Tom would express in this language as 'Jane acts freely' = the belief Tom would express in this language as 'Jane can act otherwise if she so chooses'.[25]

If this suggestion were accepted, then, to return to the point from which this discussion of the paradox of analysis commenced, the conception of a merely explicatory analysis would be in trouble. For (4)' implies that as soon as a doubt is raised about an analysis, the analysis has to be conceived as explicitly linguistic, or at any rate tied to some mode of representation of content. And if that is so, then the original presentation of the analysis as a type (C) explicatory analysis, with no reference to language or any mode of representation, would turn out to be less than fundamental. So, if this suggestion is accepted, the price to be paid for a solution to the paradox of analysis is the devaluation of the status of the type of analysis which gives rise to it.

But the suggestion need not, and should not, be accepted. The Fregean thesis that names have sense as well as reference is not a Russellian conception of names as disguised descriptions. On the contrary it is a way of expressing the traditional distinction between the 'content' and the 'object' of thought which Moore and Russell rejected. We have seen in chapter 1 how slippery this terminology can be, but the basic distinction is between that which a thought is a thought about (e.g. Venus) and the way that object is presented in the thought (e.g. as the morning star). This distinction is not one between a thing which some thought, as a matter of fact, is a thought of and the thought itself. For the conception of an object of thought is itself intentional, and though the 'content' determines the thought, it is not itself what is thought. Thus that Venus is thought of as the morning star does not make thoughts about Venus more accurately regarded as thoughts about the morning star. On the contrary, the contrast between the rigid aspect of names and the typically non-rigid aspect of the descriptions which give the mode of presentation of the objects of thought ensures that substitution of a description which gives the mode of presentation for the name of the object presented simply does not preserve the identity of thought described.[26] The Fregean thesis is that a descriptive mode of presentation plays an essential role in securing for a thought its object – it fixes the reference of the subject's thought – but it cannot supplant that object.

Once these considerations are applied to the case in question, to the significance for the identity of Susan's doubt of recognising that for her Tom's belief is presented in two different ways in language, it follows that one should not regard Susan's doubt as better expressed by (4)' than by (4). On the contrary, as Moore himself would insist, since in (4)' the content of Tom's belief is only described in non-rigid terms, whereas it is rigidly specified in (4), it cannot be right to regard (4)' as a better account of the content of Susan's doubt. What is required by this account is that it be possible for Susan to employ these two modes of presentation of Tom's belief without realising that they are modes of presentation of the same belief; and we show that we accept this requirement by acknowledging that (2) does not imply (6) or (7).[27]

In the end, therefore, the Fregean solution to the paradox of analysis does not threaten Moore's favoured type of analysis – explicatory analysis – in which there is no explicit reference to language or any mode of representation. And although its reliance on a sense/reference distinction is not compatible with Moore's own account of the structure of thought, Moore does make one comment about the paradox of analysis which fits well with the account I have offered:

> in order to explain the fact that, even if 'To be a brother is the same
> thing as to be a male sibling' is true, yet nevertheless this statement is
> *not* the same as the statement 'To be a brother is to be a brother', one
> *must* suppose that both statements are in *some* sense about the
> expressions used as well as about the concept of being a brother.
>
> (*PGEM* p. 666)

The sense in which, on my account, Moore's statements are 'about' the expressions used is that the distinct modes of presentation of the concept they are about are linguistic.

### 3: Why analyse?

If it is an important task of philosophy to analyse common-sense, as Moore's practice of philosophical analysis implies, there must be some reason why common-sense needs analysis. The account of philosophical analysis which I have presented suggests two kinds of reason: syntactic and semantic analyses will be motivated by assumptions drawn from the philosophy of language, whereas explicatory analyses will be motivated by other reasons, typically metaphysical or epistemological. Since a prominent feature of twentieth-century philosophy has been the use of theories of language with significant implications for the analysis, syntactic and semantic, of ordinary discourse, it is worth assessing Moore's relation to them, so that an account of his own reasons for engaging in philosophical analysis can emerge.

One theory is that presented by Wittgenstein in his *Tractatus Logico-Philosophicus*: central to this is the conception of the world as a world of independent facts, and of the meaning of language as fundamentally constituted from the 'picturing' of these facts by atomic sentences. With this latter idea goes the idea that all complexity in what is said derives from the use of truth-functional compounds of atomic sentences, which do not themselves picture complex facts but have their truth or falsity determined in systematic ways by the truth or falsity of their constituent atomic sentences. It follows, therefore, that a grasp of conceptual relations can be attained only through logical (syntactic) analysis which shows how familiar sentences are to be understood as truth-functional combinations of atomic sentences. The impact of this theory on the work of Russell, Ramsey, Wisdom, and others is obvious. As far as I can discern, however, it made no impression on Moore even though he regarded it as 'a work of genius'.[28]

This is a remarkable fact; Moore was frequently in contact with Wittgenstein during the period 1912–14, and it was to Moore that Wittgenstein dictated some of his early notes on logic while Moore was staying with him in Norway in April 1914.[29] Again, during the 1920s, when Ogden and Ramsey were translating the *Tractatus*, Moore studied the work carefully (*PGEM* p. 33); indeed it was he who suggested the title by which it is now known. Somehow or other, none the less, Moore managed to resist the attractions of Wittgenstein's theory to which so many others succumbed. The fact that he did so tells us much about the strength of his intellectual convictions. In one way the situation is comparable to his early refusal to go along with the fashion for Absolute idealism; but the difference lies in his attitude to the exponents of these fashionable positions. His attitude to Bradley was at best one of distant respect; but his tribute to Wittgenstein in his autobiography is unqualified:

> When I did get to know him, I soon came to feel that he was much
> cleverer at philosophy than I was, and not only cleverer, but also
> much more profound, and with a much better insight into the sort of
> inquiry which was really important and best worth pursuing, and into
> the best method of pursuing such inquiries.

(PGEM p. 33)

Moore never published any direct criticism of the *Tractatus*, but two lines of critical thought can be extracted from his writings. One concerns the contingency of existence. Wittgenstein maintains in the *Tractatus* that the individual objects which actually exist exist necessarily (cf. 2.0271). Exactly why he takes this position is disputed, but his thought is roughly that if the existence of objects were contingent, then whether a state of affairs concerning an object obtained or not would be contingent upon the existence of the object, contrary to the postulate that states of affairs are independent. Moore's objection to this, which comes out clearly in his reply to Ramsey in F&P, is simply that it is clear to him that among the objects which are as basic as any he can

215

conceive, i.e. sense-data, some which do exist simply might not have existed. There is not much of an argument here; rather the situation is comparable to that which arose concerning the idealist thesis that all relations are internal. Moore is pointing out that Ramsey's Tractarian position conflicts with a judgment that seems to us unquestionably correct; to think otherwise we would require a persuasive argument that neither Wittgenstein nor Ramsey supplied.

Moore's other objection to the *Tractatus* also comes out in his reply to Ramsey, and concerns the postulate that states of affairs, or facts, be independent. Moore here objects to Ramsey's assumption that necessarily equivalent facts are identical (F&P pp. 74–5), which is implied by this postulate. Again Moore does not argue against Ramsey's assumption, he just maintains that no reason has been given for it. Behind this scepticism, I think, there lies a rejection of the view of necessity implicit in the *Tractatus*, namely that all necessity is logical necessity. For this view conflicts with Moore's belief that in ethics and elsewhere there are synthetic necessary truths which are not truths of formal logic. This belief was central to Moore's early philosophy, and despite the caution expressed in *SMPP* concerning certain putative truths of this kind (cf. chapter 5, section 3) there is no reason to think that he changed his mind about the matter (cf. e.g. *PGEM* pp. 607ff.).

These cases are obviously contentious. But a further aspect of his views about necessity needs to be brought into the picture: his introduction and use of the concept of entailment. The origins of Moore's reflections on this topic are to be found in his unpublished review of Russell's *Principles of Mathematics*.[30] Russell had identified the deducibility relation with material implication, and Moore rightly objected to this identification, commenting: 'In short, if Mr. Russell really meant by "deduction" no more than what he says he means, his proposition, that pure mathematics can be deduced from Logic, would be profoundly unimportant.' Hence, he says, there must be another relation of implication, which he calls 'implication in the ordinary sense', which is the converse of deducibility, and as compared with material implication '*this* one has by far the greater philosophical importance. Of what nature this important relation is, it is indeed possible to doubt . . . I myself believe that it is a simple concept'.

The first place in which Moore makes public use of this concept is in E&IR, where he introduces entailment as the converse of deducibility (p. 291), and rejects both Russell's definition of it as material implication and the view that it can be defined in terms of the truth of a universally quantified material conditional (pp. 303–5). Moore also suggests here that necessity itself should be defined in terms of entailment: he proposes that 'Necessarily $(P \supset Q)$' means that $P$ entails $Q$ and that 'Necessarily $Fa$' means that $x = a$ entails $Fx$ (p. 302).

It is not clear how one is supposed to generalise from these cases; but one could take 'Necessarily $\sim P$' to mean that $P$ entails a contradiction, and then use the usual definitions of the connectives. Moore did not in the end retain this view of necessity, for he came to reject the equivalence between '$P$ entails $Q$' and 'Necessarily $(P \supset Q)$' in the light of C.I. Lewis's 'paradoxes' of strict implication: there was no denying the truth of all instances of 'Necessarily $((P \ \& \sim P) \supset Q)$', but Moore could not accept the truth of all instances of '$(P \ \& \sim P)$ entails $Q$' (RTD p. 155). Whether Moore was right about this is, of course, disputed and Lewis famously provided an impressive argument for the truth of '$(P \ \& \sim P)$ entails $Q$' from antecedently plausible principles concerning entailment.

I shall not discuss the now vast literature on entailment beyond commenting briefly on a paper by Tennant.[31] Tennant attempts to develop Moore's original thought that entailment is the converse of deducibility by putting forward a proof-theoretic account of entailment. Tennant's idea is that for first-order logic one can extract the 'entailment fragment' by deleting from standard logical theory the absurdity rule (that from a contradiction anything may be deduced; this is the representation of Lewis's first 'paradox' of strict implication as a rule of inference) and then making further adjustments. This is an attractive proposal which captures most of the intuitive judgments concerning entailment that are commonly advanced, but it applies only to entailments that depend on the logical constants of first-order logic; thus as Tennant recognises, his account does not apply to such Moorean paradigms of entailment as ' "This is scarlet" entails "This is coloured" '. If his proof-theoretic approach is to be applied to this case, therefore, one must suppose that our use of colour predicates can be formulated as a theory within which these entailments are represented as deductions. Though this seems possible, it is less easy to see how it can be applied to the synthetic entailments which Moore discerned in ethics and elsewhere; but since these are intrinsically problematic, this is perhaps no great objection.

I embarked upon the topic of entailment because of its connections with Moore's views about necessity and his reasons for not pursuing a *Tractatus*-inspired programme of logical analysis, and it is time now to return to that theme. If one combines Moore's suggestion that necessity be defined in terms of entailment with Tennant's proof-theoretic conception of entailment, one arrives at a proof-theoretic conception of necessity, somewhat reminiscent of that which Moore had advanced in N (cf. chapter 2, section 4). Although there is a sense in which, on such a view, all necessity is 'logical', because tied to the existence of deductions, the position is far removed from that of the *Tractatus*, where the conception of logic is essentially semantic; in particular, it is not tied to the implausible thesis that all necessary truths are tautologies. So quite apart from his belief in synthetic necessities, there is here a further reason for Moore's unwillingness to accept the need for a *Tractatus*-inspired programme of analysis.

As I have explained, Moore came to reject the attempt to define necessity in terms of entailment and one can ask what view of necessity one should ascribe to him thereafter. There is, however, no clear answer to this question. He employs the Leibnizian formula for it as truth in all possible worlds (*LP* p. 186); but as subsequent discussion has shown, this formula can cover a multitude of sins. Much of what Moore says suggests a modal realism comparable to his ethical non-naturalism, according to which internal relations and other modal properties are taken to constitute objective 'non-natural' facts. But it is one thing to talk in this way, and another to want to be taken at face value. I do not think that Moore had any determinate view about modal concepts beyond the negative one that he rejected the view of them inspired by Wiittgenstein's *Tractatus*, and, indeed, also the rule-folowing conception which Wittgenstein developed when he returned to Cambridge in the 1930s (cf. Moore's critical comments in 'Wittgenstein's Lectures in 1930–33' *PP* pp. 280ff.).

The other great analytic programme of twentieth-century philosophy, logical positivism, was the result of applying an empiricist epistemology to the philosophy of language presented in the *Tractatus*. The analyses thus motivated were typically semantic, employing a meta-language in which empirical criteria for the use of the concepts expressed in the object-language are described. Moore never discussed the logical positivist programme directly in his published writings, although he will certainly have been familiar with it from discussions at Cambridge and from the articles dealing with it which he published in *Mind*. But those aspects of his philosophy which descend from his early anti-empiricism are obviously incompatible with the positivist programme, most especially his ethical non-naturalism. Indeed in CIV he anticipates the positivist critique of this position:

> With regard to so-called 'objective' views they [positivists] are apt to feel not only that they are false, but that they involve a particularly poisonous kind of falsehood – the erecting into a 'metaphysical' entity of what is really susceptible of a simple naturalistic explanation. They feel that to hold such a view is not merely to make a mistake, but to make a superstitious mistake.

(CIV p. 258)

Moore here thinks it sufficient refutation of this view to observe that it cannot accommodate his conception of intrinsic value. This attitude contrasts with his later willingness to take Stevenson's emotivism seriously (cf. chapter 3, section 7); and I think this is indicative of a shift during the 1930s towards greater sympathy for the positivist position. Another possible sign of this is his apparent shift, during the 1930s, to a phenomenalist conception of the external world (which I discuss in the next chapter). None the less, his work nowhere explicitly employs positivist presumptions as reasons for philosophical analysis; indeed Moore probably realised that his criticism of William James's verificationism (cf. chapter 5, section 5) is equally potent in relation to the verificationism of the positivists. Thus what marks Moore's attitude to logical positivism was not that he became in any way a positivist; rather he was responsive to the intellectual vitality of the logical positivists, and happy to encourage them to develop their ideas even when he disagreed with them. Characteristic of this is the fact it was largely through his support that A.J. Ayer's famous positivist manifesto *Language, Truth, and Logic* was published by Gollancz[32] – an attitude which contrasts sharply with that of the dominant Oxford philosophers of the period who dismissed it contemptuously.[33]

The conclusion so far is that Moore's demand, that instead of doubting common-sense philosophers should analyse it, is motivated neither by a *Tractatus*-inspired programme of logical analysis nor by a positivist programme of semantic analysis. What then does lie behind it? Can one just say that there is nothing here beyond the desire to get sufficiently clear about what is being said to be in a position to resolve philosophical puzzles? For is not unprogrammatic piecemeal analysis precisely the mark of Moore's style of philosophical analysis? There is undoubtedly much justice in this judgment which repeats his own view about 'the justification of analysis' (*LP* pp. 165–71). His discussions of imaginary objects, for example, seem intended just to resolve philosophical puzzles about these concepts. Admittedly, Moore's analyses here presuppose, and also develop, Russell's logical and semantic theories; but they are motivated essentially by anxieties about the metaphysical status of imaginary objects.

Yet this modest account of Moore's philosophical analyses fails to account for his sense-datum analysis of perception, the most important example of analysis in his work. For this analysis cannot be presented as an attempt to clarify perceptual judgments in such a way that philosophical puzzles about the external world and our knowledge of it are removed. On the contrary, Moore's analysis is itself unclear, in that Moore could never make up his mind about what it is for a sense-datum to be *of* a material object, and, so far from removing puzzles, the analysis reinforces them. By the pragmatic criteria of clarification and puzzle-solving associated with the conception of piecemeal analysis, the sense-datum analysis must be judged a failure.

But Moore insisted upon it. Why? I think the answer lies with

Russell's 'fundamental principle' that 'Every proposition which we can understand must be composed wholly of constituents with which we are acquainted'.[34] Moore never overtly discusses this principle; but the only way to understand his sense-datum analysis is by invoking Russell's principle and Moore's belief that in sense-perception the objects we are acquainted with, or directly apprehend, are sense-data. There is one place at which he almost presents matters this way: in SJP in the course of arguing that we can only have knowledge by description of material objects because we cannot 'directly identify' them, he imagines a situation in which he is looking at a pair of coins, lying side by side; he now argues:

> It will be plain to everybody, I think, that, when I identify the one as 'This one' and the other as 'That one', I identify them only by reference to the two visual presented objects, which correspond respectively to the one and to the other. But what may not, I think, be realised, is that the sense in which I identify them by reference to the corresponding sense-data, is one which involves that every judgment which I make about the one is a judgment about the sense-datum which corresponds to it, and every judgment which I make about the other, a judgment about the sense-datum which corresponds to *it*: I simply cannot make a judgment about either, which is not a judgment about the corresponding sense-datum.
>
> (p. 235)

Why cannot I make a judgment about either coin which is not a judgment about the 'corresponding sense-datum'? Because it is only the sense-data which are directly apprehended, and every proposition which I judge must be composed of constituents which I directly apprehend. The tacit premiss Moore employs in drawing his conclusion is Russell's fundamental principle.

I shall discuss Moore's sense-datum analysis in detail in the next chapter; what concerns me here is the significance, assuming that my interpretation is correct, of Moore's reliance on Russell's principle to motivate his analysis. An initial point is that Russell's principle establishes a programme of analysis — whereby the objects of acquaintance which constitute propositions of all kinds are identified. Moore's sense-datum analysis belongs to this programme: it is not a case of piecemeal, clarificatory, analysis. This connects with the type of analysis involved. Russell formulates his principle as one concerning the limits of understanding; one might interpret this as the understanding of language, but in the first instance one should think here not of language but of thought. Russell's principle concerns what we can think. Thus any analysis which is grounded in Russell's principle will be an analysis of thoughts. Moore usually presents his sense-datum analysis as an analysis of judgments of perception, and the reference here to judgments is important; the sense-datum analysis is to specify the content of certain mental representations – our judgments of perception. Thus although not strictly a semantic analysis, the sense-datum analysis is essentially of that type, or, rather, it suggests that the type be extended to include analyses of the content of mental representations as well as of linguistic ones.

Why might Moore have adopted Russell's principle and treated it as too obvious to need discussion? I suspect that it reflects his continuing commitment to introspection as a method of analysis, on which I commented when discussing *SMPP* (cf. chapter 5, section 3). For if the content of thought is to be introspectively analysable, then there is reason to suppose that I must stand in some introspectible cognitive relation to anything that I can think about, such that I can tell by introspection that it is that thing which I am thinking. One need only now add that this introspectible cognitive relation is direct apprehension to derive Russell's principle.

This is not an intrinsically attractive line of thought. But there are other, more interesting, ways of approaching Russell's principle. In particular, Evans argued that if we consider the conditions for the possibility of thoughts about particular objects, we will find a reason for a version of Russell's principle: if I am to be able to think about Jones, I must know who Jones is.[35] As Russell himself says: 'The chief reason for supposing the principle true is that it seems scarcely possible to believe that we can make a judgment or entertain a supposition without knowing what it is that we are judging or supposing about'.[36] Obviously much here depends on what 'knowing what', or discriminating knowledge, amounts to, and Evans's claim has been much disputed.[37] But even if there is a way here of upholding a version of Russell's principle, it will only imply a Moorean sense-datum analysis of judgments of perception with further premises to the effect that we inevitably lack discriminating knowledge of such things as our hands, although we can have it of sense-data *of* our hands. Arguments for these *prima facie* implausible premises can come only from the philosophy of perception and I shall discuss Moore's attempts to provide them in the next chapter.

None the less one small critical point about the sense-datum analysis can be made here: when combined with Moore's account of the meaning of quantifiers, it runs into insoluble problems. The analysis requires us to analyse 'This is a coin' as '$(\exists x)$(this is *of* $x$ & $(\forall y)$(this is *of* $y \supset y = x$) & $x$ is a coin)' (I simplify a little here). The account of the existential quantifier given in EP (p. 121) is that a sentence of the form '$(\exists x)(Fx)$' means that there is an object to which we can truly point and say '$F$(that)'. Applying this account to the sense-datum

221

analysis, we get the result that the sentence giving the analysis means that there is an object such that we can point to it and say truly 'This is *of* that & ($\forall y$)(this is *of* $y \supset y$ = that) & that is a coin'. But now the sense-datum analysis will have to be applied to the occurrences of 'that' in this sentence, thus introducing further existential quantifiers and leading off down an infinite regress. Furthermore, the regress is vicious: for each stage of the analysis is supposed to bring us closer to an account of those things of which our apprehension is constitutive of our understanding, but since Moore's assumptions imply that no such account can be provided it is quite mysterious how we ever understand 'This is a coin'.

The source of the problem here is obvious enough: in his account of the quantifier Moore takes it that we can use demonstratives to refer to things other than sense-data; and he must allow this if the account is to elucidate the quantifier at all – it would be no help at all to be told that '($\exists x$)(Fx)' means that under certain conditions there would be a sense-datum such that we could point to it and say truly '($\exists x$)(this is *of x &* Fx)'. So if Moore is to keep his account of the quantifiers (whose general purport is hard to dispute), his sense-datum analysis of the objects of demonstrative reference must be dropped.

## 4: *Analysis and ontological commitment*

Now that a reasonably clear account of Moorean philosophical analysis has been presented, it is possible to consider its implications. There is an interesting tension in Moore's treatment of this issue in DCS. On the one hand, he says, in the light of the sense-datum analysis of judgments such as 'This is a hand', that 'there is always some *sense-datum* . . . which is *a* subject (and, in a certain sense, the principal or ultimate subject) of the proposition in question' (p. 54; cf. SJP pp. 235–6). Moore's parenthetical remark here suggests that his analysis has ontological implications. On the other hand Moore is famously emphatic in DCS that he is not at all sceptical about the truth of 'propositions which assert the existence of material things', although he is not certain as to their analysis (p. 53). This reflects his wish to analyse common-sense without challenging it, so that if common-sense declares that there are material objects, then the sense-datum analysis cannot challenge that declaration. But now it seems that Moore is denying any ontological implications to analysis, by taking it that our ontological commitments are given by the common-sense claims we accept rather than by our analyses of what is meant by them.

There is no explicit contradiction here. But Moore does, I think, contradict himself on this matter in SJP; discussing the position of phenomenalists, he writes:

They hold, in short, that though there are plenty of material things in the Universe, there is nothing in it of which it could be truly asserted that *it* is a material thing: that, though, when I assert 'This is an inkstand', my assertion is true, and is such that it follows from it that there is in the Universe at least one inkstand, and, therefore, at least one material thing, yet it does not follow from it that there is anything which is a material thing.

(p. 250)

It is not worth discussing the detailed interpretation of this passage; but it is worth articulating the way in which the conflict apparent in it is to be resolved. The first stage in doing so is the derivation of an explicit contradiction concerning the thesis that analysis has implications for the ontological commitments of our judgments. The truth of this thesis seems easy to establish. Where an analysis is syntactic, it seems clear that, in giving the logical form of the analysandum, the analysis displays the ontological commitments of the proposition expressed better than the analysandum itself. Likewise, where an analysis is semantic, if it tells us all that the analysandum can mean, then it too must surely give the ontological commitments of the proposition expressed. And, finally, where an analysis is explicatory, there seems no sense to accepting that the analysis explicates a proposition without accepting that it explicates its ontological implications.

The antithesis is now that analysis has no implications concerning the ontological commitments of the judgments analysed. This can be argued for by appealing to Moore's requirement concerning the understanding of the analysandum which I discussed in section 2. The idealist philosopher who offers an analysis of the concept of a material object has to allow that the vulgar idioms of common-sense have a legitimate role in his own language, and thus in ascriptions of content to his own judgments. It follows that despite his revisionary analysis he is committed to accepting the material object ontology of common-sense in so far as he is prepared to assent to the truth of common-sense judgments. Of course, he may wish to reject all such judgments; but such a rejection is different from offering an idealist analysis of them.

At this point the contradiction is explicit. For some cases it is easy to see what has gone wrong. Where a syntactic analysis is employed, it is liable to undermine the assumption that the judgments analysed have the ontological commitments they may appear to common-sense to have. This is characteristic of the analyses employed by Russell in his theory of logical fictions. In that context, as I argued in the previous chapter, Moore's ontological conservatism is untenable. But not all analysis is of this kind, as Russell's theory of logical constructions shows: the hypothesis of a logical construction, unlike that of a logical fiction, is not the product of syntactic (logical) analysis, and where the analysis of an apparently existential judgment is not syntactic, it does not undermine the status of that judgment as itself existential. A phenomenalist analysis of judgments concerning material objects will include no quantification over material objects; but this feature does not undermine the existential status of the judgments analysed. So for these cases the contradiction cannot be removed by supposing that analysis undermines the apparent ontological commitments of common-sense beliefs analysed.

One way to remove the contradiction in these cases would be to distinguish between the conceptual scheme which the philosopher shares with common-sense, which provides him with the material for his analyses, and the purified scheme of concepts which meet standards demanded by his philosophical theory and in whose terms he analyses the concepts he employs when in the frame of mind of common-sense. Outside his study the phenomenalist agrees that there are material objects, though once inside it he makes no such assertion (though he does not then deny their existence either). This way of coming at the matter suggests that the revisionary analytic philosopher lives a schizoid life, in which he operates with a pair of conceptual schemes, and that the tension in Moore's discussion is indicative of this schizoid state. The appearance of contradiction can then be removed by relativising the conflicting judgments to the frame of mind in which they are made — to that of common-sense and that of philosophical reflection.

I do not think that this Humean position can be regarded as a satisfactory resolution of the difficulty. It is essentially unstable, in that it does not present a single account of the analytic philosopher's commitments, and the strategy of relativising the answers offered to the philosopher's frame of mind threatens a reflective regress arising from the possibility of conducting this whole discussion in different frames of mind. What is needed is a pair of questions to which the different answers are appropriate, without any relativisation to frames of mind. Yet the difficulty is that one does not want to hold that 'exists' is ambiguous or to find oneself heading back in the direction of, say, the distinction between existence in time and 'being in the transcendental sense' characteristic of Moore's youthful idealism. None the less a distinction of some kind concerning questions about existence is unavoidable here.

A useful guide is provided by a concept characteristic of much seventeenth-century philosophy, that of *substance*; for it is characteristic of that philosophy to hold that not all that exists is a substance — only those things which are in some sense self-sufficient count as substances. It is of course much disputed by those philosophers what things are self-

224

sufficient and what this self-sufficiency amounts to. But the use of the concept shows how, alongside questions about existence, one can raise a more theoretically motivated question about the *fundamental* kinds of thing that there are. Just how 'fundamental' is to be taken here can be left open; different philosophical theories will provide different accounts. But the implication is that the distinction needed, concerning questions about the analytic philosopher's ontological commitments, is that between the kinds of thing whose existence is implied by his beliefs, including his common-sense beliefs, and the kinds of thing which his beliefs lead him to regard as fundamental kinds. Questions concerning the latter will be settled by what the philosopher says in his study; but even there he remains committed to the existence of things that are not fundamental.

This is still rather vague, but I think it suffices both to explicate and to confirm Moore's ambivalence in DCS about the ontological implications of analysis. Philosophical analysis, unless it is of the syntactic kind which leads to a hypothesis of a logical fiction, does not of itself alter one's ontological commitments; in so far as one assents to common-sense judgments one remains committed to its ontology. What assent to an analysis will typically modify are one's commitments concerning fundamental ontology, concerning, to use Moore's phrase, the 'principal or ultimate subjects' of one's beliefs.

I have focused on Moore's comments in DCS because they manifest what I take to be a genuine conflict concerning the ontological implications of analysis. But his comments here are also of interest in the light of their relationship to his views on this matter at other times. On the whole in his earlier writings he stresses the revisionary implications of philosophical analysis; thus in SSD (1914) he writes, concerning phenomenalism, that 'the fact that these assertions that the coins exist, are round, etc., will, on this view, only be true in this outrageously Pickwickian sense, seems to me to constitute the great objection to it' (p. 191). By contrast, in his later writings he seems to dismiss altogether the thesis that analysis could have any revisionary implications. Thus in VSD (1957) he says, concerning his remark in SJP that sense-data are the 'real or ultimate subjects' (SJP p. 236) of judgments of perception, that 'this expression is . . . misleading, and ought not to have been used' (VSD p. 136). We can see that this later position is a mistake. Although Moore was quite right to insist that there is a sense in which analysis cannot subvert common-sense ontology (and in the context of logical positivism this insistence was timely), it is hard to deny that most philosophical interest attaches to the questions of fundamental ontology to which philosophical analysis is directly relevant. Thus DCS emerges as the paper in which, if only implicitly, Moore strikes the mean between his earlier exaggeration of the implications of revisionary analysis, and his later conservative rejection of these implications.

### 5: Moore's paradox

Although the issues raised by the paradox of analysis are central to Moore's style of philosophical analysis, Wittgenstein bestowed the name 'Moore's paradox' upon a different thought of Moore's, one which is less central to his philosophical perspective but, arguably, of greater interest in its own right (Wittgenstein apparently told Malcolm that he regarded it as Moore's most important insight[38]). It concerns such facts as that although it may be true both that I went to the pictures last Tuesday and that I do not now believe that I did, were I to say 'I went to the pictures last Tuesday, but I don't believe that I did' I would say something which is 'perfectly absurd' (PGEM p. 543). The 'paradox' here is that in a situation in which what I thus say is perfectly true, I cannot without absurdity assert it: there are truths about me which I cannot sensibly assert of myself. This paradox calls for a different kind of solution from that required by the paradox of analysis. In that case what was wanted was a way of establishing that the premisses did not imply the paradoxical conclusion, that an analysis must be trivial if true; Moore's paradox calls for an understanding of its conclusion, that there are truths about me which I cannot without absurdity assert of myself, whereby its paradoxical appearance is dissipated.

Moore first presented his paradox in his reply in PGEM and his paper RTD. Both of these are late works, and on neither occasion does he make much of the point; he introduces it only to illustrate the distinction between what someone says, or asserts, and what he implies by saying what he does. Moore's thought is that in saying 'I went to the pictures last Tuesday' I imply that I believe this, although I do not assert that I do, and it is because of this implied belief that it is so absurd to say 'I went to the pictures last Tuesday, but I don't believe that I did'. I shall return to this account of the situation; but it is worth noting that Moore had employed the distinction between what is asserted and what is implied (or expressed) long before his explicit formulation of his paradox. In E (pp. 63–4) he had used it to argue against a naive subjectivist position to the effect that in saying that an action is wrong one is just saying that one thinks that it is wrong; Moore argues that the naive subjectivist confuses what is asserted with the thought that is implied by its assertion. This passage looks back to an earlier discussion of idealism in PE in which Moore makes essentially the same point:

> It is often pointed out that I cannot at any given moment distinguish
> what is true from what I think so: and this is true. But though I

cannot distinguish *what* is true from *what* I think so, I always can distinguish what I mean by saying *that* it is true from what I mean by saying *that* I think so. For I understand the meaning of the supposition that what I think true may nevertheless be false.

(p. 132)

Some of Wittgenstein's late remarks about Moore's paradox (which I discuss below) can be read as comments on this passage.

In *E* Moore says that in asserting that *p* one implies that one either believes or knows that *p*. And in several of his writings about scepticism he suggests that assertion implies a claim to knowledge; for example, in *C* he remarks, concerning the assertion that some dreams are just like ordinary sense-experiences:

a philosopher who does use it as a premiss, is, I think, in fact *implying*, though he does not expressly say, that he himself knows it to be true. He is *implying* therefore that he himself knows that dreams have occurred.

(C p. 249; cf. HP p. 158)

This thesis that assertion implies a claim to knowledge implies that one should be able to form epistemic versions of Moore's paradox, such as 'I went to the pictures last Tuesday, but I don't know whether I did'. That these sentences are indeed strange is widely accepted;[39] but they are not quite as strange as their doxastic counterparts, for one can in this case remove the absurdity by weakening the initial assertion, as in 'I think I went to the pictures last Tuesday but I don't know whether I did', whereas the same modification of the doxastic version obviously does not help at all. In what follows, therefore, I shall concentrate on the doxastic cases (I shall say more about the thesis that assertion implies a claim to knowledge when discussing Moore's anti-sceptical arguments in chapter 9).

For Moore, as I said, the significance of the paradoxes is that they reveal the way in which assertion implies belief. To get clear about this, we need to know what belief is implied, how it is implied, and how this implied belief explains the absurdity of the paradoxical statements. The answer to the first question seems easy: where a speaker asserts that *p*, he implies that he believes that *p*. But there is a complication here;[40] for Moore presents his paradox in two forms. In the reply it is of the form '*p* but I don't believe that *p*', and here he does indeed claim that in asserting that *p* I imply that I believe that *p*. But in RTD he presents his paradox as 'I believe he has gone out, but he has not' (p. 175), which is of the form '*p* but I believe that *not-p*', and here he says (p. 176) that what is implied by asserting that *p* is that one does not believe that *not-p*. Moore does not explain how these implications fit together; but it seems reasonable to suppose that where the belief that $p$ is implied, it is further implied that it is not also believed that *not-p*. This implication is not a straightforward matter of logic; it depends on the assumption is that the speaker's beliefs are consistent, and this is not a logical truth. But if this assumption is made, we can stick with the simple thesis that in asserting that $p$ a speaker implies that he believes that $p$.

What is the nature of this implication? The implied belief is certainly not entailed by what the speaker asserts. Nor can it be a matter of Gricean conversational implicature since the attempt to cancel it produces the paradoxical sentence.[41] Moore says that the implication rests on an inductive inference; it 'simply arises from the fact, which we all learn by experience, that in the immense majority of cases a man who makes such an assertion as this does believe or know what he asserts: lying, though common enough, is vastly exceptional' (*PGEM* pp. 542–3; cf. RTD p. 176). But this does not seem right; it suggests that the absurdity of the paradoxical sentences is comparable to that of a report of a flying pig, and also that in the mouth of a known habitual liar paradoxical sentences should not sound at all absurd. Both these implications of Moore's account are incorrect. Instead, as Burnyeat observes,[42] the implication must arise from the intention, constitutive of the speech-act of assertion, of providing one's audience with information through their recognition that this is one's intention. For since one cannot be understood as intending to inform someone that $p$ unless one is believed by them to believe that $p$, the intention to be thus understood includes the intention to be taken to believe what one asserts. Lying is of course possible; but since the liar exploits the constitutive intentions of assertion, his assertions still require the intention to be taken to believe what he asserts, and although we are not taken in by the assertions of the known habitual liar, utterances by him of the form '$p$ but I don't believe that $p$' are just as absurd as when uttered by anyone.

The implication rests, therefore, on the fact that assertion is 'expressive' of belief, in the sense that assertion entails the intention to be believed to believe what one asserts. Since the speaker also intends that the audience should believe what he asserts, and intends that the audience should recognise this is his intention, the absurdity of the paradoxical sentences arises from conflict between the propositions which the audience recognise that it is the speaker's intention that they should believe – on the one hand, the proposition asserted by the speaker, and on the other hand, the proposition that he believes what he has asserted, the implied belief, as Moore would put it. In the case of paradoxical sentences of the form '$p$ but I don't believe that $p$', the absurdity arises from the fact that what is implied contradicts what is asserted. In the case of sentences of the form '$p$ but I believe that *not-p*', there is no overt

228

contradiction between what is implied and what is asserted; but since here the implied belief that $p$ is inconsistent with the asserted belief that *not-p*, the absurdity arises from the apparent intention of the speaker that the audience should attribute obviously inconsistent beliefs to him.

On this speech-act analysis, the absurdity of Moore's paradoxical sentences arises from conflict between the beliefs which the speaker must intend his audience to form if they are to regard him as making an assertion. It does not follow that one cannot therefore make any assertion at all by uttering a paradoxical sentence;[43] for, unlike 'persuade', 'assert' is not a 'verb of success' in Ryle's sense.[44] Thus the fact that one who utters one of Moore's paradoxical sentences cannot thereby convey the information that he appears to be trying to convey shows only that his assertion is pointless.[45] None the less, in interpreting linguistic acts, we employ the principle that one should try as far as possible to make sense of the lives of those whom we seek to understand. And since the straightforward interpretation of the utterance of a paradoxical sentence attributes an obviously pointless assertion to the speaker, there is good reason to seek for some alternative interpretation. Hence confronted by an utterance of 'He's dead – I don't believe it', we interpret it as an emphatic way of saying 'He's dead, but I find it very difficult to believe that he is'; or confronted by 'I went to the cinema last night, but I don't really believe it' we interpret this as 'I suppose I must have gone to the cinema last night, but I don't remember doing so at all'; and so on.

In a letter of 1944 to Moore, following a paper to the Moral Sciences Club in Cambridge in which Moore had presented his paradox (unfortunately the paper is not among the Moore papers in Cambridge University Library, though Wittgenstein's letter is), Wittgenstein wrote:

> I should like to tell you how glad I am that you read us a paper yesterday. . . . You have said something about the *logic* of assertion. . . . It makes *no* sense to assert '$\vdash p$ is the case and I don't believe that $p$ is the case'. This *assertion* has to be ruled out and is ruled out by 'common sense', just as contradiction is. And this just shows that logic isn't as simple as logicians think it is. In particular: that contradiction isn't the *unique* thing people think it is.

The implication of this letter is that Moore's paradox shows us something about 'logic' – that it needs to concern itself not only with what is asserted (and thus overt contradictions) but also with the conditions for successful assertion. Apart from the extended use here of the term 'logic', this does not point beyond the kinds of consideration I have already discussed. But it is difficult to suppose that this is all Wittgenstein had in mind when he wrote in 1948 'Moore stirred up a philosophical wasps' nest with his paradox; and the only reason the wasps did not duly fly out was that they were too listless'.[46] What more, then, needs to be said in order to show the wasps the way out of the wasps' nest?

If one looks to *Philosophical Investigations* part II, section x, which is concerned with 'Moore's paradox' (the name derives from Wittgenstein's use of it here), and to the material in his *Last Writings on the Philosophy of Psychology*, from which part II of the *Philosophical Investigations* is distilled, Wittgenstein's centre of interest seems far removed from questions about the intentional structure of assertion. He raises such questions as 'How did we ever come to use such an expression as "I believe . . ."?'; and he seeks to use Moore's paradoxical sentences to bring out something special about the first-person present-tense uses of verbs such as 'believe', to make us realise that it is 'a most remarkable thing, that the verbs "believe", "wish", "will" display all the inflexions possessed by "cut", "chew", "run" '.[47]

I think the first step to a grasp of Wittgenstein's purpose here is accomplished by switching attention from explication of the absurdity of uttering a Moorean sentence to the question of whether a rational thinker can consciously hold a Moorean belief. For much the same reason that a rational speaker will not consciously assert a Moorean sentence, it seems clear that a rational thinker will not consciously hold a Moorean belief. For to hold a belief consciously is both to hold the belief and be aware, and thus believe, that one holds it; and no rational thinker will believe either that he both believes and fails to believe the same thing (which is required by a conscious belief that $p$ and that one does not believe that $p$) or that he both believes and disbelieves the same thing (which is required by conscious belief that $p$ and that one believes that *not-p*). In drawing this conclusion, I stress that it applies only to the conscious beliefs of a rational thinker. It is not implied that the self-deceiver cannot have beliefs that he believes he disbelieves; nor that one cannot have inconsistent beliefs. These combinations are only excluded for the conscious beliefs of a rational thinker.

Wittgenstein is not concerned to establish this thesis in his late remarks; he takes it for granted as an obvious implication of Moore's observation. Rather, he wants to elucidate the significance for us (as conscious rational thinkers) of our inability to believe certain truths about ourselves. He puts the matter nicely in a remark he did not incorporate in part II of *Philosophical Investigations*: 'The line "x is in error" has no real point for x = myself. At this point the line disappears into the dark' (remark no. 427 *Last Writings on the Philosophy of Psychology*). It is by putting the point this way that Wittgenstein reveals Moore's observation as an apparent paradox; he transforms 'Moore's absurdity' into 'Moore's paradox'. What he then wants to do is to provide us with a way of thinking about our relationship to the world whereby the appearance of paradox is removed.

In developing this Wittgenstein concentrates, not on the impossibility of believing oneself to be in error (obviously no intellectual smugness is here implied; it is only the self-attribution of specific errors that is ruled out), but on the correlative necessity of believing oneself to be in the right ('One can mistrust one's own senses, but not one's own belief' he remarks – *Philosophical Investigations* p. 190). This necessity induces a merging of one's conception of the world as it is and one's conception of the world as one believes it to be. In the case of the beliefs of others, one's own past beliefs, and of beliefs one hypothetically supposes that one might have, no such merging takes place. We might suppose that if we could take a fully third-person view of ourselves, Moorean beliefs would become possible: 'And then it would also be possible for someone to say "It is raining and I don't believe it", or "It seems to me that my ego believes this, but it isn't true". One would have to fill out the picture with behaviour indicating that two people were speaking through my mouth' (*Philosophical Investigations* p. 192). But Wittgenstein's way of putting the point shows that there is no escape here from the impossibility of the Moorean belief: even if the self divides, the point returns concerning each ego's relationship with its own beliefs.

This is about as far as Wittgenstein takes the matter in part II of the *Philosophical Investigations*; but it seems to me that the line of thought he has been pursuing leads straight back to the famous remarks about the subject in the *Tractatus* (5.63ff.). The subject of the first-person present-tense remarks that he puts us on our guard about in part II of the *Philosophical Investigations* just is the metaphysical subject of the *Tractatus*, the eye that does not appear in its own visual field; and the impossibility of Moorean beliefs shows that, for a conscious rational thinker, 'The subject does not belong to the world'. So, I suggest, Wittgenstein's view is that the way to come to terms with Moore's paradox is through a metaphysical conception of the subject. The reason that there are truths about me which I cannot believe is that because these are truths about me as a metaphysical subject, they cannot appear in my world. Any attempt to make them appear by a division of the self introduces into my world an empirical ego whose beliefs I can mistrust but who is not me.

This may seem an unnecessarily metaphysical response to Moore's paradox. Why not interpret it as just a manifestation of the error of trying to represent the fallibility of one's own beliefs within the world as one believes it to be? Wittgenstein felt that one could not leave the matter there; that would be to leave the wasps undisturbed in their nest. He sought to explore the grounds of this error, to explain how it is possible for there to be truths about us which we cannot consciously believe; and on the need for some explanation of this phenomenon he was surely right. Without one, the paradox remains unresolved. It does not follow that Wittgenstein's explanation is to be accepted. But to assess it fully one would need to set it in the context of a full exploration of the metaphysics of the self; and this is not a task to be undertaken here.

# VIII

# Sense-data and perception

*At the start of the study of perception, we find in language the notion of sensation, which seems immediate and clear: I sense red, blue, hot, or cold. It will, however, be seen that in fact nothing could be more confused.*

(M. Merleau-Ponty *The Phenomenology of Perception* p. 3)

It is hard to regard Moore's preoccupation with sense-perception as fruitful. He invested a great deal of time and energy on this topic (as his publications, lecture notes, and notebooks show), but few people now attend to this aspect of his work. This is not simply because Moore's views on this matter are now regarded as straightforwardly incorrect. Rather, as G.A. Paul observed in 1936 concerning one of Moore's puzzles about sense-data,

> The difficulty about it is not that there is a problem which we can understand and to which we are unable to find the answer; the difficulty is on the contrary to find out clearly what the problem is itself. It is the difficulty of understanding what anyone is saying who says that there *are* such things as sense-data. [1]

Before proceeding it is worth quickly gathering together from previous chapters the points that have already emerged concerning this topic. In chapters 1 and 2 I discussed Moore's emphatic anti-subjectivism, which leads him to insist that consciousness has no 'content', and that the sensible qualities apprehended in sense-experience are 'objects' of experience whose existence is independent of our experience of them. In NROP Moore still regards these as, typically, parts of material objects; but, I suggested in chapter 5, at the end of the paper this naive realist view of the matter is recognised as problematic in the light of Berkeley's argument concerning the relativity of appearances. The problem is then discussed at length in *SMPP*, where the term 'sense-datum' is introduced to describe these objects of sense-experience. Moore here takes the argument from relativity to be unanswerable and adopts an indirect realist position, according to which the sense-data directly apprehended are never parts of material objects, but are instead caused by them. This rather poorly specified indirect realist position then sets the stage for his subsequent discussions of sense-perception.

## 1: The status of sense-data

*SMPP* was not published until 1953; but in 1914 Moore presented to an Aristotelian Society symposium his paper 'The Status of Sense-Data' in which he advanced many of the views he had advanced in *SMPP*. I shall not go over all of these again, but there are also significant developments in Moore's position which make the paper a useful point of departure.

Moore starts by modifying the reference of the term 'sense-datum'. He here refers to 'patches of colour' (p. 169), and not colours themselves, as sense-data. This, I think, signals his abandonment of the view that sense-data are particularised qualities; on his new view sense-data have qualities such as colour, shape, and size, which are not themselves sense-data. In one way this modification is certainly an improvement; for whatever may be truth about the relation between particulars and their properties, it cannot be right to treat all qualities as sortals, with distinctive kinds of thing as their instances. But in the context of a discussion of sense-perception, this change is not so clearly an improvement. It leads Moore to insist that sense-experience is experience of particular objects with sensible qualities, rather than simply of sensible qualities (cf. *LP* pp. 53–7). Many of Moore's critics, such as Stout and Dawes Hicks, took the opposite view, and Moore has a regrettable tendency to dismiss their position as simply deriving from a confusion between particulars and qualities, without seeing that he has to *argue* for the thesis that sense-data are particulars and not qualities.

A related change of view apparent in SSD is his rejection here of the 'accepted view' of sense-data according to which sense-data exist only 'in the mind' of one who directly apprehends them (cf. *SMPP* pp. 40–3). In *SMPP* Moore had expressed doubts about this position, and denied that it was an analytic truth, but had been prepared to go along with it for lack of any satisfactory alternative. Much of the first half of SSD is devoted to the rejection of this position, in particular to denying that sense-data do not exist unapprehended. Moore maintains instead that we have reason to think that some sense-data exist unapprehended, or, rather, as he prefers to put it, that there is a class of 'sensibles' which includes both apprehended sense-data and further entities of exactly the same sort, which would be sense-data were they to be apprehended (thus Moore's sensibles are much the same as Russell's 'sensibilia', which first appear in his 1914 paper 'The Relation of Sense-Data to Physics';[2] I would guess that Russell is here following Moore).

Moore's argument for this position consists of an appeal to his 'instinctive belief' (p. 185) or 'strong propensity of believe' that:

> the visual sensibles which I directly apprehend in looking at this paper still exist unchanged when I merely alter the position of my body by turning away my head or closing my eyes, *provided* that the physical conditions outside my body remain unchanged.
>
> (p. 181)

This is a problematic argument.[3] The reference to the need for unchanged physical conditions implies that the instinctive belief Moore wants to support embodies the assumption that 'visual sensibles' are themselves physical. But Moore also argues here that, because of the relativity of appearances, sense-data are not physical (p. 187). As a result his instinctive beliefs lend no support to the position he actually maintains. Stout's comment on this point seems entirely just:

> From what Mr. Moore says, I gather that he would deny that the sensible, as such, can be simply identified with a quality of the thing. Either, then, his instinctive belief contradicts one of his fundamental principles, or he believes that the sensible persists without believing it to be a quality of the perceived object. In the latter case, his propensity to believe seems so extraordinary that we can hardly attach much importance to it.[4]

What underlies Moore's unsatisfactory treatment of this issue is his deep attachment to a realist conception of sense-data. He feels that if the 'accepted view' of them is adopted, such that their *esse* = *percipi*, then it will follow that they are just abstracted qualities of sense-experiences which we find it convenient to discuss by themselves. Since he rejects this conclusion he finds himself required to make it reasonable to suppose that sense-data can exist unperceived, even though his argument invokes a tacit assumption that sense-data are physical which is at odds with his official position. This inconsistency is, I think, not accidental: Moore's discussion is symptomatic of the difficulty sense-datum theorists face in defending the thesis that sense-data are objects in their own right.

In SSD Moore takes it that there are only two alternatives to the naive realism he has discarded – phenomenalism and indirect realism. He takes the chief merit of phenomenalism to be its anti-sceptical implications; but he raises several objections to it. One is just that if phenomenalism is true, then it is only in a 'Pickwickian' sense that material objects exist and have qualities such as shape. For although the phenomenalist will assent to the truth of 'That coin is circular', his analysis of it does not mention the existence of a circular coin, but concerns instead actual and hypothetical sense-experiences (SSD p. 191). This is the point which I discussed in the previous chapter (section 4) when discussing the implications of philosophical analysis; as I said there, by itself the point counts for little, since the phenomenalist also preserves his common-sense understanding of these propositions.

A different point concerns the difficulty phenomenalists face in formulating true hypotheticals concerning the sensory experiences supposedly constitutive of perceptions of unperceived objects without introducing conditions such as 'If I were to move my body' and 'If I were to turn the coins over' (SSD p. 190; cf. DCS p. 58), which make explicit reference to material objects. Moore does not develop the point very far; indeed in SSD he suggests that it may be possible to find a way around it. But in fact the objection strikes very deep: it raises the issue of the phenomenalist's conception of space and of his location in it, and thus the issue of his conception of his body, including his sense-organs, and of his causal relations with his environment. There is much to be said on these issues, but in my view there is here a conclusive objection to reductive phenomenalism.[5]

In DCS Moore briefly raises a further objection, that the phenomenalist cannot give a satisfactory account of what it is for two sensory experiences to be experiences of the same material object (DCS p. 58). He does not explain what he has in mind here, but the point seems to concern the need to be able to distinguish experiences of similar objects from experiences of the same object. This is clearly an important issue which is central to later discussions by Strawson and Evans.[6] What is not so clear is that this objection raises any issues not already raised by the previous one; for given the role of spatio-temporal continuity in constituting the identity through time of material objects, it seems to me that if the phenomenalist can give an adequate account of his location in physical space then he faces no further problems here.

These objections to phenomenalism show that Moore had good reasons for rejecting phenomenalism even when the arguments of Russell and the logical positivists made it seem unavoidable. Braithwaite remarks however that 'in his Cambridge lectures in the middle thirties phenomenalism received a far more favourable treatment than might have been expected' (A&L p. 23). The only hint of a change of mind in his published writings comes at the end of EP, which dates from the period Braithwaite alludes to: for having put forward his usual sense-datum analysis of 'This is a book' as 'This sense-datum is *of* a book', he continues (p. 125):

I do not believe, however, that 'of' here does stand for a relation, nor therefore that 'This' in 'This is a book' can be said to be short for the sort of phrase which Russell has called 'a definite description'.

Moore is here being very cryptic, but since, on his usual account of the matter, the indirect realist does interpret 'of' as standing for a relation and does treat the occurrence of 'This' in 'This is a book' as an abbreviated definite description (I say more about this below), it is pretty clear that he is here denying that he is an indirect realist. The point is not so clear with respect to the direct realist position which Moore took seriously at this time, since he does not usually formulate that position in quite the terms that he here disavows; but it is implausible to ascribe direct realism to him at this time. So it seems natural to interpret the remark in EP as an endorsement of phenomenalism, and this also fits with some of the later epistemological writings which I shall discuss in the next chapter. It would be nice to know how he proposed to overcome his own objections to phenomenalism.

In SSD, however, Moore does take his objections to phenomenalism to be sufficient reasons for rejecting it, and, as in *SMPP*, he here endorses a Lockean indirect realism (p. 195). In the final paragraph of the paper (p. 196) he acknowledges that this position gives rise to the Humean sceptical argument, but he does not here attempt to state and confront that argument beyond hinting that we can have immediate knowledge of the existence of things we do not directly apprehend, which strongly suggests the position he had proposed in *SMPP* (cf. chapter 5, section 2). That position was not worked out in a satisfactory manner in *SMPP*, but Moore does not now attempt to improve upon it, for he soon adopts a new direct realist position, which I shall discuss in the next section. When he abandoned that position (around 1921), however, he returned to the topic of indirect realism, presumably in the hope of finding here a satisfactory position to adopt, and *LP* contains notes from a series of lectures given in 1928–9 on the subject (pp. 87–103).

In discussing indirect realism in *LP* he takes as his starting-point his sense-datum analysis of 'This is a hand' which structures much of his thought about perception. Moore takes it (DCS p. 55) that there is an initial, unproblematic, stage in the analysis of 'This is a hand' whereby we take it to express the proposition expressed by 'This is part of the surface of a hand'. Beyond this initial stage, however, Moore found himself perplexed and presented the situation as one in which one had to choose between analyses characteristic of theories of three types, direct realism (type I), indirect realism (type II), and phenomenalism (type III). The analysis of 'This is part of the surface of a hand' supposedly offered by the indirect realist is of the following form:[7]

(II) $(\exists x)(xR\text{this}$ & $(\forall y)(yR\text{this}$ $\supset y=x)$ & $x$ is a part of the surface of a hand)

and for Moore, the basic issue the indirect realist faced was that of finding an acceptable interpretation here of '$R$' (or '$of$', as he often expressed it).

Before pursuing this issue, however, I want to discuss how direct realism and phenomenalism fit into this framework. For direct realism, the matter is simple: the new direct realist position of SJP and thereafter can be regarded as an instance of (II): one just takes '$R$' to be '$=$', to get (after simplification):

(I) $(\exists x)(x = \text{this}$ & $x$ is a part of the surface of a hand).

In the light of this, then, it is at least only instances of (II) for which '$R$' is not identity which are to count as indirect realist analyses. What, then, of phenomenalism? Is there another instance of (II) which we might regard as a phenomenalist analysis – e.g. the result of taking '$xR\text{this}$' to be '$\text{this} \in x$', with surfaces of material objects as sets of sense-data? Although views of this kind are sometimes regarded as phenomenalist, Moore did not usually so regard them; he treated them as forms of direct realism (obviously distinct from that captured by (I)). Whether this is right depends on how the position is developed; there are connections here with the issue of the significance of Russellian logical constructions (cf. chapter 6, section 1). However that may be, Moore did not present phenomenalism as an instance of (II); rather, his phenomenalist analysis of 'This is a part of the surface of a hand' is in terms of conditionals concerning possible apprehensions of sense-data intrinsically related to this sense-datum (DCS p. 58).

Returning now to the topic of indirect realism, because Moore is looking for an interpretation of '$xR\text{this}$' in (II) he takes it that the typical indirect realist will present his position in terms of a causal relation between material objects and sense-data. This formal requirement does not by itself rule out the supposition that this causal relation is derived from one between material objects and apprehensions of sense-data. But Moore argues that this supposition has to be rejected once one approaches the matter from the perspective of finding an analysis of 'This is a hand'; for 'when we talk of that surface, we are not talking about our *perception* of the s.d., but only of the s.d.' (*LP* p. 92). Given Moore's assumptions, what he says here is fair enough; but in fact it simply counts against taking issues concerning the details of this analysis, rather than that of 'Moore perceives his hand', as the framework for discussing the philosophy of perception. The indirect realist is not committed to

Moore's sense-datum analysis, and can therefore take the causal relation to hold between material objects and sensory experiences; and if one wants to be an indirect realist, this is surely the position to take. For there is a powerful metaphysical objection to the position Moore requires of his indirect realist: he has to accept that there is causal interaction between objects in different spaces – material objects in physical space and sense-data in private spaces. This seems as much of an *aporia* as Cartesian mind–body interaction.

Moore, characteristically, devotes most attention in his lectures to the problem of characterising adequately the requisite causal relation, in such a way that optic nerves and suchlike do not satisfy the conditions for being the objects of visual perception. Since perception is certainly a causal relation, this is a point of potential real interest and the account Moore offers is more or less that which Price was later to propound as that of a 'differential causal condition'.[8] This is certainly a useful idea, but it has now been superseded by more complex proposals, and I shall not pursue the matter.[9]

Even though Moore seems reasonably satisfied with his account of the causal relation between material objects and sense-data, he recognises that the sceptical threat remains as pressing as ever (*LP* p. 101). If our evidence concerns only the sense-data we directly apprehend, then, he suggests, we could not know anything about their unapprehended causes. For this reason an indirect realist might do better to forget about causality and take it that there is an unanalysable 'manifestation' relation between material objects and sense-data such that one can know *intuitively* (i.e. immediately) that a sense-datum is a manifestation of an unapprehended material object (*LP* p. 102). But no sooner has he stated this than he remarks that 'Some people feel a strong objection to theories of this type; & I own I myself feel very uncomfortable about it'. In an attempt none the less to reconcile himself to it, he suggests that the principle concerning immediate knowledge of unapprehended material objects to which he is here appealing is not really different from the principle which the direct realist employs when he takes it he knows that a penny which looks round is round.

This is an instance of a familiar strategy of indirect realists when confronted by the sceptical objection: they seek to argue that their position is no worse than that of direct realists, who also have to justify an appearance/reality transition (cf. NSA p. 188).[10] However, the cases are not parallel: the indirect realist has to justify belief in the existence of intrinsically unobserved objects, whereas the direct realist has only to justify belief that the conditions of present perception are such that things are as they appear to be. The direct realist can therefore rely on considerations of coherence in a way which the indirect realist cannot, since he (or, at any rate, the Moorean indirect realist) holds that sense-data are self-sufficient particulars. Stout, I think, put the point perfectly clearly in his reply to SSD:

> If, now, these particular existents were in their own nature self-complete and self-contained, so as to imply nothing beyond themselves . . . we could not through knowing them have knowledge of anything beyond them. . . . But if we find a difficulty here, it is entirely of our own making. It arises from a perfectly arbitrary assumption – the assumption that the existentially present data are in their own nature self-complete and self-contained.[11]

In his reflections on indirect realism, Moore never found a satisfactory way of avoiding Stout's conclusion.

### 2: Direct realism

I mentioned that shortly after SSD Moore changed his mind and adopted what was for him a novel direct realist theory, which then displaced his early naive realism as the alternative to indirect realism and phenomenalism. Before discussing Moore's direct realist theory, however, I shall say something about what I take direct realism to be, since the terminology in this area is not always used in the same way and it is useful to approach Moore's discussions of it with some independent ways of thinking about the matter.

The basic idea of direct realism is that we are able to perceive material objects without any intervening awareness of objects of other kinds. However, the conception here of an 'intervening awareness' needs further elucidation. This is a matter which Jackson has discussed helpfully.[12] Central to his account is the thought that in some cases a relation holds between two things *in virtue of* its holding between one of these things and something else: I live in Britain in virtue of living in Cambridge. But what is this 'in virtue of' relation? Jackson characterises it in terms of the possibility of an analytic definition.[13] Thus, according to Jackson, I live in Britain in virtue of living in Cambridge because living in a country is definable in terms of living in a district of that country. This seems acceptable; but there are other cases which imply that the requirement of definability is too strong. For example: one becomes liable to make a VAT return in virtue of running a commercial business, and someone may become able to swim in virtue of their improved health; in neither of these cases is there any implication of definability. As Jackson observes, however, that $q$ is sufficient for $p$ does not suffice for the truth of '$p$ in virtue of $q$'; for this does not capture the asymmetry of the 'in virtue of' relation. I suggest that '$p$ in virtue of $q$' is true where the fact that $q$ explains why $p$ obtains. The concept of explanation is weaker than that of definition, but it is stronger than that of a sufficient condition and since it brings with it the idea of an order of explanation, the asymmetry of '$p$ in virtue of $q$' is accounted for.

We can now put this account of the 'in virtue of' relation to work in defining the direct and indirect objects of sense-perception. Jackson's idea is that we can take it that something is an indirect object of perception just when it is perceived only in virtue of the perception of something else; and a direct object of perception is anything which is not in this sense as indirect object. One of Moore's favourite examples can be used to illustrate this. He writes in DCS:

> I hold it to be quite certain that I do not *directly* perceive *my hand*; and that when I am said (as I may be correctly said) to 'perceive' it, that I 'perceive' it means that I perceive (in a different and more fundamental sense) something which is (in a suitable sense) *representative* of it, namely, a certain part of its surface.
>
> (p. 55)

There are several assertions here, but one is, clearly, that hands are not direct objects of visual perception in Jackson's sense; for we see hands, and other opaque material objects, only in virtue of seeing something else, namely parts of their surface.

Moore's way of presenting the assertion that hands are not direct objects of sight is, however, that they are not seen directly. This way of putting the matter is dangerous, for it suggests that there two kinds of seeing – direct seeing and indirect seeing. As Jackson observes, this does not follow from the direct/indirect distinction with respect to their objects; if one thing is seen in virtue of something else's being seen it does not follow that the latter is seen in a sense in which the former is not (any more than the analogous claim follows with respect to where one is living). Moore's reason for his position is that he takes it that if the sense in which one sees a part of the surface of a hand is just that in which one sees the hand, one is committed to the absurdity that one sees part of the hand's surface in virtue of seeing a part of the surface of part of the surface (cf. *CB* pp. 320–7 for an extended argument to this effect). What is right here is that we do not want to iterate the 'in virtue of' relation in this way. But it is not necessary to discriminate senses to achieve this. For the grounds for assenting to the first claim is that seeing a material object is explained by seeing a part of its surface (that part from which light is reflected into one's eyes), and there is no reason to hold that seeing this part is in turn to be explained by seeing part of its 'surface' – whatever that might mean.

In this case, therefore, there is no cause to introduce a new sense of 'see'. Jackson further holds that an upholder of a representative theory of perception should hold that the non-material sense-data which he takes to be the direct objects of perception are perceived in exactly the sense in which material objects are perceived. However, this seems to me unnecessary: a representative theorist might want to uphold a causal analysis of the perception of material objects, but reject a similar analysis of the 'perception' of non-material sense-data, and it is not clear that he can if the perceptual relation is the same in the two cases. For this reason, therefore, I shall relax Jackson's restriction and take it that a representative theory of perception permits the hypothesis that sense-data are not perceived in the sense in which material objects and their surfaces are perceived; following Moore, I shall express this view by saying that sense-data are apprehended.

There is now an issue, largely verbal, to be resolved concerning the direct objects involved in perception. What is one to say where something is, in Jackson's sense, a direct object of perception, and yet it is perceived only in virtue of the non-perceptual apprehension by the same subject of something else? It helps here to have a term to cover both perception and non-perceptual apprehension, and I shall use the term 'perceptual awareness' for this purpose. Thus in the case envisaged the direct object of perception is not a direct object of perceptual awareness. On this way of presenting the matter, the issue between direct realists and representative theorists is whether such things as the surfaces of material objects are direct objects of perceptual awareness. The direct realist holds that this is so: the representative theorist will deny this, either because he thinks that some other things are the direct objects of perception (that is Jackson's view) or because he thinks that perception occurs in virtue of the apprehension of other things (that is the more common view, and certainly the view of the Moorean indirect realist).

It is now possible to define the naive realism characteristic of Moore's early philosophy. I take this to be the conjunction of direct realism and the thesis that the direct objects of perceptual awareness have the sensible qualities which are apparent in sense-perception. So it is held that the surfaces of material objects that are the direct objects of sight have the sensible qualities which they appear visually to have. Thus understood, naive realism is a clearly unacceptable position; the only thing that made it possible for Moore to remain attached to it during the period of his early philosophy was his being/existence distinction, whereby misleading appearances were held to 'be' even though they did not exist. As I explained in chapter 5, once Moore abandoned the being/existence distinction, he had to abandon naive realism. His immediate reaction was to become an indirect realist, and this enabled him to retain the assumption concerning sensible appearances characteristic of his naive realism.

Manifestly, there is an alternative response to the problems of naive realism: one can retain the direct realist account of the direct objects of perceptual awareness and give up the naive assumption concerning sensible appearances: one can hold that the direct objects of perception just appear to us with certain sensible qualities whether or not they actually have those qualities. Given this new assumption, the relativity and variability of appearances put no pressure on direct realism. This direct realist response, which goes back at least to Reid, was advanced in the early years of this century by Stout, Prichard, and, especially, Dawes Hicks, who gave it the name 'Theory of Appearing'.[14] I shall discuss it further in section 4 of this chapter.

What is unusual about Moore's formulation of direct realism in SJP (and thereafter) is that he combines it with a sense-datum theory, according to which sense-data are the direct objects of perceptual awareness. This sounds like a representative theory of perception; but Moore transforms the position into a direct realist one by identifying sense-data with such things as the physical surfaces we see. In order to prevent this position from falling back into naive realism, Moore now rejects the naive realist assumption concerning appearances. Given his formulation of the direct realist position, however, this denial takes a surprising form: he now denies that the sense-data we apprehend need be as they appear to be. He puts his new view in the following passage:

> What now seems to me to be possible is that the sense-datum which corresponds to a tree, which I am seeing, when I am a mile off, may not really be perceived to *be* smaller than the one, which corresponds to the same tree, when I see it from a distance of only a hundred yards, but that it is only perceived to *seem* smaller. . . . If such a view is to be possible, we shall have, of course, to maintain that the kind of experience which I have expressed by saying one *seems* different from the other – '*seems* circular', '*seems* blue', '*seems* coloured', and so on – involves an ultimate, not further analysable, kind of psychological relation, not to be identified either with that involved in being 'perceived' to be so and so, or with that involved in being 'judged' to be so and so.

(SJP pp. 245–6)

Thus, for Moore, direct and indirect realist are to agree that sense-data are the direct objects of perceptual awareness. The Moorean direct realist then takes it that sense-data are physical and that perceptual awareness is just perception; but he denies that an account of the ways things sensibly appear to us is an account of properties other than apparent properties ('seems larger' etc.) of the sense-data we perceive. The Moorean indirect realist, on the other hand, takes it that the way things appear to us is constitutive of the real properties ('is larger' etc.) of the sense-data that are the direct objects of perceptual awareness. And since he holds that this condition makes it impossible for sense-data to be physical, he takes them to be non-physical.

So far as I can see, no questions need be begged against the direct realist by formulating his position in this way as long as it is clearly understood that properties are not to be attributed to sense-data simply on the basis of the content of sense-experience. Prior to a resolution of the issue of direct vs indirect realism, the conception of a sense-datum is just that of the direct object of perceptual awareness, and nothing follows from that alone about the relationship between the properties of sense-data and the content of sense experience. Indeed it does not follow that a sense-datum is perceived or apprehended whenever someone has a sensory experience; and a direct realist will want to deny that this is so, for he will want to say that in the case of total hallucinations, nothing at all is perceived and there is therefore no direct object of perceptual awareness and so no sense-datum.

Moore, however, does not accept this; in his discussions of hallucinations and after-images (e.g. *CB* pp. 119–20, 136, 144, 146–7, 152–3; *PGEM* pp. 630, 644–7, 684–7; *VSD* pp. 133–4), he takes it for granted, prior to a resolution of the direct/indirect realism issue, that in these cases it is certain that sense-data are apprehended or perceived. This does now make it look as though the question is being begged against the direct realist. Moore might reject this charge: for at one point he suggests that there may be two kinds of sense-data, 'objective' and 'subjective' ones (e.g. *CB* p. 144), such that in hallucinations and after-images it is just subjective sense-data that are apprehended whereas in perception proper, if the direct realist is right, the sense-data perceived are objective. It is hard to see, however, that this account is satisfactory; for once it is held that in a hallucinatory experience subjective sense-data are apprehended, there seems no good reason for denying that in a non-hallucinatory, but subjectively similar, perceptual experience, similar subjective sense-data are apprehended – contrary to the thesis of the direct realist. For as far as the content of experience goes, the two experiences, one hallucinatory, the other perceptual, can be as similar as one likes; so, whatever reasons there are for supposing that in the hallucinatory experience subjective sense-data are apprehended apply equally to the perceptual experience.[15]

Had Moore extended his willingness to allow that sense-data need not be as they appear to be to embrace the issue of their existence, he would not in this way have begged the issue against the direct realist. But I detect no inclination to permit this position in his writings; on the contrary he argues that the absurdity of thinking 'This patch doesn't exist now' implies that the existence of the experience requires the existence of the sense-datum (*CB* pp. 152–3). This is, indeed, a point of some significance, which connects with issues concerning the possibility of thoughts about what does not exist which have arisen earlier. All that needs to be said here is that Moore's argument is not decisive, for it is open to a direct realist either to hold that in a hallucinatory situation there only appears to be a demonstrative thought or to hold that, although the demonstrative thought occurs, all that its occurrence implies is the existence of a place in the region indicated by the subject.[16]

For the moment we can set aside Moore's belief that in all sensory experiences one is aware of sense-data and just consider his objections to his direct realist theory. The point that most impressed him concerns double images. He put it as follows in DCS:

> A far more serious objection [to direct realism] seems to me to be
> that, when we see a thing double (have what is called 'a double image'
> of it), we certainly have *two* sense-data each of which is *of* the surface
> seen, and which cannot therefore both be identical with it; and that
> yet it seems as if, if any sense-datum is ever identical with the surface
> *of* which it is a sense-datum, each of these so-called 'images' must be
> so.
>
> (pp. 56–7)

Clearly, the central issue in this case is whether there are two sense-data. Moore here takes it as obvious that there are. But if all that is assumed is that sense-data are the direct objects of perceptual awareness, it does not follow that where one has a double image, there are two sense-data unless one has shown that the direct realist's treatment of the case as one in which a single physical surface appears double is unsatisfactory (Moore seems to have later accepted this point – LP p. 83).[17]

Moore brings forward a further battery of arguments against direct realism in LP (pp. 58ff.) concerning such matters as the time it takes for light to travel to us from the things we see and the possibility of change in the visible qualities of the surfaces we see. But since, as Moore usually acknowledges, these arguments assume that sense-data have the qualities they appear to have, they are ineffectual as addressed to the Moorean direct realist who rejects this assumption. It is, then, not surprising that once Moore had formulated the direct realist position in SJP (or rather, as I think, taken it over from Dawes Hicks), he treated it as a serious option, although he was at times more strongly drawn to indirect realism and, perhaps, to phenomenalism. In fact, during this period Moore also took it that in all sensory experiences one is aware of sense-data, so he had grounds for rejecting direct realism although he never articulated this line of thought. In his final paper, 'Visual Sense-Data' (delivered 1953, published 1957), however, he rejected direct realism for a related reason – that he was no longer prepared to allow that sense-data need not have the properties apparent in sense-experience:

And it also seems to me plain that, to say that, e.g. if I am wearing blue spectacles, a wall which is white but *not* bluish-white 'looks' bluish-white to me, is merely another way of saying that I am directly seeing an expanse which really is of a bluish-white colour. . . . If I am *not* directly seeing a bluish-white expanse which *has* some such relation to a wall which is *not* bluish-white, how can I possibly know that that wall *is* looking bluish-white to me?

(pp. 133–4)

As Moore knew well, the direct realist will dispute this final claim. So, as it stands, there is not here much of an argument against direct realism. But Moore does at least recognise that one of the fundamental points at issue between direct and indirect realist is whether or not it is correct to give an account of the content of sensory experience by supposing that we are perceptually aware of sense-data which are as things appear to us to be; and this issue is clearly related to that of whether in all sensory experiences there are sense-data of which one is aware. There are, therefore, real issues to be settled here, though they are ones to which Moore addressed himself all too infrequently. In section 4 of this chapter I shall discuss them further. But before doing so, I want to discuss Moore's conception of a sense-datum in order to try to elucidate just why he felt it essential to employ it in discussing sense-perception.

### 3: What are sense-data?

In his 1919 paper KBA Moore wrote:

I quite certainly am at this moment acquainted with many different sense-data; and in saying this, I am merely using this language to express a fact of such a kind, that nobody has ever thought of disputing the existence of facts of that kind.

(p. 180)

Why does Moore say this? Why does he think that once his talk of sense-data is properly understood, no one will dispute that he is acquainted with sense-data? One way of understanding this claim is suggested by a comparison he draws here with the thesis that it is indisputable that there are judgments:

It seems to me quite plain that what Mr. Russell has primarily meant by 'judgment' is what we all mean – a kind of fact, the existence of which no one disputes; and that even if his theory that it is a multiple relation of a certain kind is untrue, that would not at all entitle us to say that there is no such thing as what he means by 'judgment'.

(p. 179)

This suggests that Moore's attitude to sense-data is similar to his attitude to propositions in his writings from *SMPP* onwards, that although talk of propositions is an indispensable idiom for characterising the content of judgments, its employment has no determinate ontological implications (cf. chapter 7, section 1). On this interpretation, therefore, Moore's talk of sense-data is just an ontologically non-committal way of characterising the content of sensory experience, so that only someone who disputes whether we have visual experiences at all will dispute our acquaintance with visual sense-data.

Although this is an attractive line of thought, it will not do as an interpretation of Moore's position. For he repeatedly calls sense-data 'entities', 'objects', and 'things', and makes it clear that he thinks it indisputable that there are such entities/objects/things, which are the 'principal or ultimate' subjects (DCS p. 54) of our perceptual judgments. Thus he argues vehemently against the view that sense-data can be regarded as just qualities which exist 'in the mind' of one who apprehends them, and insists on the contrary that they are particulars which can be coherently conceived to exist unperceived. His 'as if' attitude to propositions is sustained by a genuine uncertainty concerning the analysis of propositional attitudes; but Moore never displayed a similar uncertainty concerning the reference to sense-data in judgments such as 'This is a hand'.

A second way of interpreting the opening passage quoted from KBA is by linking it to the conception of a direct object of perceptual awareness in the way suggested in the previous section. For it is certain that if Moore is perceiving something, then there is a direct object of his perceptual awareness. So, if we define sense-data as the direct objects of perceptual awareness, it is indeed indisputable that, if Moore is perceiving something, then he is at that time aware of, or acquainted with, some sense-data.

This interpretation certainly captures an aspect of Moore's conception of a sense-datum. As I indicated before, however, the trouble with it is that the combination of it and Moore's belief that one is perceptually aware of sense-data in all sensory experiences implies that direct realism is untenable. But this conflicts with Moore's insistence, throughout most of his life, that the sense-datum terminology be employed in a way which is neutral between direct and indirect realism. So, even allowing for Moore's failure to grasp this point, this interpretation can scarcely be exhaustive as an account of his conception of a sense-datum.

Moore, conscious that his sense-datum terminology needed explanation, offered several explanations of it. These fall into four groups.[18] In NROP and *SMPP* he proposes an introspective psychological analysis of 'What exactly is it that happens, when (as we should say) we *see* a material object?' (*SMPP* p. 29), whose answer is given in terms of what we 'did actually see' — 'this patch of a whitish colour, and its size and shape I did actually see. And I propose to call these things . . . *sense-data*' (*SMPP* p. 30; cf. NROP p. 68). This was discussed in chapter 5; despite changes in his views about what sense-data are I think that much the same act/object philosophy of mind, essentially dependent on the conclusion of RI, lies behind his other explanations of sense-data. But this is not obvious. In KBA he writes:

> If we want to indicate what sort of entities he [Russell] has meant by 'sense-data', in a way which will leave no doubt that there certainly are entities of the sort, I do not know that there is any clearer way of doing so than that which I suggested in my Presidential Address, namely, by saying that they are the sort of entities about which we make such judgments as 'This is a coin,' 'That is a tree,' etc., when we are referring to something which we are at the moment perceiving by sight or touch. Everybody can easily discover for himself the entity about which he is talking, when under such circumstances he judges 'That is a tree'. And in calling this entity a sense-datum, we by no means imply either that it is not identical with that part of the surface of the tree which he is seeing, nor yet the opposite philosophical view according to which . . . it is merely a sensation in his own mind, may not be the true one.

> (pp. 181–2; cf. SJP pp. 231–2)

The leading idea here is provided by Russell's principle, whose role in the sense-datum analysis I discussed in section 3 of the previous chapter: sense-data are the objects of acquaintance about which we make such judgments as 'This is a coin'. But what are these entities with which we are then acquainted? Moore provides a pretty clear hint as to what he has in mind when he writes that 'Everybody can easily discover for himself the entity about which he is talking, when under such circumstances he judges "That is a tree" '. What Moore has in mind is not that one should walk up to the tree in question and in that way discover its identity, but that one should attend introspectively to one's sensory experience when making the judgment. Sense-data are to be those entities, whatever they are, such that introspection reveals that sensory experience is constituted by acquaintance with them. It is just assumed that sensory experience is thus constituted.

In DCS Moore tries a different approach:

> But there is really no doubt at all that there are sense-data, in the sense in which I am using that term. I am at present seeing a great number of them, and feeling others. And in order to point out to the reader what sort of things I mean by sense-data, I need only ask him to look at his own right hand. If he does this he will be able to pick

out something (and unless he is seeing double, *only* one thing) with regard to which he will see that it is, at first sight, a natural view to take that that thing is identical, not, indeed, with his whole right hand, but with that part of its surface which he is actually seeing, but will also (on a little reflection) be able to see that it is doubtful whether it can be identical with the part of the surface of his hand in question. Things *of the sort* (in a certain respect) of which this thing is, which he sees in looking at his hand, . . . are what I mean by 'sense-data'.

(p. 54; cf. NSA pp. 181–2)

The novelty here is the attempt to identify sense-data by their supposed philosophical neutrality; sense-data are the sort of thing one sees concerning which one recognises that it is natural at first to take a direct realist view and then, 'on a little reflection', to take a more detached view of this realist thesis. In one respect this passage suggests the account of sense-data as direct objects of perceptual awareness; for the supposed neutrality of sense-data fits well with the account of sense-data as direct objects of perceptual awareness – whatever they are. But this account implies that to determine what sense-data are one needs to determine what the structure of perception is. Yet Moore just tells us to look at our right hands. There is more to his position than this account suggests.

In his article in *PGEM* O.K. Bouwsma showed that Moore's discussion here rests on his usual assumption that sensory experience is constituted by acquaintance with objects. For he showed that if we approach Moore's instructions without this assumption and try to pick out something which we are seeing about which we might feel the sort of doubt Moore describes, we fail. If, under the conditions Moore describes, and without making his assumption about the nature of visual experience, I look at my right hand, there is nothing I can pick out visually about which I find it on a little (or much) reflection doubtful whether it can be the surface of my right hand. On the other hand, once I introduce Moore's assumption that my visual experience is constituted by my 'seeing' patches of colour, then, indeed, the attitudes that Moore describes become comprehensible. But it is through that assumption that the conception of a sense-datum becomes intelligible, and not through Moore's thought-experiment by itself.

This conclusion is confirmed by Moore's response to Bouwsma in *PGEM*, where he advances the fourth type of explanation of his sense-datum terminology. He here explains sense-data simply by reference to direct apprehension, maintaining that 'I think I have always both used, and intended to use, "sense-datum" in such a sense that the mere fact that an object is *directly apprehended* is a *sufficient* condition for saying that

249

it is a sense-datum' (p. 639). By itself, one might interpret this as an account of sense-data as direct objects of perceptual awareness. That account, however, implies that one should not assume without argument that where nothing is perceived but there is still a sensory experience, sense-data are apprehended. But this is precisely the assumption Moore makes; in *PGEM* he explains direct apprehension by reference to after-images and hallucinations (pp. 629–30). Hence, since these are both sensory experiences in which nothing is perceived, the description of them as the apprehension of sense-data can only rest on the act/object conception of sensory experience presented in RI.

My conclusion is, therefore, that Moore's conception of a sense-datum is grounded in the act/object philosophy of mind he presented in RI, although it also embraces the conception of sense-data as direct objects of perceptual awareness. Moore attempted to preserve neutrality on the issue of direct realism by allowing that sense-data might appear with properties they do not actually have. But once one takes the view that the manner in which things appear to us is to be understood in terms of our apprehension of those appearances as things in their own right, it becomes quite unclear how an appearance, a sense-datum, could lack a property it appears to have. For what is this latter appearance supposed to consist of if not the possession of the property by the sense-datum apprehended? Moore could only hang on to his compromise theory of appearing by failing to think through the implications of the philosophy of mind on which his sense-datum theory is founded. Once he had been forced to think through these implications by Ducasse, whose contribution to *PGEM* directly challenged the philosophy of mind on the basis of which Moore's sense-datum theory had been constructed, he realised that sense-data understood in his terms could not appear with properties they did not possess. His realisation of this is of course the thesis of his final paper VSD; and he here goes on to draw the correct conclusion from it, that his sense-datum theory is inconsistent with direct realism. To this, of course, the direct realist will want to respond by contraposing; but then he has to provide his own alternative account of the nature of sense-experience. And it is to this issue that the next section is devoted.

### 4: The nature of sensible appearances

It is a good deal easier to treat the sense-datum theory as an Aunt Sally than it is to formulate a convincing alternative account of sensory experience. In thinking about the matter an initial issue is that of the terms in which to describe sensory experience. Moore concentrates on visual experience, and, especially in his later writings, tends to describe it in terms of what he is 'seeing', or, rather, 'directly seeing' (*PGEM*

p. 629); in a similar way, he writes of what he is 'directly hearing' (*PGEM* p. 641), and implies that the same approach could be applied to the other senses. The mark of this approach is that a type of sensory experience (e.g. visual experience) is described by using an ordinary verb of perception ('see') in a special sense. Moore sought to characterise this sense by reference to after-images and hallucinations; it is, he said, the sense of 'see' in which we see after-images and in which Macbeth saw a dagger, so that the difference between this sense and the ordinary sense is that that which we see in this special sense need not be a physical object (*PGEM* p. 630).

Moore did, however, take it that that which we are said to see in this sense, i.e. 'directly see', is an object of some kind, a sense-datum, and some of his critics think that at this point he went wrong. Thus White argues that although Moore was correct in supposing that 'see' has two uses, he was mistaken in supposing that these uses are distinguished by the types of object said to be seen (physical objects vs sense-data). Instead, according to White, these two uses of 'see' are differentiated by the fact that one '*identifies* what you see, whereas the other *describes* what you see'.[19] The distinction seems to be that where 'see' is used to identify, I am said to see *an F, a G*, etc.; whereas where it is used to describe, I am said to see something *as F, as G*, etc., but not as *an F, a G*, etc. Thus, where I am said to see a hand, 'see' is used to identify what I see; whereas where I see something or other as pinkish-grey and irregular in shape 'see' is used to describe what is seen. Moore's mistake, according to White, was to treat this descriptive use of 'see' as if it were an identifying use, in which a shape, or a patch of colour, is identified as seen.

White's distinction between identification and description matches Moore's distinction between particulars and qualities; so Moore would treat White's thesis as the thesis that visual sense-data are not particulars, but qualities. Thus we should ask what, for White, the described qualities are supposed to be qualities of. It is clear that he takes them to be at least apparent qualities of the particulars identified through identifying uses of 'see'. But what about where there is no such physical particular? White takes a catholic view of the matter: as well as physical particulars, there are non-physical ones, such as after-images and hallucinations. So there is always something to bear the apparent qualities. But if one is in this way catholic about what particulars there are, why should one not equally say that there are patches of colour, sounds, etc., even if these are not physical? When Moore says that he sees a patch of colour, why is that not the 'identifying' use of 'see' that Moore clearly intends it to be? So far as I can judge, White offers no argument at this point. However O'Connor has offered an argument: he argues that when Moore tries to present a descriptive use of 'see' as an identifying one, we can show that this is not a proper identifying use by the fact that in a case in which Moore says that he sees a patch of black, we can always go on to ask 'A patch of what?' 'What do you see a black patch of?' which shows that in fact nothing determinate has been identified by Moore's initial claim.[20]

This is not persuasive. O'Connor's question is not always appropriate, as he acknowledges in the case of someone seeing an after-image, nor is it clear what its significance is. If I claim to see a father, one can always go on to ask 'Father of whom?' 'Whom do you see a father of?'; but it does not follow that fathers are qualities and not particulars. O'Connor wants to interpret 'of' in his question as the relation between quality and particular; but other interpretations are possible. Moore typically described the relation between sense-data and physical objects by saying that sense-data were 'of' physical objects; so he would have often been prepared to answer O'Connor's questions – but no conclusions can be drawn from that fact about the status of sense-data.

O'Connor in fact seems to follow a more puritanical line than White, and hold that only physical objects can be properly identified by identifying uses of 'see'. It follows that where no physical object is seen, but there is none the less a true statement concerning what is 'seen', the use of 'see' must be merely descriptive. Though this avoids the difficulty White faced, it leaves quite unresolved the question of what these seen qualities are in this case qualities of. So at this juncture, Moore can face his critics with a dilemma: either we can only identify physical objects by identifying uses of 'see' or not. If we are not restricted to physical objects, as White maintains, then Moore can identify his sense-data this way. If we are restricted to physical objects, as O'Connor implies, then although a purely descriptive use of 'see' is thereby singled out, its use is inherently problematic – we are supposed to be able to see something as F even though we do not see anything. As I have observed, linguistic intuitions here are unreliable, but to me that sounds contradictory.

Another issue that White and O'Connor fail to address is that of how particular things can look to us to have qualities they do not have, or, to put the matter in their terms, be truly described by us as appearing with qualities they do not have. For again here one wants to ask what the apparent qualities are qualities of. *Ex hypothesi* they are not qualities of the thing seen; so how then are we to understand that in virtue of which the descriptive claim concerning what is seen is true? Moore's sense-datum theory at least offers an account here: the apparent qualities are actual qualities of the sense-datum seen. But the linguistic distinction drawn by White and O'Connor between identifying and describing uses of 'see' does no more than present the issue in new terms; it offers no alternative account of the phenomena which the sense-datum theory sought to explicate.

Some of the criticisms I have directed at White and O'Connor can, I think, be equally directed at Anscombe's similar suggestion that 'see' has two uses, in one of which it takes a 'material object' (where what we are said to see must exist if what is said is true) and in the other of which it takes an 'intentional object' (where no such existential implication obtains).[21] On this account, the characteristic mistake of Moore and others was to mistake the intentional objects of 'see' for material objects, and to think that a certain kind of thing – a sense-datum – is being said to be seen by one who is only describing the intentional objects of sight. The objection to this account is that it does not explain how 'see' can have an intentional object without a material object; nor, more simply, how 'see' can take an intentional object at all. Perhaps in the end one will judge that in some sense visual sense-data are just intentional objects of sight; but this is not a conclusion to be reached by a quick survey of some linguistic data. It requires an account of the nature of sense-experience which deals better than the sense-datum theory with the phenomena that that theory at least addresses.

But what are these phenomena? So far I have discussed two attempts to characterise visual experience through our uses of the verb 'see'. Although this approach is, by and large, that which Moore employed, it tends to provoke disputes about the use in English of 'see'. Thus it has been forcefully argued that the only proper use of 'see' is that in which, in Anscombe's sense, it takes a material object.[22] If this is correct, then one cannot discuss all aspects of visual experience simply by reference to what we are said to see; so if one were to continue in this way, it would be necessary to embark on a tedious discussion of whether it is appropriate to interpret a remark such as 'I saw some spots floating in mid-air before my eyes' with the prefix 'It seemed to me that'. In order to avoid this, therefore, I shall switch from discussing what we see to a discussion of how things look to us, and, in general, to a discussion of the nature of sensible appearances. This is, of course, not a change of subject, but only of idiom. Indeed when presenting her account of the way in which 'see' takes an intentional object, Anscombe herself remarks: 'There is such a thing as simply describing impressions, simply describing the sensible appearances that present themselves to one situated thus and thus.'[23]

Although I have switched to the question of the nature of sensible appearances to avoid the linguistic disputes that surround talk of 'seeing', even here some linguistic distinctions are useful. I start with some ideas from Chisholm, who distinguishes four uses of 'appear' and related terms:[24] (i) a doxastic use in which I might say 'It appears to me that Jones is guilty' and mean that I believe that Jones is guilty; (ii) a 'hedging' use, typically expressed by use of 'It seems to me that', in which I express an inclination to belief without actually committing myself (Moore makes all too frequent use of this idiom); (iii) a comparative use, in which I might say of a plastic object 'It looks like an apple', meaning that when viewed under certain conditions the plastic object looks the way an apple looks; (iv) a non-comparative use, in which I might say 'Under normal conditions things that are round look round', intending thereby to make a non-trivial claim about visual appearances, and not the trivial claim I would be making if my remark were taken in accordance with the comparative use of it.

Having introduced these ideas from Chisholm, I hasten to add that they are not uncontentious. Chisholm himself assigns the kind of claim which philosophers have traditionally debated in discussing sensible appearances to his fourth category, that of non-comparative 'appears'-statements; but it should not be taken for granted that there is such a category distinct from the others. One familiar critical line of thought is that this last category can be reduced to the first (or to the first and second); this gives us Armstrong's doxastic theory of sense-experience, to the effect that this is belief that one is perceiving something with a sensible property, or, more simply, belief that there is before one something with a sensible property.[25] Moore did not confront this theory as such; but his attitude to it is clear from his remark, when presenting his direct realist theory of appearing in SJP, that

> the kind of experience which I have expressed by saying one *seems* different from the other – '*seems* circular,' *seems* blue,' '*seems* coloured,' and so on – involves an ultimate, not further analysable, kind of psychological relation, not to be identified either with that involved in being 'perceived' to be so and so, or with that involved in being 'judged' to be so and so; since a presented object might, in this sense, *seem* to be elliptical, *seem* to be blue, etc., when it is neither perceived to be so, nor judged to be so.
>
> (pp. 245–6)

Moore's critical point here is surely correct; a straight finger looks bent when placed in water, but one does not judge or believe that one's finger bends on being placed in water; nor is there any inclination, even on the part of an unsophisticated child, to form such a belief – so the attempt to construe such appearances in terms of Chisholm's 'hedging' use (ii) of 'appears' is unsatisfactory. When discussing Moore's paradox I quoted Wittgenstein's remark in part II of his *Philosophical Investigations* (p. 190) that 'One can mistrust one's own senses, but not one's own belief', and this expresses neatly the conceptual gap between sensory experience and belief.[26]

It does not follow from the rejection of the doxastic theory that there is not an *a priori* connection, of a defeasible kind, between sensory experience and belief. Such a connection, would be primarily a matter for epistemology; but one might also hold that it contributes to the content of sensory experience. I shall return to this idea, but I want now to pursue a different idea to which the doxastic theory gives rise. This theory construes sensory experience as a propositional attitude, and one can suppose that it is of this form without seeking to reduce it to belief. One can just employ the idiom 'It appears sensibly to me that $p$' as an irreducible general description of sense-experience. This is not a use of 'appears' which occurs in Chisholm's list; none the less it is as legitimate as those which do. When a stick in water looks bent to me, I can say that it appears visually to me that the stick is bent, and so on. This formal proposal expresses the substantive view that sense-experience is a fundamental species of mental representation, and that what appears sensibly is just what is thus represented. The idea here is that it is the function of the senses to inform us about our environment and that it is therefore intrinsic to them that they should aim to represent for us features of it to which they are sensitive. This may seem to imply the doxastic theory; but by relying on a defeasible *a priori* connection between sense-experience and belief one can maintain the informational role of the senses while distinguishing between belief and experience.

The basic idea here of an informational theory of sensible appearances is, I think, a serious contender for the truth about them.[27] One of its attractive features is that since, on this theory, the apparent qualities of things are just predicated intentionally of the things themselves, there is here no immediate cause to invoke a special category of sensible properties which have to be understood either as qualities of the experience or of its supposed object – the sense-datum. Once thus freed from the restriction to the traditional sensible properties, we can recognise the variety and richness of sensible appearances, especially visual ones. The things we see appear visually with many of the properties we believe them to have; for although sensible appearances are not beliefs they are often influenced by our beliefs about what we are seeing – thus a table looks solid, honey looks sticky, and so on.

What would Moore have made of this account of sensible appearances? In one way it harmonises with his approach; for by treating sensible appearances as represented content, it embodies a denial that sense experience has any further qualitative content of the kind Moore repudiated. Yet in other respects it diverges sharply from Moore's approach: whereas Moore treats sensory experience simply as consciousness of a real object (a sense-datum – whatever it is), on the informational theory, the sensible appearance which constitutes the content of an experience is not regarded as a thing to which one is related by the experience. Rather, this theory implies that appearances should be conceived in whatever way is held to be appropriate for the content of

255

propositional attitudes, and this is not likely to be by regarding the content as an object to which one is related through the attitude. One might say that on this approach sensible appearances are treated as just the intentional objects of sense-experience (so that this provides one interpretation of Anscombe's thesis that visual sense-data are just the intentional objects of sight).

Another reason for thinking that Moore would have rejected this informational theory is given by the passage from SJP quoted above. For Moore here contrasts 'seems elliptical' not only with 'judged to be elliptical' but also with 'perceived to be elliptical', which one might associate with a representational conception of sensible appearances according to which to appear elliptical is to appear to be elliptical. There is a passage in VSD in which a similar point is presented:

> if you see (in the common sense) two boats on the sea, one of which is quite near and the other at a considerable distance, you may be able to say with truth both (1) that the distant boat looks much smaller than the near one and (2) that the distant boat 'looks as if it were' much larger than the near one.

(p. 134; cf. *CB* pp. 70–1)

It is plausible to suppose that the sense in which the distant boat 'looks as if it were' much larger is captured by the informational account: the distant boat appears visually to be much larger. A doxastic account of this might also be proposed; but the situation could be such that one is aware that conditions of perception are not normal and thus does not believe that the distant boat is larger even though it appears visually to be so. But what then of the sense in which the distant boat looks much smaller than the near one? Moore clearly thought that this sense was distinct, and, as he goes on to make clear, his sense-datum theory is intended to explicate sensible appearances of this other kind.

The important question here is whether there is a significant category of non-representational sensible appearances. The informational theorist may well claim that Moore's case does not establish this. He will say that it shows the need to distinguish visual representations of impersonal spatial relationships from those of spatial relationships within the subject's perspectival visual space (which is not a distinct space, but an egocentric way of regarding physical space). With this distinction one can then re-express Moore's distinction as one between (1) the fact that the nearer ship appears to occupy more visual space than the distant one, and (2) the fact that the distant ship none the less appears to be larger, i.e. to occupy a larger region of impersonal space.

I think this response is adequate for this case. There are other cases for which it cannot readily be generalised: when a shadow falls across part of my wall, the part in shadow looks darker, but I might well say, it does not look to be darker; similarly, an approaching car sounds louder as it comes closer, but, I might say, does not appear to be getting noisier. On reflection, however, I think an informational theorist can accommodate these cases by a contrast between belief and sensible appearance: one does not believe that the colour of the wall has altered, although it appears to one that it has, etc. But there are two other considerations which are more potent.

One is typified by the case of myopic vision; when I remove my spectacles, the things in front of me look blurred, but they do not look to be blurred. This case cannot be handled by the belief/appearance distinction, for it is not clear what it would mean to say that things themselves appear to be blurred. The blurring is somehow a feature the way in which things are represented visually, not of what is represented. The second point arises from a more abstract challenge, which seeks to develop the distinction between what is represented and how it is represented within sense-experience. How, it can be asked, can sensory experience have a representational content of which the subject is conscious without having non-representational features that are apparent to the subject? Sensory experience is not just representation within the head caused by the ways in which our sense organs interact with the world; it is a conscious experience whose qualitative features make it possible for it to represent to us the world. The wall I now see looks to be yellow because it *looks yellow*. Furthermore, one can ask what account an informational theorist can offer of the different ways in which the same spatial qualities (e.g. shape) manifest themselves within different kinds of sense-experience (sight and touch); for if the represented content is the same in both cases, wherein lies the apparent difference between the two experiences if not in their non-representational aspects?

These considerations are not conclusive, but they suffice to raise a question about the adequacy of the informational theory. If the mode of representation characteristic of sensory experience requires that there be features of sensory experience apparent to the subject which are not features of what is represented, these will be sensible appearances which are not the representational content of sense-experiences. In the ensuing discussion, therefore, I shall distinguish, in talking about sensible appearances, between representational appearances, for which the informational account is correct, and *phenomenal* appearances, which I shall assume to be a non-empty set of sensible appearances for which it is not.[28]

One important implication of allowing that there are phenomenal appearances is that one cannot dispense with a special category of sensible qualities in the way that the informational theory of sensible appearances makes possible. One needs to distinguish between uses of terms such as 'red' in specifying a phenomenal appearance, where I shall say that it denotes a phenomenal quality, and uses in which it is predicated of other things, typically material objects, where I shall say it denotes an objective quality. It seems clear that if phenomenal appearances are to be constitutive of the mode of representation of the different senses, the prime examples of phenomenal qualities will be Aristotle's 'special sensibles' and the indexical spatial properties requisite for a sensory field. Thus in the case of sight, one would expect the phenomenal qualities to be colour, shape, and spatial properties such as being on one's left.

This distinction between phenomenal and objective qualities is that which was overlooked by Moore in RI (cf. chapter 1, section 6), and I think it was only when his argument in RI was challenged by Ducasse in *PGEM* that he saw the need for such a distinction (cf. his response to Ducasse: *PGEM* pp. 655–6; the first entry in *CB* in which the distinction is affirmed dates from 1944 – cf. p. 225). He then adopted the familiar dispositionalist account of the relevant objective qualities, e.g. that for a material object to be red is for it to look red to a normal observer in good light (*CB* p. 225); he also proposes a similar dispositional account of objective shape (*CB* p. 326), which confirms his phenomenalist sympathies at this time. But he never published an extended discussion of the matter, nor of the related issue of the distinction between primary and secondary qualities (which is an extraordinary omission from his extensive writings on perception).

The issue of whether there are phenomenal appearances is closely connected to the dispute between direct realists and adherents of a representative theory of perception;[29] for the sense-datum theory is usually presented as an account of the nature of phenomenal appearances. But the connections here need a moment's attention. Following Jackson, I argued that the issue between direct realists and others turns on whether we perceive physical objects in virtue of perceptual awareness of anything else. So if adoption of a sense-datum theory of phenomenal appearances is to bear upon that issue, it must be accepted that we perceive what we do in virtue of things appearing phenomenally as they do. But this is, I think, implied by the hypothesis that phenomenal appearances constitute the mode of representation of sensory experience. Admittedly other factors are relevant to perception: the representational content of sense-experience is shaped by the subject's beliefs, by sub-personal hypotheses, and by sensory input that remains subconscious. But these do not falsify the 'in virtue of' claim; for in other cases where $p$ obtains in virtue of $q$ it is not required that the fact 'that $q$' provides a complete explanation. Running a business only gives rise to liability to complete a VAT return within a certain system of taxation, but this does not falsify the thesis that within such a system, liability arises in virtue of running a business.

There are two traditional accounts of phenomenal appearances: the sense-datum theory and the adverbial theory. I have already said enough about Moore's conception of the former of these; the adverbial theory is a development of the theory of appearing proposed by Dawes Hicks and others.[30] It gets its name from the idea, proposed by Ducasse (and since developed by Chisholm and Tye[31]) that the way to understand 'The stick appears (phenomenally) brown to me' is to transform it into the passive 'I am appeared brownly to with respect to the stick', which can be shortened and clarified if rephrased as 'I sense brownly, with respect to the stick'. Thus the phenomenal appearance of the stick is construed as a manner of sensing with respect to the stick, which latter relation is then interpreted causally. One range of phenomenal appearances which the adverbial theory handles in a straightforward manner is that which is typified by my myopia: that things look blurred to me when I remove my spectacles is interpreted as my sensing blurredly with respect to them; and this seems right. However, this is not a central case; and the problem for the adverbial theory is that, since sensory representations are articulated spatially, it has to provide an account of sensory fields. This point quickly emerged in the course of the correspondence between Ducasse and Moore which followed their initial debate in *PGEM* and which has now been published as an addendum to the third edition (1968) of *PGEM*. Ducasse correctly saw that Moore's argument in RI lay at the heart of his philosophy of perception, and criticised Moore's act/object conception of sense-experience, offering its place his own adverbial theory:

> The hypothesis, then, which I present . . . is that 'blue', 'bitter', 'sweet' etc. are names not of objects of experience nor of species of objects of experience but of *species of experience itself*. What this means is perhaps made clearest by saying that to sense blue is then to sense bluely, just as to dance the waltz is to dance 'waltzily'.
>
> (*PGEM* pp. 232–3)

In response, Moore rightly observed that Ducasse needs also to provide an account of the visual field, which cannot be readily provided from within the adverbial theory:

> I agree with you that there is a relation, which may naturally be called 'occupation', such that to say that a resting blue spot exists at a given time is equivalent to saying that the sensible colour 'blue' is, at that time, occupying a region in some sensible space. But then, in order that you may be seeing a resting blue spot, it is necessary that you should not only (1) be seeing the colour, blue, but also (2) seeing a region (or 'place') in sensible space, and also (3) seeing the colour blue *as* occupying that seen place. And even if the colour blue could

259

be related to your seeing as is a stroke at cricket to the hitting of it, I do not at all understand how a place could be related to an act of seeing in the same way, and still less what account could be given of seeing a colour *as* occupying a place.

(*PGEM* p. 687h)

The importance of this issue for the adverbial theory is well brought out by Jackson's 'complement property' and 'many property' problems.[32] Suppose a stick looks brown and oblong to me at the time that an apple looks red and circular; it will not do to say that in this situation I just sense brownly and oblongly and redly and circularly. There are two related points here. One, the 'complement property' problem, concerns the incompatibility of some of these properties. If the sensing of colours is a matter of different species of sense-experience, we need an explanation of how it is that these different species of experience can coexist within the same consciousness; one cannot dance the waltz, the foxtrot, etc., at one and the same time. The other point, the 'many property' problem, concerns the grouping of these properties; something looks brown and oblong at a time at which something else looks red and circular, but nothing looks brown and circular, or red and oblong.

At one level, a solution to these problems is provided by location in a sensory field. For we experience the properties as located in different regions of a sensory field, and it is this which, intuitively, makes possible experience of differentiated groups of incompatible qualities at the same time. But then Moore's challenge to Ducasse must be met: the adverbial theory must provide an account of the spatial relations constitutive of sensory fields. It is clearly not enough for the adverbial theorist just to introduce putative spatial adverbs, 'on-my-left-ly' and 'on-my-right-ly', say, as further phenomenal properties of experience (this seems to have been Ducasse's intention; cf. *PGEM* p. 687m). For this only repeats the previous problems: since sensing 'on-my-left-ly' and sensing 'on-my-right-ly' will be different species of sensing, it remains to be explained how these different species can be accomplished simultaneously and how they can combine in a discriminating way with other phenomenal qualities.

One idea here is to take 'on-my-right-ly' as a second-order property of the property expressed by 'redly'.[33] Though this avoids repetition of the old problems, treating spatial properties in this way does not explain why they offer solutions to the old problems for phenomenal properties. There are other second-order properties (e.g. those expressed by 'extremely' and 'to some degree') but the distribution of these properties among the phenomenal qualities of experience provides no solution to the 'complement property' and 'many property' problems. That can only come from some individuating feature which enables the phenomenal

260

properties to be interpreted as properties of different things. Although such a feature can always be regarded as a second-order property (just as one can so regard the property expressed by '$(\exists x)(x = a \, \& \, \ldots x \ldots )$') the individuating element requires reference to different spatial locations, or things at them, which are not themselves qualities of experience; and this is not compatible with the approach of the adverbial theorist.

In the light of this point it is easy to see the appeal of a sense-datum theory. Such a theory provides one with real objects, sense-data, located within a sensory field, of which one can predicate phenomenal qualities and spatial relations in a way which at once avoids the difficulties which beset the adverbial theory. This is the point which Moore urged against Ducasse, and it is essentially Jackson's recent argument for a sense-datum theory.[34] Yet the objections to sense-datum theories are legion. Perhaps the most telling point is simply Moore's utter failure to develop his sense-datum theory into a satisfactory philosophy of perception. As I explained in sections 1 and 2 he found himself trapped within a conceptual treadmill which condemned him to move from direct realism to indirect realism and thence to phenomenalism and then again back to direct realism and on through the cycle, without any sign of a synthesis that would enable him to *aufheben* any stage of this dialectic.

One might suppose that this point just reflects a contingent inability on Moore's part to put his act together in a satisfactory fashion, but I think that it is a consequence of difficulties inherent within his simple act/object conception of sensory experience. One familiar difficulty concerns individuation and identity:[35] How many visual sense-data am I now apprehending? How long does each last? (When I blink do I get a whole new lot?) There seems no principled way of answering these questions; but if sense-data are particulars, things in their own right with their own properties, then there ought to be. Jackson responds to this objection by suggesting that 'sense-datum' is a dummy term, like 'thing', which one should not expect to provide a criterion of identity for the things to which it applies.[36] This response belongs with Moore's neutralist conception of a sense-datum, according to which we can say that the patches of colour we apprehend are visual sense-data while leaving it open what sorts of thing these sense-data are. I have, however, argued that this conception conflicts with Moore's reliance on sense-data to give an account of the phenomenal aspect of sensory experiences irrespective of whether or not they are perceptual. So Moore needs to be able to extract criteria of individuation and identity from this phenomenal aspect alone. The difficulty is that he cannot. A sensory field can be divided up in any number of ways, and there is no clear sense to questions about its persistence.

In Moore's work this latter point comes out in his discussions of whether there are any unapprehended sense-data to which I referred in section 1; the unsatisfactory nature of these discussions shows that his conception of a sense-datum was just not that of a determinate object for which these fundamental questions of identity had any non-arbitrary answer. It was this arbitrariness which gave rise to the thesis, advanced by Paul and Ayer, that the answers to questions about the identity of sense-data are no more than a matter of alternative verbal conventions.[37] It was all very well for Moore to respond indignantly in *PGEM* (pp. 680–1) that Ayer had failed to see that his questions about the identity of sense-data arose from serious questions about the nature of sensory experience. What Moore failed to grasp is that the justice of Ayer's characterisation of the situation constituted a serious objection to his account of sensory experience.

A different problem concerns the applicability of an appearance/reality distinction to sense-data themselves. On the one hand, if they are genuine entities, whose *esse* is not just *percipi*, then the distinction ought to apply to them. For no cognitive state, however 'direct' or 'transparent', can guarantee that things are as they are apprehended. But, on the other hand, as I observed at the end of the previous section, if there is an appearance/reality distinction with respect to sense-data, then the phenomenal aspect of sense-experience is not being explicated by the properties of sense-data; it resides instead in the manner in which they appear to us. But then the sense-datum theory has achieved nothing; the appearances of things are just being redescribed as the appearances of sense-data.[38]

A related point concerns the formal conception of the perception or apprehension of sense-data as merely an act/object relationship. The difficulty is that this conception does not readily allow for awareness of an object's properties. For that seems to be awareness of the object *as* having certain properties, and awareness of $x$ *as* $F$ is implicitly propositional. But this threatens to introduce, at the level of phenomenal appearances, a notion of represented content which it was intended to explicate. One might try to avoid this by the position Moore adopted in RI, according to which, in effect, properties are themselves objects. But this does not really avoid the problem, since one still needs to be aware of different particular properties *as* properties, or parts, of one thing.

A final difficulty concerns the identity of the space within which sense-data must be actually located if the sense-datum theory is to avoid the difficulties which were insurmountable on the adverbial theory. Because of his neutralist position about the status of sense-data Moore has no unequivocal account of this matter; but at various points he makes it clear that he does not think that double images, after-images, and hallucinations (which he regards as visual sense-data) are in physical space (cf. PEW pp. 131–2; *CB* p. 233). Jackson, by contrast, who takes it that all sense-data are mental, none the less locates them in physical space (pp. 102–3), and I shall discuss this view first. It implies that when Macbeth hallucinated a dagger, a dagger-shaped visual sense-datum was actually located a few feet in front of him. This is the sort of challenge to common-sense against which it is difficult to argue. One cannot just invoke the principle that a region of physical space is occupied only in virtue of the instantiation there of some physical property; for that obviously begs the question at issue. Moore argues that location in physical space implies the possibility of observation by more than one person (PEW p. 103). But perhaps that only applies to things which are objective, and, *ex hypothesi*, the visual sensa-data of which Macbeth was aware are not. Yet there is a principle concerning change in the physical location of an object which seems cogent: that any such change requires that some force act at the place occupied by the object; otherwise why on earth should any object there move? The hypothesis that Macbeth's hallucinated dagger is located in physical space, however, violates this principle; for changes in its location will be brought about by changes in Macbeth, in his location and his frame of mind, and neither of these give rise to forces that bear on the supposed location of the visual sense-datum.

Perhaps this is still question-begging; but it is equally clear that Jackson's position constitutes a massive affront to common sense, and this fact provides a strong reason for rejecting the position. But is there any viable alternative for the sense-datum theorist? What is the non-physical alternative space within which, according to Moore, at least some sense-data are located? Moore never tells us. In the visual case there is a temptation to think in terms of a two-dimensional region 'before the mind' whose occupation by patches of colour provides us with our phenomenal 'picture' of the world.[39] Though this misrepresents depth as essentially different from other apparent spatial properties of the visual field, the pictorial analogy is potent because a picture has dual spatial properties: there is the (physical) space of the materials of the picture, and the pictorial space of the things represented in the picture which is (usually) quite distinct from the first space. Thus it provides a model for the sense-datum theorist's conception of the visual field as a mental picture with spatial features distinct from those of the physical world it represents. The trouble is that at a crucial point the analogy does not help. It is because pictures are themselves physical that they have spatial properties in addition to the pictorial space they represent; so we cannot get from them any help in understanding how the visual field can be a non-physical space in which ordinary spatial relationships obtain.

These points provide, I think, grounds for rejecting a sense-datum theory at least as strong as those offered before for rejecting the adverbial theory.[40] The problem that now arises is where one is to go from here. A line of thought that some philosophers have recently espoused seeks to account for phenomenal appearances in terms of the normal causes of the sense experiences in question.[41] This line of thought is closely related to attempts to construe phenomenal appearances in terms of Chisholm's 'comparative' conception of appearance. On that construal to say that an apple looks red to me is to say that the apple looks the way a red object looks to me under normal circumstances; what these philosophers add is a causal analysis of this comparative statement, to the effect that visual experience produced by the apple is of a kind which is normally produced in me by the presence in my visual space of a red object. There are, however, several objections to this account. One general weakness is that it is not easy to see how the kind of experience whose normal cause is here invoked is to be characterised except in terms of the phenomenal appearance involved – e.g. as the kind in which something looks red. Another point where circularity is difficult to avoid concerns the definition of a 'normal' cause. Consider the Muller–Lyer illusion; in this illusion one line looks longer than the other. What is the normal cause of appearances of this kind? Often, of course, they are a result of looking at lines of unequal length. But the cases most similar in kind to the appearance involved in a particular Muller–Lyer case are just Muller–Lyer cases in general, where the lines observed are in fact of equal length. By any ordinary standards there is nothing abnormal about the circumstances under which the illusion is usually observed, and only if 'normal circumstances' are defined as circumstances in which things are as they appear can this kind of case be systematically excluded. A final objection, which I take from Jackson,[42] concerns after-images which appear coloured in ways that nothing is, in fact, coloured – a peculiar purplish-green, say. One can go counterfactual, and propose that the visual experience is of a kind which would normally be caused by the presence of a purplish-green object if there were any such objects. But, quite apart from the intrinsic implausibility of thinking of after-images in this way, this counterfactual cannot be held to be barely true in the way in which the description of the after-image as purplish-green is. If the counterfactual is to be accepted as true, this can only be in virtue of the acceptance of other facts – such as that the particular after-image looks purplish-green.

The conclusion at this point seems to be that none of the theories which aim to provide an account of phenomenal appearances is tenable. One diagnosis of the situation must be that their topic is misconceived at the outset, i.e. that there is no important category of phenomenal appearances, and hence that the informational conception of sensible appearances as just representational must after all be accepted. Can one rest content with this?

One objection is that accounts of this kind typically rely on causality to determine what content is represented in sensory experience. Clearly, any such hypothesis is vulnerable to the objections to a causal account of phenomenal appearances. But perhaps one can also hold, in a functionalist style, that 'output', i.e. beliefs, help to determine content. This seems especially plausible in the case of spatial content: for it is not clear how an experience could represent an object as, say, in front of one unless this representation was such as to give rise to dispositions to actions targetted on that region of space. This is the hypothesis mentioned at the start of this section that, although sensory experiences are not beliefs, their *a priori* connection with belief helps to determine their content.

Yet this point does not suffice by itself to make a case for the informational approach; in particular, the intuition behind the appeal to phenomenal appearances, that the conscious aspect of sensory experience is essential to its representational content, still needs to be met. I think that the way to accommodate this is to take a step which is in one respect in the direction of a sense-datum theory; one has to introduce a conception of sensory representations, such that in having a sensory experience there is a sensory representation somehow present to one. Where this line of thought differs sharply from that of Moore is in locating these sensory representations firmly in the head; they are psychological structures, realised in neurophysiological structures of which we are at present largely ignorant. It is indeed, uncontentious, that psychological structures of this kind are involved in perceptual processes. My hypothesis is that it is by reference to them that that conscious aspects of sensory experience can be satisfactorily characterised, that in sensory experience we consciously experience them without being aware *of* them.

This last point may appear to be just evasion. What it challenges is Moore's presumption that consciousness has to be understood in terms of an act/object relationship of awareness. As I have frequently stressed, this presumption of Moore's is closely linked to his one-level conception of meaning; and the opposed Fregean sense/reference distinction provides a way of thinking about the present issue. A Fregean whose conception of sense is, unlike Frege's, psychological, will treat treat senses as types of mental representation whose presence 'in the head' determines the content of thought. My hypothesis is that sensory experience has much the same structure except that sensory representations are consciously experienced. This conscious experience constitutes the qualitative 'content' of sensory experience – but it is just a sensory mode of presentation of that aspect of the subject's environment which is represented in the sensory representation and which appears sensibly to the subject. So this qualitative 'content' itself does not appear as such to the subject (except when the subject reflects on his perception), just as Fregean senses are not what an unreflective subject thinks about. In both cases there is a psychological mode of presentation in addition to the (intentional) 'object' presented; what is distinctive about sensory experience is that the mode of presentation is consciously experienced. There is no separate category of phenomenal appearances; but the representational aspect of sensible appearances depends on a qualitative, or phenomenal, mode of presentation.

Since this hypothesis makes serious use of the conception of sensory representations it can be regarded as contributing to a representational theory of perception, though not to a representative theory in the sense defined by Jackson. But these remarks provide only the beginnings of an account which does justice to the complexities of sense-perception, and I do not pretend to have a clear grasp of all that is required. It remains to be explained, for example, why sensory representations are experienced at all – i.e. what significance the role of consciousness has here. As I said at the start of this section, it is a good deal easier to dismiss the sense-datum theory than it is to construct a satisfactory alternative.

# IX

# Knowledge and scepticism

---

*'Tis easier to forbear all examination and enquiry, than to check ourselves in so natural a propensity, and guard against that assurance, which always arises from an exact and full survey of an object. On such an occasion we are apt not only to forget our scepticism, but even our modesty too; and make use of such terms as these, 'tis evident, 'tis certain, 'tis undeniable; which a due deference to the public ought, perhaps, to prevent.*

(D. Hume *A Treatise of Human Nature* I.4.vii)

If Moore is notorious for his attachment to sense-data, he is famous for his affirmations of common-sense knowledge. When 'Moore' is introduced into a discussion of knowledge we can guess what position he will take up – he will affirm that he knows for certain that 'This is a hand', that the earth existed for many years before his birth, and so on. The truth and significance of these affirmations is disputed. But even those who deny that Moore's affirmations answer philosophical questions about the limits of human knowledge are ready to acknowledge that reflection on why this is so is an important stage in answering these questions.[1]

## 1: Perception and knowledge

In *SMPP*, where an indirect realist philosophy of perception is advanced, Moore expressed his rejection of scepticism concerning the possibility of empirical knowledge in the light of this philosophy of perception by distinguishing between 'immediate knowledge' and 'direct apprehension'. As I explained in chapter 5 it is not clear what this position amounts to, and Moore does not develop it. But at least he recognised the need to take sceptical arguments seriously in this context. When he switched to the direct realist position presented in SJP he did not discuss the relationship between empirical knowledge and sense-perception at all,

267

perhaps because he thought the position invulnerable to sceptical arguments. In truth, of course, there is a sceptical threat here, though it arises in a new form as the question of how we are to know whether a sense-datum we apprehend is physical or not.

A few years later in DCS, Moore has rejected the direct realist position and the issue of scepticism does again strike him as important. It is the difficulty of avoiding the sceptical implications of indirect realism that he gives as his reason for not endorsing this position. In his 1928–9 lecture notes, he again introduces the thought that an indirect realist might regard some empirical knowledge as immediate (p. 102), but, as I mentioned in the previous chapter, he admits that this is not a persuasive move. Hence the need to avoid scepticism may well have been significant in leading him to adopt a phenomenalist position in the mid 1930s, if indeed he did so. For in SSD he remarks (p. 190) that the great merit of phenomenalism is that it makes it possible to understand how perceptual knowledge is possible. This is not elucidated in any detail, but Moore suggests here that on this view our apprehensions of sense-data would provide us with an inductive basis for knowledge of the conditionals constitutive of the truth of material object propositions. Significantly, this view is again implied in his late paper 4FS. He here maintains that we have immediate knowledge only of our current thoughts and experiences, and of those things of which we have 'personal memory', so that our knowledge of such things as 'This is a pencil' and 'That person is conscious' is not immediate and is instead 'based on analogical and inductive arguments' (pp. 225–6). If we associate the inductive arguments with our knowledge that 'This is a pencil', we can attribute to Moore a position suggestive of phenomenalism, though there is nothing definite here.

More striking than this indefiniteness, however, is the lack, throughout Moore's numerous discussions of perception, of any definite account of how perceptual knowledge is possible in the light of his sense-datum theory. In these writings he concentrates on the reasons for his sense-datum analysis and on the issue of the metaphysical relation between sense-data and material objects; epistemological considerations are never prominent. In several of his later papers, of course, epistemological issues are central; but here the philosophy of perception is kept in the background. It is as if Moore's mind was strictly compartmentalised, and he could not make the requisite connections between issues in the philosophy of perception and epistemology. The baleful consequences of this separation are manifest in his final papers: notoriously, they end in failure, when Moore confesses at the end of C that he has no satisfactory refutation of sceptical arguments concerning the possibility of perceptual knowledge of the external world. Moore's failure here is symptomatic of his persistent unwillingness to address directly the epistemological implications of his philosophy of perception.

## 2: Differential certainty

Despite Moore's failure to explain how empirical knowledge is possible, he is famous for his anti-sceptical affirmations. One issue which his work raises, therefore, is whether it is possible to refute scepticism without showing how knowledge is possible. Certainly Moore appears to attempt such refutations. In this section I shall concentrate on the anti-sceptical strategy he employs in *SMPP*. For although it is unclear what positive account of empirical knowledge Moore offers here, it is not at all unclear that he rejects the conclusion of the Humean sceptical argument he sets out.

A central part of his strategy is the logical principle of *modus tollens*. Where the sceptic's argument is represented as of the form $p$, $p \supset q \vdash q$, Moore observes that one can equally well argue that $\sim q$, $p \supset q \vdash \sim p$, and thereby derive the falsity of the sceptic's premiss ($p$) from the falsity of his conclusion ($q$). Moore recognises, however, that by itself this possibility of reversal does not establish any anti-sceptical conclusions. In order to employ either argument to draw a conclusion one needs to have determined what premisses one is justified in accepting:

> The only way, then, of deciding between my opponent's argument and mine, as to which is the better, is by deciding which premiss is known to be true. My opponent's premiss is that Hume's principles are true; and unless this premiss not merely *is* true, but is absolutely known to be so, his argument to prove that I do not know of the existence of this pencil cannot be conclusive. Mine is that I do know of the existence of this pencil; and unless this premiss not only *is* true, but is absolutely known to be so, my argument to prove that Hume's principles are false cannot be conclusive. And moreover the degree of certainty of the conclusion, in either case, supposing neither is quite certain, will be in proportion to the degree of certainty of the premiss.
>
> (pp. 121–2)

At this point Moore's dialectical strategy looks problematic. For how can he make good his claim to know that he knows that 'This is a pencil' without begging the question against the sceptic? The reference in the final sentences to degrees of certainty, however, suggests a way around this problem: perhaps all that is required is that Moore be more certain of his claim to knowledge than the sceptic is of his premisses, and perhaps these judgments of differential certainty can be made without assuming in advance the ineffectiveness of the sceptic's argument. That is certainly how Moore develops the point in *SMPP*, and how he presents the matter in a famous passage in SJP:

> For some philosophers seem to me to have denied that we ever do in fact know such things as these [that this is a finger], and others not only that we ever know them but also that they are ever true. . . .
> But it seems to me a sufficient refutation of such views as these, simply to point to cases in which we do know such things. This, after all, you know, really is a finger: there is no doubt about it: I know it, and you all know it. And I think we may safely challenge any philosopher to bring forward any argument in favour either of the proposition that we do not know it, or of the proposition that it is not true, which does not rest upon some premiss which is, beyond comparison, less certain than is the proposition which it is designed to attack.
>
> (pp. 227–8)

The confidence which this passage manifests helps to explain why Moore did not feel that it was necessary, for the purpose of refuting scepticism, to make it clear what is the relation between perception and empirical knowledge. In his view we are more certain that we have such knowledge than we are of any philosophical theory which explains how we have it, so the philosophical theory is not necessary in order to legitimate our claim to such knowledge.

Moore's argument here embodies an appeal to common-sense; the belief that we know that 'This is a finger' is a matter of common-sense (*SMPP* p. 12), in a way in which no philosophical theory about knowledge is. But does the argument warrant the confidence which he placed in it? It certainly does not refute the sceptic to observe that he must be wrong if Moore knows that he has a finger; but that is not Moore's argument. Rather, Moore's appeal is to the fact that we are much more certain that we know such things as that 'This is a finger' than we are of the premisses of the sceptic's argument; and when we think informally about the matter this seems correct. However the point is not by itself as decisive as Moore implies. For, as Moore later noted in C (pp. 238–9), we need to distinguish between subjective certainty ('I feel certain that . . .') and objective certainty ('It is established as certain that . . .'); and once we ask which kind of certainty he is appealing to in his anti-sceptical argument, an unattractive dilemma opens up for Moore. If we say that Moore is appealing to differences in objective certainty, then the anti-sceptical conclusion follows; but we can surely ask Moore where, and how, it is established as objectively certain that he does know that 'This is a finger' without assuming in advance that the sceptic is mistaken. If then we try the subjective interpretation, which fits well with the rhetorical appeal in Moore's text, we get premises which are doubtless true, for most people anyway, and whose acceptance does not obviously beg any questions. But now the difficulty is to detach an anti-sceptical conclusion from them; for the sceptic will suggest that it is not proper for us to feel as certain as we do feel that we know that 'This is a finger', and until his arguments have been laid to rest we cannot place any rational reliance on the fact of our common-sense subjective certainty.

In *SMPP* Moore makes a further move which in one way offers help. He here suggests, albeit tentatively, that he knows immediately that he knows that 'This is a pencil' (p. 125). If we associate immediacy with infallibility, this implies the objective certainty of his claim to know that 'This is a pencil'. On this premiss, therefore, Moore could legitimately draw his anti-sceptical conclusion, since if you know the conclusion of an argument to be mistaken, and the grounds for your knowledge are not called into question by the premises of the argument (a condition obviously satisfied by immediate knowledge), you can contrapose without begging any questions. But this new argument is only as good as its new premiss; which means that it is no good at all. For, whether or not there can be any immediate knowledge, it is clear that there cannot be immediate knowledge of knowledge: claims to possess knowledge require grounds that are not self-evidently apparent. Moore's new premiss seems to arise from the conception of knowledge as an introspectible inner state of which Wittgenstein accused him in *On Certainty* (section 178): 'The wrong use made by Moore of the proposition "I know" lies in his regarding it as an utterance as little subject to doubt as "I am in pain".'

There is a different line of argument in *SMPP*, however, which has, *prima facie*, a greater chance of success. It rests on the recognition that the anti-sceptical argument is one from differential certainty; thus Moore does not need to establish the absolute certainty of his claim to knowledge, but only that it has a greater degree of objective certainty than the sceptic's premises. His argument to this effect is just that the sceptic's general premises about the limits of human knowledge can only be grounded in particular facts about what is, or is not, known; they must be based upon an 'empirical induction' (p. 143). So

> it follows that no such general principle can have greater certainty
> than the particular instances upon the observation of which it is
> based. Unless it is obvious that, in fact, I do not know of the
> existence of a material object in any particular instance, no principle
> which asserts that I cannot know of the existence of anything except

271

under conditions which are not fulfilled in the case of material objects, can be regarded as established.

(p. 143)

We cannot have good reason to assent to a general principle which overturns our convictions concerning particular cases of knowledge, since it thereby destroys our grounds for assenting to it.

Although Moore's presentation of this argument is excessively empiricist, it clearly does have some cogency, for our intuitive judgments about what in particular we do know must be relevant to the assessment of general principles concerning what we can know. None the less I do not think Moore's argument establishes more than a presumption against the sceptic. One reason is that general principles about what we can know need to take account of the means available to us for acquiring such knowledge, given that we are the kinds of being that we are. We may informally think of ourselves as possessing religious knowledge, but if, in the light of an otherwise persuasive account of the content of religious beliefs and of the kinds of being we are, we cannot provide a satisfactory account of a way in which that knowledge can be acquired, the appeal to our informal judgments achieves little. A different point is that general principles can be taken from considerations that are agreed to be decisive within one domain (e.g. mathematics), and then applied in other domains (e.g. to beliefs concerning matters of fact) with sceptical implications. Not all putative cases of knowledge are of the same kind, so there is room for critical assessments of some particular claims to knowledge on the basis of the general principles manifest in other judgments concerning particular cases.

The decisive objection to Moore's argument, however, is that it fails to take account of the normative character of the concept of knowledge. When we think of knowledge as *justified* or *warranted* belief, or of a claim to knowledge as a claim to be *right* to be sure we use normative language; indeed the expression 'claim to knowledge' itself employs such vocabulary (we do not need to 'claim to believe'). And general norms, or standards, are not grounded in particular cases in the way in which general empirical truths are. In ethical cases, there is a complex interaction between our recognition of what is appropriate in a particular case and our assent to a general principle. Moore's intuitions concerning the intrinsic value of different kinds of state of affair are certainly not arrived at by empirical induction from particular cases, though I do not commend them as a model of ethical reflection. But one has only to think of the ethical case to recognise that our assent to principles concerning what one can know is not just a matter of generalising from particular cases.

The normative character of the concept of knowledge implies that the appeal to common-sense embodied in the argument from differential certainty cannot be presented in the way that Moore presents it and does not have the conclusiveness that he attributed to it. Yet there is a rejoinder to the point which enables one to continue the argument within a roughly Moorean framework. Let it be granted, it may be said, that the concept of knowledge is normative; still one can ask where we get our standards for assessing claims to knowledge from if not from our actual practices – from the common-sense judgments concerning knowledge we unhesitatingly accept, the retrospective criticisms of knowledge claims we allow, the arguments in support of them we advance, and so on. The situation here, it will be urged, is no different from that which obtains in the ethical case, where we take our standards from reflection upon the values already inherent in social and private life. In both cases we bring to our critical reflections requirements of coherence and rationality which ensure that the standards adopted are not just descriptions of common-sense – ethical or cognitive; but equally, since these practices are the 'matter' out of which the normative standards are shaped by critical reflection, these reflections are necessarily grounded in our practices and cannot totally repudiate them. So, in the cognitive case, although recognition of the normative character of the concept of knowledge legitimates the critical assessment of claims to knowledge, and thus some limited scepticism, one cannot justify standards for knowledge which would overturn such central knowledge claims as Moore's knowledge that 'This is a hand'. There is a core of obvious judgments concerning knowledge which an account of the standards for knowledge has to respect, not controvert.

Although this rejoinder is powerful, it is not decisive. For even if a sceptic acknowledges the validity of the general line of argument, he may still object to the singling out of Moore's particular knowledge claims as constituting the core of the concept which he has to respect; instead, he may say, it is certain familiar lines of argument for and against claims to knowledge which are central to the concept (e.g. that one should be in a position to eliminate alternative hypotheses compatible with one's current evidence), and his sceptical conclusions can be regarded as just the outcome of pressing those lines of argument to the limit. So it is unfair to represent his sceptical conclusions as the result of the imposition of alien standards upon our common-sense claims to knowledge; they are instead just the outcome of the kind of critical reflection which this line of thought explicitly permits.

This response cannot be easily rejected. What it calls for is a better understanding of our concept of knowledge, for the attainment of a critically coherent reflective equilibrium in this area. One cannot settle the matter by appealing directly to our common-sense judgments in the way that Moore attempts in the passage from SJP on p. 269. A sceptic can easily say that our subjective certainty concerning such judgments does not have the significance Moore imputes to it. Although in no ordinary context would it be appropriate to challenge such a judgment and argue that it is mistaken, our rational confidence in its truth has to be able to withstand the challenge of critical arguments – precisely the challenge which Moore himself, in C, found himself unable to withstand.

## 3: Pragmatic incoherence

Another of Moore's anti-sceptical arguments is that there is an incoherence in the sceptic's presentation of his own sceptical position. In DCS he says that the position of the sceptic 'really is self-contradictory, i.e. entails both of two mutually incompatible propositions' (p. 42). But this charge is difficult to substantiate and Moore usually makes the weaker charge that there is a pragmatic incoherence in the position of the sceptic. He suggests that 'any philosopher who asserts positively that other men, equally with himself, are incapable of knowing any external facts, is, in that very assertion, contradicting himself, since he implies that he *does* know a great many facts about the knowledge of other men' (HP p. 158); i.e. there is a contradiction between between what the sceptical philosopher asserts and what he implies by asserting what he does.

Moore's argument here has two premisses: that the sceptic asserts that there have been other men who, like himself, have been incapable of knowing any external facts; and that in making this assertion, the sceptic implies that he knows that there have been other men, and thus that he knows some external facts. As he himself observes, however, the sceptic does not need to make the first assertion: he need only maintain that he himself is incapable of knowing any external facts and that, if there are any other men similar to him, then they too will be incapable of knowing any external facts (HP p. 159; LP p. 48). So the argument looks unpersuasive, even if the second premiss is granted. Moore typically counters by saying that sceptics do not in fact present their position in this qualified way (LP pp. 48–9). But this only shows that Moore's argument is often effective *ad hominem*, which will not refute the position of the careful sceptic (though it still threatens the position of the extreme sceptic who asserts that knowledge of all kinds is impossible).

Yet Moore's conclusion implies that the careful sceptic has to pay a higher price for sticking to his general principles concerning knowledge than may appear at first, and in the context of the argument from differential certainty this is a point to count against an account of the concept of knowledge which supports a sceptical conclusion. Moore uses this point in a rhetorically effective way when discussing one of Russell's sceptical arguments in 4FS. He quotes the following passage from Russell's *An Outline of Philosophy* (4FS pp. 208–9): 'When my boy was three years old, I showed him Jupiter and told him that Jupiter was larger than the earth. He insisted that I must be speaking of some other Jupiter, because, as he patiently explained, the one he was seeing was obviously quite small.' Moore now observes that since Russell is a sceptic about the external world, other minds, and memory, we should not take him here to mean what he says, since what he asserts in telling his story implies that he then knew that Jupiter exists, that his son had certain thoughts, and that the incident in question really did occur. Instead, therefore, according to Moore, Russell should only have said: '*It is highly probable* that, when my boy was three years old, I showed him Jupiter and told him that it was larger than the earth; but *perhaps* I didn't. It is highly probable that he insisted that I must be speaking of some other Jupiter; but *perhaps* he didn't' (4FS p. 209).

Moore's argument here still depends on the second premiss, that assertion implies a claim to knowledge, and that can be challenged. Before looking at that, however, I want to consider a different anti-sceptical argument in which Moore employs the same premiss about the implications of assertion. This argument is presented in C, when Moore is discussing the sceptical argument which invokes the possibility that he might be dreaming. Moore has the sceptic invoke as a premiss the claim that his (Moore's) current sensory experience is very similar to experiences he has had when dreaming (C p. 248); Moore then says that in making this claim the sceptic is implying that he knows that dreams have occurred, and objects that what is thereby implied is inconsistent with the sceptic's conclusion, that he does not know whether he is dreaming. Thus, according to Moore, the sceptic cannot argue for his conclusion without asserting premisses whose assertion by him conflicts with his sceptical conclusion.

It is not in fact obvious that there is an inconsistency in the sceptic's position. Much depends on one's attitude to the KK principle that if *a* knows that *p* then *a* knows that he knows that *p*. We do not need to use this principle to establish that if the sceptic does not know whether he is dreaming he does not know whether he knows that dreams have occurred (for if he is dreaming he does not thereby know anything). But we do need it to infer from this that the sceptic does not know that dreams have occurred; and since the principle is contentious, the attribution of inconsistency is not straightforward. On the other hand, many sceptical arguments themselves assume the KK principle: given

275

the weak closure principle $Kp$ & $K(p \supset q) \vdash Kq$, the KK principle is equivalent to the strong closure principle $Kp$ & $K(Kp \supset q) \vdash Kq$, and this is often deployed in sceptical arguments in the contraposed form $\sim Kq$ & $K(Kp \supset q) \vdash \sim Kp$ (this is how Moore sets out the dream-sceptic's argument, with 'I am not dreaming' for '$q$'). So the sceptic may well not be in a position to raise this objection to Moore's charge of inconsistency.

Let us suppose, therefore, that Moore's charge cannot be evaded by objecting to his tacit use of the KK principle. The sceptic can still object that he does not need the premiss that Moore has him use, that Moore's current sense-experience is similar to experiences he has actually had when dreaming. All he needs to assume is that Moore's sense-experience is similar to experiences that he might have when dreaming, and, he will say, he can claim to know this without claiming to know that dreams have actually occurred. After all, when Descartes introduces the hypothesis of an Evil Genius to undermine our confidence in our ordinary beliefs, he does not imply that there is such a thing, let alone that he knows that there is; he only asserts that, for all he can tell at the time, there might be.

This objection shows that Moore burdens the sceptic with unnecessary commitments, but it does not altogether evade the argument. For even if the sceptic only invokes a possibility, he still makes definite assertions concerning the consequences of this possibility, e.g. that if one were to be having a wholly realistic dream one's experiences would be qualitatively similar to ordinary sense-experiences. So if assertion implies a claim to knowledge, the sceptic, in presenting his argument, implies that he then knows what the consequences of his sceptical possibility are. And yet if his conclusion that he does not then know anything is correct, he does not know what the consequences of his sceptical possibility are. So, it appears, the sceptic cannot draw his conclusion without undermining his argument for it.[2]

One response for the sceptic at this point is to treat Moore's argument as a *reductio ad absurdum* of the hypothesis that he (the sceptic) does know such things as the consequences of his sceptical possibility. With $p$ for this hypothesis, and $q$ for other kinds of knowledge which are inconsistent with the sceptic's conclusion, he will maintain that Moore's argument can be represented as of the form $p \vdash \sim p$ & $\sim q$, from which one can properly infer $\vdash \sim p$. Thus it appears that the sceptic's argument is not undermined by his conclusion. He can legitimately represent himself as having a form of knowledge which he concludes he does not after all have. According to the sceptic, the assumption that he has this knowledge destroys itself, not his argument for the sceptical conclusion.

This is clearly a powerful response to Moore's argument. The trouble with it is that it treats the epistemic implications of the sceptic's assertion of his premises as assumptions which the sceptic makes for the sake of presenting his sceptical argument. But that is not quite how matters stand. For the sceptic does not reach his sceptical conclusion by means of a *reductio* argument; he argues from the consequences of the non-eliminability of sceptical possibilities. So, if he is to be able to detach his conclusion, he does have to assert, categorically, the premises of his argument. But then, given Moore's thesis, he must claim to know these premises, and it is not easy to understand how this claim to knowledge can be merely something assumed for the sake of argument, since the assertions which give rise to it are not.

It seems to me, therefore, that in this case, as with the previous argument for incoherence, one can find lines of thought that should be unsettling for a sceptic as long as the assumption that assertion implies a claim to knowledge is accepted. I turn therefore to this assumption. I touched on it before in chapter 7 when discussing Moore's paradox, since if the assumption is correct, sentences of the form '*p* but I do not know that *p*' should be paradoxical in the way in which sentences of the form '*p* but I do not believe that *p*' are. At an informal level, this does indeed appear right; but what remains to be discussed are both the facts which bring about this appearance, and the question of whether these facts have the anti-sceptical implications that Moore supposes. I argued that what lies behind Moore's paradox is the fact that assertion is expressive of belief, in the sense that it is constitutive of assertion that the speaker should intend his audience to take him to believe what he asserts. The issue here, therefore, is whether one can establish a similar thesis concerning knowledge, that it is constitutive of assertion that the speaker should intend his audience to take him to know what he asserts.

One can give some support to this thesis through the thought that the aim of assertion is to get one's audience to believe what one asserts. For if this is granted, then it follows that one who asserts must thereby intend to be taken not simply to believe what he asserts, but to have some reason for this belief. For unless he is so taken by his audience, they will have been given no reason to believe what the speaker asserts: that they understand the speaker to express a belief that he holds is not by itself any reason for them to adopt that belief, unless the speaker is taken to be authoritative with respect to the content of the belief – in which case this fact provides the speaker with a reason for his belief.

This point gets one some distance towards Moore's thesis that assertion implies a claim to knowledge. But in two respects it does not get one far enough. First, the thought that assertion implies that one have some reason for one's assertion falls short of the thesis that it implies a claim to knowledge.[3] The sceptic will hold that one only knows when one is in a position to eliminate sceptical possibilities, and that it is not a requirement of assertion that one should present oneself as able to eliminate these possibilities, which are not relevant to the everyday contexts in which most assertions are made and criticised. The conception of knowledge which the sceptic employs here can of course be criticised; but such criticisms are not germane to this argument since if one can show that the sceptic is wrong about knowledge, one does not need to press the charge of incoherence.

One can, however, argue that the sceptic presents his arguments and conclusions in the context of a discussion of philosophical scepticism, and in this context the standard for rational belief just is sceptic-proof knowledge. The sceptic makes assertions about the implications of sceptical possibilities, and thereby presents himself as having reasons for what he asserts; in this context does he not present himself as, by his own standards, knowing what he asserts? I do not see that he has to. He can surely hold that it suffices if he takes his reasons for his beliefs about the implications of sceptical possibilities to be conclusive as long as the arguments of philosophical scepticism are not invoked. Admittedly, he then proposes to argue that we cannot eliminate sceptical possibilities and therefore do not know such things as the implications of sceptical possibilities. But this does not undermine his argument, for his assertions concerning the implications of the sceptical possibilities are made before the issue of whether sceptical possibilities can be eliminated has been decided. Nor need his conclusion lead to retrospective doubt about his argument and thus about whether he has good reason for his conclusion. For to reassure himself concerning his sceptical conclusion, he need only suspend belief in it and run back through his argument.

The second respect in which Moore's thesis is open to criticism is that it fails to take account of the possibility of qualified, or hedged, assertions, in which a speaker explicitly disavows a claim to knowledge by means of a parenthetical verb – as in 'It is, I think, three o'clock in the afternoon'. Thus, even in a situation in which assertion is taken to imply a claim to knowledge, the sceptic need not remain silent; he can present his conclusions and arguments by making qualified assertions: he can 'quassert' them. As Moore's comments on Russell indicate, a string of hedged assertions tends to sound rather mealy-mouthed (cf. also C pp. 227–8), so I think it is preferable for the sceptic to attack the thesis that assertion implies a claim to knowledge. But the possibility of quassertion reinforces this attack: for, by showing that there is a speech-act which, though expressive of belief, does not imply a claim to knowledge, it helps to undermine the thesis that there is an intrinsic claim to knowledge in the case of assertion itself. It suggests that the issue here is basically one of linguistic conventions which can be adjusted to fit in with the beliefs and expectations of speakers and audience. The sceptic's assertions need not amount to more than what others might regard as quassertions.

For these reasons, therefore, Moore's accusation of pragmatic incoherence against the sceptic fails. The sceptic can coherently argue for his sceptical conclusion, and can equally coherently present his conclusion to others and to himself. Moore's argument relies on a thesis about assertion which, though supported by intuitive judgments about the oddity of sentences of the form '$p$ but I don't know that $p$', is itself called into question by sceptical arguments. Hence it does not provide a non-question-begging point of reference by means of which the sceptic can be refuted without grappling in detail with his arguments.

### 4: The dogmatist interpretation

In the two preceding sections I have attributed some arguments to Moore and discussed them critically. It is a feature of these arguments that they aim to deliver their anti-sceptical conclusion without showing in detail what is wrong with sceptical lines of thought, and thus without showing how knowledge is possible. As I have indicated, I do not think that Moore's arguments are persuasive, and I doubt whether his strategy can succeed. But whether or not I am right about this, my approach to Moore is liable to incur the objection that it misses the point of Moore's response to philosophical scepticism. For the dominant interpretation of Moore at present is that he does not argue a case against scepticism at all. His appeal to common sense is supposed to amount to an affirmation that one just does know such things as that 'This is a hand'. Indeed, in PEW he says:

> I certainly did at the moment *know* that which I expressed by the combination of certain gestures with saying the words 'There is one hand and here is another'. . . . How absurd it would be to suggest that I did not know it, but only believed it, and that perhaps it was not the case! You might as well suggest that I do not know that I am now standing up and talking – that perhaps after all I'm not, and that it's not quite certain that I am.
>
> (pp. 146–7)

And equally he affirms in DCS, concerning the truisms which he there claims to know:

> But do I really *know* all the propositions in (1) to be true? Isn't it possible that I merely believe them? Or know them to be highly probable? In answer to this question, I think I have nothing better to say than that it seems to me that I *do* know them, with certainty.
>
> (p. 44)

These passages certainly give some support for what I shall call the

279

'dogmatist' interpretation of Moore's response to philosophical scepticism. As I shall explain below, I believe that this interpretation is a serious mistake. None the less many of those who have written about Moore under its influence have produced interesting ideas which cast light both on Moore and on philosophical scepticism, so that although their 'Moore' is not the historical G.E. Moore their work merits careful attention. I have in mind two groups of philosophers: the first, Norman Malcolm, Alice Ambrose, and Morris Lazerowitz, set out their position in *PGEM*, where it drew a critical response from Moore. The second group derives from the influence of Thompson Clarke; apart from Clarke, its most prominent member is Barry Stroud, and their writings are responsible for the present dominance of the dogmatist interpretation.

The dogmatist interpretation of Moore is explicit in the papers by Malcolm, Ambrose, and Lazerowitz in *PGEM*; thus Malcolm sets out Moore's 'way of attacking' the philosophical sceptic in terms drawn from the passage from PEW cited on p. 278:

> (10) Philosopher: 'We do not know for certain the truth of any statement about material things.'
> Moore: 'Both of us know for *certain* that there are several chairs in this room, and how absurd it would be to suggest that we do not know it, but only believe it, and that perhaps it is not the case!'
> (Malcolm p. 347; cf. Lazerowitz pp. 374–5; Ambrose pp. 403–4)

These three philosophers agree that, considered as such, Moore's response to the sceptic is unsatisfactory. For since the sceptical philosopher will just reject the claim to knowledge which Moore makes, he can scarcely be refuted by an argument which consists only of affirming such a claim. None the less, they all agree that there is something of value in Moore's dogmatic response to the sceptic. They disagree about just what this is, but they start from a common explanation of the failure of Moore's dogmatic response, namely that the sceptic's doubt is not empirical and hence not susceptible of an empirical refutation of the kind Moore attempts (Malcolm p. 352; Lazerowitz pp. 382–3; Ambrose p. 399).

At this point all three philosophers introduce linguistic theories of the *a priori*. Malcolm takes it that since conceptual truths are not about empirical matters of fact, their truth is guaranteed by the meanings of the words used to express them, and those who assert them are really making claims about the proper use of language. Thus, according to Malcolm, 'The philosophical statement "We do not know for certain the truth of any material-thing statement" is a misleading way of expressing the proposition: "The phrase 'know for certain' is not properly applied to material-thing statements"' (p. 354). Ambrose and Lazerowitz, by contrast, take it that the sceptic is recommending a linguistic revision, albeit covertly: 'he is proposing, or recommending, that certain expressions in our language be deprived of their use . . . "knowing there are hands" . . . will not make sense' (Ambrose p. 404; cf. Lazerowitz p. 391).

Now that the sceptic has been interpreted as a linguistic philosopher, the way is open to re-introduce Moore as refuting scepticism by appealing, not to common-sense, but to ordinary language. It is not, of course, suggested that this is what Moore thinks of himself as doing; rather, the suggestion is that this is a rational reconstruction of Moore's dogmatic method which enables us to see that Moore does indeed refute the philosophical sceptic. But how does Moore's 'extraordinarily powerful language-sense' (Malcolm p. 366) enable him to refute the linguistic claims supposedly made by the philosophical sceptic? Basically, it is supposed, by a paradigm case argument. Indeed, Malcolm's paper is a paradigm case of the paradigm case argument: 'Both the philosophical statement and Moore's reply to it are disguised linguistic statements. In this as in all other cases Moore is right. What his reply does is to give us a *paradigm* of absolute certainty' (p. 354). Two considerations are introduced to reinforce the anti-sceptical implications of Moore's supposed paradigms: first, one can only learn the meaning of the expression 'It is certain that' through being shown cases of empirical certainty (Malcolm pp. 360–1): second, in the case of contrastive terms, such as 'certain/probable' and 'know/believe', the point of the contrast, and thus the meaning of both terms, would be lost if one of the pair were not allowed any proper empirical application (Malcolm pp. 364–5; Ambrose pp. 411–13).

It is not surprising that in his reply in *PGEM* Moore did not welcome this linguistic reconstruction of his arguments. He does not discuss the arguments of his critics in any great detail, because, as he makes clear, they start off on the wrong foot in ascribing to him an attempt at a dogmatic refutation of scepticism, and it is worth quoting him at some length on this matter, since what he says here is such a strong piece of evidence against the dogmatist interpretation of his position:

I have sometimes distinguished between two different propositions, each of which has been made by some philosophers, namely (1) the proposition 'There are no material things' and (2) the proposition 'Nobody knows for certain that there are any material things'. And in my latest British Academy lecture called 'Proof of an External World', which is the subject of Miss Ambrose's essay, I implied with regard to the first of these propositions that it could be *proved* to be false in such a way as this; namely, by holding up one of your hands and saying '*This* hand is a material thing; therefore there is at least one material thing'. But with regard to the second of the two propositions, which

281

has, I think, been far more commonly asserted than the first, I do not think I have ever implied that *it* could be *proved* to be false in any such simple way; e.g. by holding up one of your hands and saying 'I know that this hand is a material thing; therefore at least one person knows that there is at least one material thing'.

(p. 668)

He goes on to say:

In the case of 'Nobody knows that there are any material things' it does seem to me more obvious that some further argument is called for, if one is to talk of having *proved* it to be false, than in the case 'There *are* no material things'.

(p. 669)

These are pretty unequivocal statements; anyone who persists with the dogmatist interpretation in the face of them must hold that Moore simply does not know what he is talking about here, and that seems, to put it mildly, a difficult interpretative thesis to sustain.

Having established that his critics have all set off on the wrong foot, as far as his response to philosophical scepticism is concerned, Moore concentrates on the position advanced by Ambrose. He agrees with her that the sceptic will believe it to be self-contradictory to suppose that anyone has any knowledge of an external world, but goes on to remark, surely rightly, that in fact it is an empirical truth that we do have such knowledge (pp. 672–3). In line with his repudiation of any dogmatic refutation of the sceptic, however, he also agrees that 'no empirical evidence would have any tendency to convince the philosopher who says "Nobody knows for certain that there are external objects"' (p. 672). He does not explain how the sceptic should then be refuted; but proceeds to criticise the linguistic theory of necessity propounded by Ambrose and Lazerowitz and to reject totally their reconstruction of him, in the light of that theory, as a linguistic philosopher (p. 675).

Unfortunately, Moore did not discuss Malcolm's paper in detail in his reply. This has enabled Malcolm to believe that Moore agreed with his linguistic reconstruction of his anti-sceptical arguments.[4] Malcolm is not without excuse for this belief: for Lazerowitz has written that Moore stated this to him in conversation (A&L p. 109). However, this is simply not credible in the light of Moore's reply in *PGEM*: given that Moore explicitly states there that Malcolm starts off on the wrong foot by ascribing to him a dogmatic refutation of scepticism, it is not conceivable that Moore should none the less have accepted Malcolm's reconstruction of that dogmatic refutation, especially in the light of his comments about the Ambrose–Lazerowitz account of the matter. And if Moore's off-the-record remarks are allowed to be cited as evidence, then

I can introduce Alan White's memory of a conversation with Moore shortly before Moore's death in which Moore expressed strong agreement with his (White's) criticisms of Malcolm's linguistic reconstruction of his argument in his book.[5]

Malcolm has continued to discuss the significance of Moore's treatment of scepticism, and although these discussions are conducted under a misapprehension concerning Moore's position, they are interesting and important. The most important is his 1949 paper 'Defending Common Sense', to which Moore responded at length.[6] This response can be reconstructed from notes and letters in the Cambridge archive and from the substantial passage which Malcolm has quoted from a letter to him by Moore about the paper.[7] As Malcolm has explained, he discussed this paper and Moore's response to it with Wittgenstein while the latter was staying with him;[8] it was these discussions with Malcolm which provided Wittgenstein with the stimulus to develop the views he collected in his notes *On Certainty* (indeed there is a good deal of Malcolm in *On Certainty*). So Moore's response to Malcolm can be read as a response to parts of *On Certainty*.

In his *PGEM* paper Malcolm had maintained that Moore refutes the sceptic by bringing forward paradigm cases of knowledge. In 'Defending Common Sense', Malcolm rejects this thesis. He now argues that Moore's characteristic claims to common sense knowledge, along with the sceptic's denial of them, do not make sense at all ('Defending Common Sense' pp. 219–20; cf. *On Certainty* para. 521). Simplifying a little, Malcolm maintains that claims to knowledge only make sense when (i) there is 'a question at issue and a doubt to be removed', and (ii) it is possible to carry out an investigation in order to settle the question ('Defending Common Sense' p. 203; cf. *On Certainty* paras 58, 243). Malcolm then observes that Moore's characteristic claims precisely do not satisfy conditions (i) and (ii): Moore explicitly acknowledges in PEW that he cannot prove that 'Here is a hand', and his remarks about the absurdity of questioning whether he really does know it show that in making his claim he takes it that there is no substantive question at issue, no doubt to be resolved. So, he concludes, Moore's claims to knowledge were literally senseless.

One response to Malcolm's argument would be to insist that the context of a discussion of philosophical scepticism provides Moore with the means to satisfy Malcolm's conditions (i) and (ii); for there is here a philosophical doubt to be resolved, and the possibility of philosophical arguments which will succeed in resolving this doubt. Malcolm indeed acknowledges that this response is available, but insists, first, that a philosophical doubt is not a real doubt, and, second, that philosophical arguments are not, in the relevant sense, methods of proof. One may well find this unpersuasive, but it is certainly effective *ad hominem*: for

Moore's conception of philosophical scepticism is that it is '*compatible* with a complete absence of doubt on any subject whatever' (4FS p. 199); and he does accept that he cannot prove that 'Here is a hand'. Both of these aspects of Moore's position merit further discussion, and I shall return to them later in this chapter.

What Moore himself rejects in Malcolm's paper is the thesis that claims to knowledge only make sense where conditions (i) and (ii) are satisfied. Moore's central objection is that Malcolm has failed to distinguish the sense in which a remark is 'senseless' because in the circumstances in which it is made, making it serves no useful purpose, from the sense in which a remark is senseless because it is literally meaningless (cf. the passage from Moore's letter to Malcolm quoted on p. 172). The conclusion of Malcolm's argument requires that Moore's claims be senseless in the latter sense; but his conditions (i) and (ii) relate at best to senselessness in the former sense. This is a decisive point and, indeed, evidence of Moore's acute 'language-sense'. Two further criticisms occur in Moore's notes. First, it is absurd to suppose that claims to knowledge make sense prior to an investigation which resolves all doubts about them, but do not make sense afterwards when there is no longer any doubt. On this view, investigations and proofs would diminish knowledge by rendering claims to knowledge senseless! Second, Malcolm's condition (i) cannot really be a condition of claims to knowledge making sense. For where this condition is not satisfied, there is no doubt concerning that which is claimed to be known. But where there is no doubt, there is certain knowledge. So the concepts employed in stating condition (i) are such that failing to satisfy that condition is a sufficient condition for the knowledge which failing to satisfy the condition was supposed to show to be senseless. In his paper Malcolm recognises this difficulty and, attempts to deal with it by suggesting that where condition (i) is not satisfied, it itself makes no sense. Since this entails that wherever condition (i) makes sense at all, it is satisfied, it renders it useless for Malcolm's intentions.

On this occasion Moore's critical response seems to have persuaded Malcolm to change his mind.[9] But Malcolm persisted in maintaining that there was something special about Moore's claims to knowledge, in particular, that 'know' has a distinctive 'strong' sense in these contexts. Attributing the idea to Wittgenstein, he put this claim in a letter to Moore in the following terms: 'But you wish to maintain that nothing which has happened after this could possibly provide a reason for doubting that you *now* have two hands.' Much the same view is suggested at one point in *On Certainty* (para. 69), and Malcolm developed the position at length in several papers.[10] The weakness of this position is that, at least considered as a response to the philosophical sceptic, it seems merely dogmatic, a return to the position of 'Moore' and his dogmatic rejection of scepticism. For the sceptic does offer reasons for doubting whether one knows even such things as that 'Here is a hand', and just to insist that one cannot conceive of being mistaken about this matter is not to refute him at all.[11]

The other group of philosophers who have presented the dogmatist interpretation of Moore are those influenced by Thompson Clarke,[12] in particular Barry Stroud, who has developed it at length in *The Significance of Philosophical Scepticism (SPS)*. They agree with Malcolm in finding the dogmatic response to scepticism ineffectual; they also come close to Malcolm's reconstruction of Moore as just a defender of ordinary language, since for them Moore's work embodies the 'plain man's' response to philosophical scepticism, and ordinary language is just what the plain man speaks. However, they differ markedly from Malcolm in their attitude to Moore's plain talk; whereas Malcolm described it, in successive papers, as paradigmatic, senseless, and distinctively 'strong', Clarke and Stroud find no problem in Moore's plain talk itself. Rather, they suggest, if there is a problem about what is being said, it is a problem about the sceptic's use of language. And although Moore's plain talk is ineffectual in refuting the philosophical sceptic, its very ineffectiveness is of central importance in raising the question of what philosophical scepticism really amounts to.

Stroud brings to his discussion of Moore a distinction between 'internal' and 'external' reactions to claims to knowledge: an 'internal' reaction is one which does not question the usual criteria by which such claims are assessed: an 'external' reaction is one which embodies 'a certain withdrawal or detachment from the whole body of knowledge of the world' (*SPS* p. 117), and thus calls into question the assumption that beliefs formed where the usual criteria are satisfied constitute knowledge. Moore, as portrayed by Stroud, never gets beyond the internal reaction, and this is why he employs his dogmatic style of argument: for if one judges by the usual criteria, then of course Moore knows that 'Here is a hand', and a sceptic who raises doubts about this can be as brusquely dismissed as Moore dismisses him in the passage from PEW cited on p. 278. But the philosophical sceptic as represented by Stroud is reacting 'externally' to claims to knowledge. So, Stroud proposes, Moore did not so much beg the question against the sceptic as miss his point. But this presupposes that there is a point to be missed, and for Stroud Moore's importance is that his work (if not the man himself) raises the question of whether we can really make sense of there being an external reaction to claims to knowledge, a reaction which Moore, through some 'philosophical lobotomy',[13] cannot hear.

Indeed Clarke argues that this external reaction is incoherent. He maintains that it requires reference to a sceptical possibility which undermines all our usual criteria, and that it is essential to the

285

conception of such a possibility that an agent of deception, such as the Evil Genius, could know that this possibility obtains if it does. Since this knowledge is of essentially the same kind as that which the sceptic argues to be impossible, it follows that the sceptic's external reaction presupposes the possibility of that knowledge which it itself argues to be impossible. In a way, then, for Clarke, this vindicates Moore: 'In his practice Moore was, in one sense, the compleat philosopher.'[14] But this does not vindicate Moore's dogmatic response; for plain talk does not by itself explain why the external reaction is incoherent, and, on Clarke's approach it will be precisely this explanation which constitutes the refutation of the sceptic. So an understanding of the external reaction is still required, even though, according to Clarke, it turns out to be incoherent.

As with Moore's arguments for the incoherence of philosophical scepticism, I do not find Clarke's argument persuasive. He does not substantiate his thesis that the conception of a sceptical possibility includes the possibility of knowledge by some subject that it obtains.[15] But I shall not pursue that matter now. Instead, I want to turn to the interpretation of Moore in terms of the 'external/internal' distinction. Is Moore as deaf to sceptical arguments as Clarke and Stroud suggest? The Humean sceptical argument which Moore discusses in *SMMP* has as its aim the denial of all claims to perceptual knowledge of an external world, and Moore's discussion seems to show plainly that he understands that all ordinary criteria are called into question. Yet it may still be felt that Moore's response to sceptical arguments shows that he understood them as internal reactions to claims to knowledge, which is why his response is so ineffective.[16]

One way to justify this charge would be to invoke the passage from PEW which I quoted on p. 278 as an example of a dogmatic rejection of sceptical arguments. Now I have already quoted Moore's rejection, in his reply in *PGEM*, of this interpretation of this passage. Stroud refers to these remarks in *PGEM* (*SPS* p. 107 fn. 15), but says that he is going to disregard them! The reason he gives for this is that he thinks that Moore's response to the Humean sceptic in *SMPP* is precisely the dogmatic response which Moore later disavowed. I shall discuss the justice of this charge in a moment, but even if Stroud is correct in this respect, it is hard to see why this entitles him to interpret PEW in a way which Moore explicitly rejected. Indeed Stroud does more than just interpret PEW as intended to refute philosophical scepticism: he misrepresents Moore as here saying 'I know that there are at least two external things' (*SPS* p. 87), in the way in which he did say 'There are at least two external things'. Moore did not say any such thing in PEW.[17]

In *SMPP* Moore did affirm 'I do know that this pencil exists', so one might try to use his discussion here to justify the characterisation of his response to philosophical scepticism as merely dogmatic. This is of course how Stroud interprets Moore; he quotes a passage from *SMPP* and comments: 'The form of anti-sceptical argument described here in 1910 is precisely what Moore follows in his more famous "Proof of an External World" twenty-nine years later' (*SPS* pp. 125–6). There is a question here about what is evidence for what: since, as I have indicated, Stroud's defence of his interpretation of PEW as a dogmatic refutation of scepticism, in the face of Moore's insistence to the contrary, rests on the thesis that in *SMPP* Moore advances the dogmatic response, there is no question of his invoking PEW to support a dogmatist interpretation of *SMPP*. That interpretation has to be manifestly correct on its own. Is it? Surely not. For as I stressed in section 2 of this chapter, Moore's appeal here to common-sense knowledge is not a simple, question-begging, *modus tollens*; it rests on considerations concerning the difference in certainty we attach to claims to knowledge of particular matters of fact as compared with knowledge of the general principles concerning human knowledge invoked by the sceptic. Moore's argument is certainly not as decisive as he presents it as being; but, I suggested, it can be developed into a challenge to the sceptic to justify the standards for assessing claims to knowledge which he employs, and it is not dogmatic to think that in this respect the burden of proof lies upon the sceptic.

One might still suggest that the argument from differential certainty manifests an 'internal' response to sceptical doubt, in so far as it appeals to our subjective certainty that we do know such things as that 'This is a pencil'. But by this standard there will also be forms of philosophical scepticism which count as merely internal. For, as I argued in section 2, there are perfectly respectable, and familiar, sceptical arguments which base themselves upon features of our actual use of the concept and seek to show that if we take seriously the requirements implicit in these features, then we should reject claims to knowledge of some kind. It is just not true, as Clarke and Stroud sometimes seem to suggest, that philosophical scepticism requires the adoption of a point of view wholly external to our practice. There are quite sufficient strains within our cognitive practices for sceptical arguments to proceed solely on the basis of 'internal' criteria and requirements of consistency and rationality.

It does not follow from this that there is nothing distinctive about philosophical scepticism. But Moore also recognised this:

> And also, curiously enough, a man who denies that we ever know for certain things of a certain sort, need not necessarily feel any doubt whatever about *particular* things of the sort in question. A man who, like Bertrand Russell, believes with the utmost confidence that he never knows for certain such a thing as that he is sitting down, may nonetheless feel perfectly sure, without a shadow of doubt, on

thousands of occasions that he is sitting down. . . . I think that the common opinion that doubt is essential to scepticism arises from the mistaken opinion that if a man sincerely believes that a thing is doubtful he must doubt it. In the case of sincere philosophical opinions this seems to me certainly not the case. . . . There is, therefore, a sort of scepticism which is *compatible* with a complete absence of doubt on any subject whatever.

(pp. 198–9)

It is instructive to compare this description of philosophical scepticism with that provided by Descartes, in his reply to Gassendi:

However, we must note the distinction which I have insisted on in several passages, between the actions of life and the investigation of the truth. For, when it is a case of organizing our life, it would, of course, be foolish not to trust the senses, and those sceptics who neglected human affairs to the point where their friends had to stop them falling off precipices deserved to be laughed at. Hence I pointed out in one passage that no sane person ever seriously doubts such things. But when our inquiry concerns what can be known with complete certainty by the human intellect, it is quite unreasonable to refuse to reject these things in all seriousness as doubtful and even as false;[18]

Is Moore's distinction the same as that of Descartes? Certainly they agree that it is one thing to doubt a proposition and another thing to regard it as doubtful, and they both apply the latter description to the attitude of the philosophical sceptic. It might seem from the passage quoted that Moore, unlike Descartes, would want to apply this distinction only to propositions about particular cases (e.g. 'I am now sitting down'), but I think he is just arguing in his characteristic way from the particular to the general, and would hold that even if Russell believes it to be doubtful that there is an external world, this is still not a conclusive reason for taking him to doubt that there is. Yet there is an important difference between Moore and Descartes. Moore suggests that philosophical scepticism is essentially second-order – it is doubt whether one knows – and that this can coexist with the absence of first-order doubt. Descartes would agree that the starting-point for philosophical scepticism is doubt about what one knows; in the passage above he writes that his inquiry concerns 'what can be known with complete certainty by the human intellect'. But Descartes does not hold that doubts of this kind are compatible with the absence of first-order doubt; rather, for Descartes, the mark of the philosophical sceptic is that from theoretical inquiries into human knowledge, the sceptic finds reasons for first-order doubts which do not arise within ordinary affairs.

288

Moore's position here is to be understood in the light of his belief that
we do all know the things which the sceptic denies that we know, and
thus that the sceptic differs from us, not in not knowing what we do
know, but only in believing that he does not know what in fact he does
know. But this is a difficult position to maintain, and especially so for
Moore. For since he takes it that assertion implies knowledge, the
thought '$p$, but I do not know that $p$' is, for him, not one that can be
framed without incoherence; and yet it is something like this thought
which he takes to be distinctive of the philosophical sceptic whose
second-order doubt whether he knows that $p$ is not accompanied by any
doubt whether $p$. In section 3 I argued that Moore's thesis that assertion
implies knowledge is, in fact, mistaken. But this does not ensure that
Moore's description of philosophical doubt is unproblematic. For Moore
requires that it be possible for the philosophical sceptic to have no doubt
at all that $p$, and yet to doubt whether he knows that $p$. But in the
absence of doubt whether one believes that $p$, the content of the second-
order doubt whether one knows that $p$ must be either doubt that one is
reliable with respect to matters such as $p$ or doubt whether $p$. Since the
former of these gives me reason to doubt whether $p$, it follows that one
who entertains doubt whether he knows that $p$ has reason to doubt
whether $p$, even if, by some defensive strategy of the mind, he does not
in fact do so.

For this reason, therefore, Moore's description of philosophical
scepticism is not altogether satisfactory (although I think that the thesis
that sceptical doubt is primarily doubt whether one knows is an
important truth). In the context of the dogmatist interpretation of his
position, however, this mistake is not as important as the fact that
Moore recognised the distinctiveness of philosophical scepticism. For
implicit in this is the recognition that the sceptic's philosophical doubts
cannot be put to rest by the procedures which we employ to put to rest
first-order doubts that arise in the course of ordinary life. More needs to
be done to refute the sceptic than just to wave our hands at him. I have
already discussed some of the arguments which Moore advances to refute
the sceptic's claims; and in section 6 I shall discuss Moore's final
attempts in 4FS and C to refute scepticism. But I need first to
substantiate my rejection of the dogmatist interpretation by explaining
just what Moore is up to in his 'Proof of an External World' and his
'Defence of Common Sense'.

## 5: The 'Proof' and the 'Defence'

In the previous section I maintained that Moore's 'Proof' is not to be
understood as an attempt to refute philosophical scepticism. How then
should it be understood? Manifestly, as an attempt to prove the

existence of an external world. The important point to grasp, however, is Moore's belief that one can separate the metaphysical from the epistemic aspect of realism in such a way that one can refute the idealist who maintains that 'There are no material things' without having to refute the sceptic who maintains that 'Nobody knows that there are any material things'. This is how Moore presented the matter in his reply (*PGEM* p. 668) and he makes the same distinction in his lecture notes from 1933–4 (*LP* pp. 181–3), where he also sketches the argument of PEW:

> We might say, it has been discussed: Is Matter real? Is change real?
>
> And it seems to me that a particular answer to these questions, namely that there have been many material things, & there have been many changes, is 'presupposed' by us all in ordinary life & the sciences in the following senses.
>
> (1) *Ordinary Life*. That there have been many bodies is 'presupposed' by us all in ordinary life, in the sense that we have all, in ordinary life, often *observed* facts from which, taken together, it strictly *follows* that there are a good many bodies. For instance, I at this moment *observe* that there are a good many human bodies in this room.
>
> <div align="right">(<i>LP</i> p. 176)</div>

Yet can one separate the metaphysical from the epistemic aspect of realism? Can one prove that there is an external world without proving that one knows that there is an external world? Stroud maintains that this is not possible:

> So if what must be proved is both the existence of external things and the very possibility of knowing in general of the existence of external things, it cannot be said without further explanation that Moore proves only the first but not the second. If he does prove the first it follows that he proves the second. It is true that Moore himself does not actually claim to have proved the second, but we can see from his success in proving the first that he does also prove that knowledge of external things in general is possible.
>
> <div align="right">(<i>SPS</i> p. 137)</div>

Moore's strategy depends on the existence of a distinction between proving that *p* and proving that one knows that *p*, which Stroud here challenges. If one considers a third-person case, the existence of a distinction is obvious: to prove that *x* knows that *p* I need to prove not only that *p*, but also that *x*'s belief that *p* is a reliable guide (or something similar) to the fact that *p*. The disputed point is whether there is still a distinction when one switches back to the first-person case. Surely there is. For even though it requires only a moment's reflection to pass from proving that $p$ to conclusive evidence that I believe that $p$, no similar reflection will *prove* to me that my belief that $p$ is reliable. Certainly, in taking myself to prove that $p$, I take my belief to be reliable; but I do not thereby take myself to have proved that my belief is reliable. To prove this, I should have to prove that my proof is a good one, and I do not prove this by simply giving my proof. A mathematician who uses the law of excluded middle in a non-constructive proof that $p$ will have proved that $p$ if non-constructive proofs are good proofs; but he will not have proved this in his proof that $p$.

If one applies this line of thought to Moore's 'Proof', one takes it that in giving his proof he takes it that knowledge of an external world is possible. But he does not regard his proof as a proof that this belief is correct, as a refutation of scepticism. Yet this is not the end of the matter. For Moore does not only state his proof; he also sets out to show that it is a good one, that 'it is perhaps impossible to give a better or more rigorous proof of anything whatever' (PEW p. 146), and he takes it to be a requirement of this that he should know the premises of his proof to be true. How can he show this to be so, we may well ask, without proving that he knows that there are external things?

It is here that Moore makes the straightforward assertion of knowledge which I quoted on p. 278 – 'I certainly did at the moment *know* that which I expressed by the combination of certain gestures with saying the words "There is one hand and here is another"' (PEW p. 146). But what does he say to show that this is true? He just appeals to our ordinary convictions: 'How absurd it would be to suggest that I did not know it, but only believed it, and that perhaps it was not the case. You might as well suggest that I do not know that I am now standing up and talking – that perhaps after all I'm not, and that it's not quite certain that I am' (pp. 146–7). It is here that it looks as though Moore is attempting a dogmatic refutation of scepticism. But this interpretation, I suggest, misunderstands Moore's intent; he wants to show that his original proof is a good one, and he accepts that it will be such only if he knew its premises to be true. So he accepts that he has to show that he knows these premises to be true, and his appeal to our convictions is intended to achieve this. But it is not intended to prove that he knows these premises to be true.

This interpretation rests on a distinction between showing that one knows something and proving that one does. This may appear tenuous, but if one bears in mind Moore's purposes, it is fair enough. The important point is that where a proof of knowledge would require refutation of sceptical arguments, an exhibition of knowledge can proceed by means of an appeal to the audience's beliefs concerning what is known. Even Stroud acknowledges that Moore's appeal here is just intended to remind his audience of something they all normally take for granted – that one knows such things as that 'Here is a hand' (*SPS* p. 104). Moore would have had to be very philosophically naive, or obtuse, to suppose that one could refute the philosophical sceptic by reminders of this kind. It is as if a mathematician could seriously presume to refute the constructivist critique of classical mathematics by reminding his audience that they take for granted the truth of the law of excluded middle. Yet such a reminder could have a proper place in the presentation of a non-constructive proof; in effect, the mathematician would be saying that he was just not going to bother with the constructivist critique of his method of proof. And that is in effect, what Moore's dogmatic assertion of knowledge here amounts to: he implies that he is not going to bother here with sceptical arguments, but is just going to assume (as he reminds his audience that we all do constantly assume) that he does know such things as that 'Here is a hand'.

So far I have argued that Moore's strategy in his 'Proof' is coherent. However, I now have to confess that my account does not altogether square with remarks Moore makes at the end of the paper. In the last two pages of PEW (pp. 149–50) he attempts to disarm those critics who will object that he has not proved what he claims to prove. On my account, what he should here say is that he has not proved that he knows what he asserted by saying 'Here is one hand and here is another', and that he does not need to prove it. But this is not what he actually says: he says that he has not proved what he asserted by saying 'Here is one hand and here is another', that he cannot prove it, and that he does not need to. Some of these points are certainly right: he has not proved that 'Here is one hand', and he does not need to. It is not a requirement of a proof's being a good one that one prove the truth of all its premisses. But what is puzzling is the thesis that he *cannot* prove 'Here is a hand'; for, surely, one can prove such things. In order to prove that there is a hand before one, one would examine its relation to a human body, its tissue, and so on – the kind of examination which pathologists are best qualified to carry out. Moore alludes to the possibility of such an examination ('If one of you suspected that one of my hands was artificial, he might be said to get a proof . . . by coming up and examining the suspected hand close up'; PEW p. 149), but dismisses it as inapplicable to most cases ('I do not believe that any proof is possible in nearly all cases'). The reason he gives for this is that for him now to prove to his audience that 'Here is one hand' he would have to prove that he is not now dreaming, and this he cannot prove. Yet the question of whether or not he is then dreaming is relevant, not to the issue of whether or not there is hand before him, but to the issue of whether or not he knows that there is a hand before him. Arguably, in order to prove that he knows that there is a hand before him, he must prove that he is not dreaming. But since the question of whether or not he is dreaming is irrelevant to the truth of 'Here is a hand', it is just not true that, because he cannot prove that he is not dreaming, he cannot prove that 'Here is a hand'. Admittedly, for him to prove that 'Here is a hand' he must not then be dreaming; so to prove that his proof is a good one he would have to prove that he is not dreaming; but, I have argued, it is central to Moore's strategy in his 'Proof' that, in giving a proof, one does not have to prove that the proof is a good proof.

I believe that in these last two pages of PEW Moore confused the thesis that one cannot prove such things as 'Here is a hand' with the thesis that one cannot prove such things as 'I know that here is a hand'. It is the latter thesis which fits with his remarks about dreaming and with his general position in PEW. For he wants to insist that he can know such things as that 'Here is a hand' without having to prove that he does, and thus that his proof of an external world is a good proof even though he has not refuted the sceptic by proving that he knows its premises to be true. I shall say more later in this chapter about the thesis that one cannot prove 'I know that here is a hand'. But I want now to return to Moore's 'Proof' and briefly assess it for what it was always intended to be, a proof of the existence of an external world, a new refutation of idealism – Moore's original refutation being vitiated, in his own eyes, by his commitment there to naive realism.

In assessing Moore's proof in this light, as a proof of metaphysical realism, attention is focused on his account of what it is for there to be an external world. Moore in fact devotes most of his lecture to this topic (a fact which confirms my interpretation of it). He begins by following Kant in taking it that for there to be an external world it is necessary and sufficient that there are things 'outside of us' or 'external to our minds'; and he then explains what he takes these phrases to mean. In elucidating the former he starts from a remark of Kant's that these are things which are 'to be met with in space', and suggests that Kant has in mind here things which are perceptible by several people and such that they can exist unperceived (so that things such as after-images are excluded from this category). He then suggests that the conception of something 'external to my mind' is that of something whose existence now does not entail that I am now having any experience, and hence that the conception of something 'external to our minds' is that of something whose existence now does not entail that any of us (i.e. any human beings) are having any experiences. As he then notes, when the key terms are understood in this way, there are things which are external to our minds but not to be met with in space: Moore gives the example of the pains of animals, but the case of abstract objects is clearer. On the other hand, he takes it that anything which is to be met with in space is *ipso facto* external to our minds, and this is for him the important point, since he takes it to be obvious that things such as hands and dogs are to be met with in space.

At this point Moore has defined the issue in such a way that few philosophers will want to deny that there is an external world in the sense Moore has defined. For to deny that there is an external world, in Moore's sense, one must deny that there are objects 'to be met with in space', i.e. perceptible by more than one person and capable of existing unperceived. The crucial case is that of a phenomenalist; for if Moore's proof is to be a proof of metaphysical realism, and a refutation of idealism, it must surely be such that its conclusion is inconsistent with phenomenalism. But Moore's conclusion in this case is not one that a phenomenalist will want to dispute. Even Berkeley allows, in his third *Dialogue*, that a phenomenalist can speak with the vulgar and talk of unperceived material objects.

So far from regarding this as an objection to his proof, however, Moore would have been quite unperturbed by it. For he treats phenomenalism as primarily a view concerning the analysis of statements about the external world and thus as not challenging its existence. In his lecture notes from 1933–4 he put the point very straightforwardly: 'Berkeley did not deny that Matter is real. All he did was to give a peculiar analysis of what's meant by saying it is' (*LP* p. 179). Indeed since, as I suggested in the previous chapter, there are reasons for supposing that in the late 1930s, Moore himself was a phenomenalist, he could scarcely regard himself as arguing for a conclusion inconsistent with phenomenalism. Yet having removed all familiar epistemological and metaphysical issues from his target, it then becomes puzzling just whom Moore thought he was arguing against. I think Moore felt that he was refuting a position held by McTaggart. In his lecture notes Moore contrasts the views of Berkeley concerning the reality of matter with those of McTaggart, and just before the sentence quoted above, he writes: 'I've said some philosophers have denied that Matter is real: & at least one (McT.) certainly has.' Indeed, Wisdom has described how, when he challenged Moore concerning the purport of his proof, Moore picked up his copy of McTaggart's *Some Dogmas of Religion* and pointed to McTaggart's denial of matter there.[19] But Moore never explained what he took McTaggart's position to be, and thus what position of interest his proof was supposed to refute.

Although Moore defines the conclusion of his proof in such a way that it is consistent with phenomenalism, his way of approaching the issue fails to take account of the phenomenalist's desire to deny the existence of matter, of an external world. In PEW itself Moore comes close to recognising this when he alludes briefly to Kant's conception of 'transcendental realism':

Now Kant, as we saw, asserts that the phrases 'outside of us' or 'external' are in fact used in two very different senses; and with regard to one of these two senses, that which he calls the 'transcendental' sense . . . it is notorious that he himself felt that things which are to be met with in space are *not* 'external' in that sense. There is, therefore, according to him, *a* sense of 'external', a sense in which the word has been commonly used by philosophers – such that, if 'external' be used in that sense, then from the proposition 'Two dogs exist' it will *not* follow that there are some external things. What this supposed sense is I do not think that Kant himself ever succeeded in explaining clearly; nor do I know of any reason for supposing that philosophers ever have used 'external' in a sense, such that in *that* sense things that are to be met with in space are *not* external.

(pp. 138–9)

Moore is here dismissing what the phenomenalist will regard as the substance of his position. For he will want to say that the truth of 'Two dogs exist' just does not suffice for the existence of an external world in the metaphysically interesting sense of that thesis.

Moore's attitude here manifests his beliefs that the phenomenalist is just offering an analysis of thought about an external world and that philosophical analyses have no deep metaphysical significance. If the analysandum is such that it seems to imply that there is an external world, then its analysis can make no difference to this implication. I discussed this thesis at length in chapter 7 (section 4), and argued that although Moore is largely right to defend the ontological commitments of common-sense, he is prone to neglect the significance of philosophical analysis for questions about the fundamental kinds of thing there are. Since the issue of metaphysical realism is precisely one of this latter kind, it follows that Moore's attitude to phenomenalism, and the strategy of his proof, is a mistake. The phenomenalist is of course prepared to speak with the vulgar and assent to 'There are external objects'; but he does not regard the category of external objects as fundamental. Moore's 'Proof' is not a refutation of scepticism, nor was it intended to be. It was intended to be a refutation of idealism; as such it is a total failure.

In the light of this failure, it would be surprising if Moore's earlier 'Defence of Common Sense' were more successful. Yet it merits attention because it does not cover the same ground as the 'Proof'. For the first point to strike one in the 'Defence' is that the list of truisms with which Moore opens are *not* such things as that 'Here is a hand' and 'This is a pencil'; they are general claims about himself as mind and body (and thus incidentally expressive of his dualist philosophy of mind). He begins with a list of claims about his body, about its spatial and

295

temporal relationships with other material objects (e.g. 'the earth had existed for many years before my body was born'), and then moves on to a similar list concerning his mental states (e.g. 'I have been aware of other facts, which I was not at the time observing, such as, for instance, the fact, of which I am now aware, that my body existed yesterday'). In so far as Moore's truisms are all first-person propositions, his starting-point is reminiscent of that of Descartes. But the claims Moore makes about his body are quite unlike any that Descartes will admit as indubitable; none the less Moore does claim to 'know, with certainty' (p. 32) all of his truisms. Furthermore (and here too he departs from Descartes), he maintains he knows that he knows that 'very many (I do not say all)' people know a similar set of truisms concerning themselves (Moore takes it that the indexical feature prevents the propositions being the same for any two subjects). If we were to add that these people also know that each other knows a set of truisms, knowledge of these truisms would be 'common knowledge' in David Lewis's sense;[20] and I think that Moore does conceive of his 'common-sense' knowledge as common knowledge in this sense.

What is the nature of Moore's claim that there is common-sense knowledge of this kind? In *On Certainty* Wittgenstein, who apparently had a high opinion of DCS,[21] remarks:

> 6. Now, can one enumerate what one knows (like Moore)? Straight off like that, I believe not – For otherwise the expression 'I know' gets misused. And through this misuse a queer and extremely important mental state seems to be revealed.

This criticism rests on a misapprehension. Although Moore does claim to know his truisms, this claim is an expression of belief on his part; he is presenting an aspect of his 'philosophical position' (p. 32), which is what Muirhead had invited him to do (DCS originally appeared in the second series of 'personal statements' solicited by Muirhead and published as *Contemporary British Philosophy* (Allen & Unwin, London: 1925); Moore's contribution is unusual in not including an intellectual autobiography). Thus when he introduces his truisms, he says that 'they are, in fact, a set of propositions, every one of which (in my own opinion) I *know*, with certainty, to be true' (p. 32); similarly, at the end of his discussion of this matter he writes of 'my belief in (2)' (where (2) is roughly the assertion of common-sense knowledge) as 'this first point in my philosophical position' (p. 44). In setting out his truisms, therefore, Moore is not, as Wittgenstein suggests, supposing that introspection can reveal to one what one knows; he is only taking it that it can reveal one's beliefs about what one knows oneself and about what others know.

Moore's description of common-sense knowledge thus belongs,

therefore, in the first instance, to his description of 'the Common Sense view of the world'. He holds that it is an important feature of the common-sense view of the world that it embodies claims to knowledge: we all constantly assume that we know a set of Moorean truisms and that we know that everyone else does. But Moore does not just describe this common-sense view; he also asserts that it is correct: 'I am one of those philosophers who have held that the 'Common Sense view of the world' is, in certain fundamental features, *wholly* true' (p. 44).

In arguing for this conclusion, Moore takes it that he has two different opponents: idealists, who will contest the truth of his truisms (Moore is here unwilling to allow that idealists just present an analysis which presents no challenge to his truisms), and sceptics, who will contest his knowledge of them; the distinction is again that between metaphysical and epistemological realism. His argument against the sceptics is that concerning the coherence of their position which I discussed in section 3; and he here essays a similar argument against idealists. He argues that assertions are acts performed by people who have bodies and minds of the kind characterised by his truisms; hence if an assertion of any kind is made, including an idealist one, then there must be at least one person of whom a set of truisms is true, and, therefore, the idealist thesis must be false.

Moore's argument turns on the claim that assertions are necessarily made by people with minds and bodies as characterised in his truisms. The way for an idealist to respond to this is for him to introduce an empirical/transcendental distinction, such that he takes Moore's truisms to be 'empirically' true but, in some respects, 'transcendentally' false. Hence, he can allow, at the level of empirical truth it is correct that assertions are made by people with minds and bodies as characterised in Moore's truisms; but the same does not apply where 'assertion' is understood transcendentally. Admittedly the idealist then owes us an account of what it is for assertion, or judgment, to be understood transcendentally: but idealists have been only too ready to provide such accounts, and even if they have sometimes been unsatisfactory, it is not for reasons which have anything to do with Moore's argument.

Although Moore's arguments in DCS against idealism and scepticism are, therefore, ineffective, it has to be recognised that he does at least argue for the common-sense realism that he here presents. Hence when he maintains that, in answer to the question whether he really knows his truisms, 'I think I have nothing better to say than that it seems to me that I *do* know them, with certainty' (p. 44), he is not just dogmatically affirming the existence of common-sense knowledge. Rather, having, as he thinks, shown that idealism and scepticism are untenable, he is simply presenting his claims to common-sense knowledge as ones which he finds it reasonable to accept in the light of his belief that they are so.

The title of our common-sense knowledge as presented here by Moore rests not on indubitable foundations nor on intuitions of self-evidence but on the supposed facts that we all assume that we know these things and that there are no compelling objections (from the idealist or the sceptic) to our doing so. The thesis that we have this knowledge coheres with our best understanding of the world and our place within it.

Moore does not adequately substantiate this thesis. Quite apart from the ineffectiveness of his arguments against scepticism and idealism, Moore fails to address the possibility of significant revisions of common-sense in the light of the natural sciences. In *SMPP* he had allowed that common sense beliefs about the history of the earth have altered in the light of scientific theory, and that common-sense beliefs about space and time may not be able to survive paradoxes concerning infinity (cf. chapter 4, section 3). There is no comparable qualification of his affirmations in DCS; presumably he takes it that he has identified a hard core of beliefs which are invulnerable to revision in the light of scientific discoveries. We may well be sceptical about that (e.g. current cognitive science poses a challenge to some of Moore's common-sense affirmations about his mental states). If common-sense gets its authority from considerations of coherence, then, in principle, no feature of common-sense is beyond reasonable challenge. None the less, there does seem to be something right in what Moore goes on to say about the epistemological status of his common-sense truisms:

> We are all, I think, in this strange position that we do *know* many
> things, with regard to which we *know* further that we must have had
> evidence for them, and yet we do not know *how* we know them, i.e.
> we do not know what the evidence was.

(p. 44)

This observation is not integrated into the account of common-sense Moore presents in DCS. I shall explore it further in the final section of this chapter, where I suggest a different approach to the role of common-sense. But first I need to discuss Moore's final treatment of scepticism in his late papers, 4FS and C.

## 6: The final failure

Moore returned to the theme of scepticism in his two late papers, 4FS and C. Perhaps conscious of the misunderstandings of PEW that were soon to be published in *PGEM*, he wanted to explain just what his attitude to scepticism was, although many of the ideas were ones that he had held for some time (cf. his 1928–9 lecture notes, *LP* pp. 47–52). In both papers he makes his characteristic assertions of certain knowledge of particular things such as 'This is a pencil' and 'I have clothes on', thereby showing that he believes that scepticism is false. But he does not dogmatically assert that scepticism is false; he seeks to refute sceptical arguments. Furthermore, although he closes 4FS with a statement of the argument from differential certainty, his presentation of it is much more tentative than it had been in SJP; and although he presents the argument from pragmatic incoherence in C in a form which I discussed in section 3 he does not here take it that this argument refutes scepticism. So he does not attempt the kind of general demonstration of the unpersuasiveness, or incoherence, of sceptical arguments he had attempted before; instead he presents a critical assessment of some sceptical arguments.

He devotes much space to arguments which revolve around the concept of possibility. In C he distinguishes epistemic possibility (what is not ruled out by what is known) from logical possibility (what is not self-contradictory); once this distinction is clearly made, he observes, there is no temptation to move from the premiss that a proposition is contingent to the conclusion that it is not known to be true via the thoughts that if it is contingent, it is possible that it is false, and that if it is possible that it is false, then it is not known to be true. Similarly, in 4FS he notes that we sometimes use the expression 'It is possible for an $F$ to be $G$' to mean 'Some $F$'s are $G$'s', and he suggests that one of Russell's sceptical arguments concerning memory is fallacious because he employs this concept of possibility in his premiss, but draws a conclusion which employs the epistemic concept of possibility (4FS p. 220; cf. LP pp. 49–50).

Although both these points are fair enough, neither is central to sceptical arguments. Right at the end of 4FS, however, Moore addresses a more serious argument, which he sets out in a Cartesian manner by introducing the hypothesis of a malicious demon in the context of a foundationalist theory of knowledge. Having distinguished between immediate and indirect knowledge, he has the malicious demon interfere in such a way as to call into question our assumptions about what we know indirectly. The case he presents concerns knowledge of an external world: he takes it that we have immediate knowledge of our own sense-experiences and also of what we remember concerning such experiences, and that this knowledge is not threatened by the malicious demon. But he also accepts that we do not have immediate knowledge of an external world, and that all that we know immediately is not logically incompatible with the hypothesis that our sense experiences are being produced by a malicious demon.

Moore's response to this argument in 4FS is in several respects unclear. It is clear that he takes it that if he knows such a thing as that 'This is a pencil', then he knows that his sense-experiences are not due to a malicious demon (4FS p. 224); furthermore, he recognises that he

299

needs to say something to show how he knows this, given that the sceptical possibility is consistent with everything that he knows immediately. What he suggests is that his immediate knowledge of his present sense-experience and memory of previous sense-experiences and thoughts provide him with adequate inductive evidence to rule out the sceptical hypothesis. One puzzling feature of this suggestion is the assumption that his memory is not being interfered with by the malicious demon; for no sceptical philosopher will feel inclined to grant this without argument, and it is not clear from Moore's discussion whether he is making this assumption simply for the purpose of the argument, or whether he thinks himself entitled to make it in the light of his thesis that memory is immediate knowledge of the past. His remarks rather suggest the latter, but this just shows that Moore's thoughts about the relationship between the immediacy of a kind of knowledge and the infallibility of claims to possess knowledge of that kind are undeveloped.

Another point which arises from Moore's argument is that he has not specified in any detail what the inductive inference is to be in this case. To do this he would have had to specify what account of the relationship between sense-experience and material objects is to be assumed. The Cartesian argument is primarily directed against the indirect realist position; if that position is here presupposed then a good deal has to be assumed in order to suppose that inductive arguments help at all; e.g. 'Hume's Principles' have to be faced down. Furthermore it is notoriously difficult to justify anything more than 'more or less probable belief' in this way, rather than the 'certain knowledge' Moore wants. I have suggested, however, that Moore's remarks here fit with the phenomenalist account of the external world that he was then attracted to. Hence, as long as the issue of inductive scepticism is not introduced, there is here a plausible way of filling out Moore's position.

But perhaps inductive scepticism should be introduced. For Moore writes: 'it does seem to me very certain that I know little, if anything, with certainty with regard to the future' (4FS p. 212). Yet Moore cannot consistently combine inductive scepticism with the view that inductive arguments provide an adequate basis for certain knowledge of an external world. For there seems no reason why the phenomenalist's inductive inferences from the actual to the possible should be certain if those from past to future are not. In 4FS Moore does not appear to have a coherent view of the matter.

Let us leave aside for now the question of inductive scepticism, and ask whether a phenomenalist account of the external world would really vindicate Moore's anti-sceptical position in 4FS. Might not a sceptic reply that if he has persuaded Moore to adopt a phenomenalist account of the external world, then the substance of the victory is his? Moore of course will deny this, for he holds that the phenomenalist only differs from others concerning the analysis of propositions about an external world. But this is an oversimplification; a sceptic who does not deny that we have knowledge of an external world, but only that we have knowledge of an external world as the metaphysical realist conceives it to be, can well regard the adoption of phenomenalism as a sign of agreement with him. Certainly, not all sceptics are in this way 'metaphysical'; there are 'vulgar' sceptics as well, and I am not sure which species is the more interesting. But it is at any rate clear that phenomenalism and similar anti-realist positions just confirm the views of the metaphysical sceptic.

In C Moore returns in effect to the sceptical argument he had discussed at the end of 4FS, though again only at the end of his paper. In this case the sceptical possibility he seeks to refute is simply that he is dreaming; thus it is still the Cartesian sceptic whom he confronts. As before, he takes it that if he is to know that he is standing up, he must know that he is not dreaming. But what he says about this is a bit puzzling. He tells a nice story about a Duke of Devonshire to show that it does not follow simply from the hypothesis that he is dreaming that he is not standing up (C p. 245). He accepts, however, that if he is dreaming, he does not then know that he is standing up.[22] What is puzzling is that having distinguished between these two conditionals, he concludes that 'if I don't know now that I'm not dreaming, it *follows* that I don't *know* that I am standing up' (C p. 247). For although this would follow from knowledge of the rejected conditional ('if I am dreaming I am not standing up') and the weak closure condition for knowledge $Kp$ & $K(p \supset q) \vdash Kq$, it does not follow from knowledge of the conditional Moore accepts ('if I am dreaming I don't know that I am standing up') and the same condition. To derive it one must assume the KK principle $Kp \supset KKp$ of which Moore makes no mention; so it looks as though this is a tacit assumption of Moore's conception of knowledge in C.

I will return later to the question of the role here of the KK principle; let us now return to Moore's argument. Having accepted that he has to know that he is not dreaming in order to know that he is standing up, he faces the question as to how he is to know the former of these. In 4FS he had acknowledged that the demon hypothesis was logically consistent with all that he knew immediately, which turned out to be knowledge of his present sensory experiences and of his past experiences and thoughts; but he had urged that none the less he could certainly rule out the demon hypothesis on inductive grounds. In C he does not even try the same argument. He begins by allowing that the dream hypothesis is logically consistent with his current sensory experiences; but then he proposes that it is not logically consistent with the conjunction of these

301

experiences and his memories of the immediate past (C p. 250). Thus Moore has here gone back on the assumption which he had made in 4FS, that the sceptical possibility is consistent with all that he knows immediately. As he himself recognised (cf. his preface to PP p. 13, and Dr Lewy's footnote to C, p. 251), this position is not convincing. Only by regarding the distinction between dreams and waking life as solely a matter of coherence could one suppose there to be a *logical* relationship between the proposition that one is dreaming and propositions describing present sensory experiences and memories of past experiences. Furthermore, even a phenomenalist who relies on coherence will not take it that actual present and past experiences are by themselves *logically* sufficient to settle the matter: he will invoke possible experiences as well, and make the inference from the actual experiences to the possible ones, and thus to the conclusion concerning whether or not one is dreaming, an inductive one. Indeed that is the position suggested by Moore's remarks in 4FS. But in C he rejects it; for he here says that if his present experiences and memories of past experiences do not suffice to rule out on logical grounds the hypothesis that he is dreaming, then 'I don't see how to deny that I cannot possibly know for certain that I am not dreaming' (p. 250).

Why does Moore say this? The only reason I can think of is that he has come to see the implications of the sceptical position concerning induction which, as I observed, he advances in 4FS. But if that was his reason, it is odd that he does not discuss it; and odder still that he does not here entertain scepticism concerning memory of one's immediate past. For it is only by assuming that our present apparent memories of our past experiences are correct that it is at all plausible to suppose that present experiences and memories suffice to rule out the dream hypothesis; once scepticism about apparent memory is introduced, as it surely needs to be in the context of Moore's argument, Moore's anti-sceptical line of thought obviously collapses. There is an entry in *CB* (pp. 162–5) from this period in which he does seem prepared to entertain scepticism about memory. I do not understand why he does not take it seriously either in 4FS or C.

It is clear by this stage that Moore's last two papers, so far from providing a final settling of accounts with the sceptic, reveal Moore as quite unable to refute philosophical scepticism (though not of course himself a sceptic). What has gone wrong with Moore's deliberations on this matter? Stroud has suggested that it is his tacit assumption of the KK principle (*SPS* pp. 120–1 fn. 18). But the type of sceptical argument Moore discusses does not need to rely on it. Moore observed, quite correctly, that it does not follow from the hypothesis that he is dreaming that he is not standing up; but it does surely follow from that hypothesis that he is not wide awake and standing up. So, if weak closure is assumed, it will follow, without the use of the KK principle, that if he knows that he is wide awake and standing up then he knows that he is not dreaming. Thus by modifying very slightly his target the sceptic can mount his sceptical argument without relying on the KK principle (alternatively he can modify his sceptical hypothesis – 'If I am a brain in a vat on Alpha Centauri, then I am not standing up on Earth', etc.).

In my view, Moore's failure derives from his belief that he has to be able to be provide for himself conclusive, non-question-begging, ways of eliminating sceptical hypotheses if he is to have the knowledge he takes himself to have. If he is to know that he is standing up, he thinks, he has to be able to establish conclusively that he is not dreaming without employing any assumptions which are called into question by the hypothesis that he might be dreaming. It is for this reason that he does not appeal to our common-sense conviction that we have such knowledge; for, as he recognises, common-sense knowledge is called into question by the sceptical hypothesis. Moore's position is characteristic of those who employ an 'internalist' conception of knowledge.[23] This conception of knowledge leads naturally to the foundationalist approach characteristic of Moore's last two papers, for this at least offers the possibility of non-question-begging arguments for the disputed claims to knowledge. It is also associated with the KK principle which Moore seems to assume; if knowledge requires the ability to eliminate all alternative hypotheses, including sceptical ones, then knowledge seems to imply the ability to know that one knows. But the internalist conception is not just an affirmation of this principle; for the internalist will acknowledge the challenge posed by arguments which do not employ it.

The trouble with the internalist conception is manifest in C. There is no way in which sceptical hypotheses can be eliminated in the way required by the internalist; so a sceptical conclusion is inevitable. But was it inevitable that Moore should employ the internalist conception of knowledge? Might not his appeal to common-sense have a more effective role in the context of a theory based on an externalist conception of knowledge?

## 7: Externalism and common-sense

Despite the Cartesian tradition within which Moore approached epistemological issues, some of Moore's characteristic affirmations of common-sense knowledge point away from the internalist conception of knowledge. In PEW he insists that he certainly knows that 'Here is a hand', although he cannot prove (that he knows) it because he cannot prove that he is not now dreaming – a striking comment in the light of his later argument in C. Similarly, his remark in DCS that the (objective) certainty of his common-sense truisms is not undermined by the fact that he does not know how he knows them suggests a different approach to claims to knowledge. There is also a passage in his 1928–9 lectures in which he almost explicitly calls into question the internalist approach characteristic of 4FS and C:

> I can ask myself: Do *I* know that this is a physical thing?
>
> And I *know* (I think) that other philosophers have given the following reasons why they think I'm unreasonable if I answer that I *do* know for certain. . . .
>
> (a) You don't know for certain, anything wh. you *can* doubt. And you *can* doubt that is a blackboard. I really don't know whether I *can*. Nor do I know that if I *can*, that proves that I don't know it. [People who say this seem to me confusing 'indubitable' = not able to be doubted with 'indubitable' = known. To doubt is to believe a prop. of the form 'Perhaps this isn't a blackboard' & to believe that is to believe *you don't know it*. But mayn't you believe this, even when you do know it?]

As I have indicated, Moore does not make much use of these ideas when he is arguing against sceptical theses. The appeal to common-sense has a role in the context of the argument from differential certainty; but that argument remains inconclusive until Moore can show that his affirmations of knowledge concerning particular matters of fact are more central to our concept of knowledge than are the assumptions about it which sceptical arguments employ. This is well borne out by C, which commences with characteristic affirmations and ends in failure because Moore himself accepts the assumptions concerning knowledge which produce sceptical conclusions. What is required, then, is an alternative to the internalist conception of knowledge which can put Moore's affirmations to good use.

A central move is, obviously, the adoption of an 'externalist' conception of knowledge, according to which knowledge consists, in Armstrong's phrase, of 'some natural relation which holds between the belief-state . . . and the situation which makes the belief true. It is a matter of a certain relation holding between the believer and the world'.[24] This is pretty vague, but the vagueness does not matter here. Armstrong remarks that reliabilist theories are externalist in his sense, and this gives us enough to go on. An account of knowledge of this kind was in fact advanced by Russell in 1921 in *The Analysis of Mind*, complete with the analogy between knowledge and a reliable thermometer which Armstrong repeats (cf. lecture XIII); but I have not encountered any recognition of its significance in Moore's writings.

There are those who think that the adoption of an externalist conception of knowledge by itself removes all danger of sceptical conclusions; for, it is suggested, once it is accepted that the truth of one's knowledge claims does not require that one be able to justify them to oneself, no sceptical conclusions can be drawn from one's inability to eliminate sceptical hypotheses without question-begging assumptions. Once we conceive of knowledge as just a natural relation, we can be as reasonably confident that this natural relation obtains in particular cases as we can be that any natural relation ever obtains.[25]

In my view, however, this is too quick. Moore's observation in 4FS that philosophical scepticism is essentially a reflexive doubt whether one knows is important here. For once the first-person perspective is adopted, traditional sceptical hypotheses can be brought back into play. In a third-person case, a doubt whether $x$ knows that $p$ is typically a doubt whether $x$'s belief that $p$ stands in the appropriate natural relation to the fact that $p$, and this doubt need not induce any further doubts about the world; in the first-person case, however, there is precisely this induction of further doubts, since doubt whether one knows that $p$ gives one reason to doubt whether $p$. Thus, it seems, one cannot appeal to one's belief that $p$ in order to settle one's doubt whether one knows that $p$ without begging the question; and if the grounds for the initial doubt whether one knows are sufficiently general to cast doubt upon similar claims to knowledge, one cannot rely on those beliefs either.

But why should one doubt whether one knows in the first place? Our own experience of our own fallibility certainly raises such doubts in ordinary life. We typically banish them by considerations of coherence – by introducing other beliefs, about the world and about our place within it, by reference to which we are able to dismiss the doubt. But, as I have indicated, if a doubt is raised by reference to a consideration whose scope is sufficiently general (e.g. whether I am not now dreaming), this procedure becomes questionable; for the beliefs by reference to which the doubt is settled are themselves called into question by the doubt. But what if I do not, in fact, have any such general doubts? Does the force of sceptical considerations depend on the contingent availability of people with sufficiently general doubts? It suffices, I think, for the sceptic to provide a *reason* for a general doubt even if no actual doubt ensues. For if there is reason for a sufficiently general doubt whether one knows, then, equally, there is reason for widespread first-order doubts which will make it difficult to remove the initial reason for doubt. It is because it is only a reason for doubt that is required that the sceptic can safely adduce his hypothetical characters – the Evil Genius, the mad scientist, etc.

At this point it may seem that the adoption of the first-person perspective, combined with permissiveness towards merely hypothetical doubt, has produced a situation that, from a first-person point of view, is indistinguishable from the internalist conception of knowledge. This is not in fact the case; but the proximity of these two positions does a great deal to explain the attractiveness of the internalist conception. The reason that the positions do not quite coincide emerges if one considers what is at issue in sceptical arguments in the two cases. The internalist makes it a condition for the truth of a claim to knowledge that one should be able to silence doubts concerning it; hence unless one can silence these doubts, one does not know and, reflecting on one's situation, one should judge that one does not know. The externalist, by contrast, does not make it a condition of truth that sceptical doubts be silenced; for him, the truth of a claim to knowledge depends on whether the appropriate natural relation obtains. Instead, sceptical doubt gets its purchase by adducing reasons why one might after all not know what one takes oneself to know. In this context it is not necessary that one be able to conclusively eliminate such sceptical hypotheses; it will suffice if one can demonstrate that the doubt is, actually, unreasonable. Thus the externalist does not need to be able to prove conclusively that he is not dreaming; he need only establish that, in the light of his experience, this is an extremely implausible hypothesis.

This shows that externalism is an essential element in an anti-sceptical strategy. But given the scope of sceptical hypotheses, establishing that sceptical doubts are unreasonable is not a straightforward matter. Because these hypotheses call into question all the obvious counter-evidence, it is not easy to understand what one can appeal to without joining the ranks of those who have begged the question against the sceptic.[26] Yet it is at this point, I think, that a Moorean appeal to common-sense should be introduced. What requires care is the way in which this appeal to common-sense is to be understood; one needs to avoid the dogmatism inherent in 'Moore' as conceived under the dogmatist interpretation. I think the essential move is the application of Hume's thesis of the involuntariness of belief to Moore's affirmations of knowledge concerning particular matters of fact — that 'This is a pencil' and 'Here is a hand', etc. For the continuous, involuntary, welling-up within us of non-sceptical beliefs concerning such matters provides us with a way of breaking into the circle of argument. The involuntary arrival on the cognitive scene of fresh beliefs which conflict with sceptical doubt challenges the reasonableness of that doubt. I can frame the thought that I might now be dreaming, and I can acknowledge that there is no way in which I can conclusively establish to myself that I am not; but the fact that I find myself, willy-nilly, believing that I am sitting down and writing makes it hard for me to sustain the reasonableness of my doubt. My current perceptual beliefs provide me with ever new reasons for rejecting the doubt, and although I might wish to dismiss these new beliefs as question-begging, the fact that they are involuntary implies that, initially, I do not have the opportunity to do so. The involuntariness of common-sense belief, therefore, challenges sceptical doubt, by furnishing us with beliefs which give us reason to reject it without our acquisition of these beliefs being grounded in lines of argument that it has called into doubt.

The involuntariness of our common-sense beliefs does not by itself suffice to exhibit the unreasonableness of sceptical doubt; someone with involuntary paranoid beliefs about others can have good reasons for calling these beliefs into doubt. It is at this point that considerations of coherence come into play; the refutation of scepticism requires a good degree of coherence. In particular it is important that our common-sense beliefs should manifest a degree of reflective coherence sufficient to enable us to understand the causes of error on our own part; for in this way we incorporate an understanding .of our own fallibility within our understanding of the world instead of simply setting aside judgments which do not cohere in a potentially question-begging way. None the less considerations of coherence, and the related argument from differential certainty, cannot do all the work; it is our involuntary common-sense which primes the pump of rational self-appraisal.

This Humean account of the appeal to common-sense is not deeply alien to Moore's affirmations of certainty concerning particular judgments, although it makes no use of the epistemic content of Moore's appeals, which it would be question-begging to rely upon. In a way it embodies the argument from differential certainty, but stripped of that argument's appeal to our relative certainty concerning what we know. It is our involuntary certainties concerning particular matters of fact that give us reason to reject sceptical hypotheses. When Moore appeals to his audience to agree with him about the absurdity of doubting such things as that 'Here is one hand' (PEW pp. 146–7) or that he has some clothes on (C pp. 227–8), he is relying on the involuntary inevitability of their belief in these things. There is also a measure of agreement with Moore concerning the common-sense truisms presented in DCS. As presented by Moore, these form a heterogeneous bunch of first-person principles that give the general structure of that common-sense view of the world which Moore holds to be certainly true. The first-person content of these truisms fits well with my approach; and the 'strangeness' of our epistemological position with respect to them, whereby 'we do not know *how* we know them' is accounted for. Although our belief in them is not itself involuntary, their acceptance is due to the fact that our involuntary beliefs concerning particular matters of fact commit us to them, and what is strange here is that these general beliefs arise from particular beliefs our acceptance of which would depend upon them were we to acquire these particular beliefs by a process of reasoning from evidence.

What are not here accommodated are Moore's affirmations of objective certainty concerning his truisms. On my account, there is a sense in which these general beliefs should strike us, as we reflect on ourselves, as ungrounded assumptions. For the only reasons we can offer for them are particular beliefs which are such that, as soon we to try to assess their rationality, we have to acknowledge that this assumes the rationality of the general beliefs whose rationality we wanted to establish. Admittedly, considerations of coherence can be employed to buttress the rationality of both particular and general beliefs. But these considerations provide no grounding outside the circle of beliefs whose rationality is in question. So the best we can do is to say that the truth of these general beliefs, which are not involuntary, is implicated in the truth of particular beliefs which, in the first instance, we accept for no reason. Thus although I think that the way to confront sceptical arguments is by means of the combination of externalism and involuntary common-sense which I have presented here,[27] the result falls short of the expectations aroused by Moore's affirmations of certainty (cf. Hume's remark quoted on p. 266). Naturalism in epistemology is the means to victory over scepticism; but the price is the abandonment of self-sufficient rational certainty.

So far I have alluded to Hume in this externalist interpretation of Moore's appeal to common-sense. But there are two other philosophers whose writings show more clearly than do Hume's the nature of the resulting position. For, despite his recognition of the involuntariness of belief, Hume remained a sceptic of sorts because of his commitment to the theory of ideas. Reid, however, grasped the implications of Hume's position and presented a naturalised epistemology freed from Hume's commitment to the theory of ideas. Common-sense, for Reid, is the a priori of such a naturalised epistemology; he expressed it in the following terms:

> Such original and natural judgments are therefore a part of that
> furniture which nature hath given to the human understanding. . . .
> They serve to direct us in the common affairs of life, where our
> reasoning faculty would leave us in the dark. They are a part of our
> constitution, and all the discoveries of our reason are grounded upon
> them. They make up what is called *the common sense of mankind*.[28]

Moore read some of Reid's works when he was in Edinburgh and, as I discussed in chapter 5, they provided him with some of the stimulus for his own defence of common-sense. But just as he did not appreciate the significance for his own sense-datum theory of Reid's criticisms of the theory of ideas, he did not, alas, grasp the way in which Reid develops his appeal to common-sense in the context of a naturalised epistemology.

The other philosopher to have explored these ideas is Wittgenstein, in his notes *On Certainty*. As I mentioned when discussing Malcolm's response to Moore in section 4, the initial stimulus for *On Certainty* was the Malcolm–Moore debate, and I endorsed Moore's criticisms of those aspects of *On Certainty* which correspond with Malcolm's views. There is, however, a central feature of *On Certainty* which does not correspond to anything in Malcolm's work.[29] This is his emphasis on 'Moorean propositions', which correspond to Moore's truisms in DCS (the two sets are not quite the same, but Wittgenstein's name makes it clear that he is thinking of roughly the set Moore described; cf. also *On Certainty* section 674). Concerning these propositions Wittgenstein wrote:

> 136. When Moore says he *knows* such and such, he is really
> enumerating a lot of empirical propositions which we affirm
> without special testing; propositions, that is, which have a
> peculiar logical role in the system of our empirical propositions.

In subsequent remarks, Wittgenstein develops an account of this 'peculiar logical role' in which four points are especially prominent: (i) the truth of these Moorean propositions is assumed by us in our ordinary methods of inquiry; (ii) these propositions are not, however, *a priori* foundations from which we reason; instead they are implicit within our ways of forming particular beliefs and the general picture of the world we thereby acquire; (iii) so the certain truth of these propositions is not learnt by considering them in isolation; rather it is only through reflection on our general picture of the world that we are led to frame the Moorean propositions, and our conviction that they are correct derives from our attachment to this general picture of the world; (iv) ultimately, in fact, this attachment is grounded in the way in which we lead our lives, in what we do.

It will be clear that this account fits readily into my Humean account of Moore's appeal to common-sense and of the place of Moore's truisms within it. Where I have interpreted this appeal with reference to Hume's thesis about the involuntariness of belief, Wittgenstein emphasises the role of action or one's form of life. This is, I think, largely a difference of idiom. There are, of course, many other points in Wittgenstein's remarks and I do not suggest that all his ideas are to be understood in the light of my own perspective. In particular, at one or two points he implies that the Moorean propositions should not be regarded as true or false at all (cf. sections 191, 215), and this idea has been recently developed by Wright into the central thesis of a response to sceptical arguments.[30] In my opinion, however, this is an unnecessary metaphysical evaluation of the strange epistemological role of these propositions. From the fact that we do not determine their truth or falsity by seeing whether or not they 'agree with reality' it does not follow that they neither agree nor disagree with reality. Indeed since it is a presumption of the externalist conception that our knowledge of such propositions consists of a natural relationship with facts in which the truth of these propositions consists, there had better be such facts.

There is, however, a different aspect of Wittgenstein's ideas which raises a potential problem for any appeal to common-sense. This arises when one asks what our attitude is to be to the possibility of other forms of life, expressed by different sets of involuntary beliefs which give rise to different sets of Moorean propositions. If we are supposed to be readily able to conceive of this with equanimity, as Wittgenstein sometimes suggests in *On Certainty*, then we seem to have a form of epistemological relativism that the sceptic might well regard as a victory for him. As Moore's remarks in *SMPP* about alterations in common-sense suggest, one can appeal to considerations of coherence to avoid this consequence, for, as I stressed before, it is only involuntary beliefs that enable us to build up a reflectively coherent conception of the world and our own place within it that we can re-appraise as rational. But the question remains whether considerations of this kind guarantee uniqueness. I do not believe that there is any quick demonstration of such a guarantee. The currently popular strategy for the epistemological absolutist is to point to the explanatory power of the natural sciences and hold out the ideal of their development as a means to convergence upon a single coherent rational system of belief.[31] But there is plenty of room for doubts about the persuasiveness of such an ideal; it is not readily applicable within disciplines such as history and the social sciences, whose subject-matter is intrinsically cultural, and even in that paradigm natural science, physics, its application is disputed.[32]

These issues lie at the heart of current debates in epistemology and they carry one well beyond Moore's bare appeal to common-sense. But one can use the idea of such an appeal to represent them, as Wittgenstein does in his captivating image of Moore among the natives:

> 92. Men have believed that they could make rain; why should not a king be brought up in the belief that the world began with him? And if Moore and this king were to meet and discuss, could Moore really prove his belief to be the right one? I do not say that Moore could not convert the king to his view, but it would be a conversion of a special kind; the king would be brought to look at the world in a different way.

The fact that Wittgenstein chose Moore for this role is a symbol of the indebtedness to him which we all share.

# Notes

## Preface

1 Most notably, Alan White's book *G.E. Moore* (Blackwell, Oxford: 1958).
2 cf. T. Regan's *Bloomsbury's Prophet* (Temple University Press, Philadelphia: 1986). I have reviewed this book in *Mind* (1988).
3 A. Quinton *Thoughts and Thinkers* (Duckworth, London: 1982) p. vii.
4 In a reference McTaggart wrote for Moore when he was applying (unsuccessfully) for a professorship. It is worth remarking that Bradley, who had earlier been McTaggart's (Platonic) idea of a philosopher, was still alive at this time.
5 G. Ryle 'G.E. Moore' reprinted in his *Collected Papers* vol. 1 (Hutchinson, London: 1971) pp. 270–1; cf. also R. Braithwaite 'George Edward Moore 1873–1958' reprinted in A&L, p. 30; M. White 'Memories of G.E. Moore' *Journal of Philosophy* 1960.
6 *The Letters of Virginia Woolf* vol. 6 ed. N. Nicholson (Hogarth, London: 1980) p. 400.

## Chapter I: The refutation of idealism

1 Sidgwick's report on Moore's dissertation is preserved, along with the dissertations, in the library of Trinity College, Cambridge. The dissertations are owned by Cambridge University Library, along with many of Moore's other unpublished writings and correspondence to which I shall refer.
2 Abbreviated titles for Moore's works and a few others are employed throughout the text for the purpose of references. There is a complete guide to the abbreviations used, and the editions of the texts to which reference is made, in the list of abbreviations at the start of the book.
3 cf. B. Russell *My Philosophical Development* (Allen & Unwin, London: 1959) p. 54: 'Moore led the way, but I followed closely in his footsteps.'

4 The 'Apostles' was, and still is, an elitist society of Cambridge intellectuals whose younger members meet regularly to read papers to each other. At the turn of the century Moore was especially influential within it, and the passage from *The Longest Journey* quoted at the start of the book is a description of a meeting of the Apostles. Although the character of Ansell in the book is not a representation of Moore, the initial description of him in the passage quoted is unquestionably reminiscent of the young G.E. Moore. The society has recently become notorious through the fact that in the 1930s its members included the Cambridge spies. Most of the papers Moore wrote for the meetings of the Apostles are preserved in Cambridge University Library.

5 'In what sense, if any, do past and future time exist?' G.E. Moore *Mind* 1897 esp. pp. 238, 240; cf. F p. 202.

6 As I mentioned in note 1, the manuscripts of these dissertations are now in Trinity College library. In some parts the manuscripts are incomplete, and I shall not give detailed references when quoting from them (except when quoting from the parts which Moore published as F and NJ).

7 Most of NJ comes from chapter 2 of the 1898 Dissertation. But most of the relevant pages of the surviving copy of the dissertation (it is the one Moore retained) are missing, doubtless because they were used by Moore himself in composing NJ. So one cannot look for significant changes of phrasing between the dissertation and NJ itself.

8 I am indebted to Dr C. Lewy for making this manuscript available to me. Moore returns to the topic of Kant's arguments concerning infinity in the course of his discussion of idealism in *SMPP* (chs IX, X). Though by and large he still accepts Russell's position, he is less confident about the matter than he had been and expresses some sympathy for Kant's position (cf. pp. 198–200).

9 This letter, unlike others by Moore from which I quote, is in the possession of the Bertrand Russell archives at McMaster University, and I am grateful to them for making available to me a copy of it.

10 G.E. Moore 'Mr. McTaggart's Ethics' *International Journal of Ethics* 1903; cf. *PE* pp. 130ff.

11 *International Journal of Ethics* 1901 cf. esp. pp. 90–1, 93–4. The argument is also used in the 1898 lectures on 'The Elements of Ethics' and in an unpublished paper of 1899 on Natural Theology. Moore also advances a general endorsement of Kant's arguments in N pp. 300–1.

12 cf. R. Walker *Kant* (Routledge, London: 1987) p. 10. Moore's mistake here may well derive from McTaggart, who makes the same mistake in the first edition of his *Studies in the Hegelian Dialectic* (Cambridge University Press, Cambridge: 1st ed. 1896, 2nd ed. 1922) but corrects it in the second – cf. p. 21.

13 In his review of Russell's *Foundations of Geometry* in *Mind* 1899; 'Nativism' in B vol. 2; *PE* pp. 130–5; KI; *SMPP* pp. 153–4. Moore's influence on Russell is manifest in the latter's *The Philosophy of Leibniz* (Allen & Unwin, London: 1900) p. 14.

14 cf. B.Stroud 'Transcendental Arguments' *Journal of Philosophy* 1968; Walker *Kant*. ch. 10.

16 It was often said at the time of RI that Moore had here merely refuted 'subjective idealism', while leaving other forms of idealism unscathed (cf. e.g. H. Joachim *The Nature of Truth* (Clarendon, Oxford: 1906) pp. 61–2). Moore did not take this view, and although I do not think he here refuted any form of idealism, I think he was at least right in maintaining that Absolute idealism includes a Kantian account of the objectivity of the objects of perception.

17 F.H. Bradley *Principles of Logic* (Oxford University Press, London: 2nd ed. 1922).

18 The letter is now in Cambridge University Library.

19 H.P. Grice presented his account of meaning in 'Meaning' *Philosophical Review* 1957; his ideas were developed by D. Lewis in *Convention* (Harvard University Press, Cambridge, Mass.: 1969) ch. IV.

20 G. Frege's account of directions occurs in *The Foundations of Arithmetic* transl. J.L. Austin (Blackwell, Oxford: 1953) sections 64–8.

21 Doubts about synonymy were famously raised by W.V. Quine in 'Two Dogmas of Empiricism', reprinted in *From a Logical Point of View* (Harvard University Press, Cambridge, Mass.: 2nd ed. 1961); Moore himself aired similar doubts in some of his later writings – cf. RTD pp. 178–82 and his reply in *PGEM* p. 667.

22 Moore's terminology remains rather erratic: in NROP, published only two years after RI, Moore writes of colours, sounds etc., as 'contents' of sensation, or as 'sense-contents' (cf. pp. 68–72, 78–9). There is here no dramatic change of view from that of RI; only a change of terminology. It is perhaps significant that Moore here places quotes round most occurrences of 'content' and 'sense-content'.

23 Thus in his *Principles of Psychology* (Macmillan, London: 1890) William James distinguishes between taste as a 'subjective quality of feeling' and as an 'objective quality felt' (p. 272).

24 Compare the final sentence of this passage from RI with the following sentence from H.A. Prichard's *Kant's Theory of Knowledge* (Clarendon, Oxford: 1909) p. 124: 'It is as much a fact of our experience that we directly apprehend bodies in space, as that we directly apprehend our feelings and sensations.' Much of chapter VI of Prichard's book, from which this is taken, reads like a rewriting of RI, though there are no references to it. I think this is just a case of a realist *Zeitgeist*, if one can so speak, manifesting itself a bit later in Oxford.

25 G.E. Moore 'Mr. McTaggart's "Studies in Hegelian Cosmology"' *Proceedings of the Aristotelian Society* 1901–2; 'Mr. McTaggart's Ethics'.

26. Moore 'Mr. McTaggart's "Studies in Hegelian Cosmology"' p. 188.

27 cf. J. Wisdom's account of his conversations with Moore: 'G.E. Moore' in *Paradox and Discovery* (Blackwell, Oxford: 1965) pp. 83–4.

28 Moore treats in this way James Ward (review of *Naturalism and Agnosticism* in *Cambridge Review* 1899), R. Adamson (review of *The Development of Modern Philosophy* in *The Saturday Review* 1903), A.E. Taylor (review of *The Elements of Metaphysics* in *The Saturday Review* 1904), and W.R. Boyce Gibson

(review of *A Philosophical Introduction to Ethics* in *International Journal of Ethics* 1905).

29 Bradley op. cit. pp. 145ff.; McTaggart op. cit. pp. 8–10.

30 Moore's characterisation seems fair enough in this respect; cf. Bradley op. cit. pp. 94–6; *Appearance and Reality* (Allen & Unwin, London: 1897) pp. 521ff.; McTaggart op. cit. pp. 209ff.

31 Bradley *Principles of Logic* p. 185.

32 J. Passmore *100 Years of Philosophy* (Penguin, Harmondsworth: 1968) p. 209; P. Pettit 'The Early Philosophy of G.E. Moore' *Philosophical Forum* 1973 p. 262.

33 Moore does not, unfortunately, comment on the 'converse' of this, the thesis that George V might not have been fathered by Edward VII; the issues raised by this were famously raised by S. Kripke in *Naming and Necessity* (Blackwell, Oxford: 1980) pp. 110ff.

34 It seems to me, however, that A. Manser has committed this fallacy on behalf of Bradley; cf. his 'Bradley and Internal Relations' in *Idealism: Past & Present* ed. G. Vesey (Cambridge University Press, Cambridge: 1982) p. 193. But I do not want to exempt Bradley from all charges of fallacious argument. On p. 578 of *Appearance and Reality* Bradley seeks to prove that spatial relations are internal; as I understand his argument he moves illicitly from the premiss that it is essential to material objects that they stand in some spatial relations to the conclusion that it is essential to them that they stand in the spatial relations they actually do stand in.

35 J. McTaggart's argument is presented in *The Nature of Existence* (Cambridge University Press, Cambridge: 1927) ch. 23. There is an excellent discussion of it in D.H. Mellor *Real Time* (Cambridge University Press, Cambridge: 1981) ch. 6.

36 cf. e.g. G. Evans *The Varieties of Reference* (Clarendon, Oxford: 1982) pp. 227ff.

37 There are other lines of thought in Bradley; e.g. he hankers after a Romantic re-unification of reason, will, and the passions, as in the marvellous description of the Absolute in *Appearance and Reality* p. 172. But this aspiration scarcely constitutes an argument, let alone a demonstration of an inherent contradiction in judgment. A more serious line of argument employs premisses concerning the nature of truth and judgment to argue for the conclusion that no judgments can be wholly true, which contradicts the thesis that judgments can be true or false. Although this is an interesting line of argument, Bradley does not represent it as central to his thesis of the unreality of relations.

38 cf. Bradley *Principles of Logic* p. 96; *Appearance and Reality* pp. 32–3; *Essays on Truth and Reality* (Clarendon, Oxford: 1914) pp. 288–9.

39 *Mind* 1906 esp. pp. 532–3.

40 *Mind* 1907 pp. 229–35.

41 cf. Bradley's remark in the preface to *Appearance and Reality* (p. xiv): 'Metaphysics is the finding of bad reasons for what we believe upon instinct.'

## Chapter II: Pure realism

1 From *The Correspondence of W.B. Years and T. Sturge Moore* ed. Ursula Bridge (Routledge, London: 1953) p. 59.

2 cf. also footnote 2 to Russell's paper 'Meinong's Theory of Complexes and Assumptions', p. 21 as reprinted in B. Russell *Essays in Analysis* ed. D. Lackey (Allen & Unwin, London: 1973).

3 cf. Russell's remark in *The Principles of Mathematics* (Allen & Unwin, London: 1903) p. 493, with a reference to Moore, that 'empiricism is radically opposed to the philosophy advocated in this work'.

4 This letter is the one referred to in note 9 to chapter 1.

5 cf. 'We must accept once for all the identification of truth with reality' in F.H. Bradley *Essays on Truth and Reality* (Clarendon, Oxford: 1914) p. 113.

6 G. Frege 'The Thought' transl. A. and M. Quinton, reprinted in *Philosophical Logic* ed. P. Strawson (Clarendon, Oxford: 1967) p. 19.

7 But Russell displayed considerable anxiety on this issue: cf. Russell op. cit. pp. 49–50, 83–6, 99–100, 139–42.

8 cf. G. Evans *The Varieties of Reference* (Clarendon, Oxford: 1982) esp. ch. 1.

9 B. Russell's 'On Denoting' was first published in *Mind* 1905; 'Knowledge by Acquaintance and Knowledge by Description' in *Proceedings of the Aristotelian Society* 1910–11; it is reprinted in *Mysticism and Logic* (Allen & Unwin, London: 1917). In this latter paper Russell attributes a Fregean position to Miss Jones and criticises it as such.

10 *Mind* 1910 pp. 395–409.

11 Some years ago there was a controversy between H. Hochberg and J.O. Nelson concerning this aspect of Moore's early philosophy (the relevant papers are reprinted in part 2 of *Studies in the Philosophy of G.E. Moore* ed. E.D. Klemke (University of Illinois, Chicago: 1969)). Since neither Hochberg nor Nelson realised that Moore changed his views in 1898 concerning concepts, particulars, and universals, much of their controversy was beside the point.

12 H. Hochberg has tried to resuscitate Moore's arguments in 'Moore and Russell on Particulars, Relations, and Identity' in *Studies in the Philosophy of G.E. Moore*. I confess that I find his argument no more persuasive than Moore's.

13 cf. G.F. Stout 'The Nature of Universals and Propositions' in his *Studies in Philosophy and Psychology* (Macmillan, London: 1930); D.C. Williams 'The Elements of Being' *Review of Metaphysics* 1953.

14 cf. 'Are the characteristics of particular things universal or particular?' in *PP*.

15 Moore's unpublished review of Russell's *Principles of Mathematics*.

16 In B. Russell *Essays in Analysis* ed. D. Lackey (Allen & Unwin, London: 1973).

17 cf. R. Grossman *Meinong* (Routledge, London: 1974) p. 6.

18 A denial of 'contents' is of course later maintained by Sartre, whose conception of consciousness is in this respect remarkably similar to that of Moore; thus the notorious anti-idealist argument of the 'ontological proof' in the introduction to *Being and Nothingness* is essentially the same as that of RI.

19 Moore *Mind* 1910 pp. 395–409.
20 G.E. Moore 'Mr. McTaggart's "Studies in Hegelian Cosmology" *Proceedings of the Aristotelian Society* 1901–2.
21 cf. B. Williams 'Personal Identity and Individuation' in his *Problems of the Self* (Cambridge University Press, Cambridge: 1973); for later discussions cf. *The Identities of Persons* ed. A. Rorty (University of California Press, London: 1976).
22 I cannot locate this exact phrase in William James's *Principles of Psychology* (Macmillan, London: 1890), but it is certainly the central thesis of chapter X of that work.
23 G.E. Moore 'The Subject-Matter of Psychology' *Proceedings of the Aristotelian Society* 1909–10 p. 52.
24 ibid. p. 54.
25 But it is notable that Bertrand Russell, following Moore, makes the same claim in *The Philosophy of Leibniz* (Allen & Unwin, London: 1900) p. 24.
26 B. Russell 'Meinong's Theory of Complexes and Assumptions' in *Essays in Analysis* ed. Lackey (Allen & Unwin, London: 1973) p. 75.
27 Moore's influence is apparent in Russell's *Principles of Mathematics* p. 454 and 'Meinong's Theory of Complexes and Assumptions' pp. 26–7, 45. For a full account of Russell's views about necessity during this period, see N. Griffin 'Russell on the Nature of Logic (1903–1913)' *Synthese* 1980 esp. p. 122.
28 Russell also employs the semantic conception of necessity as universality (cf. 'Meinong's Theory of Complexes and Assumptions' pp. 26–7, 45) and Moore may have taken it from him; unlike Moore, Russell explicitly describes it as an account of necessity and juxtaposes it with the proof-theoretic account presented by Moore in N. When Russell became more ontologically parsimonious, he, like Moore, introduced reference to possible worlds and defined necessity in the Leibnizian way as truth in all possible worlds; *The Problems of Philosophy* (Williams & Norgate, London: 1912) p. 121.
29 J.S. Mill *Utilitarianism* ed. M. Warnock (Fontana, London: 1962) p. 255.
30 J.M. Keynes 'My Early Beliefs' in *Two Memoirs* (Hart-Davis, London: 1949) p. 85.

## *Chapter III: The naturalistic fallacy*

1 In *The Letters of Virginia Woolf* vol. 1 ed. N. Nicholson (Hogarth, London: 1975) p. 340.
2 P. Geach *Truth, Love, and Immortality* (London, Hutchinson: 1979) pp. 174–5.
3 The work of this school most openly indebted to Moore is *The Right and the Good* by W.D. Ross (Clarendon, Oxford: 1930).
4 Moore alludes to both sets of lectures in his autobiography, but mistakes their order: *PGEM* pp. 23–4.
5 In J. Rawls *A Theory of Justice* (Clarendon, Oxford: 1970) esp. pp. 50–4.
6 There is a distinctly Moorean quality to R.M. Hare's objection to Rawls,

that he cannot dispense with a prior analysis of moral concepts; cf. 'Rawls'
Theory of Justice' reprinted in *Reading Rawls* ed. N. Daniels (Blackwell,
Oxford: 1975) esp. pp. 81–5.

7  Although Moore says nothing explicit about Plato on this issue, the
favourable reference to Plato on p. 178 of *PE* suggests that Moore does not
impute the naturalistic fallacy to him.

8  cf. H. Rashdall *The Theory of Good and Evil* (Clarendon, Oxford: 1905) vol.
I p. 135 fn. 1. H. Sidgwick himself acknowledges the importance of Price
in his *Outlines of the History of Ethics* (Macmillan, London: 5th ed. 1902)
pp. 224–6. There is a good discussion of the work of Price and similar
'moralists', and of their relation to Moore's ethical theory, in A. Prior's
*Logic and the basis of Ethics* (Clarendon, Oxford: 1949).

9  Quoted by B. McGuinness in his *Wittgenstein: A Life* (Duckworth, London:
1988) p. 109.

10  The draft preface occurs in C. Lewy's paper 'G.E. Moore on the Naturalistic
Fallacy' which is reprinted in *Studies in the Philosophy of Thought and Action*
ed. P. Strawson (Oxford University Press, London: 1968). Inspection of
Moore's draft shows that Moore would have accepted many of the criticisms
of his position advanced by W. Frankena in his famous paper 'The
Naturalistic Fallacy', in *Theories of Ethics* ed. P. Foot (Oxford University
Press, London: 1967).

11  In Lewy op. cit. p. 139.

12  cf. P. Geach 'Good and Evil' in *Theories of Ethics* ed. P. Foot (Oxford
University Press, London: 1967); B. Williams *Morality: An Introduction to
Ethics* (Penguin, Harmondsworth: 1973) pp. 52ff.

13  Geach 'Good and Evil' pp. 71–2.

14  Ross curiously says (op. cit. p. 66) that in our use of the expression 'good
sunset' we are 'half-personalizing' the sunset, 'thinking of it as succeeding
in that which all sunsets are trying to achieve'. This is precisely the absurd
thought which a literal application of Geach's principle would require.

15  There now arises the issue as to how a unified account of these uses of 'good'
is to be attained. On this cf. J. Mackie *Ethics* (Penguin, Harmondsworth:
1977) ch. 2.

16  Sidgwick does of course regard practical reason as indefinable and in some
sense not just a natural faculty of man; cf. H. Sidgwick *The Methods of Ethics*
(Macmillan, London: 7th ed. 1907) pp. 32–4. This has implications for his
account of goodness, since Sidgwick requires that those desires definitive of
my good be 'in harmony with reason' (p. 112). The interpretation of this is
disputed, but if Sidgwick here means practical reason, then perhaps he does
not offer an entirely naturalistic analysis of goodness.

17  J.S. Mill *Utilitarianism* ed. M. Warnock (Fontana, London: 1962) p. 288.

18  Sidgwick does not himself propose this application of his account of
desirability to Mill. He holds that Mill's 'desirable' is to be interpreted as
'ought to be desired' (*The Methods of Ethics* p. 388), and anticipates Moore's
argument against Mill (p. 388 fn. 2). It would have been nice to attribute
the argument of this footnote to the young G.E. Moore, since Sidgwick says
that he is here responding to a suggestion by someone else; but the footnote
appears in too early an edition for this to be correct.

19 Mill op. cit. p. 289.

20 M. Warnock *Ethics Since 1900* (Oxford University Press, London: 2nd ed. 1966) p. 16.

21 1921 draft preface in Lewy op.cit. pp. 134–5.

22 B. Russell 'The Elements of Ethics' in his *Philosophical Essays* (Allen & Unwin, London: 1910) p. 17. Russell seems to have had a habit of taking over the title of Moore's lectures for his publications; cf. also *SMPP* and *The Problems of Philosophy*.

23 Similar proposals for the analysis of goodness had been made by C.D. Broad, in *Five Types of Ethical Theory* (Kegan Paul, London: 1930), and by A. Ewing in *The Definition of Good* (Routledge, London: 1948).

24 This essay, which was not written for the Apostles, is in Cambridge University Library.

25 For Hume as anticipating Moore's thesis that there is a naturalistic fallacy, cf. Prior op. cit. p. x; for Hume as a naturalist in ethics, cf. J. Kemp *Ethical Naturalism* (Macmillan, London: 1970). Hume himself realised that the application of the term 'natural' in ethics was a matter of controversy; cf. *Treatise* 3.1.1.

26 Moore himself writes of 'non-natural' properties only in *PGEM* (p. 581ff.). In *PE* and elsewhere he just denies that goodness is a natural or metaphysical property.

27 See Lewy op. cit. p. 137.

28 cf. B. Williams 'Internal and External Reasons' in *Moral Luck* (Cambridge University Press, Cambridge: 1981).

29 e.g. A. Flew *Evolutionary Ethics* (Macmillan, London: 1970) p. 38.

30 This is the passage in which Moore uses the phrase 'open question'; it has since been applied to the argument of section 13 of *PE*, although it does not occur there. The objection to reductionism I am here attributing to Moore is essentially that raised by Price and by Sidgwick (cf. Sidgwick *The Methods of Ethics* pp. 30–1, 375). Locke makes much the same point in his *Essay*: 'There cannot any one moral Rule be propos'd, whereof a man may not justly demand a Reason' (I.iii.4).

31 cf. Prior op. cit. pp. 7-8.

32 R.M. Hare *The Language of Morals* (Clarendon, Oxford: 1952) p. 30.

33 cf. P. Foot 'Morality as a System of Hypothetical Imperatives', reprinted in her *Virtues and Vices* (Blackwell, Oxford: 1978).

34 The 'thick/thin' distinction is due to B. Williams; cf. *Ethics and the Limits of Philosophy* (Fontana, London: 1985) pp. 129ff., to which I am much indebted throughout this chapter.

35 cf. J. McDowell 'Virtue and Reason' *Monist* 1979.

36 cf. H. Putnam *Reason, Truth, and History* (Cambridge University Press, Cambridge: 1981) pp. 206–8.

37 ibid. p. 208. It is worth stressing that Putnam only rejects Moore's argument; he is content to accept Moore's anti-reductionist conclusion, though for no discernible reason. His discussion of Moore's position is conducted under some substantive misapprehensions concerning it, but they do not, I think, affect the point of his objection to Moore's argument.

38 cf. A. MacIntyre *A Short History of Ethics* (Routledge, London: 1976) p. 251.

39 cf. *PGEM* p. 17. H. Sidgwick's lectures were published posthumously as *Lectures on the Ethics of Green, Spencer, and Martineau* (Macmillan, London: 1902).

40 cf. E.O. Wilson *On Human Nature* (Harvard University Press, London: 1978). But the piece of his which I have found most helpful is an essay on 'The Evolution of Ethics', written in collaboration with M. Ruse, in *New Scientist* 17 October 1985, and further references are to this essay.

41 Wilson and Ruse 'The Evolution of Ethics' p. 52.

42 ibid. p. 52.

43 cf. M.A.E. Dummett 'The Reality of the Past' in *Truth and Other Enigmas* (Duckworth, London: 1978) pp. 359–61.

44 ibid. pp. 360–1.

45 S. Blackburn *Spreading the Word* (Clarendon, Oxford: 1984) ch. 6.

46 But there is a substantive argument against supervenience by P. Winch in 'The Universalizability of Moral Judgments' in his *Ethics and Action* (Routledge, London: 1972).

47 S. Blackburn 'Supervenience Revisited' in *Exercises in Analysis* ed. I. Hacking (Cambridge University Press, Cambridge: 1985).

48 cf. Williams *Ethics and the Limits of Philosophy* ch. 8.

49 *Butler's Sermons* ed. W.R. Matthews (Bell, London: 1949) p. 64.

50 H.A. Prichard 'Does Moral Philosophy Rest on a Mistake?' in *Moral Obligation* (Clarendon, Oxford: 1968) esp. pp. 16–17.

51 Sidgwick *The Methods of Ethics* p. 102.

52 Rawls op. cit. pp. 34–5.

53 cf. J. Feinberg 'Rawls and Intuitionism' in *Reading Rawls* ed. N. Daniels (Blackwell, Oxford: 1975).

54 Williams 'Internal and External Reasons'.

55 Moore uses this argument in *PE* (p. 201) against subjectivist accounts of beauty. The argument is presented in much the form that Moore employs it in *E* by Sidgwick (cf. *The Methods of Ethics* p. 27), from whom Moore doubtless took it. But it was not invented by Sidgwick; it occurs in the work of Richard Price, from whom Sidgwick may well have taken it.

56 Published in 1923 by Routledge, London.

57 Hare op. cit.

58 cf. Williams *Ethics and the Limits of Philosophy* pp. 124–6.

59 Blackburn 'Supervenience Revisited' p. 56.

60 cf. Blackburn *Spreading the word*; Williams *Ethics and the Limits of Philosophy* ch. 8. D. Wiggins's paper 'Truth, Invention, and the Meaning of Life' (*Proceedings of the British Academy* 1976) is an important example of work in this area.


## Chapter IV: Ideal utilitarianism

1 The term 'ideal utilitarianism' comes from H. Rashdall *The Theory of Good and Evil* (Clarendon, Oxford: 1905). Rashdall alludes to *PE*, but makes it clear that he arrived at his views independently (p. vii). Moore wrote a dry and ungracious review of the book (*Hibbert Journal* 1907–8 pp. 447–8), but

later referred to it favourably in *E* (p. 133).

2 H.A. Pritchard cf. 'Duty and Ignorance of Fact' in *Moral Obligation* (Clarendon, Oxford: 1968) esp. pp. 34–5.

3 cf. T. Nagel *The View from Nowhere* (Clarendon, Oxford: 1986) pp. 164ff.; D. Parfit *Reasons and Persons* (Clarendon, Oxford: 1984) pp. 54–5. The agent-neutral/agent-relative distinction is apparent in Bernard Williams's discussion of promise-keeping in *Utilitarianism: For and Against* (Cambridge University Press, Cambridge: 1973) pp. 88–9; it is also hinted at by R. Nozick in *Anarchy, State, and Utopia* (Blackwell, Oxford: 1974) note to p. 29. I think that Prichard had something like the agent-relativity of obligations in mind when he insisted that obligation is an attribute of agents and not of ends (*Moral Obligation* pp. 92–5); and there are close similarities between agent-relativity and Broad's conception of 'self-referential altruism' (*PGEM* pp. 51ff.) to which Moore unfortunately made no response in his reply to his critics.

4 Nozick op. cit. pp. 28ff.

5 Deontologists such as Ross of course included some positive duties among their list of *prima facie* duties. None the less, even for him, the emphasis is on the negative duty of avoiding evil rather than doing good; cf. W.D. Ross *The Foundation of Ethics* (Clarendon, Oxford: 1939) p. 75.

6 cf. e.g. P. Foot 'Utilitarianism and the Virtues' *Mind* 1985; S. Scheffler 'Agent-centred Restrictions, Rationality, and the Virtues' *Mind* 1985; Nagel op. cit. pp. 159ff.

7 Thus Nagel op. cit. pp. 175ff.; C. Fried *Right and Wrong* (Harvard University Press, London: 1978) ch. 1; and, of course, G.E.M. Anscombe 'Modern Moral Philosophy' *Philosophy* 1958.

8 It is notable that both Nagel and Fried switch from the claim that we are primarily responsible for what we intend to do to the claim that we are likewise responsible for what we choose to do without realising that they thereby undermine the significance they attach to the foresight/intention distinction. cf. Nagel op. cit. p. 183; Fried op. cit. p. 25.

9 cf. S. Scheffler *The Rejection of Consequentialism* (Clarendon, Oxford: 1982); M. Slote 'Satisficing Consequentialism' *Aristotelian Society Supplementary Volume* 1984.

10 cf. Williams op. cit.

11 cf. B. Williams *Moral Luck* (Cambridge University Press, Cambridge: 1981) pp. ix–x.

12 cf. H. Rashdall *The Theory of God and Evil* (Clarendon, Oxford: 1905) vol. I pp. 189ff.; W. Ross *The Right and the Good* (Clarendon, Oxford: 1930) pp. 134–5.

13 But F.M. Cornford did draw precisely this consequence in his delightful Moorean essay *Micro-cosmographica Academica* (Bowes & Bowes, Cambridge: 8th ed. 1970): 'Even a little knowledge of ethical theory will suffice to convince you that all important questions are so complicated, and the results of any course of action are so difficult to foresee, that certainty, or even probability, is seldom, if ever, attained. It follows at once that the only justifiable attitude of mind is suspense of judgment' (p. 14).

14 cf. A. Adkins *Merit and Responsibility* (University of Chicago Press, Chicago:

1975) for a discussion of this theme in Greek ethical thought.

15 Nuclear weapons have now altered the situation; Moore's argument has no purchase against a pessimist who can now destroy the whole human race!

16 Moore probably took this point from McTaggart; cf. *Studies in Hegelian Cosmology* (Cambridge University Press, Cambridge: 1901) p. 99.

17 R.M. Hare *Moral Thinking* (Clarendon, Oxford: 1981) ch 2, 3.

18 In his review of *PE* in the *Independent Review* 1904.

19 Prichard op. cit.

20 H.A. Prichard 'Does Moral Philosophy Rest on a Mistake?' in *Moral Obligation* (Clarendon, Oxford: 1968).

21 A point made almost at once by Rashdall in response to *PE*; op. cit. p. 79 fn.

22 B. Williams *Problems of the Self* (Cambridge University Press, Cambridge: 1973) p. 258.

23 Moore has another attempt at showing that egoism is self-contradictory in *PGEM* (pp. 611ff.); but, as Broad showed, his argument is fallacious – cf. A&L pp. 371ff.

24 T. Nagel *The Possibility of Altruism* (Clarendon, Oxford: 1970).

25 Nagel *The View from Nowhere* p. 159.

26 B. Williams *The Project of Pure Enquiry* (Penguin, Harmondsworth: 1978) pp. 245ff.

27 'Is there a Duty to Hate?', delivered in 1900; the manuscript is in Cambridge University Library.

28 cf. Ross *The Right and the Good* p. 71.

29 In the *Independent Review* 1904.

30 cf. J. Passmore *Man's Responsibility for Nature* (Duckworth, London: 1976) ch. 1.

31 G.E. Moore 'Is Goodness a Quality?' *PP* pp. 94–5.

32 C. Bell *Civilisation* (Chatto & Windus, London: 1928) ch. IV.

33 ibid. pp. 198–9.

34 cf. J.M. Keynes 'My Early Beliefs', in *Two Memoirs* (Hart-Davis, London: 1949).

35 C. Bell *Old Friends* (Chatto & Windus, London: 1956) p. 30.

36 L. Woolf *Sowing* (Hogarth, London: 1960) pp. 147–9.

37 Bell *Civilisation* p. 168.

38 In the final entry in *CB* (pp. 409–10) Moore says more about the way in which non-human animals make voluntary movements. His comments here depart from the position presented in *E* and are quite perceptive.

39 Reprinted in J.L. Austin *Philosophical Papers* (Clarendon, Oxford: 3rd ed. 1979). Austin took (without acknowledgement) his central criticism of Moore from Prichard's paper 'Duty and Ignorance of Fact'; cf. p. 33.

40 D. Dennett *Elbow Room* (Clarendon, Oxford: 1984) p. 144.

41 cf. R. Chisholm's review of Austin's *Philosophical Papers* in *Mind* 1964; D. Pears: 'Ifs and Cans' in his *Questions in the Philosophy of Mind* (Duckworth, London: 1975).

42 cf. P. van Inwagen 'The Incompatibility of Free Will and Determinism' in *Free Will* ed. G. Watson (Oxford University Press, Oxford: 1982) and his *An Essay on Free Will* (Clarendon, Oxford: 1983).

43 cf. esp. A. Gallois 'Van Inwagen on Free Will and Determinism' and J. Narveson 'Compatibilism Defended', both in *Philosophical Studies* 1977.

44 Van Inwagen *Essay on Free Will* p. 68.

45 cf. Chisholm op. cit. and 'Human Freedom and the Self', in *Free Will* ed. G. Watson (Oxford University Press, Oxford: 1982) esp. pp. 26–7.

46 I take this way of thinking about Chisholm's argument from B. Aune 'Hypotheticals and "Can": another look', in *Free Will* ed. G. Watson (Oxford University Press, Oxford: 1982). The basic idea of such a triad is due to K. Lehrer, cf. his 'An Empirical Disproof of Determinism' in *Freedom and Determinism* ed. Lehrer (Random House, New York: 1966). Lehrer's argument is slightly different from Chisholm's and in my view Moore can plausibly deny the consistency of Lehrer's triad in any sense other than that provided by the determinist.

47 J. Locke *Essay concerning Human Understanding* II.xi.13.

48 cf. J. Feinberg 'What is so Special about Mental Illness?' in *Doing and Deserving* (Princeton University Press, Princeton: 1970) esp. pp. 288–9.

49 H.G. Frankfurt 'Freedom of the Will and the Concept of a Person' in *Free Will* ed. G. Watson (Oxford University Press, Oxford: 1982) p. 90.

50 cf. H.G. Frankfurt 'Alternate Possibilities and Moral Responsibility' *Journal of Philosophy* 1969.

51 ibid. p. 837.

52 cf. D. Davidson 'Freedom to Act' in his *Essays on Actions and Events* (Clarendon, Oxford: 1980) pp. 79ff.

## Chapter V: Pure realism rejected

1 Letter to Desmond MacCarthy, June 1900.

2 cf. F. Dretske 'Conclusive Reasons' in *Essays in Knowledge and Justification* ed. G. Pappas and M. Swain (Cornell University Press, Ithaca, NY: 1978).

3 In the sense of the 'external/internal' contrast discussed by A. Goldman in 'The Internalist Conception of Justification' in *Midwest Studies in Epistemology* vol. 5 ed. P.A. French, T.E. Uehling, and H.K. Wettstein (University of Minnesota Press, Minneapolis: 1980).

4 Moore uses similar language to affirm a naive realist position in *SMPP* (p. 137): 'And moreover, at the moment when I do look at my hand, I find it very difficult to believe that that the colours which I see are not *really on* the surface of the hand – in the very same place in which the surface of the hand – the material object – is. The conviction that these things are so seems to me so overwhelming.' A reference in Moore's early notes implies that he is here quoting from Lotze (some of whose writings Moore studied as an undergraduate); but I have not been able to find any talk of similar 'overwhelming convictions' in Lotze's writings.

5 Lorenz Kruger has recently called attention to the fact that Moore's treatment of philosophy as a collection of problems is a distinctive feature of a conception of the subject which owes much to Moore and Russell; cf. his 'Why do we Study the History of Philosophy?' in *Philosophy in History* ed. A. Rorty, J.B. Schneewind, and Q.R.D. Skinner (Cambridge University

Press, Cambridge: 1984).

6 Russell alludes to Moore's lectures in the preface to *The Problems of Philosophy* (1912), and Moore's influence on the first four chapters of Russell's book is obvious. It was Russell's use here of Moore's conception of a sense-datum that fixed the 'sense-datum' terminology for later philosophers; sense-data were whatever satisfied the Moorean theory Russell here presented.

7 Originally published in *Mind* (1905); my page references are to it as reprinted in *Logic and Knowledge* ed. R. Marsh (Allen & Unwin, London: 1956).

8 T. Reid *Essays on the Intellectual Powers of Man* (Edinburgh, 1785) p. 594.

9 This is central to chapter 2 of Essay VI ibid.

10 I take it that Moore does indeed change his mind in the course of his lectures, in that he shifts from the pure realist view of propositions upheld in chapter III to the 'as if' theory of chapter XIV. In his (1953) preface Moore suggests that chapter III can also be understood in terms of the 'as if' theory, and thus that there is no essential conflict between his positions in chapters III and XIV. But this is not a tenable interpretation of chapter III, which includes an emphatic commitment to an ontology of propositions (cf. the passage quoted on p. 160 of this book); furthermore on p. 300 Moore writes of a change of view about things which *are* but do not exist that is best explained by a genuine change of mind concerning propositions.

11 Upholders of D. Lewis's concrete realism concerning possible worlds will not be moved by this argument; cf. *On the Plurality of Worlds* (Blackwell, Oxford: 1986). But I find Lewis's position incredible (and unnecessary).

12 Russell *Logic and Knowledge* pp. 46–7.

13 B. Russell *Principia Mathematica* (Cambridge University Press, Cambridge: 1910) p. 43.

14 cf. B. Russell 'The Nature of Truth' *Mind* 1906; 'On the Nature of Truth' *Proceedings of the Aristotelian Society* 1906–7, parts (i) and (ii) of which are reprinted in *Philosophical Essays* (Allen & Unwin, London: 1910), and form the basis of chapter XII of *The Problems of Philosophy* (Williams & Norgate, London: 1912).

15 F.P. Ramsey *The Foundations of Mathematics* (Routledge, London: 1931) p. 143.

16 Page references are to the 1907 edition (Longman, London).

17 This point is forcibly made by S. Haack in 'The Pragmatist Theory of Truth' *British Journal for the Philosophy of Science* 1976, esp. pp. 233–4.

18 This is the response Haack attributes to James. She acknowledges that it is not satisfactory.

19 James himself was not impressed by Moore's arguments. Referring to WJP he wrote to H.M. Kallen of 'Moore's pretentious fiasco in the last Aristotelian Society proceedings'; *The Meaning of Truth* (Harvard University Press, London: 1975) p. 305. By contrast James had a high opinion of Russell's critical essays, which are contemporary with Moore's; cf. chapters iv and v of Russell's *Philosophical Essays*. Russell's essays are more sympathetic to James than WJP is, but they just focus on the thesis that truth of a belief consists in its possession of practical value. James replied quite effectively to Russell in *The Meaning of Truth* (esp. ch. XIV).

20 cf. esp. 'The Reality of the Past' in M.A.E. Dummett's collection *Truth and Other Enigmas* (Duckworth, London: 1978).

## Chapter VI: Logic and fictions

1 P. Strawson *Introduction to Logical Theory* (Methuen, London: 1952).

2 Quoted by N. Malcolm in 'Moore and Wittgenstein on the Sense of "I Know"' in his collection *Thought and Knowledge* (Cornell University Press, Ithaca, NY: 1977) p. 174.

3 B. Russell *Our Knowledge of the External World* (Allen & Unwin, London: 1922) p. v.

4 The second editionn of S. Stebbing *A Modern Introduction to Logic* was published in 1933 (Methuen, London). J. Wisdom's *Logical Constructions* first appeared as a set of articles in *Mind* during the period 1931–3; in 1969 these were republished as a book by Random House (New York), and my page references are to this reprint.

5 B. Russell *Principia Mathematica* (Cambridge University Press, Cambridge: 1910) p. 66.

6 Stebbing op. cit. pp. 155–6.

7 Russell *Principia Mathematica* p. 81.

8 cf. B. Russell 'The Relation of Sense-Data to Physics' in *Mysticism and Logic* (Allen & Unwin, London: 1917) p. 115.

9 cf. Russell's 'supreme maxim in scientific philosophising': *'whenever possible, logical constructions are to be substituted for inferred entities'*; ibid. p. 115.

10 Wisdom op. cit. p. 46.

11 From Russell's 'Lectures on the Philosophy of Logical Atomism', reprinted in B. Russell *Logic and Knowledge* ed. R. Marsh (Allen & Unwin, London: 1956) p. 232.

12 In his addendum to his reply in *PGEM* Moore suggests that when 'exists' is predicated of physical objects it does not always have the meaning which it has when predicated of sense-data; in the former case it can mean 'is a physical object', which it never means in the latter case (*PGEM* pp. 686–7). This implausible view about an ambiguity in 'exists' does not, I think, occur elsewhere, and it is best regarded as an aberration into which Moore is tempted by difficulties in his sense-datum theory.

13 cf. e.g. M. Sainsbury *Russell* (Routledge, London: 1979) p. 82.

14 As of course Lewis recognizes; cf. D. Lewis *On the Plurality of Worlds* (Blackwell, Oxford: 1986) ch. 4.

15 Russell *Principia Mathematica* p. 175; cf. his 'The Relation of Sense-Data to Physics' p. 115.

16 F.P. Ramsey *The Foundations of Mathematics* (Routledge, London: 1931) p. 143.

17 The arguments propounded here by Ramsey and Moore look forward to more recent debates about the necessity of identity initiated by S. Kripke and others; Moore's position anticipates Kripke's distinction between strong and weak necessity – cf. *Naming and Necessity* (Blackwell, Oxford: 1980) pp. 109–10. In a recent note Allen Hazen reformulates Moore's refutation

of Ramsey in the modern idioms of modal logic (giving due credit to
Moore): cf. 'A Fallacy in Ramsey' *Mind* 1986. Incidentally, Moore did not
take the thesis of the necessity of numerical identity and difference from
Ramsey; it is, for example, explicit in CIV – cf. pp. 262–3.
18 G. Evans *The Varieties of Reference* (Clarendon, Oxford: 1982) pp. 173,
199–200. Much the same position is developed by J. McDowell in *'De Re
Senses'* in *Frege: Tradition and Influence* ed. C. Wright (Blackwell, Oxford:
1984). The position is criticised by S. Blackburn in *Spreading the Word*
(Clarendon, Oxford: 1984) pp. 316ff. and by H. Noonan in 'Russellian
Thoughts and Methodological Solipsism' in *Language, Mind and Logic* ed. J.
Butterfield (Cambridge University Press, Cambridge: 1986).
19 Moore faced a similar difficulty concerning tense. He recognised early on
both the token-reflexiveness of tensed utterances and the irreducibility of
tense (cf. *CB* pp. 87–9, 97–9). But, because of his one-level theory of
meaning, he could never develop a satisfactory account of the matter.
20 J.L. Austin *Sense and Sensibilia* (Clarendon, Oxford: 1962) p. 70.
21 cf. e.g. W.V. Quine *Word and Object* (MIT Press, Cambridge, Mass.: 1960)
section 32.
22 D. Lewis 'Truth in Fiction' in his *Philosophical Papers* vol. 1 (Oxford
University Press, Oxford: 1983) pp. 265–6.
23 ibid.
24 Kripke op. cit. pp. 80–1.
25 cf. G. Evans 'The Causal Theory of Names' in his *Collected Papers*
(Clarendon, Oxford: 1985).

## Chapter VII: Philosophical analysis

1 Reprinted in A&L p. 25.
2 J. Wilson *Logical Constructions* (Random House, New York: 1969) p. 50.
3 A. Duncan-Jones 'Does Philosophy Analyse Common Sense?' *Aristotelian
Society Supplementary Volume* 1937 p. 147.
4 *Aristotelian Society Supplementary Volume* 1919 p. 193.
5 cf. B. Russell 'Lectures on the Philosophy of Logical Atomism' in *Logic and
Knowledge* ed. R. Marsh (Allen & Unwin, London: 1956) p. 226.
6 ibid. p. 226.
7 The way to see this is to recognise that Quine's 'relational' construal of
propositional attitudes is a notational variant of Russell's theory; hence the
difficulty about the need for a multiplicity of such attitudes which arose for
Quine. This was removed by the use of a Tarski-style reduction to one
single relational form for each attitude, one of whose terms is a sequence
(the number of whose members can vary from case to case); cf. J. Wallace
'Belief and Satisfaction' *Nous* 1972.
8 R. Carnap *Logische Syntax der Sprache* (Springer, Vienna: 1934); translated as
*The Logical Syntax of Language* (Kegan Paul, London: 1937).
9 J.M. Keynes *Formal Logic* (Macmillan, London: 4th ed. 1906); cf. esp. part
II ch. 1. I myself doubt whether Moore's interpretation of Keynes is correct.
10 For an account of the history of the translation argument, see C. Lewy

*Meaning and Modality* (Cambridge University Press, Cambridge: 1976) p. 8, n. 2.

11 cf. W.V. Quine *Word and Object* (MIT Press, Cambridge, Mass.: 1960) p. 214.

12 I take this idea from Lewy op. cit. pp. 48ff.

13 cf. H. Field 'Mental Representation' in *Readings in Philosophy of Psychology* ed. N.J. Block vol. II (Methuen, London: 1980).

14 D. Davidson 'On Saying That' in his *Inquiries into Truth and Interpretation* (Clarendon, Oxford: 1984).

15 cf. D. Davidson 'Quotation', in *Inquiries into Truth and Interpretation* (Clarendon, Oxford: 1984). Moore sketched the basic idea of a demonstrative theory in an entry in his 1941–2 notebook (*CB* pp. 167–8). The idea was, I believe, first set out publicly by C. Whiteley, in 'Names of Words: A Note on *Analysis* Problem No. 10' *Analysis* 1956–7. cf. also A. Prior *Objects of Thought* (Clarendon, Oxford: 1971) pp. 60–1.

16 Davidson 'On Saying That' pp. 98–9.

17 ibid. p. 99.

18 The thesis that linguistic self-reference should be employed in a statement of the quotational analysis is argued for by T. Burge in 'On Davidson's "Saying That"' in *Truth and Interpretation: Perspectives on the Philosophy of D. Davidson* ed. E. Le Pore (Blackwell, Oxford: 1986).

19 cf. Prior op. cit. ch. 2; W.V. Quine *Philosophy of Logic* (Prentice-Hall, Englewood Cliffs, NJ: 1970) pp. 32–3.

20 Field op. cit.

21 cf. the accounts offered by R. Montague himself in 'English as a Formal Language' in his *Formal Philosophy* (Yale University Press, New Haven, Conn.: 1974).

22 A. Church *Journal of Symbolic Logic* 1946 pp. 132–3.

23 The generalisation is set out by Church in 'A Formulation of the Logic of Sense and Denotation' in *Structure, Meaning, and Method* ed. P. Henle, H.M. Kallen, and S.K. Langer (Liberal Arts, New York: 1951) pp. 3–24.

24 cf. D. Davidson 'Theories of Meaning and Learnable Languages' in *Inquiries into Truth and Interpretation* (Clarendon, Oxford: 1984) p. 15.

25 This kind of solution to the paradox of analysis was advocated by Prior in *Objects of Thought*.

26 The 'rigid/non-rigid' distinction comes from S. Kripke, *Naming and Necessity* (Blackwell, Oxford: 1980) cf. esp. the preface.

27 M.A.E. Dummett has denied that this requirement can be met. But he offers no argument for this thesis; cf. *Frege: Philosophy of Language* (Duckworth, London: 1973) p. 95.

28 Wittgenstein submitted the *Tractatus* for the Ph.D. degree and Moore was an examiner for this. According to Braithwaite (op. cit. p. 30), Moore concluded his report with the comment: 'I myself consider that this is a work of genius; but even if I am completely mistaken and it is nothing of the sort, it is well above the standard required for the Ph.D. degree.'

29 These notes are appendix II in the edition of Wittgenstein's *Notebooks 1914–16* edited by G.E.M. Anscombe and G.H. von Wright and translated by Anscombe (Blackwell, Oxford: 1961).

30 Moore's unpublished review of Russell's *Principles of Mathematics*.

31 N. Tennant 'Entailment and Proofs' *Proceedings of the Aristotelian Society* 1979–80.

32 In a letter to him written in 1935, and now preserved among the Moore papers in Cambridge, Sir Roy Harrod writes, concerning the book, 'The possibility of its appearance is largely due to a very handsome testimonial which you wrote for him about a year ago.'

33 cf. A.J. Ayer *Part of My Life* (Oxford University Press, Oxford: 1977) p. 166.

34 B. Russell 'Knowledge by Acquaintance and Knowledge by Description' in *Mysticism and Logic* (Allen & Unwin, London: 1917) p. 159.

35 G. Evans *The Varieties of Reference* (Clarendon, Oxford: 1982) ch. 4.

36 Russell 'Knowledge by Acquaintance and Knowledge by Description' p. 159.

37 cf. S. Blackburn *Spreading the Word* (Clarendon, Oxford: 1984) pp. 316ff.; H. Noonan 'Russellian Thoughts and Methodological Solipsism' in *Language, Mind and Logic* ed. J. Butterfield (Cambridge University Press, Cambridge: 1986).

38 N. Malcolm *Ludwig Wittgenstein: A Memoir* (Oxford University Press, Oxford: 2nd ed. 1984) p. 56.

39 cf. e.g. J. Hintikka *Knowledge and Belief* (Cornell University Press, Ithaca, NY: 1962) pp. 78ff.

40 cf. J. Williams 'Moore's Paradox: One or Two?' *Analysis* 1979.

41 H.P. Grice 'The Causal Theory of Perception' in *Perceiving, Sensing, and Knowing* ed. R. Swarz (Anchor, New York; 1965) esp. pp. 444–51.

42 M.F. Burnyeat 'Belief in Speech' *Proceedings of the Aristotelian Society* 1967–8 esp. pp. 232–3.

43 This is the conclusion drawn by M. Black in 'Saying and Disbelieving' in *Philosophy and Analysis* ed. M. MacDonald (Blackwell, Oxford: 1954) p. 116. E.H. Wolgast takes a similar view in chapter iv of *Paradoxes of Knowledge* (Cornell University Press, London: 1977).

44 G. Ryle *Concept of Mind* (Penguin, Harmondsworth: 1963) p. 125.

45 Here, therefore, I agree with one of the earliest commentators on Moore's paradox, A. MacIver; cf. his 'Some Questions about "Know" and "Think"' in *Philosophy and Analysis* ed. M. MacDonald (Blackwell, Oxford: 1954) p. 95.

46 L. Wittgenstein *Culture and Value* trans. P. Winch (Blackwell, Oxford: 1980) p. 76.

47 Why does Wittgenstein include 'wish' and 'will' here? What would be the paradoxical sentences for them? In his paper 'Some Paradoxes of Counterprivacy: G.E. Moore, Socrates, Descartes', Andre Gombay has argued that the Socratic paradox that no one willingly does wrong is the analogue of Moore's paradox for the case of the will; cf. 'Some Paradoxes of Counterprivacy' *Philosophy* 1988. I am indebted to Gombay's paper for some of the ideas in the last part of this section.

## Chapter VIII: Sense-data and perception

1 G.A. Paul 'Is There a Problem about Sense-Data?' as reprinted in *Perceiving, Sensing, and Knowing* ed. R. Swartz (Anchor, New York: 1965). Paul had studied with Moore in Cambridge, and contributed an attractive account of Moore's work to *The Revolution in Philosophy* (Macmillan, London: 1956).
2 B. Russell 'The Relation of Sense-Data to Physics' in *Mysticism and Logic* (Allen & Unwin, London: 1917).
3 Moore presents much the same argument in 'Are the Materials of Sense Affections of the Mind?' *Proceedings of the Aristotelian Society* 1916–17. In this case the reply to Moore by Dawes Hicks in the same symposium both criticises Moore effectively and advances the alternative 'theory of appearing' in a persuasive way. For another argument by Moore for the same thesis, cf. *CB* p. 79.
4 G.F. Stout 'The Status of Sense-Data' *Proceedings of the Aristotelian Society* 1913–14 p. 402.
5 The classic statement of this objection is 'The Problem of Empiricism' by R. Chisholm in *Perceiving, Sensing, and Knowing* ed. R. Swartz (Anchor, New York: 1965).
6 cf. P. Strawson *Individuals* (Methuen, London: 1959) ch. 2; G. Evans 'Thinking of Objects' in his *Collected Papers* (Oxford, Clarendon: 1985).
7 I simplify DCS a bit here, and also follow the accounts given in *LP* (p. 87) and *EP* (p. 123).
8 H. Price *Perception* (Methuen, London: 1932) p. 70.
9 For a recent discussion of the matter see F. Dretske *Knowledge and the Flow of Information* (Blackwell, Oxford: 1981) pp. 153ff.
10 For a recent instance of the strategy see F. Jackson *Perception* (Cambridge University Press, Cambridge: 1977) pp. 147–51.
11 Stout op. cit. p. 390.
12 Jackson op. cit. ch. 1.
13 ibid. p. 18.
14 cf. Stout op. cit.; H.A. Prichard *Kant's Theory of Knowledge* (Clarendon, Oxford: 1909) pp. 72ff., Dawes Hicks op. cit.
15 The point I have been pressing was in effect made by A.J. Ayer in his 1945 paper 'The Terminology of Sense-Data' reprinted in Ayer's *Philosophical Essays* (Macmillan, London: 1954). Ayer's paper drew a response from Moore, in the addendum, pp. 677–87, to his reply in *PGEM*. Ayer responded, quite effectively to my mind, in a long footnote on pp. 83–6 of the reprinted paper.
16 cf. G. Evans *The Varieties of Reference* (Clarendon, Oxford: 1982); J. McDowell 'De Re Senses' in *Frege: Tradition and Influence* ed. C. Wright (Blackwell, Oxford: 1984); S. Blackburn *Spreading the Word* (Clarendon, Oxford: 1984); H. Noonan 'Russellian Thoughts and Methodological Solipsism?' in *Language, Mind and Logic* ed. J. Butterfield (Cambridge University Press, Cambridge: 1986).
17 Mace raised this issue in his contribution to *PGEM* (p. 294). Moore did not respond to this aspect of Mace's paper in his reply in *PGEM*, but he discusses it in an entry in *CB* (pp. 234–5). He clearly does not want to

concede the point, but in fact offers no substantive objection to it.

18 Alan White thinks he gives six: cf. *G.E. Moore* (Blackwell, Oxford: 1958) pp. 153–64. But the criteria of individuation in this matter are not precise.

19 ibid. p. 176.

20 D.J. O'Connor *The Metaphysics of G.E. Moore* (Reidel, London: 1982) p. 103.

21 cf. G.E.M. Anscombe 'The Intentionality of Sensation: A Grammatical Feature' in vol. 2 of her *Collected Papers* (Blackwell, Oxford: 1981).

22 cf. F. Dretske *Seeing and Knowing* (Routledge, London: 1969) pp. 43ff.

23 Anscombe op. cit. p. 15.

24 R. Chisholm *Theory of Knowledge* (Prentice Hall, Englewood Cliffs, NJ: 1966) pp. 30–2.

25 D.M. Armstrong *Perception and the Physical World* (Routledge, London: 1961) p. 128; *A Materialist Theory of Mind* (Routledge, London: 1968) p. 236.

26 For further arguments against the doxastic theory see Jackson op. cit. ch. 2.

27 An account of this kind is advanced by J. Hintikka in 'Information, Causality, and the Logic of Perception' in *The Intentions of Intentionality and Other New Models for Modalities* (Reidel, Dordrecht: 1975).

28 This distinction is similar to Peacocke's distinction between 'sensational' and 'representational' properties of experience; cf. C.B. Peacock *Sense and Content* (Clarendon, Oxford: 1983) ch. 1.

29 Thus when J.R. Searle maintains that the representational content of sense-experience is 'determined by' by the 'phenomenal properties' of sense-experience (*Intentionality* (Cambridge University Press, Cambridge: 1983) p. 61) he needs to provide an account of the nature and role of these phenomenal properties. In fact he says nothing at all about them, and thus fails to provide any alternative to the representative theories of perception he criticises.

30 The basic idea of the theory of appearing is in principle consistent with a purely representational account of appearances. But in practice the views of Dawes Hicks and others are best interpreted in the light of the adverbial theory.

31 cf. C.J. Ducasse 'Moore's Refutation of Idealism' in *PGEM*; Chisholm *Theory of Knowledge* pp. 95ff.; M. Tye 'The Adverbial Approach to Visual Experience' *Philosophical Review* 1984.

32 Jackson op. cit. pp. 60–9.

33 Tye op. cit. pp. 218ff.

34 Jackson op. cit. ch. 4.

35 cf. W.H.F. Barnes 'The Myth of Sense-Data' in *Perceiving, Sensing, and Knowing* ed. R. Swartz (Anchor, New York: 1965) pp. 148ff.

36 Jackson op. cit. pp. 117–18.

37 Paul op. cit. pp. 276ff.; Ayer op. cit. p. 80.

38 This is essentially the 'logical howler' of which G. Ryle sought to convict the sense-datum theory; cf. *The Concept of Mind* (Penguin, Harmondsworth: 1963) pp. 203ff.

39 cf. M.A.E. Dummett's reference to our 'essentially two-dimensional visual impressions'; cf. 'Common Sense and Physics' in *Perception and Identity* ed.

G. MacDonald (Macmillan, London: 1979) p. 33.

40 For further arguments, cf.D.M. Armstrong 'Perception, Sense Data, and Causality' in *Perception and Identity* ed. G. MacDonald (Macmillan, London: 1979).

41 cf. Peacocke op. cit. pp. 20–1; R. Kraut 'Sensory States and Sensory Objects' *Nous* 1982.

42 Jackson op. cit. p. 35; he raises a battery of further objections on pp. 34–7.

## Chapter IX: Knowledge and scepticism

1 cf. B. Stroud *The Significance of Philosophical Scepticism* (Clarendon, Oxford: 1984) pp. 99–100.

2 I take this to be the point of T. Nagel's discussion on pp. 87–8 of *The View from Nowhere* (Clarendon, Oxford: 1986), cf. esp. fn. 13 on p. 88. Nagel does not recognise that his line of argument is essentially Moorean; as a disciple of Thompson Clarke, he regards Moore as having failed completely to understand the issue of philosophical scepticism (cf. fn. 1, p. 69). I explain in the next section why this interpretation of Moore is a mistake.

3 cf. E. Curley *Descartes Against the Sceptics* (Blackwell, Oxford: 1978) pp. 50–1.

4 For an excellent early critique of them, in the context of Malcolm's discussion in *PGEM*, cf. R. Chisholm 'Philosophers and Ordinary Language' *Philosophical Review* 1951.

5 cf. A. White *G.E. Moore* (Blackwell, Oxford: 1958) ch. 1. White is here unfair to Malcolm in taking him to be advancing the 'defence of ordinary language' as an interpretation of Moore's argument, rather than as a rational reconstruction of it. Since he himself allows (p. 34) that Malcolm's appeal to ordinary language is a 'legitimate extension' of Moore's argument, his disagreement with Malcolm is not great. On the other hand, Malcolm was equally unfair to White in his review of the book (in *Mind* 1961); so there is a degree of rough justice in the situation.

6 N. Malcolm 'Defending Common Sense' *Philosophical Review* 1949.

7 cf. N. Malcolm 'Moore and Wittgenstein on the Sense of "I Know"' in *Thought and Knowledge* (Cornell University Press, Ithaca, NY: 1977) pp. 173–4.

8 ibid. pp. 171–4.

9 In a letter to Moore written in 1949 while Wittgenstein was staying with him, which is now in the Cambridge archive, Malcolm accepts something like Moore's distinction between the two kinds of senselessness. Malcolm seems to have gone back on this point: in his 1974 paper 'Moore and Wittgenstein on the Sense of "I Know"' he rejects Moore's distinction and, invoking Wittgenstein's authority, reverts to very much the position of his 1949 paper.

10 cf. N. Malcolm 'The Verification Argument' in *Knowledge and Certainty* (Prentice-Hall, Englewood Cliffs, NJ: 1963) and, in the same collection, 'Knowledge and Belief' and 'Direct Perception'.

11 cf. H.G. Frankfurt 'Philosophical Certainty' *Philosophical Review* 1971.

12 T. Clarke's response to Moore is set out in his famous paper 'The Legacy of

Scepticism' *Journal of Philosophy* 1972.

13 ibid. p. 757.

14 ibid. p. 759.

15 cf. Stroud op. cit. pp. 270–1.

16 J.W. Cook, in 'Moore and Scepticism' in *Knowledge and Mind* ed. S. Shoemaker and C. Ginet (Oxford University Press, Oxford: 1983), argues that Moore's concern with scepticism was metaphysical, but that his response to such scepticism was wholly dogmatic and therefore ineffective.

17 C. Wright similarly misrepresents Moore in 'Facts and Certainty' *Proceedings of the British Academy* 1985 p. 434.

18 *The Philosophical Writings of Descartes* vol. II transl. by J. Cottingham, R. Stoothof, and D. Murdoch (Cambridge University Press, Cambridge: 1984) p. 243.

19 cf. J. Wisdom *Paradox and Discovery* (Blackwell, Oxford: 1965) pp. 83–4.

20 D. Lewis *Philosophical Papers* vol. 1 (Oxford University Press, New York: 1983) pp. 165–6.

21 cf. N. Malcolm *Ludwig Wittgenstein: A Memoir* (Oxford University Press, Oxford: 2nd ed. 1984) p. 67.

22 For a good discussion and defence of this thesis, cf. Stroud op. cit. ch.1.

23 This terminology is of course not to be confused with Stroud's 'external/internal' distinction.

24 cf. D.M. Armstrong *Belief, Truth, and Knowledge* (Cambridge University Press, Cambridge: 1973) p. 157.

25 cf. D.H. Mellor *The Justification of Induction* (Cambridge University Press, Cambridge: 1988).

26 This is very well brought out by Wright in section 1 of 'Facts and Certainty'.

27 But there are other necessary conditions for escaping scepticism, such as a metaphysics and philosophy of mind which explains how knowledge is possible. In the case of mathematics, for example, this condition is not easily met.

28 T. Reid *An Inquiry into the Human Mind* ed. T. Duggan (Chicago University Press, Chicago: 1970) p. 268.

29 Except in Malcolm's 'Moore and Wittgenstein on the Sense of "I Know"', which is explicitly derivative.

30 Wright op. cit.

31 cf. B. Williams *Ethics and the Limits of Philosophy* (Fontana, London: 1985) ch. 8; N. Jardine *The Fortunes of Inquiry* (Clarendon, Oxford: 1986).

32 cf. N. Cartwright *How the Laws of Physics Lie* (Clarendon, Oxford: 1983) esp. introduction; I. Hacking *Representing and Intervening* (Cambridge University Press, Cambridge; 1983) pp. 217–19.fp

# Appendix

*The Elements of Ethics* (1898) and *Principia Ethica* (1903)

The text of *PE* is divided into sections. The following table shows how those sections in chapters 1–3 which are taken more or less unchanged from *The Elements of Ethics* occurred there, and also which sections in these chapters do not occur in the earlier work. Very little of chapters 4–6 of *PE* occurs in the earlier work, although many of the ideas developed in chapters 4 and 5 occur there.

PE *chapter 1*

*Sections*

| | |
|---|---|
| 1–7 | from *EE* lecture 1 |
| 8–9 | from *EE* lecture 2 |
| 10 (1st paragraph) | new |
| 10 (rest)–11 | from *EE* lecture 1 (follows on from *PE* 7) |
| 12 | from *EE* lecture 3 |
| 13 | new |
| 14–15 | from *EE* lecture 2 (follows on from *PE* 9) |
| 16–23 (end) | new |

PE *chapter* 2

*Sections*

---

| | |
|---|---|
| 24–5 | new |
| 26 | from *EE* lecture 2 and 5 |
| 27–30 | from *EE* lecture 2 (follows on from *PE* 15) |
| 31–5 (end) | new |

---

PE *chapter* 3

*Sections*

---

| | |
|---|---|
| 36–7 | new |
| 38–44 (1st paragraph) | from *EE* lecture 3 (follows on from *PE* 12) |
| 44 (rest) | from *EE* lecture 4 |
| 45 (1st paragraph) | from *EE* lecture 3 (follows on from *PE* 44) |
| 45 (rest) | from *EE* lecture 4 (follows on from *PE* 44) |
| 46–8 (part) | from *EE* lecture 3 (follows on from *PE* 45) |
| 48 (rest) | from *EE* lecture 4 (follows on from *PE* 45) |
| 53–65 (end) | largely new |

# Index